WARRIOR CHURCHMEN OF MEDIEVAL ENGLAND 1000–1250

WARRIOR CHURCHMEN OF MEDIEVAL ENGLAND, 1000–1250

THEORY AND REALITY

Craig M. Nakashian

THE BOYDELL PRESS

© Craig M. Nakashian 2016

All Rights Reserved. Except as permitted under current legislation no part of this work may be photocopied, stored in a retrieval system, published, performed in public, adapted, broadcast, transmitted, recorded or reproduced in any form or by any means, without the prior permission of the copyright owner

The right of Craig M. Nakashian to be identified as the author of this work has been asserted in accordance with sections 77 and 78 of the Copyright, Designs and Patents Act 1988

First published 2016
The Boydell Press, Woodbridge
Paperback edition 2019

ISBN 978 1 78327 162 7 hardback
ISBN 978 1 78327 433 8 paperback

The Boydell Press is an imprint of Boydell & Brewer Ltd
PO Box 9, Woodbridge, Suffolk IP12 3DF, UK
and of Boydell & Brewer Inc.
668 Mt Hope Avenue, Rochester, NY 14620–2731, USA
website: www.boydellandbrewer.com

A catalogue record for this book is available
from the British Library

The publisher has no responsibility for the continued existence or accuracy of URLs for external or third-party internet websites referred to in this book, and does not guarantee that any content on such websites is, or will remain, accurate or appropriate

To Zöe, Meran, and Pelin

Contents

Acknowledgments		viii
List of Abbreviations		ix
Introduction: Churchmen and Warfare		1

Part I: Prescriptive Voices of the Debate

1	Clerics and War in the First Millennium	27
2	Papal Centralization and Canonical Prescriptions	64
3	The Epic Archetype: Evidence from Chivalric Literature	100

Part II: The Debate in Practice

4	The Norman Conquest: Odo of Bayeux and Geoffrey of Coutances	125
5	Negotiating a New Anglo-Norman Reality	158
6	The Civil War between Stephen and Matilda	184
7	The Angevins, Part I (Henry II and Richard I): Royal Servants	207
8	The Angevins, Part II (Richard I, John, and Henry III): Crusaders for King and Christ	229

Conclusion: The Thirteenth Century and Beyond	254
Bibliography	261
Index	288

Acknowledgments

There are far too many people to thank for their help and support in writing this manuscript, but I am especially grateful to my friends and colleagues at the University of Rochester who offered me countless hours of guidance, support, and insight. I especially wish to thank Richard Kaeuper, David Walsh, William Hauser, Kira Thurman, Daniel Franke, Peter Sposato, Paul Dingman, Chris Guyol, and Sam Claussen. Their advice on this project was invaluable and I am truly in their debt. I would also like to thank the new friends I met along the way of this project, including Jeff Hass and Daniel Gerrard, who kindly read drafts of the project and offered very valuable corrections and comments. My editor, Caroline Palmer at Boydell & Brewer, has been exceedingly patient while this project matured, and it would not have succeeded without her care and support. Finally, my colleagues and students at Syracuse University, Southeast Missouri State University, and Texas A&M University-Texarkana gave me numerous opportunities to question and refine my questions and approaches, and I am in their debt.

I could not have prepared this book without the help I received from the staff at Rush Rhees Library and the Rossell Hope Robbins Library at the University of Rochester, especially Alan Unsworth, and the staff at the John Moss Library at Texas A&M University-Texarkana, especially Mari Overlock and Neisha Federick. I would especially like to thank Professor Richard Abels of the United States Naval Academy for his invaluable comments and corrections, Professor Michael Prestwich for his care and guidance both during and after my time at the University of Durham, and Professor Theodore South, without whom I never would have become interested in medieval history.

My family has been completely supportive of my decision to become an historian, and I would like to thank my parents, step-parents, in-laws, and my sister, Lauren. Finally, and most importantly, I wish to thank my wife Zöe, my son Meran, and my daughter Pelin. They have consistently provided love, support, and levity during this process.

Abbreviations

ASC   *The Anglo-Saxon Chronicle*, ed. and trans. Michael Swanton (Phoenix, 2000)
EHR   *The English Historical Review* (1886–)
HH   Henry of Huntingdon, *Historia Anglorum*, ed. and trans. Diana Greenway (Oxford, 1996)
HSJ   *The Haskins Society Journal* (1989–)
MGH   *Monumenta Germaniae Historica*
MTB   *Materials for the History of Thomas Becket*, ed. J.C. Robertson and J.B. Sheppard, 7 vols. (London, 1875–85)
PL   *Patrologia Latina*
RS   Rolls Series: Rerum Britannicarum Medii Aevi Scriptores, or Chronicles and Memorials of Great Britain and Ireland during the Middle Ages, 99 vols. (London, 1858–1897)

Introduction: Churchmen and Warfare

In his *Historia de rebus Anglicis*, William of Newburgh, the twelfth-century English Augustinian canon and chronicler, recounted an amazing, and possibly apocryphal, story of two bishops going to war. One, Bishop Wimund, was portrayed as a villainous rogue; the other, an unnamed Scottish bishop, was the very model of episcopal humility and fortitude. What these two bishops had in common was that they both led armies onto the field of battle and personally fought. Whereas Bishop Wimund aggressively fought for plunder and conquest, the humble bishop fought against him in order to defend his flock. Both bishops used military violence to achieve their ends, but William judged each very differently. He opted to use the story to demonstrate the dangers of worldliness and avarice among churchmen, rather than to make a commentary on clerics involved in war. Modern historians, such as Nancy Partner, have seen William as a largely traditional cleric bemoaning the lure of worldly service among the prelates of his time.[1] John Gillingham elaborates by pointing out that, while William was generally opposed to clerics taking on active secular jurisdictions in violation of the Third Lateran Council, he also praised Bishop Hubert Walter of Salisbury – himself an active warrior bishop and chancellor of England (who is discussed in chapter 8).[2]

For Gillingham, Newburgh's praise of Hubert is incongruous, based on the general ideology that clerics should not be interested in 'secular' activities; but, as will be seen in this book, simply engaging in military activities was not the same as being 'secular' or 'worldly', provided a cleric did so for salutary reasons. Observers often complained about clerics becoming too 'worldly' or even 'knightly', but this condemnation did not necessarily encompass all warrior-clerics. If a cleric's primary identity and manner of behavior remained humble (rather than materialistic or 'knightly') he could avoid condemnation (or even garner praise) while utilizing the levers of secular and military power. Men such as William of Newburgh

---

[1] Nancy Partner, *Serious Entertainments: The Writing of History in Twelfth-Century England* (Chicago, 1977), 85–6.
[2] John Gillingham, 'Historian as Judge: William of Newburgh and Hubert Walter', *EHR* 119 (Nov., 2004), esp. 1276–7.

could clearly see active military violence by churchmen as a morally neutral activity, being either condemnable or laudable depending on the circumstances. On the other hand, many clerical reformers, who were seeking to disassociate clerics from warfare, did not generally make such distinctions. For them, clerics had virtually no legitimate role in battle or war, regardless of the cause or conflict. Modern historians often tend to assume that the voices of the reformers were normative reflections of how the medieval world ought to have been, since it often dovetails with our own conception of Christianity as an inherently pacifist religion. The fact that William showed greater ambivalence demonstrates that there was a wider discourse on these issues than we often assume.[3]

Let us return to our opening anecdote to see these medieval debates clearly. Wimund was a monk of Séez who became the bishop of Sodor and Man in the 1140s.[4] Wimund was not content, however, with the dignity of his episcopal office, and he became 'inflated with success' and began to desire to accomplish 'great and wonderful things'.[5] According to Newburgh, Wimund claimed that he was actually the dispossessed heir to the earldom of Moray (through his relationship to the Scottish royal family), so he collected 'a band of needy and desperate men' and sought to win it back through military force.[6] He incited his people to violence, and led them in plundering the surrounding areas. Wimund used hit-and-run tactics to avoid the army of the Scottish king, and he caused widespread destruc-

---

[3] Lawrence Duggan argues that this ambivalence can be seen in canon law to a greater extent than is generally assumed. That conclusion will be considered in greater detail throughout this book; however, his point that historians have often erroneously treated the views of clerical reformers as normative is well taken. See Lawrence G. Duggan, *Armsbearing and the Clergy in the History and Canon Law of Western Christianity* (Woodbridge, 2013), 1. For an excellent review of Duggan's work, see Daniel Gerrard, Review of *Armsbearing and the Clergy in the History and Canon Law of Western Christianity*, by Lawrence G. Duggan, EHR 130 (April, 2015), 410–12.

[4] For some brief notes on his consecration, see *Councils and Ecclesiastical Documents relating to Great Britain and Ireland*, ed. Haddan and Stubbs, Vol. 2, Pt. 1 (Oxford, 1873), 189–90.

[5] William of Newburgh, *Historia de rebus Anglicis*, ed. and trans. Joseph Stevenson, *Church Historians of England, Stevenson*, Vol. 4, Pt. 2 (London, 1856), 431. 'Nec contentus episcopalis dignitate officii, animo iam ambulabat in magnis et mirabilibus super se; eratque ei cum corde vanissimo, os loquens ingentia.' See William of Newburgh, The 'Historia Rerum Anglicarum', ed. Charles Johnson (New York, 1920), 20. The entire section discussing Bishop Wimund runs from pages 19 to 21. I have provided the original language of quotations that are of particular importance for the arguments of this book.

[6] William of Newburgh, Stevenson, 431. See Melissa Pollock, *The Lion, the Lily, and the Leopard: The Crown and Nobility of Scotland, France, and England and the Struggle for Power (1100–1204)* (Turnhout, 2015), 109, note 234.

tion.⁷ Newburgh likened him to Nimrod, 'a mighty hunter before the Lord, forgetting that his episcopal office required of him to be, with Peter, a fisher of men.'⁸ He made it clear that Wimund was a warrior who took an active role in the fighting and that this was in violation of his status as a churchman. Newburgh chastised Wimund for abandoning his episcopal role in favor of becoming a brigand.

This part of the story was not overly remarkable, since one would expect a clerical author to condemn a bishop who forsook spiritual ministrations to become a violent warlord. The tale becomes much more intriguing after William introduces the man who defeated Wimund in battle. This man was a bishop 'of singular simplicity' who was able to repress Wimund's audacity for a time.⁹ The catalyst for his resistance was Wimund's attempt to extort tribute from him, and in reply the anonymous bishop gathered an army and met him in battle:

> Whereupon spiriting up his people, superior only in faith, for in other respects he was greatly inferior, he met him [Wimund] as he was furiously advancing, and himself striking the first blow in the battle, by way of animating his party, he threw a small hatchet, and, by God's assistance, he felled his enemy to the earth, as he was marching in the van.¹⁰

The humble bishop not only checked the assault of Wimund's army; he wounded Wimund in the process, and forced his army to flee. Wimund used to boast of this defeat, saying 'that God alone was able to vanquish him by the faith of a simple bishop.'¹¹

William presented this humble, unnamed bishop as the manifestation of God's will striking down the proud and vicious Wimund. This bishop not only assembled a military force against Wimund, but led it onto the field of battle himself, and then struck the first blow by hurling an axe into the enemy throng. William's

---

⁷ 'Excurrebat in provincias Scotiae, rapinis et homicidiis cuncta exterminans.' William of Newburgh, Johnson, 20.

⁸ William of Newburgh, Stevenson, 431. 'iam quasi Nembroth robustus venator coram Domino, dedignatus iuxta episcopalis officii debitum hominum esse piscator cum Petro.' William of Newburgh, Johnson, 20.

⁹ William of Newburgh, Stevenson, 431. 'Cum ergo in omnibus prosperaratur, essetque iam ipsi etiam regi terribilis, quidam episcopus vir simplicissimus eius impetum mirabiliter ad tempus repressit.' William of Newburgh, Johnson, 20.

¹⁰ William of Newburgh, Stevenson, 432. 'Cohortatus ergo populum suum, illi cum furore venienti sola fide maior, nam in ceteris longe impar, occurrit, et pro suorum animatione primum ipse belli dans iectum, iactata securi modica, hostem in fronte gradientem Deo volente prostravit.' William of Newburgh, Johnson, 20.

¹¹ William of Newburgh, Stevenson, 432. 'quod solus eum Deus per simplicis episcopi fidem vincere potuisset.' William of Newburgh, Johnson, 20.

treatment of the unnamed bishop made it clear that this embrace of personal violence in battle by a cleric was not merely excusable, but laudable and honorable. He was defending his flock from the ravages of Wimund, and William created a common-sense exception to the canonical prohibition of churchmen fighting in warfare.[12] The unnamed bishop did the right thing by defending his region against Wimund, just as Wimund was clearly in the wrong for his aggression. Wimund was wrong for being violent, destructive, and worldly; the unnamed bishop was right for being brave, humble, and ready to defend his people. Wimund's primary fault was his avarice and worldliness; the unnamed bishop's primary virtue was bravery. Wimund used violence for ill; the unnamed bishop used it for good.[13]

Given the circumstances laid out by William of Newburgh, we see a debate over what the ideal military role was for a man of the church in the Middle Ages. Was a holy man meant to uphold the seemingly pacifist notions that many saw as the bedrock ideals of Christianity, or was he meant to support worthy causes through whatever means were necessary, including those bloody and violent, or did acceptability fall somewhere in between? The discourse over clerics and warfare often became conflated with that over the dangers posed to their spiritual well-being by courtliness and worldliness. The argument was part of a larger conflict between clerics who saw active political service as a part of their ecclesiastical mission, and those who saw it as a hindrance or worse. For secular clerics especially (such as bishops), the balance between serving God and providing service in administration was difficult to maintain, and a number of these men wrestled with the propriety of such service. As the above vignette shows, the answer was far from clear, and far from cut and dried. The traditional interpretation by modern historians (based on the perspective of the clerical reformers of the high Middle Ages) was that clerics usually had to participate in secular service, but they should not have embraced it. In general they ought not to have participated in warfare, and those who did were essentially 'secular' and 'worldly', and were thus less 'clerical'. Anna Comnena, daughter of Byzantine Emperor Alexius I famously remarked on the relative 'barbarity' of Latin clerics who fought and

---

[12] This exception is despite his general acceptance of the importance and power of canon law. Nancy Partner writes, 'Popes may be harried and misguided and their court a quicksand bog for money and time, but Rome in its full authority (and in its familiar sins) stands central to the *Historia* and to the *Historia's* world.' See Partner, *Serious Entertainments*, 79.

[13] While Wimund was curbed for a while, he soon began ravaging again. The king granted him a province and monastery to hold, but his pride and insolence turned the people against him, and they endeavored to capture him. They blinded and castrated him, and he ended his days at the monastery of Byland, where Newburgh intimates that he met him. He finished his days in solitude, though he still boasted that if he had even just the eye of a sparrow, his enemies would fear him. See William of Newburgh, Stevenson, 432.

prayed simultaneously.[14] However, despite these prescriptive condemnations, the reality was that contemporaries vigorously debated proper clerical military behavior, and clerical military actions fell along a disputed spectrum running from open condemnation through neutrality to justification and approval. Just as in broader debates over licit violence by knights, clerics' involvement in warfare was praised or criticized for various reasons, and not merely determined by how closely they adhered to canonical ideals. Men such as Peter of Blois, writing in the late twelfth and early thirteen centuries, even came down on both sides of the fence, as circumstances dictated.[15]

Reformers could be concerned with clerics who were overly worldly in their interests and actions, they could be concerned with clerics who actively dealt with bloodshed, either in warfare or justice, and they could be concerned with those who did both. However, we are dealing with two interrelated, but still separate, discussions on worldliness and bloodshed. While both were the targets of ecclesiastical reformers, in the cases of a number of the clerics considered below worldliness was seen as a greater threat to their ability to remain spiritually pure.[16] Active service in warfare did not automatically mean that a cleric was considered worldly. 'Worldly' clerics were those who actively embraced the trappings of warfare, knightliness, and an ostentatious lifestyle. Clerics who fought out of necessity or a higher calling of service, and who maintained humility, would often be praised, or at least not criticized, by contemporaries. We should thus be careful not to make the mistake of assuming that all military action was automatically seen as evidence of worldliness.

Among our first actions, however, should be creating a working definition of a fighting churchman. Let us deal with the second term first. When dealing with consecrated and recognized church leaders such as bishops, it is reasonably easy to assume that these men were seen as clerics, but what of the mass of other 'clerics' in medieval society, and what of actions undertaken by men in lower grades of the clergy? To be a clergyman in the Middle Ages meant to be separated from the broader laity through your ability to perform certain rites in the church.[17] The

---

[14] Anna Comnena (Komnene). *The Alexiad*, ed. and trans. Elizabeth A. Dawes (London, 1928), 256. Comnena's concerns are addressed more fully in Chapter 2.

[15] John D. Cotts, 'Peter of Blois and the Problem of the "Court" in the Late Twelfth Century', *Anglo-Norman Studies* 27, ed. John Gillingham (Woodbridge, 2005), 70.

[16] John Cotts does an excellent job of contextualizing this discussion in regards to Peter of Blois, though we will see it reflected in a number of the ecclesiastical authors in this study. Peter was conflicted about whether clerics could remain pure while serving at court, and his letters tend to reflect that ambiguity in his arguments. See Cotts, 'Peter of Blois', 69–82.

[17] Julia Barrow, 'Grades of Ordination and Clerical Careers, c.900–1200', *Anglo-Norman Studies* 30, ed. C.P. Lewis (Woodbridge, 2008), 41–2. See also a brief discussion of this issue in Duggan, *Armsbearing and the Clergy*, 11.

Carolingian period was vital for fixing the clerical grades and ranks for the rest of the Middle Ages, and the result was that by the early part of the eleventh century the 'higher orders' were usually considered to include sub-deacon, deacon, and priest, though there was some question regarding the status of sub-deacon.[18] For the purposes of this study, men in those grades and beyond will be considered 'churchmen' broadly, as most contemporaries would have seen them as such. I am also using the terms 'churchman' and 'cleric' in non-technical, common-usage senses. If a contemporary was likely to consider someone a man of the church, I have followed suit – though I recognize that canon laws had specific penalties and allowances based on the particular grade and legal status of an individual within the ecclesiastical hierarchy.[19]

As for the 'fighting' part, there was a broad spectrum of 'military' activities that a churchman could participate in, from recruitment tours through physical combat, and pretty much everything in between. For the purposes of this study, we are limiting ourselves to those activities that were seen as being directly related to battle and fighting – leading troops in battle, on campaign, or directing military actions in the face of the enemy. Thus, we will discuss clerics who actively aided war efforts as generals and soldiers, but not those who supported wars through financial roles (such as Ranulf Flambard, bishop of Durham) or through preaching (such as Bernard de Clairvaux).[20] I believe that this defini-

---

[18] Barrow, 'Grades of Ordination', 47–9. The role of the acolyte changed throughout the period as well, and by the twelfth century represented the highest grade usually progressed to for those wishing to remain in minor orders and serve in professional capacities. For a discussion of the status of sub-deacons specifically, see John St. H. Gibaut, *The Cursus Honorum: A Study of the Origins and Evolution of Sequential Ordination* (New York, 2000), 253–6.

[19] Jean Dunbabin further distinguishes clerks from clerics, though both were covered by the Latin term clericus, writing that a 'clerk' was 'a non-servile male of at least seven years of age, who was sufficiently learned in Latin to read the psalms and sing the responses in a church service, who was required to wear the clerical habit and tonsure ... who had renounced the bearing of arms, who was justiciable in the ecclesiastical courts, was exempted from secular tolls and tallages, and who might or might not in the future intend to become a cleric.' See Jean Dunbabin, 'From Clerk to Knight: Changing Orders', *The Ideals and Practice of Medieval Knighthood II: Papers from the Third Strawberry Hill Conference 1986*, ed. Christopher Harper-Bill and Ruth Harvey (Woodbridge, 1988), 27.

[20] For further definitions, see Hugo Schwyzer, 'Arms and the Bishop: The Anglo-Scottish War and the Northern Episcopate, 1296–1357' (Ph.D. diss, University of California – Los Angeles, 1999), 11 and Daniel Gerrard, 'The Military Activities of Bishops, Abbots, and other Clergy in England, c. 900–1200' (Ph.D. diss, University of Glasgow, 2010), 35. I thank Dr. Gerrard for sharing elements of his forthcoming manuscript *The Church at War* with me.

tion captures the larger cultural conversation among contemporaries regarding warrior churchmen.[21]

So, if there was a debate among contemporaries regarding fighting clerics, what factors influenced their reactions? We can see a number of interrelated justifications in the evidence, including royal service, obligations based on land- and office-holding, political partisanship, a shared sense of elite culture between prelates and secular nobles, and the interactions of clerics with ideas of masculinity derived from chivalric identity. While all of these factors will be examined, our primary cipher for understanding the clerics in this study will be their service (or lack thereof) to the king of England. We shall see that the justification for clerical military actions based on royal service came from long-held ideas of proper clerical support for kings, as well as from a growing interest in the precedents and legal principles of Roman law, whereby defense of oneself and the *patria* was deemed a legitimate purpose for the use of force.[22] Royal service was an opportunity for clerics to take active military roles and to avoid condemnation, since many clerical authors were inclined to support royal power. Many ecclesiastical observers, relying on Old Testament exemplars, saw the king as the chief guarantor of peace and stability, and thus worthy of support (if not always in the form of active military service).[23] The defense of one's region, or church lands and personnel, could also serve as a justification for military service. There was an increasing awareness

---

[21] Lawrence Duggan complains that modern historians have often conflated 'the whole spectrum of behavior ranging from personal armsbearing to direction of troops from afar' and have thus assumed 'that none of it was licit in the law of the Church.' He notes, however, that contemporaries often made the same assumptions. Duggan, *Armsbearing and the Clergy*, 2 and 14. Cf. Gerrard, Review of *Armsbearing*, 410.

[22] For the importance of Roman law on royal power and military legitimacy in the High Middle Ages, see Gaines Post, *Studies in Medieval Legal Thought: Public Law and the State, 1100–1322* (Princeton, 1964), esp. 241–309, 434–561. For a good overview of medieval political ideology, see Walter Ullman, *Law and Politics in the Middle Ages* (Ithaca, 1975). See also Peter Stein, *Roman Law in European History* (New York, 1999); Stephen Kuttner, 'The Revival of Jurisprudence', *Renaissance and Renewal in the Twelfth Century*, ed R.I. Benson and Giles Constable (Cambridge, MA, 1982), 37–67; W.P. Müeller, 'The Recovery of Justinian's Digest in the Middle Ages', *Bulletin of Medieval Canon Law*, NS 20 (1990), 1–30; Kenneth Pennington, *The Prince and Law, 1200–1600* (Berkeley, 1993). For the development of this idea in canon law, see James Brundage, 'The Hierarchy of Violence in Twelfth- and Thirteenth-Century Canonists', *The International History Review* 17 (1995), 670–92, esp. 674–7; Duggan, *Armsbearing and the Clergy*, 123–7.

[23] See Matthew Strickland, 'Against the Lord's Anointed: Aspects of Warfare and Baronial Rebellion in England and Normandy 1075–1265', in *Law and Government in Medieval England and Normandy: Essays in Honour of Sir James Holt*, ed. G. Garnett and J. Hudson (Cambridge, 1994), 56–79, esp. 60–1.

as to the legitimacy of actions on behalf of the king, or on behalf of the *patria*. The growing interest in and awareness of Roman law, with its powerful defenses of *patria*-based warfare, helped to accelerate and to reinforce this phenomenon.

In addition to the basic utility of royal service, political partisanship was also an important determinant for the acceptability of fighting clerics. The political ideology and loyalties of the clerics involved, and of the authors writing about them, had a major effect on whether a particular behavior was considered acceptable.[24] Causes that were considered laudable would generally lead to the clerics involved being praised, or at least not overtly criticized, by those observers who shared that political outlook. Behavior that was criticized in a political opponent would be either praised or overlooked in a political ally. If a cleric engaged in activities considered beneficial to the author, or generally salutary to the broader political beliefs of the author, that cleric would usually be praised for his actions.

There was often a commonality of elite culture between the upper reaches of the ecclesiastical and secular hierarchies, in so far as those two groups were actually exclusive.[25] High-ranking bishops and abbots usually either came from the nobility or interacted with the nobility once they gained office.[26] Chivalric culture largely embraced warrior prowess as a core virtue of the warrior ethos, and as a licit and salutary method for Christians to gain honor.[27] From an early age sons were immersed in a world of chivalric virtues, and while some famously turned their backs on it (such as Guibert de Nogent), others were heavily influenced by the valorization of swinging a strong right arm in defense of God and King. These were families in which pieces of chivalric literature like the *Song of Roland* were known and recited, where artistic endowments to churches depicted saints,

---

[24] For a discussion of this phenomenon during King John's reign, see Ralph V. Turner, 'King John in His Context: A Comparison with His Contemporaries', *HSJ* 3, ed. Robert B. Patterson (1991), 183–95.

[25] Andrew Romig has considered this common noble culture in regards to the construction of masculine identity. See Andrew Romig, 'The Common Bond of Aristocratic Masculinity: Monks, Secular Men, and St. Gerald of Aurillac', *Negotiating Clerical Identities: Priests, Monks, and Masculinity in the Middle Ages*, ed. Jennifer D. Thibodeaux (Basingstoke, 2010), 39–56. See also Katherine Allen Smith, 'Spiritual Warriors in Citadels of Faith: Martial Rhetoric and Monastic Masculinity in the Long Twelfth Century', *Negotiating Clerical Identities: Priests, Monks and Masculinity in the Middle Ages*, ed. Jennifer D. Thibodeaux (Basingstoke, 2010), 86–110, especially 87.

[26] Constance Bouchard has argued that there was a basic belief that high-ranking clerics ought to come from the elite segments of society. She wrote, 'When someone from a less exalted background *did* become bishop, very unfavorable remarks were usually made about him.' See Constance Bouchard, *Strong of Body, Brave and Noble: Chivalry and Society in Medieval France* (Ithaca, 1998), 157.

[27] Richard W. Kaeuper, *Chivalry and Violence in Medieval Europe* (Oxford, 2001), 129–60.

and even Christ, as knights armed for war.[28] Men could certainly have taken some elements of noble culture with them into the church, and used them to justify manly and personal involvement with legitimate military activities.[29] The focus on prescriptive religious doctrine that has dominated the study of this topic oftentimes does not take these aspects of warrior culture into account, or, if it does, it minimizes them as less legitimate motivators of clerical action than the aforementioned doctrinal sources (especially canon law).[30]

Warfare was also a core function of the 'masculine' ideal prevalent in medieval society. The construction of masculinity and the gendering of behavior is an area that has become increasingly important for the study of the Middle Ages, and is of importance to the questions raised by this study. Recent works have begun to disentangle the complex issues surrounding the construction of an ideal masculinity for clerics, and how those identities interacted with the broader contours of medieval society.[31] Clerics were faced with a particularly difficult problem of

[28] Saint Michael was depicted as a knight fighting the Devil on the façade of the church of Anzy-le-Duc in Burgundy. See Bouchard, *Strong of Body*, 124. Archbishop Turpin was shown unhorsing an enemy on a lintel at Angoulême cathedral. Thomas of Lancaster saw tourneying as fine, and even saw Christ as a tourneyer. 'Picturing Christ as a victorious tourneyer for humanity, he says 'Le turnoy estoit pur nous quant il par turment tourna nostre dolour en joie (the tourney was for us when he by his torments turned our sorrow into joy).' Richard W. Kaeuper, *Holy Warriors: The Religious Ideology of Chivalry* (Philadelphia, 2009), 41. Christ was also often depicted as a knight in native Welsh poetry, as well as in numerous Anglo-Saxon sources. See Lindsey O'Donnell, 'Rendering unto Caesar: Ecclesiastical Identity in Thirteenth-Century North Wales' (M.A. thesis, University of Missouri-Columbia, 2004), 79–80. See also Graham D. Caie, 'Christ as Warrior in Old English Poetry', *War and Peace in the Middle Ages*, ed. Brian Patrick McGuire (Copenhagen, 1987), 13–24. Christ was also depicted wielding a sword at Auxerre cathedral. These are but a few representative examples of such imagery.

[29] One very interesting area that needs to be studied further is the phenomenon of clerics getting into conflict with one another over the bearing of episcopal crosses in rival territory. There are accounts of violence accompanying these attempts, and one cannot help but be put in mind of the similar secular phenomenon of nobles riding with banners unfurled in rival lands. There seems to be a commonality of culture at work here, in addition to any political considerations.

[30] Gerrard makes this point explicitly, and wisely expands it to include the use of land tenure as a motivator for clerical warfare. Gerrard, 238–9. See also Matthew Strickland, *War and Chivalry: The Conduct and Perception of War in England and Normandy, 1066-1217* (Cambridge, 1996), 55–97. For a good rejoinder against Strickland's 'utilitarian' reading of law, see James Brundage, Review of *War and Chivalry* by Matthew Strickland, *American Historical Review* 103 (1998), 862–3.

[31] See, for example, *Masculinity in Medieval Europe*, ed. D.M. Hadley (London, 1999); *Negotiating Clerical Identities: Priests, Monks and Masculinity in the Middle Ages*, ed. Jennifer D. Thibodeaux (Basingstoke, 2010). See also Hugh M. Thomas, 'Shame, Masculinity, and the Death of Thomas Becket', *Speculum* 87 (October, 2012), 1050–88.

fitting themselves into a masculine gender that was, to a large extent, based on and reinforced by the ability to wield weapons and have sexual intercourse.[32] To that effect, some authors, such as Andrew Miller, have argued that medieval society saw knightliness as the embodiment of masculinity, and by definition therefore, clerical identity as inherently feminine.[33] In this regard, according to R.N. Swanson, the willingness of clerics to use weapons despite the canonical prohibitions was an example of these clerics refusing to appear 'non-masculine'.[34]

In this construction of masculinity, however, we see shades of the distinction between fighting in war and being considered worldly. Clerics who sought to defend their masculinity in the face of knightly derision often did so by arguing that clerics ought to demonstrate their superiority to knights in their self-control, leadership, humility, and spiritual prowess, rather than to become more 'knightly'.[35] Katherine Allen Smith argues that clerics, especially monks, sought to portray their own warfare (defined as spiritual conflicts with demons) as inherently more dangerous (and thus more 'manly') than secular warfare.[36] She writes that there was always a difference, however, between spiritual and secular warfare: 'Spiritual combat was purifying where worldly warfare could imperil one's soul; worldly knights were all too prone to vices like greed, vanity and wrath while the *miles Christi* turned humility, obedience and chastity into formidable weapons.'[37] Her point is well taken, and it also demonstrates why some clerics who fought in

---

[32] P.H. Cullum, 'Clergy, Masculinity and Transgression in Late Medieval England', *Masculinity in Medieval Europe*, 182; Andrew G. Miller, 'Knights, Bishops and Deer Parks: Episcopal Identity, Emasculation and Clerical Space in Medieval England', *Negotiating Clerical Identities*, 206; Thomas, 'Shame, Masculinity, and the Death of Thomas Becket', 1052.

[33] Andrew George Miller, 'Carpe Ecclesiam: Households, Identity and Violent Communication ("Church" and "Crown" under King Edward I)' (Ph.D. diss, University of California – Santa Barbara, 2003), 341.

[34] R.N. Swanson, 'Angels Incarnate: Clergy and Masculinity from Gregorian Reform to Reformation', *Masculinity in Medieval Europe*, 168.

[35] Maureen Miller and Scott Wells have shown that clerics could embrace the 'manly' aspects of their status, including their use of spiritual weapons, through an emulation of Moses. Maureen Miller, 'Masculinity, Reform, and Clerical Culture: Narratives of Episcopal Holiness in the Gregorian Era', *Church History* 72 (2003), 25–52; Scott Wells, 'The Warrior *Habitus*: Militant Masculinity and Monasticism in the Henrician Reform Movement', *Negotiating Clerical Identities*, 66–71. Ruth Mazo Karras, however, argues that clerics were not employing military language and metaphors to compete with secular models of masculinity, but rather to transcend them. See Ruth Mazo Karras, 'Thomas Aquinas's Chastity Belt: Clerical Masculinity in Medieval Europe', *Gender and Christianity in Medieval Europe*, ed. Lisa M. Bitel and Felice Lifshitz (Philadelphia, 2008), 52–67.

[36] Smith, 'Spiritual Warriors in Citadels of Faith', 88–9.

[37] Ibid., 103.

secular wars were praised (those who did so without falling victim to worldliness) while others were condemned. Indeed, Bernard de Clairvaux reinforced this ideal in discussing the Templars when he claimed that a holy warrior needed to be humble and pious, and to avoid worldliness in order to gain God's favor. He also complained that secular knights dressed their horses and themselves frivolously, and questioned whether these 'trinkets' were not better served adorning women.[38] Odo of Cluny's *Life of St. Gerald of Aurillac* portrays the saintly count as doing those things expected of him – leading armies, doing justice, etc. – but with the countenance of a monk through his embrace of humility and simplicity.[39] Odo went so far as to defend the use of righteous violence, claiming that Gerald's glory was not clouded by his military actions.[40] These concerns about masculinity, and the cleric's place within the male gender, form an important backdrop for many of the cases considered later in this book.

The emergence of a strong, centralized, and relatively independent papacy and clerical estate in the eleventh and twelfth centuries has led some historians to downplay the broader cultural influences at work on guiding both clerical behavior and the reactions of others to fighting clerics. An excellent example of this comes from David Knowles's book, *Thomas Becket*. Knowles argues that the Gregorian reforms had created and perpetuated

> a reorganization and centralization of church government which made of the clergy a class rigidly separate from the lay estate, with extensive rights and privileges, and a system of discipline and law which ultimately claimed exclusive jurisdiction over all clerics, and considerable control over the laity in spiritual and quasi-spiritual matters.[41]

From the standpoint of law, Knowles is certainly correct. This characterization would have also been very familiar and agreeable from the cultural standpoint of ecclesiastical reformers such as Gregory VII and Bernard de Clairvaux. In fact, Knowles went so far as to argue that the eleventh century represented Europe

---

[38] Bernard de Clairvaux, 'In Praise of the New Knighthood', *The Cistercian Fathers Series: Number Nineteen, The Works of Bernard of Clairvaux*, Vol. 7, Treatise 3, trans. Conrad Greenia (Kalamazoo, MI, 1977), chapter two. See also Andrew Holt, 'Between Warrior and Priest: The Creation of a New Masculine Identity during the Crusades', *Negotiating Clerical Identities*, 185–97.

[39] Andrew Romig, 'The Common Bond of Aristocratic Masculinity: Monks, Secular Men and St. Gerald of Aurillac', *Negotiating Clerical Identities*, 39–56.

[40] Ibid., 46, note 51, 'Nemo sane movetur, quod homo Justus usum praeliandi, qui incongruus religioni videtur, aliquando habuerit. Quisquis ille est, si justa lance causam discreverit, ne in hac quidem parte gloriam Geraldi probabit obfuscandam.'

[41] David Knowles, *Thomas Becket* (Stanford, 1971), 11–12.

moving from 'childhood' into 'adolescence' and included campaigns against 'widespread abuses in Church and society, such as clerical marriage and incontinence, gross immorality in towns, simony in elections of all kings and excessive wealth among prelates', culminating in the popularity of the Cistercian monasteries and the power of Bernard de Clairvaux.[42] According to Knowles, the 'old' way of doing things was for the ecclesiastical and secular spheres to intertwine, but by the 1160s this was outmoded and old-fashioned, and the twelfth century was 'an age of faith *par excellence,* an age in which both Catholic faith and discipline had a greater influence upon the minds and actions of men than at any other time in the middle ages, imposing sanctions and ideals upon all, whatever their practice might be.'[43] Christopher Tyerman has reinforced this interpretation by arguing that the warrior-bishops of the twelfth century were anachronistic. They 'represented an old habit which, if anything, was dying out, as the logic of Gregorian separation of functions and powers seeped into law, custom and expectations', though he grants that some (such as Bishop Despenser of Norwich in the fourteenth century) lingered on as throwbacks to a bygone age.[44] Knowles and Tyerman (among others) present the views of clerical reformers as normative for medieval society and largely establish a cultural consensus where everyone agreed on proper clerical ideology and culture, but not everyone lived up to it. However, as will become clear in the subsequent chapters, a narrative that adopts the position of ecclesiastical reformers as representative of a consensus creates a normative bias against clerics (and laymen) who did not fit into these clear and distinctive categories. As much as reformist contemporaries would have wished it, there was a great deal more cultural discussion, both in behavior and in the acceptance of that behavior, than is often conceded.

The following chapters examine significant churchmen in England during the Anglo-Norman and Angevin periods, precisely when these Gregorian reforms were taking root, and the arguments over acceptable clerical behavior were at their height. While we will focus primarily on clerics active on royal campaigns or on behalf of the king, we should not ignore the fact that these churchmen could be involved in military affairs for a variety of reasons, including those outlined above. A cleric could embrace the use of force because of his noble background, his sense of duty to the king, his political interests, his sense of masculine identity, and out of obligations deriving from his lands and position in royal government. Multiple motivations certainly existed, and we will discuss them as they pertain to

---

[42] Ibid., 18–19.
[43] Ibid., 58–60.
[44] Christopher Tyerman, 'Were There Any Crusades in the Twelfth Century', *EHR* 110 (Jun., 1995), 558.

each individual cleric presented. However, one unifying theme for the clerics who were given positive treatments in the sources was their adherence to the legitimate ruler, most often the king, or their actions on a widely accepted campaign, such as the Third Crusade.

I am also not suggesting that this book represents a comprehensive catalogue of all militarily minded churchmen in medieval England. There were numerous clerics who played roles in warfare who do not appear in these pages. Men such as Ranulf Flambard, bishop of Durham at the turn of the eleventh and twelfth centuries, or Hugh du Puiset, also bishop of Durham in the later twelfth century, were important to the wars of their periods. However, I have excluded them because they did not (as far as we know) fight, lead, or direct men on campaign. I am examining how contemporaries viewed clerics who fought or led men on campaign, not how important such clerics were to the war effort. By focusing on the most well-known examples of warrior-clerics, I believe that I have provided a representative sample sufficient to draw some larger conclusions as to the nature and acceptability of clerical military action. One could argue, of course, that the clerics cited here are singular, isolated examples that represent only a small number of churchmen 'behaving badly'. While it is true that only a minority of clerics actively fought in war, there were enough of these men figuring prominently in the cultural imagination of the period that we can reasonably draw inferences as to a broader cultural phenomenon at work. Furthermore, these men were not obscure clerics hidden away in out-of-the way monasteries but, rather, major prelates of the realm, and among the most well-known figures of their day. Thus, while the number of clerics who fought or led men on campaign was not a majority, they were certainly common enough to elicit a great deal of debate.

I have chosen to focus my attention on England for a number of reasons. Much admirable work has been done on the warrior-clerics of other regions, especially medieval Germany, and I do not seek to replicate those studies, but instead to expand the discussion to England.[45] German bishops have often been portrayed as singularly warlike and bloodthirsty, and considering their prevalence during

---

[45] See Friedrich Prinze, *Klerus und Krieg im Früheren Mittelalter* (Stuttgart, 1971); Friedrich Prinze, 'King, Clergy and War at the Time of the Carolingians', *Saints, Scholars and Heroes: Studies in Medieval Culture in Honour of Charles W. Jones*, Vol. 2 (Collegeville, MN, 1979), 301–29; Tim Reuter, '*Episcopi cum sua militia*: The Prelate as Warrior in the Early Stauffer Era', *Warriors and Churchmen in the Middle Ages: Essays Presented to Karl Leyser*, ed. Tim Reuter (London, 1992), 79–94; David Bachrach, *Religion and the Conduct of War c.300–1215* (Woodbridge, 2003); *A Warrior-Bishop of the Twelfth Century: The Deeds of Albero of Trier*, trans. Brian A. Pavlac (Toronto, 2008); Benjamin Arnold, 'German Bishops and Their Military Retinues in the Medieval Empire', *German History* 7 (1989), 161–83.

the period in question, it is hard to argue against the proposition that German bishops often found themselves in the thick of warfare. Modern historians (and some contemporaries) seemed to think that through their actions, the German prince-bishops succeeded in carving out an exception to the normal canonical prohibitions on clerical warfare.[46] The German examples are often contrasted with the prelates of other realms, where it was assumed that warrior-churchmen were less accepted.[47] Again, this idea has its roots in the medieval world itself – in the ninth century, Archbishop Hincmar of Rheims claimed that English bishoprics did not have the landed endowments of German ones, and thus did not owe the same level of military service, and in the thirteenth century Richard, earl of Cornwall complained that England lacked the kind of warrior-bishops common in Germany.[48] However, it goes too far to argue that warrior-clerics were a peculiarly German issue, or that they were isolated cases native only to the wilds of Germania. In fact, throughout the period under our study there were always Anglo-Norman and Angevin clerics (and French, Spanish, etc.) actively engaged in warfare, leading men into battle, and fighting in battle themselves. These men were not shunted off into the exile of social irrelevance but, rather, were usually operating at the highest echelons of power and influence.

Many historians have considered these issues individually, but there has not been a comprehensive study. The existing scholarship on this topic has tended to fall into one of four major categories:

1. consideration of warrior-clerics from the perspective of canon law, such as Frederick Russell's *The Just War in the Middle Ages* or Lawrence Duggan's *Armsbearing and the Clergy in the History and Canon Law of Western Christianity*;
2. consideration of clerical military action within the context of the crusades, such as Jonathan Riley-Smith's *The First Crusade and the Idea of Crusading*;

---

[46] Prinze, 'King, Clergy and War at the Time of the Carolingians', 312–15.

[47] Nicholas Vincent, *Peter des Roches: An Alien in English Politics, 1205–1238* (Cambridge, 1996), 138.

[48] For Hincmar, see Janet L. Nelson, 'The Church's Military Service in the Ninth Century: A Contemporary Comparative View', *The Church and War*, ed. W.J. Sheils, *Studies in Church History* 20 (London, 1983), 15–19; For Richard of Cornwall, see Arnold, 'German Bishops', 166–7. He quotes Richard as saying to his nephew Edward, '"Look what spirited and warlike archbishops and bishops we have in Germany; I would count it not at all unprofitable to you if such were created in England, by whose attention you would be secured against importunate assaults of rebellion."' The original quotation is in *Annales Monastici*, I, ed. Luard, RS 36 (London, 1864), 394. It reads, 'Ecce quam animosos et bellicosos archiepiscopus et episcopos habemus in Alemannia; non multum vobis inutile reputantes, si tales in Anglia createntur, quorum ministerio uti possetis secure contra importunes rebellium vestorum incursus.'

3. biographies of individual clerics, such as H.E.J. Cowdrey's magisterial *Gregory VII, 1073–1085*;
4. and contextualizing warrior-clerics in larger studies of military history, as in David Bachrach's *Religion and the Conduct of War*.

While each of these areas is worthy of study, and this project would have impossible without them, what I propose to do here is to build on the foundation set by these historians and to try to fit these clerics into a wider cultural context that does not treat them from a pre-established normative position.[49]

The first approach tends to suffer from an over-reliance on highly prescriptive texts, and can oftentimes get bogged down in legal minutiae that may not be reflective of broader cultural influences. Due to the nature of the evidence, studies that focus on canon law can also betray a normative bias that the canonistic position was the universally accepted way for a cleric to behave, rather than seeing canon law as one among several influences over licit clerical behavior. Clerics who did not fit that mold are depicted as anachronisms or criminals. Such a focus on intellectual traditions can over-emphasize such sources, which, while fundamental to our understanding of perceptions of approved clerical behavior, do not tell the entire story. While it was not necessarily noteworthy when canon law was ignored, I am arguing that ignoring the canonistic prohibitions on warrior-clerics did not automatically render someone unfit for ecclesiastical office in the eyes of contemporaries, nor always irrevocably stain their reputations.[50] We see an example of this in a celebrated letter from Baldwin of Flanders to Innocent III praising the roles played by the bishops of Soissons and Troyes at the siege of Constantinople. Baldwin wrote that the two bishops' banners were the first to reach the walls, and that the bishops performed well in leading the attack. Baldwin was praising the military actions of these clerics in a letter to the pope, designed to elevate them in his eyes.[51]

---

[49] Duggan's book has been cited above. For the rest, see Frederick Russell, *The Just War in the Middle Ages* (Cambridge, 1975); Jonathan Riley-Smith, *The First Crusade and the Idea of Crusading* (Philadelphia, 2009); H.E.J. Cowdrey, *Pope Gregory VII 1073–1085* (Oxford, 1998); Bachrach, *Religion and the Conduct of War*. This book, as well as the forthcoming book by Daniel Gerrard, will seek to bridge these historiographical gaps. For an initial attempt, see Craig M. Nakashian, 'The Political and Military Agency of Ecclesiastical Leaders in Anglo-Norman England: 1066–1154', *The Journal of Medieval Military History* 12 (2014), 51–80.

[50] Gerrard makes this point very effectively, writing, 'It is not enough to juxtapose an individual's behaviour with a church council and declare it either canonical or uncanonical.' Gerrard, 16.

[51] Norman Housley, 'Recent Scholarship on Crusading and Medieval Warfare, 1095–1291: Convergence and Divergence', *War, Government and Aristocracy in the British Isles*

Consideration of warrior-clerics in the light of the crusades helps to contextualize their actions as they pertained to Christian warfare, but it can also present these clerics as a largely crusade-based phenomenon or as somehow a more common phenomenon on crusade than in warfare in Europe. While the crusades did certainly complicate the discourse over warrior-clerics, and brought in additional arguments over legitimacy, such clerics existed prior to and after the crusades, and their basic reception by contemporaries does not seem to have been overly influenced by the intervening religious wars. There is a possibility that because the warfare of the crusades was usually seen as more generally licit than conflicts between Christians, warrior-clerics on crusade received proportionally more positive assessments from contemporaries, but this approval was because crusading warfare was often seen as among the most licit forms of war for all combatants, not just clerics.[52]

Biographical sketches of individual clerics are extremely useful, but such an approach can lead historians to treat these clerics as exceptional, and therefore minimize the broader cultural implications of their activities. Certainly some authors have considered these questions, especially Constance Bouchard in her 1979 book *Spirituality and Administration: The Role of the Bishop in Twelfth-Century Auxerre*.[53] In her study of the episcopal see of Auxerre, Bouchard outlined the careers of the bishops who reigned from the eleventh through the thirteenth centuries. She examines much of the same sort of evidence as the current study – though in twelfth-century France rather than England – and she uncovers much of the same debate. For instance, in writing about the episcopate of Hugh of Noyers (1183–1206), Bouchard discussed his comfort with secular affairs and his willingness to engage in military activities as he saw fit. Eustache, a canon of the cathedral and the official biographer of Auxerre, wrote Hugh's entry in the *Gesta pontificum Autissiodorensium*. The biography was actually fairly critical of Hugh's secular ways and outlook, but in an interesting twist, Eustache praised Hugh for his use of military force to crush heresy.[54] In a campaign against the heretic Capuciati, Hugh organized a noble army to eliminate them. 'In Eustache's words, Hugh decided

---

c.1150–1500: *Essays in Honour of Michael Prestwich*, ed. Chris Given-Wilson, Ann Kettle, and Len Scales (Woodbridge, 2008), 205–6.

[52] As mentioned above, Jonathan Riley-Smith considers the role of clerics in the First Crusade in Riley-Smith, *The First Crusade and the Idea of Crusading*. See also James Brundage, *Medieval Canon Law and the Crusader* (Madison, 1969); *The History of Medieval Canon Law in the Classical Period, 1140–1234: From Gratian to the Decretals of Pope Gregory IX*, ed. Wilfried Hartmann and Kenneth Pennington (Washington, D.C., 2008).

[53] Constance Brittain Bouchard, *Spirituality and Administration: The Role of the Bishop in Twelfth-Century Auxerre* (Cambridge, MA, 1979).

[54] Bouchard, *Auxerre*, 99.

that when all political and Catholic disciplines were threatened with extermination, it was no time for "bland exhortations" but for "great undertakings." He rode out heavily armed, captured all the Capuciati in the Auxerrois.'[55] Eustache clearly saw Hugh's violent suppression of the Capuciati as worthy and acceptable, and he approved of Hugh's active use of military violence in this case, while still complaining about his broader embrace of secularity.[56]

Hugh's military priorities may account for his rocky relationship with the secular lords of the area. His embrace of warfare led him to take steps that earned the ire of his largely friendly biographer Eustache. He was criticized by Eustache for disallowing peasants around his family castle of Noyers to use the castle chapel because he was afraid that they might be spies in disguise.[57] Hugh was thereby elevating his military and defense-minded priorities over the clerical and spiritual responsibilities incumbent upon him as the bishop. He was also the sort of bishop who jealously guarded his rights and was very comfortable taking the secular side in arguments against the church hierarchy.[58] Eustache made a point of discussing Hugh's love of the company of knights, 'the bishop, he said, often discussed military tactics with them, feeling "such affection" for them that, when they were at home, he acted as only one among them, though when they went out he was careful to preserve his prerogatives.'[59] Preserving his prerogatives meant protecting his episcopal interests, but there is no indication that he did not behave as a knight in the company of knights, even in public. Robert of St.-Marien, on the other hand, 'criticized Hugh, as Eustache had not, for a love of "heavy spending" and of "knightly deeds," as well as for his "lack of clemency" and "immoderate exactions."'[60]

Finally, military histories have tended to fit clerics into the larger military machine, with the nature of their unique positions within chivalric and ecclesiastical culture unexamined. Institutional and military examinations tend to consider the size, effectiveness, and logistics of ecclesiastical contributions to armies, but not the larger cultural questions. An excellent example of this approach is

---

[55] Ibid., 102.
[56] It should be mentioned that another author, Robert, a canon of St.-Marien, condemned Hugh for his use of violent methods, but he also condemned any use of force against the heretics, so there was no evidence that Hugh's ecclesiastical status made his use of force worse. See Bouchard, *Auxerre*, 99–103.
[57] Bouchard, *Auxerre*, 108–9.
[58] Ibid., 107.
[59] Ibid., 109.
[60] Ibid., 110. In a foreshadowing of the case of Philip of Dreux in chapter 8, Hugh's election to Sens was quashed by Innocent III in favor of Peter of Corbeil because Hugh refused to recognize the interdict proclaimed against Philip II. It was the political opposition of the pope that cost him further ecclesiastical position, not his militaristic behavior.

David Bachrach's insightful and important study, *Religion and the Conduct of War*, in which he focuses on how clerics fit into the broader institutional use of military force. While Bachrach's book contains a huge amount of evidence of clerical involvement in warfare, and fits this involvement into the military campaigns and endeavors admirably, he examines clerical contributions to warfare almost entirely from the perspective of how it aided the morale of soldiers and armies. He begins his study with a first-century Roman officer who explained that soldiers who believed the gods were supporting them fought harder and had stronger morale, and he continues this meme throughout the period of his focus.[61] His book is invaluable for seeing how religion could be used to bolster military effectiveness, but where it does consider broader cultural trends, it tends to accept the idea that clerics fighting in battle or campaign were essentially 'criminals'.[62]

The interaction between clerical and knightly culture has been considered by Richard Kaeuper in *Holy Warriors: The Religious Ideology of Chivalry*, but generally from the perspective of lay knights and clerical authors writing about how knights ought to behave vis-à-vis piety and prowess. Kaeuper, following on the work of Richard Southern, does an excellent job of explaining the importance of examining 'basic ideas old and new, lay and clerical', rather than relying on only the governing authorities – in our case, canon law.[63] There were wider cultural currents and eddies that informed clerical (and lay) behavior, and without studying these ideas, or at least accounting for them, we cannot get an accurate image of how behavior was influenced, and how it was justified. Kaeuper also quotes Southern's argument that society was always in flux, with secular and clerical society feeding off one another. He wrote, 'Yet, as R.W. Southern has cautioned, clerical patterns were neither absolutely dominant nor static and "the theories and mechanisms of secular society also developed. The world did not stand still while the clerical ideal was realized."'[64] The dynamic interactions of medieval society made the concept of licit clerical behavior in relation to military affairs far more complicated than most reformers and canonists would have wished.

One thing that has become apparent in a study of existing scholarship is that military action by clerics has become conflated with 'secularity', both by modern scholars and by some medieval observers. Medieval critics of secular clerics could also criticize these clerics for being warriors, but the root cause of the opposition to these clerics was not always aversion to clerical warriors, but rather an aver-

---

[61] Bachrach, *Religion and the Conduct of War*, 1.
[62] Ibid., 172–5, especially note 11.
[63] Ibid., 6.
[64] Ibid. Original in R.W. Southern, *Western Society and the Church* (Harmondsworth, 1970), 41.

sion to secular service in general. Caesar of Heisterbach, writing in the 1220s, criticized the German bishops for wielding both spiritual and material swords.[65] He was complaining that this focus on secularity was making the German bishops less valuable as spiritual pastors because they had to think more about secular affairs, rather than spending time ministering to the spiritual well-being of their parishioners. Military action itself was not the primary problem; rather, it was the secularity in general that distracted them from their spiritual purpose. These two issues were not coterminous, and secularity was almost always seen as a greater problem for clerics than active service in war.

The Anglo-Norman monastic author Orderic Vitalis devoted some of his most colorful imagery to the issue. Orderic condemned in the strongest possible terms what he saw as covetousness, worldliness, and an overt desire to curry favor with secular rulers among ecclesiastical lords. He wrote, 'There were even some churchmen, wise and pious in outward appearance, who waited on the royal court out of covetousness for high office, and, to the great discredit of their cloth, shamelessly pandered to the king.'[66] This shameless pandering was unbecoming of the dignity of the church, and served to undermine the position of the ecclesiastical hierarchy vis-à-vis the king and the secular lords. It also served to distract them from their spiritual duties.[67] He went on to complain about churchmen who served the king out of hopes for 'bishoprics and abbeys, the provostships of churches, archdeaconries, deaneries, and other ecclesiastical offices and honours, which should have been granted only on grounds of piety and holy learning.'[68] Orderic united his disapproval of the worldliness and avarice of clerics with his reformist opposition to lay investiture and the granting of church offices by laymen. Orderic saw as the worst example of this covetousness Thurstan, abbot of Glastonbury. Thurstan had sought to introduce a new liturgy into his monastery, and when his monks resisted he led a group of soldiers into the church and attacked the monks violently, even to the point of having the soldiers shoot arrows into the monks huddled around the altar.[69] For Orderic, Thurstan represented the worst example of what could happen when secular rulers intruded their own candidates into ecclesiastical positions. His condemnation of Thurstan was not based only on his violence (though this was probably his greatest sin in Orderic's eyes), but

---

[65] Reuter, 'Episcopi cum sua militia', 79.
[66] *The Ecclesiastical History of Orderic Vitalis*, ed. and trans. Marjorie Chibnall, Vol. 2 (Oxford, 1999; reprint 2002), 269.
[67] Ibid.
[68] Ibid.
[69] Ibid., 271. Interestingly, Thurstan's only punishment came from William I, who transferred him to a different monastery in Normandy. He eventually returned to Glastonbury by paying a fine to William Rufus.

also on his secularity and the novelty of his proposed liturgical changes. In any case, Orderic saw his suspicions of churchmen who were elevated for their secular service confirmed.

Orderic then contrasted Thurstan's behavior with that of Guitmund, a 'venerable' monk at La-Croix-Saint-Leufroi.[70] Guitmund represented what a 'good' cleric ought to do when faced with secular rulers intruding into what Orderic saw as purely ecclesiastical affairs. When asked by William I to remain in England so that he could be given a wealthy ecclesiastical office, Guitmund responded,

> Read the Scriptures, and see if there is any law to justify the forcible imposition on a people of God of a shepherd chosen from among their enemies. We must first have a full ecclesiastical election by those who are to be governed, and then if that is canonical it must be confirmed by the fathers of the church and their fellows; otherwise it should be charitably corrected. How can you expect to avoid sin if you bestow on me and others, who had fled from the world and renounced all temporal goods for love of Christ, the spoils that you have seized by war and bloodshed? It is a fundamental law for men of religion to abstain from all plunder and refuse to accept booty even when it is offered as a reward for just service.[71]

Guitmond rejected William's overture on the grounds that neither was it William's place to grant ecclesiastical office, nor would it be becoming for Guitmund to accept the fruits of the conquest of England, since they were stained by blood. Eventually, Guitmund begged leave to return to Normandy to live a life of poverty, 'For Christ the good shepherd warns us, Woe to the rich men of this world who enjoy vain and useless pleasures.'[72]

Guitmund focused his condemnations on two things: the enjoyment of earthly pleasures and the advancement of earthly concerns over those of the spirit. The fact that the proposed benefice had been seized in war made it all the worse. Guitmund, however, refrained from making a specific condemnation of warfare. While this certainly does not indicate support for warrior-clerics, considering the fact that there were a number of clerics who were active in military affairs during and after the conquest (including Remigius of Lincoln, Geoffrey Coutances, Odo of Bayeux, and Wulfstan of Worcester), one could reasonably have expected him to offer such a condemnation. Instead, he focused on the problem of worldliness and secularity. With these two examples, Orderic was making a statement on how

[70] Ibid.
[71] Ibid., 273.
[72] Ibid., 279.

different clerics responded to the motivation of those clerics who reserved their primary loyalty to a secular ruler, as opposed to God. Worldliness, secularity, avarice, and pomp were to be condemned, whereas humility, spiritual purity, and mercy were to be extolled. The positive or negative depiction of clerics, warlike or otherwise, essentially came down to their adherence to these virtues or vices. This is how a Geoffrey of Coutances could receive mixed reviews, and a Wulfstan of Worcester could be considered nearly a saint in his own lifetime. One was perceived as worldly, and the other as humble.

Secular service was a fact of life for medieval clerics, and the debate over whether it was a great boon or a great threat never truly ceased. A simple fact of medieval society was that clerics, as major land-holders and men of regional or national power, had little choice but to be cognizant of the political power structure. The arguments between those who embraced this secular service, those who acquiesced to it, and those who deplored it probably filled many hours of talk in taverns and halls, and gave great motivation for comment by medieval authors. The embrace of war on behalf of the king was cast in this same mold. Those who were predisposed to resent clerical involvement in secular power would criticize it, and those who saw little problem with secular service usually would not.

The book is divided into two parts. The first, The Prescriptive Voices of the Debate, examines some of the most important and popular prescriptive voices of the discourse over licit clerical military behavior in western Europe. Chapter 1 lays out the evidence from the early church (beginning with the Gospels) and examines evidence up through the beginning of the eleventh century, ending with the Peace and Truce of God movements in France. Chapter 2 continues this examination by considering the evidence from the mid-eleventh-century papal reformers, the crusades and Military Orders, and the codification of canon law up through the *Liber Extra*, compiled under the orders of Pope Gregory IX. Chapter 3 examines warrior-clerics from the perspective of chivalric literature (such as the *Song of Roland*, the *Song of Aspremont*, and *William in the Monastery*), allowing us to gain an insight into the *mentalité* of the chivalric elites of medieval society. In general, the evidence from these epic tales supports the idea that while there was opposition to clerics fighting in war for petty, materialistic reasons, there was also a significant amount of support for those who fought in licit and laudable causes. There was also an almost universal condemnation of clerics, whether they fought or not, who were perceived as worldly, greedy, and hypocritical. As will be seen through other evidence, worldliness and avarice were almost always condemned, but active service in warfare was not always seen as evidence of either of those sins but, rather, could actually have salutary effects.

The second part, The Debate in Practice (chapters 4 through 8), begins our examination of actual English prelates from the Conquest in 1066 through the death of Peter des Roches in 1238. These clerics are arranged in chronologically thematic groups, providing the opportunity to examine actual experiences within the prescriptive ideologies developed and discussed in Part I. We can also see that, despite all of the changes in prescriptive ideals, there was not much change in how warrior-clerics were perceived over the nearly two-century period under study. Odo of Bayeux (d. 1095) and Peter des Roches (d. 1238) were subject to many of the same pressures, ideals, and defenses, despite the great distance in time. In each period we can see clerics who actively supported their sovereigns being given much more positive treatments than those who did not, even when the support involved active military service. We will also see that there was some difference in the treatment of clerics who directed men on campaign, versus those who swung weapons in combat.[73] While there were distinctions between fighting and leading in the prescription sources, John France argues that it was functionally difficult to make such a fine distinction on the battlefield. He writes that medieval commanders were often expected to be in the front ranks of their armies so as to inspire their men.[74] Considering the very personal nature of medieval combat, leading men in battle and actively fighting in battle were most probably largely indistinguishable for contemporary observers. Directing men on campaign could have provided some insulation from the visceral and bloody work of the battlefield, but once on the battlefield, that distinction would have probably been rendered moot.

There are two additional aspects to the issue that we should consider. The first is that the demeanor of the cleric in question mattered. Ostentatious clerics who dressed and behaved extravagantly often came in for criticism, while their humbler colleagues were praised, and this was true regardless of their actions on or off the battlefield. As shown in the example of the bishop of Sodor and Man, two bishops could meet on the field of battle, and there could be one who was in the right, and one who was in the wrong, despite canonical prohibitions against both their fighting. Medieval chronicles (and literature, and images, etc.) are full of grasping, worldly, avarice-ridden clerics being humbled by God or man, and so this theme was certainly popular and persuasive. The second crucial aspect was the political persuasion of the observer. The clerics in this book were generally

---

[73] Reuter, 'Episcopi cum sua militia', 80–1.

[74] John France, *Western Warfare in the Age of the Crusades, 1000–1300* (Ithaca, 1999), 139–49; John France, 'Property, Warfare, and the Renaissance of the Twelfth Century', *HSJ* 11 (2003), 73–4. There is evidence that some knights chafed under clerical command, and perhaps the refusal or inability of some clerical commanders to actively fight contributed to this. One is reminded of the famous complaint of a knight at the battle of Falkirk in 1298 that Bishop Antony Bek, commanding one of the army's divisions, ought to go back to his church to say Mass, and leave the fighting to the knights.

praised for serving the king, and clerical observers were usually predisposed in favor of the royal power. This was because of the general view that God's will had placed the king in power, and that his consecration with holy oil imparted some element of sanctity to his power and rule. Concomitant with this basic respect for royal authority, a growing awareness and interest in Roman law helped to elevate the ideal of serving the legitimate ruler and defending the *patria*.

Ultimately, contemporary sources featured an ongoing debate over how active clerics ought to be in military affairs. Ecclesiastical ideology was not only expressed by canon law, and the arguments were influenced by many factors that went beyond these traditional sources of prescriptive evidence. Clerics were seeking to unify Christian ideology with chivalric elite culture, or at least to influence the latter through the former. Periodically, reform movements radically sought to change clerical behavior, and they were occasionally focused on clerical warriors, but their preferred targets were secularity, simony, and nicholaitism. Warrior-clerics, to the extent that they were a concern, were lower down the list. Clerics were not uniformly condemned for their use of military force and instead were generally judged on the legitimacy of the cause, their political affiliation, or the political program of the person commenting on them. In many ways, clerics were judged in these cases in much same the way as secular nobles were, with their clerical status proving to be no absolute barrier to the acceptability of their use of military violence.[75]

---

[75] In regards to lay violence, Kaeuper writes, 'In short, the undoubted Christianization of violence and war loaded one side of a balance for which the other side carried a weight of continuing Christian doubt about war and surprisingly brisk denunciation of specific knights or even the Order of knighthood. This duality of view was undoubtedly tilted in favor of sanctified violence, but even if the doubtful view was less emphasized it persisted throughout the Middle Ages. [See Ralph of Niger] Tension and paradox were not ended by reform popes, learned canonists, peace movements or the preaching of crusade. The evident lack of crusading success after the first great effort, in fact, led to fairly widespread doubts about divine favor for the enterprise; preachers found it harder to get a receptive audience and win converts; some portion of the faithful seemed to believe only in defensive war against the Saracens. Searching critiques of knightly violence continued alongside much sanctification of warfare. The clerical view was usually modulated according to the perpetrator of violence, the victim of the violence, and, above all, the authority justifying it.' Kaeuper, *Holy Warriors*, 14.

PART I

Prescriptive Voices of the Debate

CHAPTER 1

Clerics and War in the First Millennium

CHRISTIANITY had, from its earliest days, an uneasy relationship with violence. Christ preached turning the other cheek to one's enemy, but he also drove the moneychangers forcibly out of the Temple.[1] While many Christians subscribed to a prescriptive condemnation of clerics who actively fought or engaged in military battles and campaigns, there were always clerics who ignored these prescripts and took on such roles, with greater or lesser relish depending on the cleric in question. This chapter surveys the most important texts, trends, and laws of the church as they pertained to military activity and the use of arms by clerics over the first thousand years of Christianity. The goal is to illuminate the creation of a set of prescriptive rules for the military behavior of clerics, with the tacit understanding that the reality of clerical behavior was far different.[2] What will be shown is that, while military force by clerics was never openly accepted within the canonical tradition, there was much more ambivalence over it in the broader cultural discourse than has normally been considered. The debate over whether violence was licit for Christians, let alone clerics, was well under way in the period prior to the acceptance of Christianity by Constantine.[3] After the adoption of Christianity by the Roman Empire, military activity by Christians had to become legitimated (though this did not necessarily have to extend to clerics). Early councils, in fact, legislated against the participation of clerics in warfare, though with the dissolution of Roman, and later Carolingian, power, clerics nevertheless took on a larger role in defending their regions and in carving out noble holdings, both of which often involved the use of military power.

[1] Matthew 21:12–17 and 5:3–11.
[2] Duggan sees law as the most valid way to understand the broader contours of cultural discourse, especially as compared to relying on individual commentators and authors. He writes that law was, 'an investigation not of what theologians and others believed the clergy ought to do, but rather of what ecclesiastical laws permitted, required, or forbade them to do.' He is right in a sense, but he understates the prescriptive and idealized nature of what law represented, especially a law so frequently ignored without consequence. See Duggan, *Armsbearing and the Clergy*, 90.
[3] Shean has an excellent discussion of early Christian attitudes towards warfare and the Roman military, see John F. Shean, *Soldiering for God: Christianity and the Roman Army* (Leiden, 2010), 71–103.

The presumed ideals of the Christian church were, on the surface, antithetical to an embrace of violent warfare, thus the early arguments in the church were over whether Christians in general could be soldiers.[4] Many modern historians portray the early church as uniformly pacifist, or nearly so, and that with the embrace of the religion by Constantine and the Roman government, accommodations had to be made by the religion regarding violence. This basic narrative pervades most treatments of the first few centuries of Christianity, especially among those who wish to find support for modern pacifism in the dictates of the early church.[5] Early Christianity, however, was full of contradictory and competing ideals and voices, voices that decried violence, as well as those that exulted in it as a tool for the advancement of God's righteous will on Earth. These contradictions are mostly found in texts that are a few centuries removed from Christ's life, but some elements of them can be found even in the foundational texts of the religion. As early as the Gospel stories of Christ, as we will see below, one can detect a lack of clarity as to the role of active violence within the temporal world, as well as larger questions regarding the role of the temporal world within the larger scheme of the universe and God's domain. Evidence could be found on both sides of the ledger regarding the embrace of military service and violence within the church, and for those seeking justification from their predecessors for current actions there was no shortage of supporting evidence.

Christianity, especially in the modern age, has a strong tradition of Christ as the compassionate pacifist, who taught his followers to love their neighbor and turn the other cheek rather than to seek vengeance and perpetrate violence. This Christ was trumpeted by authors of a pacifist nature as early as the writings of Tertullian (c.160–c.220). However, for readers who sought to justify violence in advancing

---

[4] Numerous biblical quotations were cited by medieval authors as guides to behavior. This brief survey highlights only the clearest and most important, those that directly comment on military violence and the role of the church in the world. Also, medieval authors used the examples of Joshua, Gideon, David, Judas Maccabeus, and others from the Old Testament to justify holy licit violence. For much of what follows, see Carl Erdmann, *The Origin of the Idea of Crusade*, trans. Marshall Baldwin and Walter Goffart (Stuttgart, 1935; Princeton, 1977), 273.

[5] See especially John Driver, *How Christians Made Peace With War: Early Christian Understandings of War* (Scottdale, 1976). For a more even treatment of the tensions inherent within early Christian thought both before and after Constantine, see Jean-Michel Hornus, *It Is Not Lawful for Me to Fight: Early Christian Attitudes Toward War, Violence, and the State*, trans. Alan Kreider and Oliver Coburn (Scottdale, 1980). For a very different take, as well as an invaluable historiographical introduction, see Adolph Harnack, *Militia Christi: The Christian Religion and the Military in the First Three Centuries*, trans. David McInnes Gracie (Philadelphia, 1981; originally published 1905). John Shean discusses these assumptions in Shean, 71.

Christian themes, Christ's own actions and words could prove a fertile ground as well. Among the most famous of Gospel quotations that could be used in support of clerical violence was Matthew 10:34–36.[6] Matthew related Christ's exhortation to his disciples that discord and violence were necessary for the kingdom of God to be established. He wrote, 'Do not think that I have come to bring peace to the world. No, I did not come to bring peace, but a sword.'[7] The church brought a sword to the world, and peace could be achieved only after the discord and violence had played out. Medieval Christians and clerics could argue that they were playing their part in bringing about the peace of the church through recourse to warfare. Christ continued by explaining that he came to set sons against their fathers, and to set daughters against their mothers. He finished by saying that 'a man's worst enemies will be the members of his own family.'[8] The violent and socially disruptive nature of this message was even more pronounced when we recall the strong societal ties provided by the Roman family, and especially the power and authority of the Roman father (*pater familias*) over his family.

However, Matthew also provided a counterpoint to this reasoning earlier, in chapter 10. When Christ warned his disciples of the persecutions and hardships they would face, he explained that he was sending them out to be sheep among the wolves.[9] As part of this analogy, he cautioned them to be 'as gentle as doves' and to 'run away to another' town when men came to persecute them.[10] While this refusal to fight against persecutors was itself a courageous rejection of cultural mores, and an invitation for additional violence, it probably would not have filled those medieval observers who saw physical vigor as the proper response to aggression with admiration. Christ was at times explicit in his rejection of violence, and thus the hands of pacifists were strengthened through the reliance on Christ's numerous references to non-violence. Nevertheless, these quotations, written within lines of one another, could be used to justify polar opposites of behavior.

The arrest of Jesus in the garden, a scene recounted by all four of the orthodox Gospel writers, offered the clearest example of the tensions between pacifism and violence in Christianity. Christ's own reaction to Judas's betrayal showed

---

[6] Translations are taken from the *Holy Bible: Today's English Version with Deuterocanonicals/Apocrypha*, American Bible Society (New York, 1978). All Latin biblical quotations are from the Vulgate.

[7] Matthew 10:34. 'Nolite arbitrari quia pacem venerim mittere in terram: non veni pacem mittere, sed gladium.' See also Luke 12:51–53; 14:26–27.

[8] Matthew 10:35–36. 'veni enim separare hominem adversus patrem suum, et filiam adversus matrem suam, et nurum adversus socrum suam et inimici hominis, domestici ejus.'

[9] Matthew 10:16; Mark 13:9; Luke 21:12.

[10] Matthew 10:16, 10:23.

acceptance and concern for his followers. His peaceful surrender was directly contrasted with Peter's violent resistance. As the armed crowd moved to take Jesus into custody, 'Simon Peter, who had a sword, drew it and struck the High Priest's slave, cutting off his right ear.'[11] In John's Gospel, Christ immediately chastised Peter and said '"Put your sword back in its place! Do you think that I will not drink the cup of suffering which my Father has given me?"'[12] In Luke's Gospel, Christ declared '"Enough of this!"' and healed the man's ear.[13] In Matthew's Gospel, Christ responded to the attack on the servant by declaring '"Put your sword back in its place ... All who take the sword will die by the sword."'[14] Christ's chastising of the sword-bearer and his ominous warning that he who lives by the sword dies by the sword was seized upon as a condemnation of violence and a rejection of its use.

However, this very same episode could be used to justify holy violence in its proper time and place. Immediately following his warning that living by the sword leads to death by the sword, Christ continued, '"Don't you know that I could call on my Father for help, and at once he would send me more than twelve armies of angels? But in that case, how could the Scriptures come true which say that this is what must happen?"'[15] Christ is not rejecting violence per se but, rather, is rejecting violence in this particular situation as interfering in the necessary condemnation and execution that he must suffer in order to fulfill the Scriptures. He must be seized and killed in order that his suffering, death, and resurrection would redeem mankind. His statement that armies of angels could appear to defend him, if he so desired, further reinforces the idea that violence is justifiable in the right circumstances. Mark's Gospel fails to record any condemnation from Christ surrounding the attack on the servant. After the disciple (Peter) strikes off the High Priest's servant's ear, Christ directs his ire at the High Priest and his followers for coming to arrest him armed, as though he was an outlaw.[16]

The Garden of Gethsemane is of central importance to our study, since it was used by canonists such as Gratian to condemn clerical involvement in warfare, and also to justify licit Christian violence by St. Bernard de Clairvaux. Whereas Gratian used the Garden as an example of why clerics ought not to fight in secular wars, for St. Bernard, the fact that Christ told Peter to put his sword in its place, and that he could call on an army of angels, showed that Christ was not pacifistically condemning violence in all times and places but, rather, only in that time and

---

[11] John 18:10.
[12] John 18:11.
[13] Luke 22:51.
[14] Matthew 26:52.
[15] Matthew 26:53–54.
[16] Mark 14:47–49.

that place. After all, if Christ had never wanted Peter to use the temporal sword, he would have told him to abandon it entirely. Instead, by allowing him to keep it on his belt, he tacitly acknowledged that it would be used in the future, or that a place existed for it in the ideal plan. While St. Bernard used this example to justify *Christian* violence, rather than *clerical* violence, the establishment of the former places pressure on the latter.

Arguments in the early church, as indicated above, focused on questions of the legitimate employment of violence by Christians. With the reign of Constantine and recognition and elevation of Christianity by imperial officials, this argument was largely settled.[17] A Christian empire could not afford to promulgate the idea that violence and military service were antithetical to the Christian message and salvation. This was underscored at the Council of Arles in 314, one of the first Church councils held after Constantine legalized and officially recognized Christianity. The third canon of the council forbade Christians in the military from laying down their arms during peacetime, thus reinforcing the idea that being a Christian and fulfilling one's duty as a Roman citizen were not at odds.[18] The argument had been shifted to military service and violence by those who had become clerics, and especially those who had become monks. The Council of Nicaea of 325 created a penance system for those who had renounced the world and then returned to it. For those who had 'cast off their military belts' and then afterwards ran back 'like dogs to their own vomit', they must spend thirteen years doing penance.[19]

---

[17] As James Brundage points out, arguments about violence prior to Constantine were over its licit use by Christians. After Constantine, the arguments were over when a Christian government could use violence legitimately. See James Brundage, *Medieval Canon Law* (New York, 1995), 14–15. Shean does a good job of illuminating the fact that early Christianity always had members who supported the active use of military violence. Shean, 86–105. Alan Kreider also pushes back strongly against the notion that early Christianity was inherently pacifist. See Alan Kreider, 'Military Service in the Church Orders', *The Journal of Religious Ethics* 31 (Winter, 2003), 415–17. Cf. Gerrard, 20. Gerrard writes, 'Despite the difficult conditions in which it had to operate, the Primitive church was wholly pacifist in its philosophy, expecting to be persecuted for its beliefs and to offer no physical resistance.'

[18] Arguments swirl around the meaning of this canon. Those seeking to find evidence of universal pacifism point to it to reinforce the idea that Christians were *expected* to lay down their weapons during war, but not peace. Others, chiefly following Harnack, read it to mean that Christians were obviously forbidden to lay down weapons during war, but that even during peace they had to fulfill their military duties. Harnack's interpretation is to be preferred, since rampant desertion of Christians during wartime would not have been allowed by Roman officials, regardless of the newly emerging détente. See Harnack, 87–8. Cf. Hornus, 172.

[19] *Decrees of the Ecumenical Councils*, ed. Norman P. Tanner, Vol. 1: Nicaea I to Lateran V (Washington, D.C., 1990), 11–12.

Katherine Allen Smith has demonstrated that there was intense debate in the early church over concerns that some biblical, especially Old Testament, imagery was too violent and might inspire warfare.[20] Indeed, early monks borrowed the imagery and descriptions from St. Paul to cast themselves as warriors of Christ. These texts were crucial to 'the creation of a distinctly monastic ideal of spiritual combat.'[21] For early monks, the violent and military imagery of the Old and New Testaments gave them a roadmap for how to combat demons and spiritual enemies of Christ. This spiritual warfare was important, especially since they were 'banned from bearing weapons and participating in actual warfare, monks' unquestioned prowess in liturgical combat gave them power over the evil forces that threatened all Christians and reinforced their self-perception as the defenders of Christendom.'[22] Monks, sidelined from the physical warfare against the enemies of the church, valorized their own prowess in the (spiritual) conflicts still open to them.

On the other hand, exceptional need could compel clerics to take active roles in warfare, though ideally this would be done through leadership and inspiration, rather than through personally shedding blood. We see an excellent example of this from the fifth-century visit to Britain by Bishop (later saint) Germanus of Auxerre. While visiting the island to combat the Pelagian heresy, Germanus (a former soldier and the leader of the expedition) took part in a battle against Pictish invaders.[23] The initial account of the battle comes from Constantius's *Life of Saint Germanus*, a Gaulish source dating from around 480. Constantius made no effort to downplay Germanus's actions in battle, and instead focused attention on them. That being said, however, Germanus's victory over the Picts was miraculous, bloodless, and a sign of God's favor. Thus, Constantius (and later authors such as Bede) created a balance whereby clerics could be valorized for their roles in battle, but only if those battles were sufficiently sanitized to avoid transgressing broader cultural concerns about bloodshed by churchmen.

According to Constantius, the mere presence of the saintly bishops in the Britons' camp lent an element of holy war to the campaign, with the assumption

---

[20] Katherine Allen Smith, *War and the Making of Medieval Monastic Culture* (Woodbridge, 2011), 10–16.

[21] Ibid., 9. For a broader discussion of monks borrowing military imagery, see 72–96.

[22] Ibid., 10.

[23] For an excellent overview of the visit, and his battle against the Picts particularly, see Michael E. Jones, 'The Historicity of the Alleluja Victory', *Albion: A Quarterly Journal Concerned with British Studies* 18 (Autumn, 1986), 363–73. Cf. Michael E. Jones, 'St. Germanus and the *Adventus Saxonum*', *HSJ* 2 (London, 1990), 1–13. See also Bachrach, *Religion and the Conduct of War*, 19–21. Bede also discusses this event, though he relies heavily on the account of Constantius. See *Bede's Ecclesiastical History of the English People*, ed. Bertram Colgrave and R.A.B. Mynors (Oxford, 1969), 62.

that God would favor the Christian side in battle. He wrote that 'to have such apostles for leaders was to have Christ Himself fighting in the camp.'[24] Constantius was speaking allegorically, but the implication of the allegory was such that if Christ was taking an active part in the warfare, why could not his appointed servants? Germanus himself saw it as such when he declared to the assembled Christian army that he would serve as their war-leader in the upcoming battle. He then proceeded to arrange the army according to his military expertise of terrain and tactics, and took personal command. As the Pictish force approached, the bishops led the assembled army in three successive chants of 'Alleluja!' This broke the will of the pagans, who fled in terror, and many were drowned in a nearby river.[25] For Constantius, and later Bede, the battle was a great victory for Christianity, made even more miraculous by the fact that it was achieved 'without bloodshed and … gained by faith and not by force.'[26] For Michael Jones, this is evidence that while some churchmen made peace with military service, it never extended to clerics bearing arms themselves nor to clerics shedding blood, whereas for David Bachrach, the account of the battle was an example of the power that religion had as a motivator and morale booster for Christian armies[27] They are certainly correct that Bede and Constantius saw the victory as more glorious for being bloodless (though still mortal for the pagans), and that it is evidence of the crucial role that religion could play in the morale of a Christian army. However, we should also highlight the importance of the fact that Germanus was willing to take on a personal role as a military commander, despite (or perhaps because of) his position as bishop, and that in the eyes of contemporaries, God stood with him in this violent endeavor.

Germanus's generalship is an important contrast to the common canonical prohibitions on clerics involving themselves in war. Canon 7 of the Council of Chalcedon in 451 reinforced the prohibition against clerics, both secular and regular, taking active military roles, decreeing 'that those who have once joined the ranks of the clergy or have become monks are not to depart on military service or for secular office. Those who dare do this, and do not repent and return to what, in God, they previously chose, are to be anathematized.'[28] This is a clear canonical prohibition on clerics becoming soldiers; however, it is also concerned with secularity. The canon

---

[24] Jones, 'The Historicity of the Alleluja Victory', 364.
[25] Ibid., 364–5.
[26] Ibid., 365.
[27] Ibid., 366; Bachrach, *Religion and the Conduct of War*, 20–1.
[28] *Decrees of the Ecumenical Councils*, Vol. 1, 90, 'Qui semel in clero deputati sunt aut monarchorum vitam expetiverunt, statuimus, neque ad militiam neque ad dignitatem aliquam venire mundanam aut, hoc temptantes et non agentes poenitentiam, ut redeant ad hoc, quod propter Deum prius elegerunt, anathematizari.'

assumes the existence an organized, professional military, and clerics who joined the military would be taking on another profession in addition to their clerical calling. Thus, the primary problem was the taking on of an onerous profession that would undermine their dedication to their clerical calling and would undermine their clerical identity with a soldier's one. This interpretation is reinforced by the fact that the canon also prohibited clerics to depart 'for secular office', and by canon 3 of the same council, which stated that no cleric 'should either manage property or involve himself as an administrator of worldly business' unless he was unavoidably taking care of minors, or he was appointed by the local bishop.[29] This is evidence of a broader pattern among early reformers to disassociate clerics from secular entanglements, except in cases of exceptional need. Concurrent with this was the formulation of a clerical *ordo* as a cultural, and legal, justification for the separation of clerics from worldly concerns and the dangers of worldliness. This period saw an increasing acceptance of the idea that clerics represented a separate group within society. Enlisting in the military, with its forced deployments, long term of service, oaths to secular powers, and system of hierarchical authority outside of the church would have been anathema to this process.

This canonical prohibition, focused as it was on the professional aspect of soldiering, became increasingly at odds with the realities in western Europe during the demise of Roman imperial authority in the West. The fifth and sixth centuries saw increasing need for leadership, politically and militarily, at the local and regional level in many places within the soon-to-be-former Roman Empire. The role of bishops as local leaders and military commanders increased in the period after Roman control effectively ended in the West, especially in France.[30] While the chief concern of the canon seems to be that cleric should not attempt to hold two full-time professions at one time, in general the canons sought to prevent clerics from engaging in warlike activities overall. However, churchmen who were faced with the collapse of political power and military protection could have embraced active roles in defending their regions or cities and could have gained comfort from other Christian sources, notably the military imagery of the psalms. In them, God appears as 'unmistakably a warrior; armed with a sword, shield, and bow, and riding in a chariot surrounded by an innumerable host', and who would thus have appealed to Christian leaders under siege.[31] Reformers such as Augustine and Cassiodorus thus undertook to recast these images as purely

---

[29] Ibid., 88.

[30] Friedrich Prinze, 'King, Clergy and War at the Time of the Carolingians', *Saints, Scholars and Heroes: Studies in Medieval Culture in Honour of Charles W. Jones*, ed. M.H. King and W.M. Stevens, Vol. 2 (Collegeville, 1979), 307–8, 312–13. See also Duggan, *Armsbearing and the Clergy*, 19.

[31] Smith, *War and the Making of Medieval Monastic Culture*, 24–5.

spiritual metaphors.[32] We can see some reflection of the reality that clerics were taking active military roles in the fact that while the canons continued to legislate against armed clerics, they no longer always listed specific punishments along with the condemnation.[33] A good example comes from the Fourth Council of Toledo (633), which forbade the use of arms by clerics in insurrections.[34] The return of a reasonably centralized state under the Carolingians in France brought these arguments back to the forefront.

Reformers saw in the Carolingians, and especially Charlemagne, an opportunity to use the centralization of the state as a tool against warrior-churchmen. Reformers sought to more clearly distinguish between acceptable and unacceptable military roles for churchmen, and they relied on the twin concerns regarding clerics holding two full-time 'professions', as well as those involving bloodshed. At the Concilium Germanicum of 742, clerics were forbidden from taking part in war, unless they were merely ministering to the troops, though at a council at Soissons in 744 the impetus against armed clerics slowed, and there were no canons promulgated against them (though abbots were allowed on campaign only if they accompanied the soldiers derived from their lands).[35] St. Boniface complained to Pope Zacharias that bishops in the Carolingian kingdom 'fought armed in the army and spilt the blood of pagans and Christians, that they were drunkards, negligent in their office and addicted to hunting.'[36] The Pope extolled the Old Testament example of Moses praying alongside Joshua as he fought the Amalekites as a demonstration that prayers, not swords, were the proper weapons of clerics.[37] Each of the new 'elites' of Carolingian society would thereby gain the

---

[32] Ibid. Augustine's interpretation was fundamental to later exegesis. See 26-8. For an interesting discussion of the evolving nature of Augustine's contextual assumptions underpinning his beliefs, see R.A. Markus, 'Saint Augustine's Views on the "Just War"', *The Church and War*, ed. W.J. Sheils, *Studies in Church History* 20 (London, 1983), 1–13.

[33] Prinze, 'King, Clergy and War', 302–3. Prinze also very effectively argued that a more subtle interpretation of the existing canons can demonstrate far more debate over warrior-clerics than appears at first glance.

[34] 'De clericis qui in quacumque seditione arma volentes sumpserint.' Gerrard, 24. Gerrard also mentions that despite not being a widely disseminated canon, it did find its way into the canonical collection of Lanfranc and was thus known in England. Gerrard provides a valuable overview of the canonical prohibitions during this period. See Gerrard, 19–25. Cf. Bachrach, *Religion and the Conduct of War*, 7–31.

[35] Prinze, 'King, Clergy and War', 305–6.

[36] Ibid., 306. Original in MGH Epp sel. 1, 83 which read in part, 'et qui pugnant in excercitu amati et effundebant propria manu sanguinem hominum, sive paganorum sive christianorum.'

[37] Dominique Barthélemy, *The Serf, the Knight, and the Historian*, trans. Graham Robert Edwards (Ithaca, 2009), 169. Barthélemy sees this example as evidence of an attempt

honor of fighting on behalf of king and Christ, and clerics would do so in a way singularly reflective of their profession and position, but they would no longer be personally shedding blood.[38] A knight becoming a cleric was seen 'not as a farewell to arms but as a change of arms' from one militia to another.[39]

Pepin's son Charlemagne was influenced by clerical reformers to minimize the roles of armed clerics, but he too saw a need for clerical involvement in warfare at some level, as the Carolingian military machine relied on retinues and soldiers from ecclesiastical landholdings, as well as the spiritual power of their prayers.[40] There was thus a conscious attempt to find a middle ground between the prescripts of clerical reformers who sought to completely separate clerics from warfare, and the Carolingian rulers who relied on the clerics for military support. Charlemagne, and the later Carolingians, sought to ameliorate, in the eyes of reformers, some of the more egregious examples of churchmen fighting by granting large numbers of exemptions from personal military service to clerics, and by separating personal service from the service owed from their lands.[41] Many clerics availed themselves of every opportunity to avoid service, and the Council of Ver in 844 supported the idea that bishops should appoint a suitable layman to lead their retinues of soldiers when they could not or would not attend themselves.[42] Prinze saw Charlemagne, drawing on the precedents of Pepin III, as creating a distinction between upper prelates and lower priests in terms of military service, with the former being allowed on campaign, but the latter being forbidden arms entirely.[43] Thus, as Prinze argued, there developed a distinction between both the canonistic sources and the acceptability of clerical

---

to create an 'Old Testament-style kingdom governed in a Gelasian spirit ... in which combat through prayer counted as much as arms.'

[38] Barthélemy develops these ideas into a broader discussion of the creation of twin elite statuses, with increasing distinctions between the lay and spiritual. Ibid., 169-73.

[39] Ibid., 174.

[40] Bachrach, *Religion and the Conduct of War*, 33-49.

[41] Prinze, 'King, Clergy and War', 306.

[42] Janet L. Nelson, 'The Church's Military Service in The Ninth Century: A Contemporary Comparative View?', *The Church and War*, ed. W.J. Sheils, *Studies in Church History* 20 (Oxford, 1983), 20.

[43] Prinze, 'King, Clergy, and War', 315. He wrote that Charlemagne had 'checked the radical application of ecclesiastical prohibition of war for the clergy at the Synod of Soissons in 744 and at the same time created an area free of punishment for the prelate's military service ... It is no more and no less than the conscious separation of an aristocratic "prelates' church" from the general hierarchy. Episcopi and abbates appear in the capitularies closely linked with the comites and the missi but nevertheless clearly and sharply distinguished from the bulk of the clerici for whom the canonical prohibition on the bearing of arms remained valid.' For more treatment of this topic, see 315-18.

military service, but also between the upper prelates of the church and the lower members. Bishops and abbots possessed the political power to insulate themselves from canonistic retribution to a much greater degree than priests and monks, and their political actions were likely to be judged primarily as political, rather than as ecclesiastical.[44] Pepin's solution, and Charlemagne's continuation of it, sought to create a canonistic distinction between bishops and priests within the confines of the ecclesiastical system, and sought to minimize the direct involvement of churchmen in battle, if not in larger military contexts. According to Astronomus, Louis the Pious's sympathetic biographer, it was Louis who finally persuaded the upper clergy to renounce their arms and to embrace the spreading Rule of St. Benedict.[45] Charles the Bald in 865 demanded military service from the churches in Burgundy, but the order demanded only that the king's representatives, the *missi*, 'are to be responsible for ensuring that each bishop, abbot and abbess should send his or her men there on time with the whole quota required, each contingent along with its banner-man (*guntfanonarius*) who, together with our missi, is responsible for his comrades.'[46] This order would seem to indicate that the appearance by the retinues on campaign was increasingly seen as more important than personal leadership by clerics (many of whom would have been aged and without military training). Instead the upper clergy would aid the Frankish kingdom's war efforts through prayers, as well as men and materials from their lands. We can see the same evidence of this shift in the letter Lupus of Ferrières wrote to congratulate Abbot Odo of Corbie for his stalwart defense against a Viking raid in 859. In addition to his congratulations, he cautioned the young abbot's exuberance in battle. Writing that Odo's habit of pitching himself unarmed into the fray scared Lupus, he suggested that Odo be content 'with only putting your troops in position – for that's as much as is suitable to your vow – and leave it to the fighting-men (*armati*) to carry out their "profession" with instruments of war.'[47] For Lupus, Odo's actions in battle were against the basic profession of a cleric, and his decision to fight unarmed (assuming we trust Lupus's report), while making it less likely to shed blood, did not make his actions acceptable. While Lupus's letter fit clearly into the narrative constructed above of a lessening of cultural support for direct clerical involvement in military violence, the fact that young Abbot Odo saw otherwise is evidence of a more tangled reality.

---

[44] Janet Nelson argued that the Carolingians understood that bishops and abbots had to lead their military retinues on campaign, and this leadership role was 'never questioned by any Carolingian churchman: so firm was the *Einstaatung* of the Frankish Church.' See Nelson, 'The Church's Military Service in The Ninth Century, 20.
[45] Barthélemy, 170.
[46] Nelson, 'The Church's Military Service in the Ninth Century', 21.
[47] Ibid., 23.

Odo implicitly saw his role as defending both the bodies and souls of his monks, and his outlook was explicitly stated by Ruotger, author of the *Life of Saint Bruno* (archbishop of Cologne 953–65). He claimed that saving souls and saving lives were both important functions of the bishop. Speaking against those who criticized prince-bishops such as Bruno, Ruotger wrote,

> If anyone who is ignorant of the divine dispensation objects to a bishop ruling the people and facing dangers of war and argues that he is responsible only for their souls, the answer is obvious: it is only by doing these things that the guardian and teacher of the Faithful brings to them the rare gift of peace and saves them from the darkness in which there is no light.[48]

For Ruotger, protecting the flock on Earth was just as important as making sure their souls were heading for Heaven. The church councils of the ninth century and beyond, however, saw no gray area regarding warrior churchmen. Pope Nicholas I saw clerical involvement in bloodshed and war as inherently antithetical to the clerical identity. Nicholas (and these church councils) was reacting against what he saw as the prevalence of military behavior among clerics during the Carolingian period. The councils of Meaux in 845, Paris in 846, Ticino in 876, and Metz in 888 legislated against clerics (or those seen to be of the clergy) who went about armed or armored, and this prohibition was taken up in the canonical collections of Burchard, Ivo, and Gratian.[49] Nicholas also declared that soldiers of the world and soldiers of the church were inherently different, and it was not right for them to mingle their responsibilities.[50] For him it was 'ridiculous' that a layman would interfere with the Mass, or that clerics would take up arms and fight.[51] While these councils did not eliminate such behavior, they did help to lay the foundation for the codification of canonical prohibitions in the eleventh and

---

[48] Ruotger, *Vita Brunonis Archiepiscopi Coloniensis*, MGH SS rer. Germ. N.S. 10:23–4. I would like to thank John France for directing me to this source. The entire passage reads, 'Causantur forte aliqui divine dispensationis ignari, quare episcopus rem populi et pericula belli tractaverit, cum animarum tantummodo curam susceperit. Quibus res ipsa facile, si quid sanum sapient, satisfacit, cum tantum et tam insuetum illis presertim partibus pacis bonum per hunc tutorem et doctorem fidelis populi longe lateque propagatum aspiciunt, ne pro hac re quasi in tenebras amplius, ubi non est presentia lucis, offendant.'

[49] For these and other developments, see Gerrard, 26–30. See also Duggan, *Armsbearing and the Clergy*, 97.

[50] Tomaž Mastnak, *Crusading Peace: Christendom, the Muslim World and the Western Political Order* (Berkeley, 2002), 22–3.

[51] Ibid. Duggan explains that Nicholas also forbade clerics to even aid in keeping watch for pirates. See Duggan, *Armsbearing and the Clergy*, 97.

twelfth centuries. They also fed into the arguments present in the attempts by clerics to create peace in their regions – a phenomenon that has come to be known as the 'Peace of God'.[52]

Beginning in southern France, and eventually spreading northwards, these church councils attempted to minimize the violence plaguing their society.[53] Although discussing a common 'movement' might convey too much organization and structure to this phenomenon, we can certainly see that there were common concerns regarding these ideas, concerns that manifested themselves most clearly in France during the tenth and early eleventh centuries. While these councils eventually may have formed the basis for a papal effort in the mid-eleventh century to centralize control over the reform movement, and to advance papal interests alongside it, the initial councils were extremely limited in their scope and their reach (indeed, Ernst-Dieter Hehl posits that the Reform Papacy paid little attention to the 'movement' until the pontificate of Leo IX).[54] The first such gathering is attributed to Bishop Guy of Le Puy, who convened a council in 975 to impose 'peace' on his diocese.[55] He sought to restrain the secular nobility who were pillaging churches and attacking the poor, but he did not promulgate official canons, nor did he seek to expand the reach of his council into neighboring dioceses by bringing in his fellow bishops.[56] His was very much a localized effort.

[52] This section merely contextualizes these councils and activities within the larger scope of the cultural debate over warrior churchmen. For the Gelasian implications of the Peace/Truce of God ideology, see Mastnak, 2–21. Cf. Barthélemy, 203–7. See also Strickland, *War and Chivalry*, 70–5.

[53] Many historians dispute the notion that these councils represented a 'movement'. Kathleen Cushing sees too much diversity in the various councils to claim any coherence, whereas Dominique Barthélemy thinks that separating the northern and southern councils is itself too artificial. See Kathleen Cushing, *Reform and Papacy in the Eleventh Century: Spirituality and Social Change* (Manchester, 2005), 39–45; Barthélemy, 152 and 204. There was also geographical diversity, with councils in Aquitaine, Burgundy, and the Auvergne, though Bull argues that the particular character of Aquitanian society could explain much of why there was such a focus on disarming the clergy. See Marcus Bull, *Knightly Piety and the Lay Response to the First Crusade: The Limousin and Gascony, c.970–c.1130* (Oxford, 1993), 24–31. Cf. Amy G. Remensyder, 'Pollution, Purity, and Peace: An Aspect of Social Reform between the Late Tenth Century and 1076', *The Peace of God: Social Violence and Religious Response in France around the Year 1000*, ed. Thomas Head and Richard Landes (Ithaca, 1992), 282, esp. n. 7.

[54] Ernst-Dieter Hehl, 'War, Peace and the Christian Order', *The New Cambridge Medieval History*, ed. David Luscombe and Jonathan Riley-Smith, Vol. 4 (Cambridge, 2004), 194.

[55] For an interesting contextualization of Guy as a displaced Northerner, see Bernard S. Bachrach, 'The Northern Origins of the Peace Movement at Le Puy in 975', *Essays on the Peace of God: The Church and the People in Eleventh-Century France*, ed. Thomas Head and Richard Landes, *Historical Reflections/Réflexions Historiques* 14 (Fall, 1987), 405–21.

[56] Cushing, *Reform and Papacy*, 39.

Additionally, he did not rely purely on ecclesiastical power, but also brought the secular military power of his family to bear.[57] While this council served as an important precedent for later peace councils in its use of the oath of peace, the ready acceptance by the bishop to use military force to ensure that his political priorities were met was also precedent setting, and would reach its apogee in the Peace League of Bourges (discussed below).

Traditionally, scholars have seen these councils as an attempt by the church to replace the declining power of the Carolingian kings and to combat local anarchy.[58] More recently, however, historians have interpreted them as an attempt to separate the clergy from the laity, as well as to 'purify' clergymen of the 'pollution' of secular life.[59] The traditional view, best expressed by H.E.J. Cowdrey, sought to locate the quest for 'peace' in the church's attempts to bring order to the post-Carolingian anarchic period. Cowdrey saw the creation of peace councils as an attempt by the church to legislate some form of legal defense for those members of society who were deemed defenseless, namely peasants, churchmen, and widows, in the face of unrestrained internecine warfare.[60] He went so far as to write that 'The Peace councils were the churchmen's self-defense, so far as any was possible.'[61] Thomas Bisson rightly points out that a cause deriving from anarchic conditions would also help to explain the geographical limitations of the phenomenon. It explains its center in the areas of post-Carolingian authority of southern France, and would especially explain its absence from the relatively centralized and orderly kingdom of England.[62]

Cowdrey, however, was also instrumental in helping to lay the groundwork for the idea that the peace councils were designed to do more than simply curb violence; they wanted to fundamentally remake Christianity and to purify the

---

[57] Ibid.
[58] On the other hand, Constance Bouchard has argued that, at least regarding the eleventh-century, historians often over-emphasize the destructive potential of territorial princes, and not the constructive role they could play in social and ecclesiastical reform and order. See Constance Bouchard, 'Laymen and Church Reform Around the Year 1000: The Case of Otto-William, Count of Burgundy', *Journal of Medieval History* 5 (1979), 1–10.
[59] For a general discussion of this argument, see Barthélemy, 169–73.
[60] H.E.J. Cowdrey, 'The Peace and the Truce of God in the Eleventh Century', *Past and Present* 46 (Feb., 1970), 42–6. For a further elucidation of this view, see Marcus Bull, *Knightly Piety*, 23; Thomas N. Bisson, 'The Organized Peace in Southern France and Catalonia, ca.1140–ca.1233', *The American Historical Review* 82 (Apr., 1977), 291–3.
[61] Cowdrey, 'Peace and Truce', 46.
[62] Bisson, 'The Organized Peace', 292. For a contrary view arguing that the decline of royal authority did not lead to 'anarchy', see Goetz, 259–61. He argued that while royal authority declined, ducal and major secular authority did not, and thus order was essentially protected.

clergy.⁶³ Amy Remensnyder has taken this idea further, arguing that the principal areas of concern for clerical reformers were the elimination of the buying and selling of church offices (simony), clerical marriage and concubinage (nicholaitism), and clerics who went about armed – all things that smacked of secularity and worldliness to the reformers.⁶⁴ The councils in question certainly did condemn simony, clerical marriage, and arms-bearing clergy, though they did not give equal weight to each one and, in fact, focused the lion's share of their energy and attention on eliminating the first two.⁶⁵ The various peace councils did not always promulgate canons against all three abuses, and as Remensyder points out, the peace councils most often linked condemnations of simony and clerical marriage, rather than the banning of arms.⁶⁶ That being said, reformers, when they did address the issue of clerical armsbearing, were uniformly opposed to it.⁶⁷

The first of the peace councils to actually propagate canons was the 989 Council of Charroux, convened by Gunbaldus, archbishop of Bordeaux. This council proclaimed that three offenses were to be punished with excommunication: the violent invasion of churches, the theft of cattle from the poor, and assault on unarmed clergy.⁶⁸ The protection afforded to unarmed clerics was continued at

---

[63] Cowdrey, 'Peace and Truce', 50.
[64] Remensnyder, 'Pollution, Purity, and Peace', 280–1. See also Anne Llewellyn Barstow, *Married Priests and the Reforming Papacy: The Eleventh Century Debates* (New York, 1982); James Brundage, *Law, Sex and Christian Society in Medieval Europe* (Chicago, 1987), esp. 182–7, 214–28, 251–3, 314–19, 342–3, 401–5.
[65] For the primacy of simony as an area of concern, see Barthélemy, 283. Duggan also makes this point effectively for a later period. See Duggan, *Armsbearing and the Clergy*, 150. Actual actions taken against clerics, such as deposition, are focused primarily against simoniac and married clergy. Cf. Smith, *War and the Making of Medieval Monastic Culture*, 44. 'Like their fellows who married or committed simony, clerics who bore arms were anathematized as impure disruptors of the church's ideal peaceful state. While the contemporary reconceptualization of Christian knighthood rendered bloodshed by lay warriors acceptable and even praiseworthy under certain circumstances, a monk or priest who armed himself "like a warrior (*ut miles*)" – even to defend ecclesiastical property – rendered himself unfit to touch liturgical objects or administer the sacraments.'
[66] Remensnyder, 'Pollution, Purity, and Peace', 285–6. While numerous councils did legislate against the bearing of arms by the clergy, especially the councils of Coyaca in 1050, Compostela in 1056, and Tours in 1060, the sheer volume of effort directed against clerical marriage and simony indicate that these two abuses were a higher priority than the banning of arms.
[67] Duggan, *Armsbearing and the Clergy*, 100–1.
[68] Hans-Werner Goetz, 'Protection of the Church, Defense of the Law, and Reform: On the Purposes and Character of the Peace of God, 989–1038', *The Peace of God: Social Violence and Religious Response in France around the Year 1000*, 264. Among the inherent difficulties in using the evidence of the peace councils to garner a cultural

subsequent councils, and this same legal status and protection was later afforded to widows, monks, nuns, noblewomen, and any of their unarmed companions.[69] What is most striking about this protection is that it excluded not just clerics bearing weapons, but also those wearing armor. The canon makes it clear that an attacker who 'robs, or seizes, or strikes a priest, or a deacon, or any man of the clergy [*ex clero*] who is not bearing arms (that is, a shield, a sword, a breastplate, or a helmet), but who is simply going about his business or remaining at home' is excommunicated.[70] A cleric, therefore, who even tried to protect himself by wearing mail, or a helmet, excluded himself from this special category of 'defenseless' persons. Preventing clerics from even wearing armor to defend themselves could be evidence that these councils were interested in preventing clerics from transgressing the social boundaries between themselves and lay warriors. On the other hand, forfeiting the protection of the 'peace' councils as a result of wearing armor also undercuts the idea that they were primarily focused on limiting the shedding of blood by clerics, as presumably armor would not be effective as an offensive weapon. These early councils, and those that continued this protection, ought to be seen as an initial attempt to protect the unarmed members of society, but focused on the clerics themselves. It should be recalled that it was only later that this same protection was extended to non-clerics. Overall, the upshot of these pronouncements was that clerics who opted to defend themselves with swords and armor could not do so with church law.

A passage from the *Historiarum* of Rodulphus Glaber, composed in the late 1030s, supports the idea that these early peace councils only later morphed into efforts to protect more than just the clergy. Glaber wrote that 'The most important [sacred commitment] was to observe an inviolable peace so that men of either condition, whatever previous threats had hung over them, could go anywhere completely tranquil and without arms.'[71] This broad protection was not a feature of the earliest peace councils, and is thus best seen as a later extension of the original ideal, which was to protect the clergy. These initial attempts to protect the clergy, however, were done against the backdrop of clergymen who were armed to protect themselves. The legal reality might have changed with the ascendancy of a

---

understanding of licit behavior is the fact that the word 'arms' (*arma*) had various meanings in the Middle Ages, and was not always limited to weapons, but could also refer to armor.

[69] Ibid.

[70] Thomas Head, 'The acts of the council of Charroux (989)', *The Peace of God: Social Violence and Religious Response in France around the Year 1000*, 327. See Smith, *War and the Making of Medieval Monastic Culture*, 46.

[71] Richard Landes, 'Rodulphus Glaber on Events in the Year 1033', *Peace of God: Social Violence and Religious Response in France around the Year 1000*, 338.

particular political group, but the cultural norm did not always follow. Katherine Allen Smith quotes Glaber's story regarding Hervé, treasurer of Saint-Martin in Tours, in discussing this change. Hervé claimed to have been visited by St. Martin, who complained about the previous generations of monks who fought with weapons in war (*armis ... militaribus famulantes*) and who sometimes died from wounds in battle (*trucidati in prelio deciderunt*). Martin was only able, with difficulty, to rescue them from Hell.[72] Glaber was seeking to disassociate monks from war (to save their souls), and for him these councils were an attempt to accomplish that feat.

Hans Goetz argues that reformers sought to entice clergy to give up their arms by offering them legal protections, or rather, by not extending the protections of the peace movement to armed clergy. Anyone aiming to disarm clerics needed to offer something in return, in this case, the promise to excommunicate their attackers.[73] In Goetz's formulation, these legal protections were necessary to counterbalance the loss of personal defensive capacity that clerics had formerly possessed. Katherine Allen Smith sees these prohibitions as being fairly effective, and she largely dismisses those bishops and abbots who 'sometimes' armed themselves and led armies against belligerent local lords, since they risked being considered 'arms-bearers'.[74] Churchmen who ignored these pronouncements were stripped of the protections of clergy, and were fair game in warfare. The evidence shows, though, that some clerics continued to prefer the protection afforded by a sword or heavy stick rather than that offered by a nascent peace council. These armed churchmen were also in danger of transgressing the boundaries between vocational classes. The reformers sought to class clerics with the other 'helpless' members of society – peasants, townsmen, and women.[75] That this protected status was later afforded to non-clerics, and also extended to anyone who went about unarmed, tends to support the argument that these councils and this movement were primarily interested in stamping out disturbers of the peace, with a possible secondary motivation of reforming and purifying the clergy.[76]

While the peace councils in their southern French form did not exist in England, the absence of these councils did not mean that there was an absence of attempts to disarm clerics. Instead, the absence of peace councils demonstrates the relative lack of social disorder in England, which reinforces the idea that the peace councils primarily were trying to create social order, not only to reform the

---

[72] Smith, *War and the Making of Medieval Monastic Culture*, 42.
[73] Goetz, 266.
[74] Smith, *War and the Making of Medieval Monastic Culture*, 44.
[75] Ibid., 44–5.
[76] Goetz, 278.

clergy. There is ample evidence that English clerics went about armed and played active roles in warfare during the period. The evidence from England, when taken in conjunction with that of France, demonstrates that there was a wide-ranging effort to disarm clerics, and an equally wide-ranging effort to oppose that disarmament. The relative stability or instability of the region did not determine whether these clerics took up arms, as the debate over armed clerics predated the collapse of the Carolingian state, and post-dated the re-establishment of centralized royal power in England.

Janet Nelson has shown that there were numerous examples of ninth-century Anglo-Saxon bishops and abbots leadings royal armies, fighting, and being killed in battle.[77] We do not need to recount every instance of clerics fighting in England during this period, but we do want to highlight a well-known example, that of Ealhstan, bishop of Sherborne. Ealhstan, brother of King Ecgbert of Wessex, was one of the most important and successful royal commanders in Wessex. His diocese, Sherborne, was an important bishopric, and had strong royal ties by serving as the burial place for Anglo-Saxon kings during this period.[78] He served as a royal commander in campaigns designed to expand West Saxon control over England, as in 823 when he served as a general alongside the king's son Aethelwulf and earldorman Wulfheard.[79] Later, in 845, during a period of Danish raiding in England, Ealhstan once again led the defense. At the battle of the river Parret, Ealhstan, along with earldorman Eanwulf and earldorman Osric, led the English army to victory over the Danes and slaughtered a great number of them.[80] Ealhstan died in 867, after ruling his diocese and serving as a royal commander for fifty years.[81] Asser, in his biography of King Alfred, added that Ealhstan had ruled his diocese honorably, and John of Worcester, writing three hundred years later, followed him in writing that the bishop 'had ruled with honour (*honorabiliter*)' and was 'buried in peace at Sherborne.'[82] Asser had recorded earlier, with great anger, that Eahlstan had joined a conspiracy against King Æthelwulf (led by his son Æthelwald) while the king was in Rome.[83] However, as Keynes points out, in

---

[77] Anglo-Saxon bishops and abbots led royal armies in 825 and 848, and bishop Heahmund was killed at Meretun in 871. Nelson, 'The Church's Military Service in the Ninth Century', 18.

[78] *The Chronicle of John of Worcester*, ed. R.R. Darlington and P. McGurk, trans. Jennifer Bray and P. McGurk, Vol. 2 (Oxford, 1995), 277. While John of Worcester was a twelfth-century observer, he incorporated information regarding Anglo-Saxon England from the Anglo-Saxon Chronicle and Asser's Life of King Alfred, among other sources.

[79] ASC, 60–1.

[80] Ibid., 64–5.

[81] Ibid., 68–9.

[82] *John of Worcester*, 2, 282–3.

[83] Asser, *Life of King Alfred*, trans. Simon Keynes and Michael Lapidge (London, 2004), 70.

recording Ealhstan's honorable death, Asser (who might have then been bishop of Sherborne himself) wanted to afford more respect to a man who had served in one of the most powerful bishoprics in the country.[84] This brief career sketch of Bishop Ealhstan helps to demonstrate that warrior-clerics were not unheard of in Anglo-Saxon England, a fact that is confirmed by the celebrated military actions of notable clerics in both 1016 and 1066.

While the relatively peaceful nature of English society (or, at least, avoidance of internecine warfare) probably lessened the importance of personal military ability for English clerics, they were still expected to contribute to the defense of the realm, both through their landholding and their personal stature in the kingdom. While some contemporary observers, such as Archbishop Hincmar of Rheims, claimed that English bishops did not have the same military responsibilities as their continental counterparts, due to a lack of landed endowments, a glance through the Anglo-Saxon Chronicle demonstrates this to be false.[85] The contents, including military hardware, of surviving wills of prelates demonstrate this, as do the attempts by reformers to prevent clerics from engaging in warfare. The simple possession of such items does not, of course, represent evidence of direct military action, nor even an endorsement of such violence by clerics, but it arguably represents a familiarity with warfare and a recognition of the role played by clerics in support of royal campaigns. The earliest of the wills comes from Bishop Theodred of London, and dates from between 942 and 951. He granted to his lord, among other things, 'four horses, the best that I have, and two swords, the best that I have, and four shields and four spears ...'[86] The inclusion of the phrase 'the best that I have' indicates that Bishop Theodred not only possessed more swords, horses, etc., than he was leaving to his lord, but that he was also cognizant of their relative value and qualities. This theme is reinforced by the terms of Bishop Arfwold of Crediton's will. Bishop Arfwold left an immense amount of military gear and equipment to a variety of people, including to fellow clerics. His will read, in part, 'And he grants to his lord four horses, two saddled and two unsaddled, and four shields and four spears and two helmets and two coats of mail ...'[87] The bishop also left horses and tents to several people, including Alfwold the monk. He left his kinsman Wulfgar three coats of mail, among other valuables. He also left a man

---

[84] Ibid., 77, n. 55.
[85] Nelson, 'The Church's Military Service in the Ninth Century', 15–19. See the *ASC* entries for 825 and 848.
[86] *Councils and Synods with Other Documents Relating to the English Church*, ed. Dorothy Whitelock, M. Brett, and C.N.L. Brooke, Vol. 1, Pt. 1 (Oxford, 1981), 76–7. 'and four hors so ic best habbe, and to suerde so ic best habbe, 7 foure schelda and foure spere'.
[87] Ibid., 384. 'he geann his hlaforde feower horsa, twa gesadelode 7 twa unsadelode, 7 feower scyldas 7 IIII spera 7 twegen helmas 7 twa byrnan...'.

named Cenwold 'a helmet and coat of mail.'[88] The amount, variety, and value of the military equipment even elicited a comment from Dorothy Whitelock, the editor of this section of the document. She writes,

> Alfwold's will is remarkable for the amount of military equipment and the number of horses he bequeathes [sic], in addition to his heriot and a large ship. One wonders whether he was a fighting bishop. Homilists would not have needed to preach as they do against the clergy taking part in military affairs if this did not sometimes take place, and two ecclesiastics, Bishop Eadnoth of Dorchester and Abbot Wulfsige of Ramsey, were killed at Ashingdon in 1016.[89]

Her point, however, that the prevalence of military equipment in his goods demonstrates the necessity of reformers' efforts against armed clergy is well taken. Reformers do not generally agitate against something that is not truly happening, and not seen as a powerful threat to their preferred world-view.[90]

The efforts of the reformers themselves might indicate a broader involvement of clerics in the warfare of Anglo-Saxon England. Among the most fervent reformers was Abbot Ælfric of Eynsham. While he spent most of his time fulminating against the lack of chastity among the clergy, he also disparaged their use of arms.[91] He firmly believed in the tripartite division of society (warriors, clergy, peasants), and thus saw the roles of warriors and clergy as inherently separate.[92] Ælfric was somewhat following on the intellectual work of King Alfred (d. 899), who himself wrote in his translation of Boethius's *De consolatio Philosophiae* that

---

[88] Ibid., 385. 'helm 7 byrnan'.

[89] Ibid., 383. For an even greater example of military profligacy, see the will of Ælfric, archbishop of Canterbury, who left his best ship, along with sixty helmets and coats of mail to the king. *Councils and Synods*, 1, 1, 239.

[90] Gerrard sees these wills as evidence of a probable military role for these prelates, rather than just their retinues. See Gerrard, 34–5.

[91] For an example of his opposition to clerical marriage and concubinage, see his pastoral letter to Wulfsige III, Bishop of Sherborne, *Councils and Synods*, 1, 1, 193–212. In this text his focus is on chastity, which he claims that Christ Himself established alongside His religion. His condemnation of clerics bearing arms is contained in a list of other disagreeable behaviors, including swearing oaths and starting 'strife'. Timothy Powell illuminates Ælfric's support for the 'Three Orders' ideology, and his arguments against armed clerics in Timothy E. Powell, 'The "Three Orders" of Society in Anglo-Saxon England,' *Anglo-Saxon England* 23 (1994), 103–32, esp. 110–15. I wish to thank Richard Abels for pointing out these and the following materials to me.

[92] J.E. Cross, 'The Ethic of War in Old English' in *England Before the Conquest: Studies in Primary Sources Presented to Dorothy Whitelock*, ed. Peter Clemoes and Kathleen Hughes (Cambridge, 1971), 269–82, esp. 273. Cf. Powell, 'Three Orders', 110.

a king must have men of various orders to make his kingdom work. He wrote that 'he must have praying men, fighting men and working men.'[93] According to Timothy Powell, Alfred did not explicitly rank these three orders, though one must assume that he saw the work of the warriors and clerics to be superior to that of the peasants. For Alfred, each of the orders supported his attempts to rule the kingdom effectively, and thus each of them was a royal servant. This elevation of royal service as a licit cause would explain why a number of English clerics put active service on the battlefield on behalf of the king ahead of the prescriptive condemnations of canon law.[94] In most of his works, however, Ælfric seemingly did not agree with Alfred's interpretation, and he did not simply condemn clerics bearing arms in battle, he condemned clerics bearing any sort of arms at all, and he condemned clerics participating in warfare in any fashion. These ideals derive not only from his belief in the proper division of society, but also from a broader abhorrence of violence, even for laudable ends.[95]

In a letter to Wulfstan, bishop of Worcester and archbishop of York, dating from between 1002 and 1005, he clearly laid out his pacifist opposition to clerics' involving themselves in warfare, and he grounded his reasoning in both Scripture and the concept of the distinct *ordines* of medieval society. Ælfric, like fellow reformers Adalbero of Laon and Gerald of Cambrai, saw medieval society as being composed of *oratores*, *bellatores*, and *laboratores*, each with their own unique, and non-transferable functions. Gerald and Adalbero had complained that the Peace of God 'movement' was illicitly undermining the king's exclusive right and responsibility to maintain the peace.[96] Indeed, Ælfric described these functions as *anum*, or 'only', thus reinforcing the exclusivity of each *ordo*.[97] He explained that once a man was called to the 'spiritual militia', even if he was currently bearing secular arms, he had to put them aside and take on only the spiritual arms and armor afforded by God.[98] Furthermore, once a man had taken on the armor

---

[93] Powell, 'Three Orders', 103. Powell points out that Alfred added this interpolation to Boethius.
[94] Alfred saw the value in obtaining Heaven's blessing prior to battle, and relied on the martial prowess of warrior saints. See John R.E. Bliese, 'St. Cuthbert's and St. Neot's Help in War: Visions and Exhortations', *HSJ* 7 (1997), 39–62.
[95] James W. Earl, 'Violence and Non-Violence in Anglo-Saxon England: Ælfric's "Passion of St. Edmund"', *Philological Quarterly* 78 (1999), 138–41.
[96] Hehl, 'War, Peace and the Christian Order', 192.
[97] Powell, 'Three Orders', 116. Cf. Hehl, 'War, Peace and the Christian Order', 185.
[98] *Councils and Synods*, 1, 1, 252. Adalbero had spoken of the three orders as they existed in their rightful labors. See the original in *PL*, 141.782. Interestingly, Barbara Rosenwein argued that Adalbero had only monks in mind when he wrote of the clerical order, because secular clerics had been subsumed into the laity. 'Priests had been carrying arms since the Viking invasions. The only really religious life was the monastic.' See

and weapons of God, he could not rejoin the secular army. It was impossible to wield both types of weapon at the same time, because a man who shed blood was incapable of performing the sacred Mass. Ælfric then went on to write that not even a walking stick was permitted to a cleric if it could or would be used to strike someone.[99] His justification for this position was Christ's chastisement of Peter in the garden of Gethsemane, as well as the canons of the church, which he largely garnered from a surviving Carolingian capitulary.[100]

Ælfric, in a subsequent letter to Wulfstan dating from 1006, went even further. He wrote to Wulfstan, in English (intending the letter to be disseminated to local clergy), that a priest 'may not bear weapons nor go into battle, for the canon tells us: if he is slain in war or because of some dispute, on no account may mass be celebrated for him or prayers offered for him; but yet one may bury him.'[101] This position goes well beyond simply decrying clerics who went about armed; it condemns clerics who took part in military activities at all. This undermines the distinction that canonists sought to create between clerics who fought personally and those who 'merely' led armies. While later canonists tried to create a stark difference between these two related activities, Ælfric represented an early voice condemning all warrior-clerics, and his 'voice' would not be silenced throughout the subsequent debates over clerical activities in warfare.

Ælfric also complained about the biblical examples used by defenders of armed clerics, such as the book of Maccabees and the example of Peter in the Garden of Gethsemane. In a homily discussing the importance of the Maccabees, he accepted that the wars of the English against the invading Danes qualified as 'just wars', but he argued that clerics were better served by emulating the meekness of Christ and by focusing on struggling with Satan, rather than physically struggling in warfare. He saw the role of the *oratores* as vital to the health and survival of Christian society, and superior to that of the *bellatores*, since fighting against Satan and his minions for the souls of the people was clearly more important

---

Barbara H. Rosenwein, 'Feudal War and Monastic Peace: Cluniac Liturgy as Ritual Aggression', *Viator* 2 (1971), 152. For a good overview of Adalbero's tripartite theory and its path to acceptance, see Constance Bouchard, *Strong of Body, Brave and Noble: Chivalry and Society in Medieval France* (Ithaca, 1998), 29–30. See also Georges Duby, *The Three Orders: Feudal Society Imagined*, trans. Arthur Goldhammer (Chicago, 1980), 21–55.

[99] *Councils and Synods*, 1, 1, 252. 'Nec saltim baculo licet episcopum quemquam percutere'.
[100] For Ælfric's main source of canons, see 195.
[101] *Councils and Synods*, 1, 1, 296–7. 'Ne mot he waepnu werian ne to gefeohte faran, forþon þe se canon us segð: gif he ofslagen bið on folces gefeohte oþþe for sumere ceaste, þaet man nateshwon ne mot him maessian fore ne him fore gebiddan; ac bebyrian swaþeah.'

than fighting the Danes to preserve their worldly bodies.[102] The Maccabees, while laudable in their own time, had ceased to become exemplars with the coming of Christ. Ælfric wrote, "'No holy servant of God after our Saviour's passion would ever defile his hands by fighting ...'"[103] In a letter to Archbishop Wulfstan of York, written between 1002 and 1005, he further explained that those called to clerical service must put aside physical arms in favor of spiritual ones.[104] Prior to the year 1000, therefore, reformers sought to shift examples of Old Testament warriors from justifying physical warfare to spiritual; the example of Christ must take preeminence over that of the Maccabees.[105]

Ælfric also sought actively to answer his critics who used the New Testament to justify clerical warriors. There were those who pointed out that St. Peter had, in fact, carried a sword with which he struck off the ear of the Jewish servant in the Garden of Gethsemane. Ælfric's rejoinder was, 'But we say in truth that the righteous Saviour, and those who followed him, did not go armed or with any warfare.'[106] He knew that he was on weak ground with this argument, since Peter clearly had a sword, even if Christ told him to put it away. Furthermore, Ælfric admitted that there were priests who advocated being armed, and based themselves on New Testament examples. He understood, as Powell argues, that the traditional prohibitions against armed clerics were failing, and he was seeking to develop arguments that would be persuasive, even in the face of increased invasion and national instability.[107] His discussion moved far beyond condemnation of criminal clerics and provides insight into the intense debates grounded in the Scriptures that probably were swirling around this entire topic during the period. Ælfric, in his reformist zeal, represented one facet of this debate. The armed clerics to whom he addressed himself represented another. Many others existed along this disputed spectrum of legitimate behavior. Ælfric himself recognized the disputed nature of the question of armed clerics, and reflected it in his commentary on the Testaments prepared for the layman Sigeweard (though also designed for a broader lay audience). In this commentary, Ælfric reinterpreted the notion of the three *ordines* of society as three legs of a stool (following Alfred), each playing an important role in supporting the king and his rule. He did not focus on the

---

[102] Powell, 'Three Orders', 111.

[103] Ibid., 112.

[104] Ibid.

[105] Nicholas Morton details the arguments surrounding the use of Maccabees around the year 1000. See Nicholas Morton, 'The Defense of the Holy Land and the Memory of the Maccabees', *Journal of Medieval History* 36 (2010), 278–9.

[106] *Councils and Synods*, 1, 1, 297. 'Ac we secgað to soþan þaet se soðfaesta Haelend, ne þa þe him folgodon, ne ferdon gewaepnode, ne mid nanum wige'.

[107] Powell, 'Three Orders', 121.

clergy's need to avoid warfare, preferring to discuss the warrior's requirement to engage in it, which reflects the audience for the commentary.[108] We do a disservice to the evidence if we determine that one is normative without acknowledging the support for the various opposing viewpoints.[109]

Ælfric was faced with trying to balance between lay figures who often saw no reason why wealthy, powerful clerics should not actively aid them in warfare alongside the secular nobles, ecclesiastical reformers (like himself) who saw the shedding of blood by clerics in warfare as antithetical to the priesthood, and finally clerics who themselves saw their duty to serve the king, or defend their regions and flocks, as primary, and therefore would utilize military violence of their own volition. Indeed, as Powell points out, some clergy saw supporting the king as their duty, and as an honorable undertaking, even including military activity.[110] Archbishop Wulfstan represented a more pragmatic approach to the strictures of canon law when faced with difficult political realities. Wulfstan himself held two offices in plurality (the bishopric of Worcester from 1002 to 1016 and the archbishopric of York from 1002 to 1023), but he did so only due to the unsettled political situation within England during the time, and 'when this difficult situation was resolved through the unification of country in 1016 under the Danish king Cnut' he surrendered the see of Worcester.[111] Wulfstan adopted this same balance and reasonably relaxed attitude with regard to armed clerics.[112] While Wulfstan only explicitly condemned clerics who bore weapons into churches, his own canonical collections contained reasonably explicit condemnations of armed clerics, following on the Carolingian examples cited above. A cleric who bore arms in warfare and died could not have prayers said on his behalf, and 'indeed it is to be declared in every way to priests and deacons that they are not to carry weapons, but rather to trust in the protection of God than in weapons.'[113]

---

[108] Ibid., 115. See also Simon Keynes, 'An Abbot, an Archbishop, and the Viking Raids of 1006–7 and 1009–12', *Anglo-Saxon England* 36 (Dec., 2007), 166–7.

[109] Powell makes this point effectively in criticizing Prinze for moralizing against armed clerics. Powell, 'Three Orders', 126–9.

[110] Ibid., 128.

[111] Joyce Hill, 'Two Anglo-Saxon Bishops at Work: Wulfstan, Leofric and Cambridge, Corpus Christi College MS 190', *Patterns of Episcopal Power: Bishops in Tenth and Eleventh Century Western Europe*, ed. Ludger Körntgen and Dominik Waßenhoven (Berlin, 2011), 146. Hill also makes the argument that we should not see Wulfstan's holding of multiple offices as evidence of corruption or greed, since he was doing it for the greater good of England. This is very much in keeping with the arguments probably advanced by clerics using warfare to defend their religion, king, or regions.

[112] Powell, 'Three Orders', 120, 124.

[113] *Wulfstan's Canon Law Collection*, ed. J.E. Cross and Andrew Hamer (Cambridge, 1999), 167. The original reads, 'Et ideo omnimodis dicendum est presbiteris et diaconibus ut

While the debate was thus advancing in England, we find another fascinating insight into the complex discourse surrounding how and when clerics could licitly take up arms in the *Liber Miracula Sancte Fidis*, edited by Bernard of Angers between 1013 and 1020.[114] Bernard collected and arranged a series of miracle stories surrounding St. Foy, and especially focused on the village of Conques in southern France, where he traveled in 1013. Bernard arranged the miracle stories into a series of thematic groups, with the first book comprised mainly of miracles surrounding the myriad terrible things that would befall those who attacked St. Foy or her people. In chapter twenty-six of this group, Bernard recounted the story of a certain monk, Gimon, who was renowned not only for defending St. Foy, but for taking the fight to her enemies. The chapter, titled *De Gimone monacho quam viriliter contra malefactores santé Fidis agebat* (How the Monk Gimon Fought Courageously Against Sainte Foy's Enemies), runs for only four pages in the edited volume, but it is remarkably illuminating for how a southern French monk, and northern French clerical author, could approach the quandary of how clerics ought to utilize military violence. Gimon was a monk and former prior of Conques (probably between 930 and 959), and according to Bernard he was possessed of a 'fierce and manly heart' (*virilis animi ferociam*) when he had lived in the secular world, and he maintained this disposition within the monastery (not unlike the fictional William of Orange in the epic *William in the Monastery* discussed in chapter 3).[115] Gimon used his manly heart to defend the monastery, physically and violently, against those seeking to do St. Foy harm, and to seek 'vengeance against evil-doers.'[116] Pursuant to that purpose, Gimon kept, in addition to the clothing 'suitable' (*congrua*) for a monk, a 'cuirass, a helmet, a lance, a sword, and all kinds of instruments of war … to the same end he had a fully equipped war-horse in the stable.'[117] Bernard's description brings up one of the basic incongruities of Gimon's actions. Clearly Gimon kept weapons, armor, and horse handy (and he was right to do so, according to Bernard), but these items were not normally acceptable for a monk.

Gimon served as the primary defender of the monastery, at least according to Bernard. Whenever danger threatened the monastery, Gimon 'immediately

---

arma non portent, sed magis confidant in defensione Dei quam in armis.' Cf. Keynes, 'An Abbot', 11–12.

[114] *The Book of Sainte Foy*, trans. Pamela Sheingorn (Philadelphia, 1995), 24–5. For the original language, see *Liber Miraculorum Sancte Fidis*, ed. A. Bouillet (Paris, 1897).

[115] Sheingorn, 93; Bouillet, 66.

[116] Ibid.

[117] Sheingorn, 93–4; 'Ille in dormitorio preter cetera indumenta moniali habitui congrua, toracam, cassidem, contum, gladium, omneque bellicum instrumentum…simulque in stabulo bellatorem equum habebat apparatum', Bouillet, 66.

took up the duty of defender. He rode at the head of his armored ranks, leading the campaign, and with his own daring he heartened the spirits of the fearful, giving them strength to face manfully either the reward of victory or the glory of martyrdom.'[118] Gimon was serving in a variety of roles when faced with imminent violence. He was a war-leader, leading his 'armored ranks' into the enemy army. His bravery inspired his men to attack the enemy manfully by leading from the front. Unlike the traditional role of the cleric as a morale booster through oration and invocations of God's will, Gimon's ability to inspire came from the same military virtues that secular warriors looked to – bravery and selfless disregard for physical well-being.

Gimon understood his role to be as a defender of Christianity and his monastery, regardless of the canonical and cultural prohibitions on clerics taking an armed role in combat. Bernard reinforced Gimon's interpretation by portraying him quite positively, but also by explicitly presenting the argument that violence in defense of a good cause was perfectly acceptable. In supposedly quoting Gimon, Bernard wrote 'that no one who wanted to be worthy of leadership should become cowardly, but rather, when necessity demanded, should battle forcefully against wicked invaders so that the vice of cowardice would not creep in disguised as patience.'[119] Earlier in the section, Gimon also explained that vanquishing 'false Christians who had attacked Christian law and willfully abandoned God' was a more important duty than subduing 'those pagans who had never known God.'[120] For Gimon, the defense of Christianity, especially against pseudo-Christian malefactors, was a primary goal of all good Christians, including (and perhaps especially) the clergy. As Amy Remensnyder has pointed out, southern France in this period had moved beyond the orbit of the Carolingian power, even though the monastery at Conques itself looked back to Charlemagne as its legendary founder.[121] Exacerbated by the unsettled nature of public order in

---

[118] Sheingorn, 94; Bouillet, 66. 'ipsemet statim functus officio defensoris, ferratam aciem in expedition antecedens ducebat, atque audacter trepidantium animos, aut de victorie premio, aut de martyrii gloria viriliter confortabat'.

[119] Sheingorn, 94; Bouillet, 66–7. 'Nec debere aliquem qui se prelatione velit esse dignum, fieri ignavum, quin, si necessitas instat, contra improbos pervasores strenue dimicet, ne videlicet sub pacientie specie, vitium irrepat ignavie.'

[120] Ibid. 'asserens etiam multo majore debito falsos christianos esse debellandos, qui christianam legem impugnantes, sponte Deum reliquerant, quam ipsos paganos, qui numquam Deum noverant.'

[121] Amy G. Remensnyder, *Remembering Kings Past: Monastic Foundation Legends in Medieval Southern France* (Ithaca, 1995), 153–5; 207–8. Remensnyder also points to the example of the monastery of Sorde, which forged diplomas late in the twelfth century claiming that Charlemagne established it on his way to Roncevaux, and that the martyred archbishop Turpin was buried there on his return. This is an explicit

southern France at the time, Gimon saw an important military role for clerical leaders seeking to defend their regions and flocks. This defense was not only necessary, but also laudable and valorizing. Gimon (according to Bernard) derided those who complained that clerics ought to emulate Christ by turning the other cheek. He even went so far as to compare such arguments to cowardice, and to see them as underhanded ways of undermining the defense of Christianity. This is an explicitly chivalric rationale, and it is interesting that Gimon saw the conflict in such stark militaristic terms.

Bernard explained that Gimon's reputation for effective violence and military ability served to protect the monastery by discouraging attacks.[122] While the power of his reputation is important, perhaps even more fascinating was that Gimon was known to invoke the power of St. Foy if he was in danger of losing. However, instead of appealing to her mercy and power, he sought to gain her favor by threatening and shaming her, as one would a recalcitrant knight. Bernard wrote that Gimon would approach the tomb and address her in a 'down-to-earth' fashion, and he would even go so far as to threaten 'to flog the sacred image and even to throw it in a river or well unless Sainte Foy avenged herself on the evildoers immediately.'[123] Bernard was careful to point out that Gimon was humble while doing this, since it was important to demonstrate that he was not worldly and haughty while insulting the saint, but rather that his great love of Christianity and his great reverence for her power caused him to act in such a fashion. Gimon was utilizing all tools for the defense of Christianity, even those that would normally be met with opprobrium and complaint, and Bernard portrayed it as worthy and laudable.

Bernard specifically wrote a section to justify Gimon's military activities, recognizing that some observers would experience deep-seated uneasiness with a warlike monk. He argued that Gimon should not have been criticized for speaking so brusquely to the saint, since his actions were beyond reproach 'except that

---

linking by the monastery of itself to the world of the *chansons de geste*, and to the best literary example of a warrior-cleric. See page 194. She also points out a number of other examples, including that found in the *Gesta Karoli Magni* from Lagrasse in which Archbishop Turpin supposedly chose 100 knights to serve as monks, then led them into battle at Narbonne, 'Bellowing as a battle cry the name of their abbey, they cleave the Muslims with as much relish – and success – as any of Charlemagne's peers.' See page 197.

[122] Sheingorn, 94.
[123] Sheingorn, 94; Bouillet, 67. 'atque vulgari more adversus sanctam Fidem causabatur, ea utique usus confidential, qua noverat se nequaquam ab ea facile contempni. Nam etiam sacram imaginem verberare et vel in flumen sive puteum precipitare, nisi se sancta Fides de malefactoribus quam mox vindicaret, minitabatur.'

he used to go on expeditions armed.'[124] Bernard was trying to balance Gimon's full-throated defense of a licit cause (the defense of the monastery and interests of St. Foy) with his violation of canonical prohibitions. His mechanism for creating a synthesis between these two positions was by focusing on Gimon's intentions. Arguing that they derived from his 'moral excellence' and his fervent desire to protect the faith and his flock, they should not be seen as an 'assault on the monastic rule.'[125] He finishes with a flourish of righteous indignation against monks who were NOT as brave as Gimon, writing, 'If only lazy monks would put aside their cowardly sloth and act as bravely to the advantage of their monasteries! Instead, they parade the handsome habits of their order on the outside, while making a hiding-place for iniquity on the inside!'[126] Monks who resisted the temptation to defend themselves against attack were not practicing Christian restraint; rather, they were cowards. Furthermore, they were guilty of worldly pride in their desire to parade around in their habits, but this outward pride masked an inner cowardice and worldliness. Bernard was taking aim at critical monks by turning the probable complaints against Gimon against them, and accusing them of the very same failings that they would probably accuse Gimon of, but casting them as even worse, since these false defenders of Christianity were undermining the viability of the faith. Gimon's use of arms might be problematic, but the monks' cowardice in the face of attack was shameful.

Bernard finished this section by appealing to his audience in language reflective of the dangerous and unsettled nature of Gimon's region. Gimon needed to take up arms to defend himself and Christianity, because he was surrounded by those who made war on the church, on clerics, and who ignored the legal protections possessed by these figures. He characterized these attackers as Antichrists who ignored the legal position of bishops and monks, and who treated them as 'shit' (*sterquilinio*). For Bernard, who was better served to be the strong arm of God's judgment upon these enemies of Christ than his own clerical servants? He wrote, 'If God's avenging omnipotence should employ the hand of any of His own servants to strike down and slaughter one of these Antichrists, no one could call it a crime.'[127] Bernard gave his audience a full-throated defense of the idea that in some circumstances, clerics not only could, but should take up arms and defend

---

[124] Sheingorn, 95.
[125] Ibid.
[126] Sheingorn, 95; Bouillet, 68. 'Neque ille judicabitur, nisi ex intentione qua id agree videbatur. Et utinam monachus desidiosus, deposita ignavia, ad utilitatem sui monasterii sic fortiter ageret, potius quam sui ordinis habitum honestum preferens extrinsecus, iniquitatis latibulum faceret instrinsecus.'
[127] Ibid. 'si quosdam vindex omnipotencia per alicuius sui servi manus, cuiuscumque etiam ordinis strage deiecerit, nemo id crimini asscribere poterit.'

themselves, their friends, and their religion. Bernard also uses the example of Saint Mercurius using a lance to pierce Julian the Apostate to argue that if a saint could utilize violence in defense of Christ, surely Christ could arm Gimon to do the same.[128] Gimon's defense of the monastery was not antithetical to Christ's wishes; Christ Himself furnished Gimon with the means to protect the monastery. Canonical prohibitions against armed clerics should not, in Bernard's estimation, extend to circumstances whereby the cleric was actively defending Christianity.

Following on the example of Gimon defending Conques, we come to one of the most interesting episodes from this entire period – the so-called Peace League of Bourges. The League was an attempt by Archbishop Aimon de Bourbon of Bourges to create and maintain peace in his region. His actions, recorded by Andrew of Fleury in his *Miracula sancti Benedicti*, are of fundamental importance to our understanding of some of the motivations behind the peace councils and of clerical conceptions of licit violence in general. The actions of Archbishop Aimon and his army have been largely ignored or explained away as an aberration by modern historians. The overt use of military violence by the clergy to create and enforce peace flies in the face of the prevailing narrative of the peace councils as part of a larger attempt to purify the clergy and separate them into their legitimate *ordo*. This latter interpretation has, unfortunately, led to the marginalization of this event, and a desire to undermine its legitimate implications. While the Peace League was certainly exceptional in its scope and ambition, it was in keeping with the ideology of the peace councils, and contemporary accounts of it support the conclusion that warfare by clerics could be considered permissible under the right circumstances.

In the late 1030s, Aimon de Bourbon, archbishop of Bourges, convened a council in which he sought to create peace throughout his region.[129] His initiative built on the logic of the previous peace councils, which had legislated against the attacking of churches, pillaging of the peasantry, and harming of unarmed clergy, and had sought to maintain the peace through the forced swearing of oaths by

[128] Ibid. Bernard also discussed Gimon's use of the power of prayer to defeat the enemies of the monastery, but he did not see such efforts as sufficient. See also Elizabeth Lapina, *Warfare and the Miraculous in the Chronicles of the First Crusade* (University Park, 2015), 55.

[129] Aimon aimed to create peace through force, see Albert Vermeesch, *Essai sur les origines et la signification de la commune dans le nord de la France (XIe et XIIe siècles)* 30 (Heule, 1966), 28; cf. Guy Devailly, *Le Berry du Xe siècle au milieu du XIIIe: Etude politique, religieuse, sociale et économique* (Civilisations et Sociétés, 19; Paris, 1973), 145–8. Devailly, following the Chronicle of Déols, casts Archbishop Aimon into the milieu of a warring noble, rather than as a partisan for peace. See especially 146–7. Both images that emerge of Aimon support the argument that warfare was an accepted part of his lifestyle as archbishop.

the leading men of a region. Aimon took the next step and created 'a military force composed largely of the so-called unarmed, that is, both clerics and the *inermis vulgus*, or commoners. Some nobles and their armed retainers also chose to join.'[130] His creation of an army based on mutual oaths of loyalty and promises to maintain the peace, all under the direct supervision of the archbishop and with the active military contributions of the clergy of the region, was an important assertion of the role of clerics in maintaining peace. Archbishop Aimon's approach was certainly unique in its overt use of armed clerics to fight armed enemies, but it goes too far to suggest that this was only a one-time, isolated event, and thus not relevant to the larger cultural milieu of the eleventh century. In fact, the archbishop's army represented the natural and logical progression of the early peace movement, and could have been foreseen as far back as the council at Le Puy in 975. As mentioned above, at that council Bishop Guy of Le Puy forced the nobles of his region to swear an oath to keep the peace, but also arrayed his family members around him as a military force designated to maintain that sworn peace. It is not a large step to move from directing family members to keep the peace to directing the peace army in person.

Aimon's creation of the Peace League itself also demonstrates an argument in favor of the acceptability of clerics' directing and partaking in violence for a cause considered holy or legitimate. His followers did not label him a pariah for having done this work, nor was he ousted from the mainstream of Christian thought or culture. That his utilization of violence drew so little criticism might indicate that an important and significant portion of the clerical hierarchy accepted clerical military force. Our contemporary author, Andrew of Fleury, does criticize the archbishop for trying to use sacred power to solve a secular problem, it is true; but

---

[130] Thomas Head, 'The Judgment of God: Andrew of Fleury's Account of the Peace League of Bourges', *The Peace of God: Social Violence and Religious Response in France around the Year 1000*, 221. Head's account remains among the best treatments, in English, of the Peace League of Bourges, though he does beg the question in assuming that clerics were fundamentally pacifist. He wrote that the peace councils asked 'what nonviolent measures can be taken to coerce armed powers to stop fighting'. He then drew parallels to the 'sex strike' by Athenian women during the Peloponnesian war and to modern-day anti-nuclear activists. This leads him to treat the Peace League as both an ideological and behavioral outlier. For other treatments of the Peace League of Bourges, see Vermeesch, 25–48. For his commentary on the inherent paradox of using violence to create peace, see 40–1; cf. Roger Bonnaud-Delamare, *L'idée de paix a l'époque carolingienne* (Paris, 1939), especially pages 477–80. For an overview of the region in this period, see Devailly, *Le Berry*. Barthélemy asserts that the peasants and clerics were derided for violating the 'normality' of their expected roles, but also that this demonstrates that knights did not have an effective monopoly on military violence. See Barthélemy, 280.

it is also true that Andrew himself was opposed in this belief by the partisans of the Peace of God movement.[131]

Examining the actual formation of the Peace League will reveal what the archbishop was trying to do, and how it illuminates the debate over licit clerical violence. First and foremost, Aimon had altered the traditional oath sworn at the peace councils, and had changed it from a passive promise not to break the peace, to an active promise to use military force to enforce the peace.[132] This meant that the archbishop was actively creating a peace militia, under his own command, in order to prevent recalcitrant nobles from waging private warfare in his area. Andrew of Fleury noted that this oath was expansive and directed at all men of the region, knightly, clerical, or peasant. He specifically mentioned that the clergy were required to swear as well, 'Nor were ministers of the sacraments excepted, but they frequently took out banners from the sanctuary of the Lord and attacked the violators of the sworn peace with the rest of the crowd of laypeople.'[133] This is a remarkable account, not least because it shows clerics expected to appear on the battlefield as combatants, though Andrew does try to specify their role as having a more spiritual component than the 'crowd of laypeople.'

The Peace League of Bourges demonstrates the tacit acceptance of clerical warfare by the archbishop and his adherents. Likewise, Andrew of Fleury's account shows he was proud of the League's early accomplishments; whatever his initial reservations, he extolled its virtues as evidence of the proud knights' being overcome by the meek commoners and clergy.[134] Only later, after the destruction of the castle of Beneciacum, and the slaughter that ensued, did Andrew grow more critical of Aimon and the League. The Peace League's army, which the archbishop led personally, captured the castle and then engaged in merciless slaughter of those huddled within, sparing neither women nor children.[135]

---

[131] Head, 'The Judgment of God', 222. It is also important that Andrew himself came from a knightly family in the area of Orleans, so he might have been opposed to the archbishop's 'intruding' on the proper domain of the knightly class. Head also makes a point that Andrew had idolized the previous archbishop of Bourges, Gauzlin of Fleury, and that Aimon's deviation from Gauzlin's policies, quite apart from the Peace League, 'might have been in itself sufficient to earn him bad marks from the monastic author.' See 224, n. 16.

[132] Head, 'The Judgment of God', 224.

[133] Ibid. Original in Vermeesch, 29 n. 54. Andrew of Fleury wrote, 'Non excipiuntur ipsi sacrorum ministry, sed a sanctuario Domini correptis frequenter vexillis, cum cetera multitudine populi, in corruptores invehuntur iuratae pacis.'

[134] Head, 'The Judgment of God', 225; original in Vermeesch, 29 n. 54.

[135] Vermeesch, 33 n. 62. It read, 'Nullam miserationis venam eliciebat caterva infantium ad ubera pendens matrum, inter ipsa instanti carnifici arridens tormenta, flebilis genitricis querelis nescia interque ipsa pia parentis oscula excepti, rogo vitae excedebant termino.'

In this event Andrew detected overreaching pride and arrogance on the part of Archbishop Aimon, and thus he thought that God withdrew his sanction from the archbishop's military actions.[136] The agent of his vengeful judgment was the secular noble Odo of Deols, who met the Peace League in battle and destroyed it. In the course of the destruction of the archbishop's army, Andrew reported that more than seven hundred clerics were killed, and the archbishop himself was severely wounded.

Andrew portrays clerics who fought in the right cause and in the right fashion as acting in an acceptable manner. In the case of the Peace League, God apparently agreed for a time, until the leaders of the League fell victim to the sin of pride, and showed none of the virtue of mercy in the capture and destruction of Beneciacum. There was no blanket condemnation of the involvement of clerics in the fighting, or of the archbishop for acting as a general. We can be sure that the clerics and archbishop took active roles in the battle because of the attention paid by Andrew to their casualties, and his earlier statement of their having to bear arms along with the laymen. Had the archbishop shown mercy at Beneciacum, and had he not succumbed to avarice, Andrew's account of the Peace League would have very probably continued in the positive vein in which he began (though he would still have to explain its eventual defeat). Andrew treats the archbishop in much the same fashion that he would have a secular noble, and in this basic similarity we can detect the tacit acceptance of clerical violence. Andrew saw no fundamental distinction between the archbishop and a secular noble when it came to keeping the peace.[137] They were judged by their actions and motivations, not by the prescripts of their specific *ordo*.[138]

[136] Hehl reinforces this point in his discussion of the Peace of God. See Hehl, 'War, Peace and the Christian Order', 190.

[137] In fact, a strain of this pragmatic reasoning can be detected earlier in the compilation in regard to the reach of royal justice. In a very interesting story, David Rollason discussed a case whereby a settlement could not be reached in a case involving control over serfs. The monks suggested that it be resolved through trial by battle, whereas the opposing party disputed this 'on the grounds that it was an unsuitable method of resolving a dispute concerning Church property'. When this argument prevailed, St. Benedict struck the offending lawyer dumb. Clearly the fact that the monks had suggested the violent approach to settling the dispute, and the fact that St. Benedict took action to this end on their behalf, suggests a clear acceptance of violence as a means to achieving a desired end. See David Rollason, 'The Miracles of St Benedict: A Window on Early Medieval France', *Studies in Medieval History presented to R.H.C. Davis*, ed. Henry Mayr-Harting and R.I. Moore (London, 1985), 82.

[138] In fact, Andrew later does complain about peasants riding on mules who were impersonating knights, and Vermeesch suggested that this was because it violated a sense of proper *ordo*. However, even if this was the case, it would make it all the more remarkable that he did not have similar condemnations of clerics who fought. Apparently

Thomas Head alluded to this point in his analysis of Andrew's tale. In reacting against earlier historians' use of the Peace League of Bourges episode to demonstrate either Andrew's own conservative, knightly biases, or his acceptance of a growing sense of trifunctionalism in medieval society, Head made the point that Andrew's opposition to the League at the end 'was rather a carefully organized and argued exposition on the logic of saintly patronage, in particular as it functioned for the abbey of Fleury.'[139] In this conception, Andrew saw the use of force as theoretically permissible, but considered that the clerics and others in the peace movement had forfeited their divine protection through their own iniquity.[140] The use of force in pursuit of justice had a long and glorious tradition within chivalric societies. Furthermore, God withdrew his protection because the archbishop and his men had violated their own oaths when they mercilessly destroyed Beneciacum.[141]

We should consider this notion of a just cause's making violence legitimate, since the archbishop clearly used this argument in his justification of the Peace League. Andrew of Fleury also included a supposed speech by Archbishop Aimon in which he offers his explanation for the Peace League. The archbishop claimed that he had formed it in order to combat the pillaging of churches, the instigators of rapes, and the oppressors of monks and clerics. He explicitly swore to use force to oppose the oppressors and breakers of the peace, and he promised to use the relics of St. Stephen to gain God's favor in this endeavor.[142] This sermon, recorded with pride by Andrew, was promulgated by the other bishops in the dioceses. There was no evidence of opposition or complaint from his suffragan bishops, so we can reasonably assume that they were in agreement with the archbishop as to the legitimacy of his actions.[143]

If the actions of Archbishop Aimon de Bourbon of Bourges represented an active approach to ensuring peace in a region, the attempt to create a 'Truce of God' represented another tack. While they were not direct reactions to the Peace League of Bourges, the peace councils held after 1038 definitely took a stance that more actively opposed the involvement of clerics in warfare. While most councils continued to promulgate canons that protected unarmed clerics only,

---

Those who Worked could not fight, but Those who Pray were under no similar restriction. Cf. Barthélemy, 280.

[139] Head, 'The Judgment of God', 226–8. Cf. Rollason, 'The Miracles of St Benedict', 77–8. Cf. Duby, 'The Three Orders', 186–90.
[140] Head, 'The Judgment of God', 228.
[141] Ibid., 229.
[142] Vermeesch, 29–30.
[143] Indeed, Aimon was not censured, nor deposed, for his actions. He, in fact, remained archbishop until his death in 1070. See Devailly, *La Berry*, 148.

such as Toulouges (1027), Vic (1033 and 1068), and Narbonne (1054), we do see an increasing focus on more strident attempts to disarm the clergy.[144] The councils of Gerona (1068) and Clermont (1095), for instance, explicitly forbade clerics from using secular arms.[145] Amy Remensnyder interpreted these councils as demonstrating that the similar aristocratic backgrounds of the secular and ecclesiastical lords meant that prohibitions of violence aimed at one had to be aimed at both in order to be effective. She writes, 'This latter, active type of prohibition may have related in part to the upper clergy's membership in exactly the arms-bearing noble class whose violence was regulated in the peace provisions', and that these prohibitions against the aristocratic use of arms would by necessity have to be applied to the aristocratic bishops as well.[146] She is certainly correct that the exalted social backgrounds of some of the highest-ranking ecclesiastical lords would probably have influenced their behavior towards an acceptance of warfare. As Richard Kaeuper demonstrates, these aristocratic knights were also forging independent relationships with piety, and could try to cast their own knightly behavior as inherently pleasing to God.[147] It would not be hard to imagine that aristocratic clerics were forging independent justifications with licit military violence.

Archbishop Wilfrid of Narbonne provides one of the most celebrated cases cited by those arguing that a broad consensus sought to eliminate armed clerics with as much fervor as simoniacs and married clergy.[148] Viscount Berengar of Narbonne strongly condemned Archbishop Wilfred for taking up arms against him and ravaging his lands. Berengar was also quick to point out that Wilfred had done these things after having publicly sworn to forego the use of secular arms. At a council in 1043, Wilfred apparently had '"renounced all military weapons and all worldly military activity. He [had] placed under the pain of excommunication and anathema himself as well as all the bishops of his diocese if they ever took up arms from that day forth."'[149] Despite Wilfred's renunciation soon afterwards '"he himself used weapons like a knight [*ut miles*], his loins girded not with a girdle but with a

---

[144] Remensyder, 'Pollution, Purity, and Peace', 286.

[145] The councils of Le Puy in 990/994 had also forbidden clerics from bearing secular arms. However, the argument advanced by Professor Remensnyder and others is that the campaign to actively disarm the clergy gained steam in the middle part of the eleventh century. See Remensnyder, 'Pollution, Purity, and Peace', 286; cf. Duggan, *Armsbearing and the Clergy*, 24–9.

[146] Remensnyder, 'Pollution, Purity, and Peace', 286–7. See also Cowdrey, 'The Peace and Truce', 52–4.

[147] Kaeuper, *Holy Warriors*, 24.

[148] Remensnyder, 'Pollution, Purity, and Peace', 287; cf. Roger Bonnaud-Delamare, 'Les institutions de la paix au Aquitaine au XIe siecle', *La Paix. Recueils de la Societe Jean Bodin* 14 (Brussels, 1961), 423

[149] Remensnyder, 'Pollution, Purity, and Peace', 287.

sword.'"¹⁵⁰ Remensnyder concludes from this that 'clearly, then, at this point the prohibition of bearing weapons embraced bishops as well as the lower clergy.'¹⁵¹ One implication of this example is that it engages quite clearly with the rhetoric of reform, and it demonstrates a desire to take secular arms out of the hands of the clergy. However, it also shows that the archbishop and his suffragan bishops were quite comfortable using arms and relying on them to bring about their desired policy outcomes. This fact, and the fact of the argument, underscores the intense debate, especially in southern France, and tension that separated those who saw arms as a licit avenue of political projection from those who wanted to limit them to lay hands.

We should tread very carefully here before extrapolating from this particular event to a larger cultural context. Unlike the Peace League of Bourges, which, though singular, became wide ranging, encompassing many actors, this particular case represented one individual complaining about another. Remensyder also points out that we cannot trust Berengar as a source, as he was a mortal enemy of Wilfred. However, her argument that his bias should not matter, since he assumed that the charge of 'being armed' would be damaging, is a fair point.¹⁵² One could make an equally compelling case that Berengar's true complaint went beyond a zeal for clerical reform. Wilfred had sworn to renounce arms, and had enjoined his suffragan bishops to do the same. He then violated this oath by taking up arms and destroying large sections of territory under Berengar's control. In chivalric terms, Wilfred had become *disloyal* in ignoring his sworn oath. Nobility operated within a cultural milieu that prized honorable behavior; however, one twisted it to fit his needs, and one of the most important attributes of honor was the virtue of loyalty to one's sworn word. We can see the importance of this in the fact that the reforms were targeted at the upper clergy because of their membership in this rarified social order. However, Berengar was also reacting to Wilfred's perfidy in much the same way that he would have done to a secular noble who had broken a similar oath.¹⁵³

---

¹⁵⁰ Ibid.
¹⁵¹ Ibid.
¹⁵² Ibid., 287 n. 30.
¹⁵³ It is an important point to remember that laymen played crucial roles in the Peace and Truce of God councils. As H.E.J. Cowdrey pointed out, for instance, Duke William V of Aquitaine had summoned the council of Poitiers 1000/1014 and was an active participant in the peace movement. See Cowdrey, 'The Peace and Truce', 59–61. Layman definitely would have preferred clerics to be disarmed, and they also would have preferred limiting fighting, since it would hinder their underlings from causing disturbances. William's actions were later taken on by Duke William of Normandy in a fashion designed to maximize his control over the duchy. The Peace and Truce of God movements were very useful for laity seeking to monopolize the use of force and their own roles in providing public order. Cowdrey pointed out that this same phenomenon happened in Barcelona. See Cowdrey, 'The Peace and Truce', 62–3.

So, if that was the case, why would Berengar condemn Wilfred's use of arms, if the true offense was the breaking of the oath? It is an important question, and a valuable opportunity to discuss a basic premise of human political nature. There was a faction within the intellectual culture that sought to disarm the clergy, of that we can be sure, and Berengar saw the opportunity to enlist their aid by casting Wilfred in a light designed to elicit their opprobrium. Merely complaining that Wilfred had broken his oath would not have engendered much sympathy from the reformers for Berengar's case; he needed to focus on Wilfred's use of warfare. Furthermore, we must consider whether Berengar would have raised a similar complaint if Wilfred had violated his oath against bearing arms in order to come to his aid, rather than to attack him. There is little evidence that Berengar was a crusader against armed clergy, except in this particular case where one of his traditional enemies had harmed him. Ultimately, this incident is best seen in the light of contemporary politics, rather than as a demonstration that the wind had shifted definitively against armed clerics.

The case of Wilfred is an example of modern historians following the leads of eleventh-century reformers. These reformers were focused on showing that their opponents were not 'true' clerics or Christians. Remensnyder demonstrates this by illuminating that, for reformers, status as a cleric derived from an acceptance of the reform position. She writes, 'Clergy who did not respect the parameters of their category became monsters – anomalies contradicting the social order and contravening peace. In other words, a cleric tainted by any of the three abuses was no longer a cleric.'[154] She applies this reasoning to Wilfred's case, arguing that by violating the precepts of his *ordo*, he had forfeited his position as archbishop. Berengar had condemned Wilfred for various crimes prior to the council of 1043, including devastating the area, but,

> Only after having described Wilfred's oath at the council did Berengar accuse him of transgressing social categories by acting 'like a knight'. Here the viscount highlighted the ontological opposition between cleric and *miles* which had been expressed in the oath. Arms, as Peter Damian had written, were reserved for the laity. Thus, by disarming Wilfred, the peace council of 1043 rendered him a cleric in a new way.[155]

---

[154] Remensnyder, 'Pollution, Purity, and Peace', 289–90. She also explained that this new ideal has persisted to the present day. For an earlier incarnation of this idea, see Cowdrey, 'The Peace and Truce', 50.

[155] Remensnyder, 'Pollution, Purity, and Peace', 290–1. Damian wrote that 'Si sacerdos arma corripit, quot utique laicorum est, quid meretur.' 291 n. 45; original in Epistolae 4.9; *PL* 144: 314–15.

While there is certainly merit in this argument, that a sharper definition of *ordo* was emerging in the mid-eleventh century, and that there were more than a few people who argued that fighting was the province of knights only, it would be too much to suggest that it represented a consensus or universal viewpoint. Also, no evidence suggests that Wilfred's condemnation by the council led to his deposition from his position as archbishop, unlike the numerous examples of clerics' being deposed for being simoniac and for concubinage.[156] This disparity ultimately provides one of the most important points for understanding the eleventh-century reform movements. While reformers did not want to see clerics bearing arms, their efforts against armed clerics were not advanced with the same fervor as those against simoniac and unchaste clerics. This could represent ambivalence regarding the utility of churchmen in warfare (since sometimes that violence was directed towards good outcomes), or it could be reflective of a relatively small number of clerics participating in war. Additionally, as the papacy gained centralizing power over the normative understanding of Christianity, the focus of reform remained on simony and concubinage, and became even sharper with time.

---

[156] For efforts to depose simoniac and married clergy, see Remensnyder, 'Pollution, Purity, and Peace', 289. Note that there are no examples listed of clerics being deposed for being armed. Prinze discusses the deposition of warrior-clerics in Germany, most famously Gewilib of Würzburg, though the examples are few. Prinze, *Klerus und Krieg*, 66–9; cited in Powell, 'Three Orders', 126.

CHAPTER 2

Papal Centralization and Canonical Prescriptions

Gerbert d'Aurillac, later Pope Sylvester II, reigned as pope for only four years, from 999 until 1003, but he represents not only an excellent example of how the papacy sought to maximize its authority, but also how it viewed the role of warfare. Gerbert's life, career, and political activities, in fact, demonstrate a good baseline of acceptable clerical behavior vis-à-vis warfare for the start of our period of study, at least from the perspective of a man well connected to papal politics. Gerbert was a scholar, an abbot, an archbishop, and eventually a pope. His actions were dictated by a sense of political expediency and are demonstrative of the importance of political pragmatism in determining licit behavior among the higher clergy. Gerbert was fully immersed in the secular affairs of his region and period, and his letters give us insight into the value of warfare to the clergy. What emerges, in brief, is that clergy (including Gerbert) could be comfortable taking on leading military roles in those violent times. This should not be surprising as we have already seen efforts and exhortations of some of the clerical reformers directed against just such behavior. Through the use of his letters, written either in his own name or on behalf of others such as Archbishop Adalbero, we see that Gerbert not only tailored his responses based on what was likely to best serve him politically, but that he also utilized violence and military action to achieve his political goals and those of his allies and friends.

Major clerics, including Gerbert himself, played leading roles in the warfare raging in France and Germany during this period. Between 985 and 990, many of Gerbert's letters are concerned with the incessant warfare between Lothair of France, Hugh Capet, Otto of Germany, as well as numerous other lords, such as Count Godfrey of Verdun and Duke Thierry of Upper Lorraine, and many prelates, including Adalbero, bishop-elect of Verdun (and son of Count Godfrey) and Adalbero, archbishop of Metz (and brother to Duke Thierry).[1] The clerics in particular were seen as vital to the wars, as Gerbert addressed letters specifically to them, including one in which he exhorted bishop-elect Adalbero, in the name of his father, to 'guard all strongholds from the enemy' and manfully

---

[1] *The Letters of Gerbert with his Papal Privileges as Sylvester II*, trans. Harriet Pratt Lattin (New York, 1961), #54.

to resist the Franks wherever he could.² After Verdun had fallen, he wrote a similar letter to Adalbero, archbishop of Metz, in his own name, recommending an attempt to recapture the city.³ Gerbert did not see it as a violation of the clerical *ordo* to engage in military campaigns or to lead men in battle. There is only one letter where Gerbert expressly complained about having to lead an army; but his complaint was not predicated on moral opposition, but because he saw such campaigns and concerns as a tedious and an unwelcome burden upon his time.⁴ Gerbert's acceptance of a military role for clerics was despite his approval of the division of medieval society into *ordines*, though he conceived of a dualistic distinction between secular and clerical, rather than the labor-based, tripartite distinction of Adalbero of Laon. A belief in distinct *ordines* separating the spiritual and temporal did not, in and of itself, necessitate an adoption of the reformist concepts of monopolies on types of labor (and thus a shutting out of clerics from war).

The middle of the eleventh century has long been understood to have been an important transitional moment in the cause of clerical reform. This is most evident in the elevation of Bruno, bishop of Toul, to the papacy as Pope Leo IX on February 12, 1049.⁵ Leo IX was among the most active of the 'reform' popes, and his papacy advanced the cause of the reformers regarding clerical chastity and simony. However, Leo was not as effective in curbing warrior-clerics, perhaps because of his welding of these reforms to the attempts to maximize papal authority and jurisdiction, as well as his own background in the imperial chancery and as a soldier-cleric.⁶ While a vocal group, including men such as the gifted theologian Peter Damian, agitated for disarming clerics, and while they would succeed in getting at least some prohibitions enshrined in the canonical collections compiled under these popes, many contemporaries tacitly accepted warrior-clerics during the period, an acceptance that only grew in importance with the embrace of papal-directed warfare under Leo IX, Gregory VII, and Urban II.

The preeminence of actions directed against simony and clerical marriage was evident throughout the period, though there were efforts to include the disarming

---

² Ibid.
³ *Letters of Gerbert*, #65. For a similar letter to Adalbero, archbishop of Rheims, see #96.
⁴ *Letters of Gerbert*, #102.
⁵ Cushing, 65.
⁶ Ibid., 73–5. Hannah Vollrath argues that the importance of forcing clerics to be chaste grew during the eleventh century onwards, and that the broader reform movement was targeted against simony and sex. Even within that narrow focus, however, there was significant debate. See Hannah Vollrath, 'Was Thomas Becket Chaste? Understanding Episodes in the Becket Lives', *Anglo-Norman Studies* 27, ed. John Gillingham (Woodbridge, 2005), 208. See also Duggan, *Armsbearing and the Clergy*, 24–9.

of clerics among the top items on the papal agenda. Leo IX accepted condemnations of armed clerics in prescriptive legislation, so long as he was able to advance his own legislative agenda, and so long as the priority of enforcement was under his control and directed according to his priorities. The 1049 Council of Rheims demonstrates Leo's compromise with the more extreme reformers who wanted to eliminate entirely clerical involvement in warfare. Leo IX opened the council of Rheims by forcing all attending clerics to swear that they were not simoniacs, but the council also included a condemnation of clerics who engaged in warfare or bore arms.[7] Only one cleric, however, Hugh of Langres, was actually deposed for anything resembling warfare. One of his crimes was the bearing of arms, but he was also condemned for selling church offices, murder, adultery, sodomy, and genital torture.[8] He was deposed, fled the council, but eventually begged for forgiveness in Rome, and was reinstated to his position (though he died before resuming it). Developments at the later councils of Florence and Lyons, as recalled by Bonizo of Sutri, further showed the focus on simony and sexual activity by reformers. At both councils many bishops were deposed for both offenses, largely through the efforts of Hildebrand (later Pope Gregory VII). The council of Lyons even witnessed a 'miracle' whereby the simoniac archbishop of Embrun was unable to state publicly that he believed in the Holy Trinity, because the power of the Holy Spirit prevented him.[9] There were, however, no celebrated accounts of clerics' being deposed for being warriors.

Two developments in the 1050s further demonstrate this focus of attention on simony and clerical marriage, and the relative minimization of armed clerics as a cause célèbre for the popes. The first comes in the move to invalidate the sacraments performed by simoniac clerics. The French Cardinal Humber of Silva-Candida, in his *Three Books Against the Simoniacs*, published in 1057 or 1058, sought to deny the sacramental power of simoniac clerics, which would have caused major upheaval with the rights and powers of the church with disputed clerics (not to mention the souls of their parishioners).[10] While Humbert's position was an extreme (even too extreme for Peter Damian), it is demonstrative of the fervency of the efforts directed against simony. In contrast, the sacraments performed by warrior-clerics were not similarly called into question. Furthermore, Leo IX's own use of warfare demonstrates his acceptance of its utility. The pope personally led a campaign in 1053 against the Normans, and was imprisoned for a

[7] Cushing, 95, 125.
[8] Ibid., 126–7.
[9] *The Papal Reform of the Eleventh Century: Lives of Pope Leo IX and Pope Gregory VII*, trans. I.S. Robinson (Manchester, 2004), 195–200. The original may be found in Bonizo of Sutri, *Liber ad amicum*, ed. E. Dümmler. MGH Ldl 1, 590–2.
[10] Robinson, *Papal Reform*, 3–4.

year at Benevento following the defeat of his army. A quick examination of how contemporaries reacted to this papal embrace of military action will demonstrate the unsettled nature of the debate.

The anonymous author of the Life of Leo IX, written probably around 1060, presented Leo's campaign and his background as a warrior-cleric with great pride, though the author was careful to avoid any mention of Leo's personally engaging in the fighting. He wrote that at the age of 23 Bruno/Leo was part of the Imperial army of Conrad II leading the contingent of soldiers owed by his bishop. The biographer wrote that, 'Bruno was charged with the command and organisation of the forces of knights bringing aid to the emperor from Toul, nevertheless in all things saving his order.'[11] Furthermore, the biographer explained that Bruno was wise in the ways of secular action, and that this was a great source of pride and admiration. He organized the troops, set the camp, and dispensed the pay to the soldiers. At no time did the biographer claim that Bruno led the troops into battle, or that he himself was armed, but his active involvement in the campaign and his overt military activities would have garnered criticisms from his contemporaries such as Humbert of Silva-Candida and Peter Damian.[12] The biographer seemingly anticipated this criticism, and offered a preemptive defense of Bruno's actions by falling back on the scriptural advice to 'render unto Caesar' those things that were owed him, and by making clear that he did these things 'saving his order', meaning that he never embraced the knightly or worldly aspects of warfare.

In 1026 Bruno was elevated to the bishopric of Toul, largely for his Imperial service, though the author stressed that his election was due to popular elevation and acclaim, not simony. In seeking to inoculate Bruno from the charge of having been a simoniac, the biographer instead, perhaps unwittingly, lent credence to the idea that simony and warrior-clerics were not equally problematic for eleventh-century reformers. Bruno's 'spontaneous' elevation and acclamation by the people of Toul was in reflection of his noted abilities as a military commander. In fact, the letter sent to the emperor stressed the difficult military position of Toul, and

---

[11] Ibid., 108.
[12] See Ferminio Poggiaspalla, 'La chiesa e la partecipazione dei chierici alla guerra nella legislazione conciliare fino alla Decretali di Gregorio IX', *Ephemerides iuris canoni* 15 (Rome, 1959), 146. He writes, 'Di questo spirito erano anche Attone di Vercelli, il quale scrive che usare le armi, far bottino, devastare le campagne, uccidere e ferire, non e azione da preti, ma diabolica (e la guerra privata in ispecie, che era il flagello di quei tempi tristi, giustificava davvero questa qualifica), S. Pier Damiani, che non esita a disapprovare l'operato di Leone IX che, se pur per giusta causa, aveva preso le armi contro i Normanni.'

asked that they be given a man who could defend them.[13] Bruno's advancement to the bishopric because of his military abilities, and the fact that the author chose to highlight this aspect of his résumé in order to downgrade the possibility that he had benefited from simony, further underscores the fact that some contemporaries saw clerics with military abilities as a net-positive.

The biographer's account of the 1053 Benevento campaign also claimed that Leo's undertaking was holy and Christian. Leo raised the forces himself to lead against the Normans, but according to this account, once he had assembled the army he remained at the castle of Civitate, while the army engaged the Normans in battle. His presence on campaign, but not in active combat, fits the narrative that the biographer sought to create regarding Leo's involvement with warfare. The biographer had a vested interest in keeping Leo in the centrist position in the debate over warrior-clerics. He was present on the campaign that was sold as a holy war against the Normans, as Leo himself told the Byzantine emperor in a letter, but he was not going so far as to fight personally, thereby possibly assuaging some of his reformist critics.[14]

We can see a continuation of this debate by looking at two other later accounts of this battle, those written by Bishop Bonizo of Sutri and Bishop Bruno of Segni. Both of these accounts were written thirty to forty years after Leo's pontificate, and can thus show us how views of clerical involvement in warfare had evolved from the mid-1060s. Bishop Bonizo was writing in order to explain why the Gregorian reformers had suffered a number of setbacks in their conflict with the Holy Roman Emperor, and he considered the question of whether it was licit for Christians to use military violence. He heaped praise on virtuous Christians, and especially clerics, who in the past had fought manfully for Christ. He specifically recalled Pope Benedict IX (admittedly, not a paragon of papal rectitude) sending John I, bishop of Oporto, on a campaign with the Holy Roman Emperor with the instructions that, if the emperor was willing, this bishop ought to carry the papal banner in 'the front line of battle.'[15] After justifying in general terms the presence of clerics on battlefields and military campaigns, he recounted Leo's campaign against the Normans. As a result of the numerous unchristian acts of the Normans, Leo 'struck them first with the sword of excommunication and then

---

[13] Robinson, *Papal Reform*, 109–10.

[14] Ibid., 149–53, esp. 149–50. Duggan makes this point clearly as well regarding warrior-clerics in general. He complains that modern historians assume that the entire range of military activities (from aiding military endeavors to actively fighting) were equally faulted in canon law (which they were not), but then he explains that this conflation of military activities was also present among contemporaries. Duggan, *Armsbearing and the Clergy*, 2 and 14.

[15] Robinson, *Papal Reform*, 181.

judged that they must be punished with the material sword.'[16] His attempt failed, but those who fought for the pope and died were shown to have been martyrs through numerous signs and miracles.[17] Clearly, Bonizo was not just excusing Leo's presence on the battlefield, but was extolling it and equating it with a fulfillment of God's will. Bonizo's decision not to engage with the question of whether Leo was present on the battlefield itself, or whether he was 'armed', demonstrates that these questions were not differentiated as clearly as canonists (and historians) would like to believe. Bonizo's exuberance in defending Leo's actions in general regarding this campaign gives a clear indication of his view of whether clerics could be involved in justifiable wars.

Bishop Bruno of Segni offered a slightly different take on the involvement of Leo in warfare, though not in the way that modern historians often present it. In his most famous account of the battle and Leo's defeat, Bruno wrote,

> He therefore assembled an army, of modest size indeed but composed of brave knights of his own nation, and went to fight against the Normans. He *had* indeed *a zeal for God, but* perhaps *it was not enlightened.* Would that he had not gone there in person, but had only sent an army there to defend righteousness![18]

The traditional interpretation of this passage is that Bruno was horrified at Leo's presence on the campaign and that this was because of canonical prohibitions of such behavior. I.S. Robinson writes that Bruno's condemnation of Leo's presence was 'An allusion to the canon law tradition that clergy should not be involved in secular warfare, which Leo IX himself had confirmed in his Council of Rheims c. 3.'[19] While this may have been true, we can also interpret Bruno's complaint to be a reaction to the results of the battle. Bruno was probably reacting negatively to Leo's presence because the papal army lost and Leo was captured. The defeat of a divinely inspired army, and one accompanied by the pope himself, gave the Normans a huge propaganda (not to mention military) victory. How could the pope's cause be said to be licit when God seemingly withdrew His support? Additionally, Leo's capture and year-long imprisonment set back the

---

[16] Ibid., 192–3.

[17] Ibid., 193. Smith argues that the 'use of papal armies by Leo IX (r. 1049–54) against the Normans of Apulia in 1053, and by the rival popes Alexander II and Honorius II during the Cadalan Schism of the early 1060s, raised thorny moral questions about church-sanctioned war, and prompted some churchmen to condemn lay participants as wicked mercenaries.' Smith, *War and the Making of Medieval Monastic Culture*, 101.

[18] Robinson, *Papal Reform*, 383.

[19] Ibid., 383, n. 48.

reform movement precipitously. Again, we must consider how Bruno would have reacted, had Leo led his army to a great and resounding victory. It is unlikely that he would have bemoaned Leo's presence on the field of battle.

Clerical direction of, and involvement in, military affairs was not uncommon during the Gregorian papacy (with the crusades providing an excellent example), but there was never a consensus on its acceptability. Pope Gregory VII saw no contradiction in leading Christendom spiritually and militarily.[20] Among his chief ideological opponents was Peter Damian, who had criticized Pope Leo for going on campaign, and who continued to oppose clerical involvement in warfare.[21] Robinson posits an evolving standard of acceptability over time in which Damian's complaint 'indicates how the behavior which had seemed fitting in 1025, when Leo – at that time, the young deacon Bruno – had led the Toul contingent to the aid of the Emperor Conrad II, had ceased to be acceptable in the eyes of the advanced reformer of 1053.'[22] With Gregory VII we see an even clearer elucidation of this debate. While Gregory's reign was defined by his conflict with Henry IV of Germany and the papal efforts against lay investiture, he also devoted great energy to advancing the cause of reform in eliminating simony and enforcing clerical chastity. A perusal of his letters and the canons of his councils demonstrates this two-fold focus on the traditional areas of reform interest, but also demonstrates the concurrent lack of interest in stamping out armed and warrior-clerics.[23] Gregory, and his successors, also directed much of their attention against the elimination of lay investiture. This focus did not allow much time to spare for prosecuting clerics who were active in warfare, nor would such a focus have fit Gregory's ideology. Gregory saw utility to the use of military violence in righteous causes by clerics, and he was not willing to acquiesce to a monopolization of licit violence by lay officials. Gregory VII was not interested in getting clerics off the battlefield or out of military affairs; in fact, he sought a greater role for himself (and, by extension, bishops) in directing and organizing warfare on behalf of the church and against his enemies (such as Henry IV). Gregory VII was essentially

---

[20] Smith, *War and the Making of Medieval Monastic Culture*, 102.
[21] Hehl, 'War, Peace and the Christian Order',196.
[22] Robinson, *Papal Reform*, 181.
[23] For an excellent overview of these areas of interest, as well as a review of primary evidence, see Cowdrey, *Pope Gregory VII*, esp. 543–6 and 550–3. As a possible indication of Gregory's tacit acceptance of warfare one can note that Ermenfrid, bishop of Sion, the legate who had promulgated the penances for clerics who fought at Hastings, eventually gravitated to the camp of the anti-pope Clement III, who was open in his criticism of Gregory's embrace of warfare. See H.E.J. Cowdrey, 'Bishop Ermenfrid of Sion and the Penitential Ordinance following the Battle of Hastings', *The Journal of Ecclesiastical History* 20 (1969), 232–3.

a more famous version of the German and French bishops who raised armies.[24] Indeed, according to Duggan, while Gregory's effect on canon law might have been minimal, he did succeed in militarizing the broader clerical culture.[25]

Gregory's conflict with Emperor Henry IV of Germany, and the subsequent creation of the anti-pope Clement III in 1080 (formerly Wibert of Ravenna), demonstrates how pragmatism and politics affected the acceptance or denial of clerical involvement in warfare. Wibert and the German bishops complained that Gregory had sullied the papal office by embracing warfare against Emperor Henry, and thus his propensity to use military force to achieve his aims was directly criticized by one of Henry's adherents, Wenrich of Trier, in 1081. He wrote,

> They declare that … you incite to bloodshed secular men seeking pardon for their sins; that murder, for whatever reason it is committed, is of small account; that the property of St. Peter must be defended by force; and to whomsoever dies in this defence you promise freedom from all his sins, and you will render account for any man who does not fear to kill a Christian in Christ's name.[26]

Wibert himself condemned Gregory's use of military violence by referring to the Gospel of John 18:11, whereby Christ ordered Peter to put his sword away in the Garden of Gethsemane. On the other hand, one of Gregory's own partisans, John of Mantua, in language later adopted by Bernard of Clairvaux to defend the crusades, reinterpreted this biblical passage to demonstrate that Christ had not categorically rejected the use of the sword by the church. Mantua's argument is worth quoting at length. In a letter to one of Gregory's staunchest allies, Countess Matilda of Canossa, he wrote

> Notice what the Lord said to Peter when he rushed for his sword: 'Put up thy sword into the sheath.' He who commanded that the sword be kept in the sheath did not command that it must be entirely cast away: 'Do not fling it away, but return it to its place.' The place of the sword is the righteous power which is not divided from the authority of St. Peter. Peter by his divine power delivers the sword when his vicar praises and strengthens the secular powers. [Christ] ordered him to put the sword in *this* sheath so that he, who was a priest, might not perform a military action with his own hand. But just as [Peter] himself repressed with the heavenly sword, do you [Matilda] –

---

[24] Hehl, 'War, Peace and the Christian Order', 198.
[25] Duggan, *Armsbearing and the Clergy*, 112–13.
[26] I.S. Robinson, 'Gregory VII and the Soldiers of Christ', *History* 58 (June 1973), 180.

but with the secular sword – exercise vengeance against the heresy which is subverting the greater part of the world.[27]

John was rejecting the use of the sword by clerics *personally*, but was endorsing the idea that military action by secular lords ought to be directed by clerics, and specifically the pope. This cohabitation of the religious and secular power in the hands of the pope was supported by a number of leading canonists, including Anselm II of Lucca. It also set an important precedent for the involvement of clerics in warfare. Opponents probably recognized the slippery-slope aspect of this argument. While men like John, and Bernard later, could argue that clerics ought only to *direct* the secular sword, rather than wield it themselves, this proved to be a fine line that could easily and licitly be crossed in individual circumstances. Once clerically directed violence was accepted as licit, admirable, and holy, it became much harder to argue categorically against clerics engaging in combat themselves, and virtually impossible to prohibit them from leading armies on the battlefield.

The culmination of this papal embrace and redirection of the 'reform' movement came in the pontificate of Urban II and the launching of the crusades. His most famous council, at Clermont in 1095 (where he essentially called for what became the First Crusade), also promulgated a number of canons pertaining to the question of warrior-clerics. However, reconstructing the actual pronouncements of the council at Clermont is frustratingly difficult, especially considering its importance and effect. There was no official publication of canons; rather, some of the clerics who attended recorded and disseminated the canons, thus there were different versions of the Clermont canons circulating in the twelfth century and beyond. Only one English monk was present, and this delayed the diffusion of these canons in England.[28] This was especially evident in the matter of armed clerics. In the group of collections that Somerville identified as belonging to northern France, there was a relatively simple canon stating that clerics should not bear arms.[29] According to Katherine Allen Smith, in defining the crusade

---

[27] Ibid., 186. For an excellent overview of Matilda's support of Gregory, see David J. Hay, *The Military Leadership of Matilda of Canossa, 1046–1115* (Manchester, 2008), 59–116.

[28] Robert Somerville, *Councils of Urban II*, Vol. 1, *Decreta Clarmontensia* (Amsterdam, 1972), 54, n. 37. For Urban's focus on simony, incontinence, and lay investiture as the world abuses of the clergy, see Francis J. Gossman, *Pope Urban II and Canon Law*, The Catholic University of America Canon Law Studies, No. 403 (Washington, D.C., 1960).

[29] Somerville, *Councils of Urban II*, 1, 74. We should also note that far more attention was paid, once again, to eliminating simony. Of the fourteen texts and collections that Somerville examined, only four contained the prohibition on clerical arms-bearing, whereas ten reiterated the prohibition on simony.

Urban II drew a distinction between secular and spiritual warfare, 'and in so doing defined the two activities as the rightful prerogatives of different groups.'[30] However, in the Anglo-Norman world, most of the dissemination of the canons came through the writings of William of Malmesbury and Orderic Vitalis, and neither made specific mention of the prohibition on armed clerics. Thus, on the one hand Urban was calling for clerically directed warfare, while on the other he was calling for clerics themselves to be disarmed. As noted with Gregory VII, the endorsement of religiously directed violence often over-shadowed the canonical prohibition on personally swinging the sword. This was especially true since Urban linked the call to crusade with a renewal and reinvigoration of the Peace and Truce of God, where clerics did take leading roles in managing warfare.[31] Indeed, the papal representative on the crusade, Bishop Adhémar of Le Puy, was intended by Urban to be an active participant in the military affairs of the campaign, if not to actively fight in the battles.

Evidence from English councils during the later eleventh and early twelfth centuries reinforces the larger trends evident in the continental councils. Two councils in 1070, organized and supervised by Bishop Ermenfrid of Sion, and two cardinal priests, John and Peter, legislated on what they considered the misbehavior of the clergy.[32] While the focus was on simony, they also legislated against clerical involvement in warfare. At the Council of Winchester in April of that year, the twelfth canon forbade monks who had renounced their habits from being accepted either into another convent or into the secular military.[33] A month later, the legatine council of Windsor refined this prohibition to the bearing of arms specifically, declaring that no cleric ought to bear arms.[34] These two councils taken together mark a clear belief that clerics ought to have nothing to do with military affairs, a probable result of the reformist zeal of Ermenfrid, and his angst over rampant clerical involvement in the campaign to conquer England and clerics' active participation in the battle of Hastings. The focus placed on clerical fighting at Hastings by the ordinances of penitence promulgated by Ermenfrid himself, either in 1067 or 1070, gives a good indication of their prevalence. In the process of assigning penances for the killing at Hastings, Ermenfrid included a specific section addressing the military actions of clerics.

---

[30] Smith, *War and the Making of Medieval Monastic Culture*, 103.
[31] Somerville, *Councils of Urban II*, 1, 102–3.
[32] For their probable identities, see *Councils and Synods with Other Documents Relating to the English Church*, ed. D. Whitelock, M. Brett, and C.N.L. Brooke, vol. 1, pt. 2: 1066–1204 (Oxford, 1981), 563–4.
[33] Ibid., 575–6.
[34] Ibid., 581. 'Ut nullus clericus secularia arma ferat.'

The clerks who fought, or who were armed for fighting, must do penance as if they had committed these sins in their own country, for they are forbidden by the canons to do battle. The penances of monks are to be determined by their rule and by the judgment of their abbots. Those who fought merely for gain are to know that they owe penance as for homicide. But those who fought as in a public war have been allotted a penance of three years by their bishops out of mercy.[35]

The penances imposed on the clerics were harsher than those for laymen. Clerics who fought 'for gain' were treated as though they committed homicide, whereas this same penalty attached itself to those who killed someone after William was consecrated as king. The clerics who fought 'as in a public war' were given three years of penance, as opposed to the year of penance for each enemy slain in battle for laymen, and the three years of penance for killing while out pillaging.[36] That distinction, with a lesser punishment for fighting in a 'public war' versus for personal gain, is an important indicator of the importance that intention played in determining the reception of warrior-clerics. Those fighting on behalf of the king (or another licit public campaign) were in a much stronger cultural position than those fighting 'illegally'. Ermenfrid represented the reformist agenda, and he managed to get this legislation passed through his authority as papal legate. However, we should note that the very necessity of this legislation indicates the prevalence of clerics fighting at Hastings, including men such as Bishop Odo of Bayeux, Bishop Geoffrey of Coutances, and Remigius of Fécamp, later bishop of Lincoln. We should note that while the penance was an exception to the general rule (it was not repeated), it nevertheless represented an interesting illumination of the reformist end of the spectrum of debate.

We can see the exceptional nature of the penitential legislation fairly clearly in the Council of London, held between December 25, 1074 and August 28, 1075. In this council, presided over by the great canonist Lanfranc, archbishop of Canterbury, many of the earlier canons from the councils of Windsor and Winchester in 1070 were re-issued; however, this did not include the canons regarding the involvement of clerics in warfare. Since this council had as one of its purposes the moving of episcopal centers to more defensible locations in light of the growing concerns of rebellion in 1075, it is arguable that the non-re-issue of

---

[35] Ibid., 583–4. The Latin reads, 'De clericis qui pugnaverunt aut pugnandi gratia armati fuerunt, quia pugnare eis illicitum erat, secundum instituta canonum acsi in patria sua peccassent peniteant. Penitentia monachorum secundum regulam suam et abbatum iudicia statuantur.' For the translation used here, see *English Historical Documents*, 2, ed. Douglas and Greenway (London, 1953), 606–7.

[36] *English Historical Documents*, 2, ed. Douglas and Greenway, 606–7.

these canons was a clear indication that clerical involvement in warfare was not seen to be a major problem. The leading roles played by clerics in crushing the 1075 rebellion demonstrate the importance of this choice.

This same tension between reality and the ideological wishes of some clerical reformers was again on display in 1138. At the Council of Westminster held in December, overseen by the papal legate Alberic, cardinal bishop of Ostia, a canon was promulgated that forbade clerics from bearing arms.[37] It followed Pope Nicholas I in arguing that a man could not be both a knight of Christ and knight of the secular world at the same time. The most interesting aspect of this canon was that it was issued four months after the battle of the Standard, in which Archbishop Thurstan of York marshaled the English barons to fight the Scots, and sought to lead them personally into battle. Furthermore, he ordered the priests of his diocese to lead their parishioners into battle, bearing crosses (which would probably not be considered 'weapons' in the traditional sense). Daniel Gerrard sees the pronouncements of this council as convincing evidence for active fighting by clerics at the battle.[38] This was not simply a case of an ideal failing to be reflected by the 'sinful' world but, rather, a case whereby Thurstan was almost uniformly lauded for his military role. Lastly, the fact that the papal legate Alberic was replaced the following year by the very embodiment of a warrior bishop, Henry of Blois, bishop of Winchester, indicates that this debate was very much ongoing. The reformers were generally very successful at getting bans on clerical armsbearing enshrined in canon law and conciliar legislation, but they were less successful in translating this legal prohibition into a broader cultural condemnation.

This debate continued unabated throughout the twelfth century. At the 1175 Council of Westminster, canon six forbade clerics from being engaged in any activities that involved the shedding of human blood.[39] While this was mostly directed at judicial proceedings that involved bloodshed, it could equally apply to the leading of men on the field of battle, or to engaging in active military activities of any kind. The eleventh canon reiterated the earlier prohibitions of clerics bearing arms, as reflected in councils of Windsor and Westminster, and the canonical collection of Gratian.[40] This council was promulgating canons against armed or warrior-clerics despite, or because of, the prevalence of such clerics, most famously Geoffrey Plantagenet, illegitimate son of Henry II, bishop-elect of Lincoln, and later the archbishop of York. While there is no evidence that

---

[37] *Councils and Synods*, 1, 2, 777.
[38] Gerrard, 45; Douglas Senette, 'A Cluniac Prelate: Henry of Blois, bishop of Winchester (1129–1171)' (Ph.D. diss., Tulane University, 1991), 124
[39] *Councils and Synods*, 1, 2, 986.
[40] Ibid., 988.

the council was promulgating these canons against him personally, it certainly underscores the problem faced by clerical and canonical reformers. Men such as Geoffrey were not only actively fighting in warfare, but they were generally being lauded for it by chroniclers and rewarded for it by rulers, regardless of the illegality (determined by the councils) of that behavior.[41]

The introduction of crusading warfare and the knightly-monastic military orders heightened the debate over clerics and war in the twelfth century.[42] While England played a fairly minor role in the crusades prior to the Third Crusade (led by Richard I), the crusades and Military Orders still had a major effect on the cultural and intellectual discussion surrounding warrior-clerics in England.[43] The 1095 church council at Clermont has already been discussed for its specific relevance to arms-bearing by clerics, but we should also consider the relevance of the crusades to the cultural and legal acceptance of clerics doing precisely what the council indicated that they should not, namely, bearing arms. The crusades had the effect of crystallizing a number of arguments and debates over the legitimacy of warfare and the interaction of 'just war' theory with the emerging notion of 'holy war'.[44] H.E.J. Cowdrey makes an interesting argument that it is anachronistic for us to assume that contemporaries saw 'holy war' and 'just war' as being inherently linked. He argues that this linkage dates only to the later part of the twelfth and early part of the thirteenth centuries. They began the period as separate ideas, but by the end of the first century of the crusading period, 'they were being drawn together in an association that has in many respects persisted until modern times.'[45] This linking of holy war with just war, just in time for the Third Crusade, could have affected perceptions of the roles played by Hubert

---

[41] Though it falls outside the specific scope of this book, there is an example of a thirteenth century English council legislating against armed clerics, the legatine council held at St. Paul's in 1268. Clerics were forbidden from bearing arms, exacting vengeance, or committing violent crimes. See *Councils and Synods with Other Documents Relating to the English Church*, ed. F.M. Powicke and C.R. Cheney, Vol. 2, Pt. 2: 1265–1313 (Oxford, 1964), 751–2.

[42] For a discussion of the roots of crusader ideology, see Jean Flori, 'Ideology and Motivations in the First Crusade', *The Crusades*, ed. Helen Nicholson (Basingstoke, 2005), 15–36.

[43] The best overall survey of England's role in the crusades remains Christopher Tyerman, *England and the Crusades* (Chicago, 1988). See also Simon Lloyd, *English Society and the Crusade, 1216–1307* (Oxford, 1988), 9–10.

[44] As H.E.J. Cowdrey has argued, 'few would disagree that the experience of the crusades had profound and indelible effects upon the views of western Christians about the morality of warfare.' H.E.J. Cowdrey, 'Christianity and the Morality of Warfare during the First Century of Crusading', *The Experience of Crusading*, Vol. 1, ed. Marcus Bull and Norman Housley (Cambridge, 2003), 175.

[45] Ibid.

Walter, bishop of Salisbury and Baldwin, archbishop of Canterbury, and could have made their military actions seem more licit to contemporaries. On the other hand, Jonathan Riley-Smith argues that for Urban II, there was no question that the crusader effort he was directing was inherently 'just', as he saw all wars waged to 'liberate' Christian lands from the Muslims as 'just wars'.[46] The crusading efforts did not, therefore, have the 'grey area' of acceptability that plagued warfare between Christians. Churchmen who fought in the crusades, while still transgressing canonical prohibitions, could defend their actions as having, at least, occurred in a conflict whose legitimacy was generally accepted.

In his call for military force to protect Christianity, Urban II saw that there was a clear and defining distinction within Christian society between laymen and clergy, hinging on the ability to bear arms.[47] In his conception of the crusade, the major roles would be played by men who were explicitly warriors, and participation by non-combatants was something to be regulated and avoided, rather than encouraged. The pope envisioned that his legate, Bishop Adhémar of Le Puy, would govern the expedition. Urban wrote of his role,

> And we have constituted our most beloved son, Adhémar, Bishop of Puy, leader of this expedition and undertaking in our stead, so that those who, perchance, may wish to undertake this journey should comply with his commands, as if they were our own, and submit fully to his loosings or bindings, as far as shall seem to belong to such an office.[48]

Bishop Adhémar was also a unifying figure for the disparate crusader forces, until his death at Antioch in 1098.[49] Thus, Urban created what he considered to be an agreeable balance – secular warriors fighting enemies of Christ at the behest and direction of His clergy. This distinction, while clear to the pope, seemed less so to many of the clerics on the crusade, including Adhémar.[50] Indeed, observers such

---

[46] Jonathan Riley-Smith, *Idea of Crusading*, 17–18.

[47] James Brundage, 'Crusades, Clerics, and Violence: Reflections on a Canonical Theme', *The Experience of Crusading*, Vol. 1, 148.

[48] See August. C. Krey, *The First Crusade: The Accounts of Eyewitnesses and Participants* (Princeton, 1921), 42–3. 'et carissimum filium Ademarum, Podiensem episcopum, huius itineris ac laboris ducem, uice nostra constituimus, ut quibus hanc uiam forte suscipere placuerit, eius iussionibus tamquam nostris pareant atque eius solutionibus seu ligationibus, quantum ad hoc negotium pertinere uidebitur, omnio subiaceant.' See *Epistulae et Chartae ad Historiam Primi Belli Sacri Spectantes*, ed. Heinrich Hagenmeyer (Innsbruck, 1901), 136–7.

[49] Riley-Smith, *Idea of Crusading*, 79–80, 87–9.

[50] John France argues that Urban II had not intended Adhémar to function as a commander-in-chief. See John France, *Victory in the East: A military history of the First*

as Anna Comnena remarked (disapprovingly) upon the military prowess of the Latin clerics.

Comnena's celebrated account of the First Crusade, the Alexiad, contains vivid descriptions of western clerics fighting in battle, which according to Anna was a horrible violation of their holy station. After commenting on the prowess of a Latin priest, Comnena explained that Latin mores were different (and inferior) to those of the Byzantines,

> the Latin barbarian will simultaneously handle divine things, and wear his shield on his left arm, and hold his spear in his right hand, and at one and the same time he communicates the body and blood of God, and looks murderously and becomes 'a man of blood,' as it says in the psalm of David.[51]

The Latin priests were not concerned about mixing the sacred and secular, and did not see the shedding of blood as polluting their ability to perform the Mass. Comnena also notes that the Latin clerics were driven by a chivalric interest in military prowess, much like the knights they fought alongside. While there is no commentary from Comnena on this bellicose cleric's background, his demeanor and embrace of war was clear. From him, she extrapolated about the warlike tendencies of the Latin clerics in general (and a demonstration of why they were 'less Christian' than the Byzantines). She wrote,

> For this barbarian race is no less devoted to sacred things than it is to war. And so this man of violence rather than priest, wore his priestly garb at the same time that he handled the oar and had an eye equally to naval or land warfare, fighting simultaneously with the sea and with men.[52]

The cleric Comnena described fits into the broader cultural discourse illuminated elsewhere in this book. While Urban had been clear about wanting to separate clerics from the fighting, if not from the directing of warfare, clerics on the crusade itself could transgress those boundaries without penalty.

Beyond the actions of the lower-ranked clerics, Bishop Adhémar set the standard for how a high-ranking churchman could gain the admiration of contemporaries for his use of military violence, and, as reportedly the first man to take the

---

Crusade (Cambridge, 1996), 97. See also Hans Eberhard Mayer, *The Crusades*, trans. John Gillingham (Oxford, 1988), 38.
[51] *The Alexiad*, 256.
[52] Ibid.

cross, we might consider him the first actual crusader.[53] His actions on the crusade as a military commander and his subsequent death at the siege of Antioch in 1098 created an exemplar of behavior for clerical crusaders. Adhémar was almost uniformly respected by chroniclers and historians. He was praised for helping the poor, advising the rich, and leading the army well. His roles as preacher, pastor, and soldier were all laudable for contemporaries.[54] At the siege of Nicaea on May 21, 1097, he commanded the right flank of Raymond of St.-Gilles' army, and at the battle of Dorylaeum on July 1, 1097, he came to the rescue of Bohemund and attacked the Turkish forces from the flank, driving them from the field and saving the day for the Christian army.[55] His actions, and subsequent death at the siege of Antioch in 1098, made him into a martyred hero for the Christian army. During the subsequent battle to capture Jerusalem, the chronicler Raymond of Aguilers claimed that the near-saintly and now-ghostly Adhémar was seen fighting in the front rank of the Christian army scaling the walls of the holy city, imagery that evokes the tales of saintly combatants coming to the aid of the Christian forces outside of Antioch earlier in the campaign.[56] Brundage concludes that Adhémar was 'a capable, imaginative, resourceful military commander in the field.'[57] Adhémar's experience and example offers a good insight into the paradigmatic tensions inherent in churchmen who fought in causes generally perceived as laudable. Urban's call for a holy war to free Eastern Christendom was met with an enthusiastic response, and the ultimately successful nature of the campaign seemed to demonstrate God's approval. For many contemporaries, churchmen who actively aided that endeavor were on the right side of the conflict. While Riley-Smith may be correct that Adhémar never personally bore arms, as it was against canon law, his successful generalship and posthumous cutting and thrusting reinforced the broader cultural acceptance of warrior-clerics in a just cause.[58] Adhémar became one of the most revered and influential figures of memory of the whole crusade, a bishop whose deeds echoed in the halls of both the nobility and the clergy.

[53] Mayer, *The Crusades*, 9.
[54] James Brundage, 'Adhémar of Puy: The Bishop and his Critics', *Speculum* 34 (Apr., 1959), 201.
[55] *Robert the Monk's History of the First Crusade*, trans. Carol Sweetenham (Aldershot, 2005), 110. Cf. Brundage, 'Adhémar of Puy', 204. Mayer questions the military value of Adhémar's flank attack. See Mayer, *The Crusades*, 47.
[56] Raymond of Aguilers, *Historia Francorum qui ceperunt Iherusalem*, Recueil des Historiens des Croisades 3 (Paris, 1866), 300. 'In hac die domnus Ademarus, Podiensis episcopus, a multis in civitate visus est; etiam multi de eo testantur, quod ipse primus murum ascendens, ad ascendendum socios atque populum invitabat.'
[57] Brundage, 'Adhémar of Puy', 211.
[58] Riley-Smith, *Idea of Crusading*, 82, 117. Cf. France, *Victory in the East*, 332–3.

For English prelates on crusade, Adhémar's experience was more the norm, rather than the exception. The warfare of the crusades, being directed against non-Christians, did not raise the same ethical and moral dilemmas for chroniclers as warfare against Christians. Therefore, since the use of military violence by churchmen was often judged on the perceived justice of the cause towards which it was directed, fighting on crusade had a higher likelihood of being deemed acceptable by contemporary observers. For men such as Hubert Walter and Peter des Roches, their military actions on crusade were almost uniformly praised in the surviving literature, even if their near-identical actions in domestic warfare were greeted with more suspicion. In fact, one can detect some angst among lay participants of the crusades in the very fact that clerics did not fight enough. Gerald of Wales, a royal clerk for Henry II and assistant to Archbishop Baldwin of Canterbury's recruitment campaign in Wales for the Third Crusade, recorded a snide but telling remark from Henry II regarding the role of churchmen on crusade. In response to the request for assistance from Patriarch Heraclius of Jerusalem in 1185, Henry supposedly responded, "'These clerks can incite us boldly to arms and danger since they themselves will receive no blows in the struggle, nor will they undertake any burdens which they can avoid.'"[59] Inherent in Henry's answer is the conflict between the active role clerics played on crusade, whether to merely incite some to fight (as canon law allowed) or to take up arms vigorously themselves against the Saracens. The evidence of English prelates indicates that many contemporaries very much approved of the more muscular approach of men such as Adhémar, Hubert, and even the fictional Turpin (to be discussed in the next chapter), even if it flew in the face of canonical restrictions.

The preaching of the Third Crusade in England, coupled with the decision to raise a special tax on non-crusaders, led to a rush of wealthy and powerful clerics and laymen alike to take the cross.[60] This rush to avoid the tax did not actually result in many clerics making the journey to Jerusalem, with only Hubert Walter and Baldwin of Canterbury making the journey. Their devotion and loyalty was contrasted by Richard of Devizes, a monk of Winchester, with clerics who merely "'saluted Jerusalem from afar.'"[61] While this was not an overt call for clerics to

---

[59] Christopher Tyerman, *England and the Crusades*, 45. "'Audacter,' inquit, "nos clerici ad arma et pericula provocare possunt, quoniam ipsi ictus in discrimine nullos suscipient, nec ulla quae vitare poterunt onerosa subibunt." See Giraldi Cambrendis, *Opera* 8, ed. George Warner, RS 21, 207.

[60] Tyerman, *England and the Crusades*, 64. Cf. John Gillingham, *Richard I* (New Haven, 1999), 114–16.

[61] Tyerman, *England and the Crusades*, 64. Devizes mocks Walter, the archbishop of Rouen, for only 'salutata a longe Ierosolyma'. See Richard of Devizes, *De rebus gestis*

hack and slash their way to the Holy City, the men who did just that were considered the heroes, while the men who avoided going to Jerusalem had their devotion questioned. Active service in the army was important for all crusaders, whether cleric or lay. Tyerman writes, 'The halfhearted were, in any case, no use on campaign. According to the possibly romanticised account of Richard of Devizes, the king's experience with the archbishop of Rouen prompted him to purge his army at Messina of all except those able and cheerfully willing to bear arms.'[62] For the king, a prelate on crusade had better be an active participant and willing to pull his weight militarily. It is no coincidence that the prelates who fought with Richard throughout the crusade, such as Hubert Walter, were rewarded with advancement and greater political power, while also garnering the equivalent of a 'good press' from chroniclers and crusade observers.[63] For the English, during the period under study, the reality was that churchmen who militarily contributed to the crusade were held up as heroes by contemporary observers.

In addition to the crusades, we should consider how the establishment of the Military Orders, such as the Knights Templar, who were fighting 'a twofold war both against flesh and blood and against a spiritual army of evil in the heavens', as Bernard of Clairvaux so memorably described them, affected the perception and behavior of churchmen in warfare.[64] Membership in these orders often conferred some element of holiness on the participant in the eyes of contemporaries, and for Duggan the creation of the Military Orders was part of the 'revolution' of the early twelfth century in favor of warrior-clerics, but we ought to be cautious of considering the members of these orders as 'churchmen'.[65] For some, the very fact of their being able to bear arms 'legally' separates them from clerics. In contrasting them with medieval monks, Katherine Allen Smith writes that monks 'held themselves to be superior to all lay arms-bearers, even the most pious crusaders and members of the Military Orders, whose spiritual warfare was tainted by physical violence and bloodshed.'[66] Alan Forey goes even further, arguing that members

---

Ricardi Primi, in *Chronicles of the Reigns of Stephen, Henry II and Richard I* 3, ed. Richard Howlett, RS 82, 404.

[62] Tyerman, *England and the Crusades*, 65. Devizes wrote, 'Ex factis huius archiepiscopi rex factus instructior, purgavit exercitum, non permittens secum quemquam venire, nisi qui bene posset, et bono animo vellet, arma portare'. Richard of Devizes, *Chronicle*, 404.

[63] Tyerman, *England and the Crusades*, 68–9; Ralph V. Turner, *Men Raised from the Dust* (Philadelphia, 1988), 16–18; Ralph V. Turner, 'Richard the Lionheart and English Episcopal Elections', *Albion* 29 (Spring, 1997), 1–13.

[64] Bernard of Clairvaux, *Treatises III*, trans. Conrad Greenia (Collegeville, MN, 1977), 127–8.

[65] Duggan, *Armsbearing and the Clergy*, 104–5.

[66] Smith, *War and the Making of Medieval Monastic Culture*, 156.

of the Military Orders were essentially laymen, despite their monastic lifestyle. He writes that the canonical prohibition on fighting clerics was irrelevant, 'for the Templars and the members of later military orders who fought were not clerics. In all of these orders a distinction was made between chaplains and lay brethren, and only the chaplains received the tonsure and were *clerici*.'[67] The problem for contemporaries, according to Forey, was how to reconcile the very active nature of the military lifestyle with the reserved expectations of the monastic one, especially in light of the increasing polarization of distinct *ordines*.[68] Once again, the question was not of violence, necessarily, but of lifestyle.

It is probable that most contemporaries often saw these men as holy warriors, and it is true that members of the lay elite certainly, at times, preferred to bequeath money and land to them instead of to traditional monastic houses. The kinship between Templars (and others) and lay knights was most probably closer than that between Templars (and others) and traditional monks, though members of the Military Orders could not marry, nor pass on property, much like monks. There was confusion, however, over what this new vocation constituted. William of Tyre thought of the Templars 'as religious, as the equivalent of regular canons or priests living in a religious community, and he stated that their military vocation was the creation of the patriarch and prelates – in other words, that the concept of the first Military Order sprang from the Church.'[69] Earlier authors, such as Simon, monk of St. Bertin, saw the first Templars as crusading knights who had remained in the Holy Land.[70] Simon argued that the Templars were restrained in their use of arms, and would resort to violence only in defense of holy sites.[71] Many contemporaries even saw the emergence of this Order as the reinvigoration of the institution of knighthood, an argument also presented recently by Sam Conedera. He stresses that the creation of the Templars, specifically, must be seen as an effort to reform knighthood, rather than to create a new monastic vocation.[72] John of Salisbury praised them as latter-day Maccabees, but 'this did not allow them to usurp the rights of ordained priests. Being holy warriors gave them some

---

[67] Alan Forey, *The Military Orders from the Twelfth to the Early Fourteenth Centuries* (Toronto, 1992), 9–10.
[68] Ibid., 11–14.
[69] Helen Nicholson, *The Knights Templar: A New History* (Stroud, 2001), 23.
[70] Ibid., 24–6.
[71] Ibid., 24. For the original, see Simon de St. Bertin, 'Gesta abbatum Sancti Bertini Sithensium', ed. O. Holder-Egger, in *MGH SS*, Vol. 13, 649. 'armis tantum contra insurgentium paganorum impetus ad terram defendendam uterentur, quando necessitas exigeret.'
[72] I would like to thank Dr. Conedera for discussions on this topic. See Sam Zeno Conedera, *Ecclesiastical Knights: The Military Orders in Castile, 1150–1330* (New York, 2015), 1.

status, but not as much as priests.'[73] Alexander the Minorite, in his *Expositio in Apocalypsim*, equated the Military Orders with the armies of heaven spoken of in Revelation 19:14.[74] The Templars seemingly resembled the holy warriors of the later books of the Bible, but were not members of the traditional clergy.

Nicholson has argued that the very fact that members of these orders were often themselves knights helped to create this additional kinship with the members of the nobility, and those aspiring to be in the nobility.[75] Indeed, in the tripartite notion of medieval society, 'the Military Orders appeared a heaven-sent means for knights to win salvation.'[76] A number of nobles opted to become members of the Military Orders on their deathbeds (including William Marshal in 1219), whereas in an earlier time, they would have joined a traditional monastic order. Nicholson saw their military function as a defining characteristic: 'The Military Orders were religious foundations ... [but unlike] many other religious orders, they were lay orders, where most of the members were never ordained to the priesthood. This was because of their military function; priests are forbidden to shed blood.'[77] Thus for a knight or aspiring knight, the Military Orders offered a path to holiness akin to a monastic order, but with the added bonus of a continuing opportunity to practice the vocation for which they had trained and to participate in the chivalric and valorizing practice of violence. On the other hand, two of the primary complaints from some clerical observers about the Military Orders were based on the general 'contempt for the knightly class and a belief that religious men should not shed blood.'[78] The tensions inherent in these two suggestions from Nicholson underscore the broader issues at work with institutions such as the Templars, Hospitallers, and others. Contemporaries were torn as to what, exactly, these men were, and where they fit into the idealized image of society.

The members of the Military Orders did not easily fit into one social category or the other. They were primarily knights, or at a minimum warriors, and thus were mostly at home with the secular lay elite, but they also lived according to a Rule, and were theoretically beholden directly to the pope in much the same manner as churchmen. James Brundage argues that these men 'were not exactly monks, nor were they canons-regular, nor were they clerics, yet in some respects their way of life resembled elements of each of these conventional religious groups.'[79]

---

[73] Nicholson, *Knights Templar*, 37.
[74] Helen Nicholson, *Templars, Hospitallers and Teutonic Knights: Images of the Military Orders, 1128–1291* (Leicester, 1993), 40.
[75] Ibid., 62.
[76] Ibid., 13.
[77] Ibid., 1.
[78] Ibid., 35.
[79] Brundage, 'Crusades, Clerics, and Violence', 153.

In their way of life they emulated religious groups such as the Cistercians, but Brundage distinguishes them from traditional religious orders through their military activities and use of arms. Canon law, according to Brundage, had 'strictly forbidden clerics, monks, and canons-regular to carry weapons at all, much less to fight with them.'[80] Thus, from the perspective of canon law, Templars and other members of Military Orders were not churchmen in the traditional sense. As support, Brundage points to the standard gloss of Gratian's *Decretum* by Johannes Teutonicus in which he explained that the members of the Military Orders were neither clerics nor laymen but, rather, akin to lay brethren who had special dispensation to bear arms.[81] The Templar rule outlawed certain 'worldly' activities, such as hunting and ostentatious dress, but allowed violence, thereby furthering the evidence that worldliness and military service were not coterminous.[82]

We can see the arguments and complaints about the Military Orders in the twelfth century as perhaps microcosms of the arguments over militarily active churchmen. While Templars were not clerics in the traditional sense, they did transgress those same ideological boundaries as monks. Men such as Bishop Anselm of Havelburg (d. 1158), himself an Augustinian canon, considered the members of the Military Orders as 'holy laymen', whereas Otto of Freising and Richard of Poitou, a monk of Cluny, saw them as a new kind of knights.[83] They were following the basic conception of the Templars as laid out by Bernard of Clairvaux in *De Laude Novae Militiae*, in which he repeatedly referred to the Templars as knights, and contrasted them with traditional knights, rather than with clerics. For Bernard these men were modern-day Maccabees, ready to do violence upon the enemies of God.[84] Others, such as William, archbishop of Tyre, were somewhat more troubled by the conception. William of Tyre was one of the best-informed contemporary observers of the Military Orders in action, but he was also one of the most critical.[85] William 'believed that clergy generally should

---

[80] Ibid., 154; Burchard, *Decretum* 2. 211–12, Ivo, Decretum 5. 332–4, 6. 286–7, Ivo, Panormia 3. 16.
[81] Brundage, 'Crusades, Clerics, and Violence', 155.
[82] Forey, 192–5.
[83] Nicholson, *Templars, Hospitallers and Teutonic Knights*, 37–8.
[84] Morton, 'Maccabees', 283. The Maccabees were a popular comparison for crusaders and members of the Military Orders, though early observers were torn as to the value of this comparison. Fulcher of Chartres favorably compared the members of the First Crusade to the Jewish military heroes, whereas for Guibert de Nogent, the fact that the Maccabees were Jews, rather than Christians, was reason enough to shy away from linking the crusaders to them. See Morton, 280–2.
[85] Helen Nicholson, 'Before William of Tyre: European Reports on the Military Orders' deeds in the East, 1150–1185', *The Military Orders: Welfare and Warfare*, ed. Helen Nicholson, Vol. 2 (Aldershot, 1998), 111 and 116–17. Nicholson also draws some

not fight, [but] he approved of the Military Orders provided that they fulfilled their function effectively, and were obedient to their bishops.'[86] For William, the basic guiding principle on clerical involvement in warfare was contained in the biblical story of the Garden of Gethsemane in which Christ tells Peter to put away his sword. This story was also the basis for Gratian's condemnation of militarily active churchmen. William wrote about a cleric in 1182 who was killed by an arrow during a battle. He wrote, 'Carried away by his zeal for secular interests, he [Godfrey of Villeneuve] was struck by an arrow and perished. It is indeed just, according to the word of the Lord that "all they that take the sword shall perish with the sword."'[87] William's canonical interpretation of clerical violence did not affect his support for the Military Orders, as he separated them from traditional clergy.

Other contemporaries were more concerned about the use of violence within the Military Orders, as evidenced by a contemporary debate over the militarization of the Hospitallers.[88] Master Gilbert of Assailly (r. 1163–1169/70) was apparently an avid warrior who had involved the Order in a number of military endeavors during his period in office. According to Lambert of Wattrelos in his *Annals of Cambrai*, Gilbert led his own troops into battle during King Amalric's attack on Egypt in 1168.[89] There was disquiet over this military role during Gilbert's rule, as well as those of his successors Jobert (1172–77) and Roger des Moulins. In a series of letters, Pope Alexander III 'between 1168 and 1180 reminded the Hospitallers that their first duty was to care for the poor and that arms-bearing should take place only in times of crisis.'[90] Thus, when Jobert wrote to Archbishop Henry of Reims, he stressed the spiritual work that the Hospitallers did, rather than their increased military activities.[91] Ultimately, for the purposes of this study, members of the Military Orders were not automatically 'churchmen' by virtue of their membership in the Order. There were debates, however, over whether these

---

interesting connections between William's work and that of Walter Map. See page 112.

[86] Nicholson, *Templars, Hospitallers and Teutonic Knights*, 45.
[87] William of Tyre, *A History of Deeds Done Beyond the Sea*, trans. Emily Babcock and August Krey (New York, 1943), 475. He was citing Gratian's classic invocation against warrior-clerics. See Gratian, *Decretum*, c. 23 q. 8.
[88] Jonathan Phillips, 'Archbishop Henry of Reims and the Militarization of the Hospitallers', *The Military Orders: Welfare and Warfare*, Vol. 2, 83–4. For a good overview of the militarization of the Hospitallers, see Helen Nicholson, *The Knights Hospitaller* (Woodbridge, 2003), 1–17.
[89] Nicholson, 'Before William of Tyre: European Reports on the Military Orders' Deeds in the East, 1150–1185', *The Military Orders: Welfare and Warfare*, Vol. 2, 116.
[90] Phillips, 'Archbishop Henry of Reims', 85.
[91] Ibid., 88.

orders should be as violent as they were, especially the newly militarized Hospital, which indicates even more concern with military violence and the 'church', even if only tangentially through the medium of the Military Orders.

The final section of this chapter will examine briefly the various canonical collections from the beginning of the eleventh century to the early period of the thirteenth century.[92] Our purpose will not be to comprehensively review canon law but, rather, to examine only the most commonly utilized canonical collections, beginning with that of Burchard of Worms in the beginning of the eleventh century, and culminating with the *Liber Extra* of Gregory IX in 1234. While there was certainly no 'single voice' to what we broadly call 'canon law', at no point did the canonists endorse overt clerical military violence.[93] We must also bear in mind that not all collections were available to all clerics at all times, and thus the question of diffusion and transmission of specific canonical collections further complicates our understanding of when and where particular canons were known.[94] While the canonical tradition never overtly embraced armed clerics, some collections and canonists made a distinction between clerics engaging in military activities generally and those personally bearing arms. Penalties were harsher for clerics who were personally 'armed', though this conventionally meant either weapons or armor, than for those who served as military commanders or advisors. These collections, therefore, represent a legislative compromise between reformers who sought to disassociate clerics from warfare entirely, and those who saw an acceptable military role for clergy. Finally, we have to consider the problem that throughout much of this period, there was no one idea of what comprised 'canon law'. There were a variety of different 'canonical' collections and 'it is, indeed, essential to grasp that there was no *one* collection used by the reformers; thus there could be no monolithic unity, no single mentality that could assert itself over others who were also of

---

[92] I am indebted to James Brundage for discussing some the finer points of canon law with me. His suggestions and corrections were extremely helpful. For a brief overview of this same period, see Duggan, *Armsbearing and the Clergy*, 128–33. Daniel Gerrard's forthcoming book on clerics and war will deal with the canonical source materials more fully.

[93] Gerrard, 31–2. Gerrard makes the point quite well that we cannot create a single voice for canon law, but as there was consistent condemnation for warrior-clerics in the canons, I believe we can make an exception in this case.

[94] For a valuable demonstration and discussion of this effect, particularly as it relates to the *Collectio Lanfranci*, see Nicolás Alvarez de las Asturias, 'The Use of the *Collectio Lanfranci*: The Evidence of the Manuscripts', *Bishops, Texts and the Use of Canon Law Around 1000: Essays in Honour of Martin Brett*, ed. Bruce C. Brasington and Kathleen G. Cushing (Aldergate, 2008), 121–8.

mind to reform.'⁹⁵ In practical terms, this meant that subsequent collections of canon law usually did not entirely replace earlier ones. Gratian's *Decretum*, published between 1139 and 1150, came closest to achieving dominance over other collections, and legal dominance was finally achieved by the *Liber extra vagantium* of Gregory IX, issued in 1234.⁹⁶ The very fluidity of canon law, and the non-exclusive nature of multiple collections (especially prior to 1234), meant that reformers, secularists, and compromisers could usually find some support for their positions.

Canon law was an important factor in both the creation of behavioral exemplars and attempts to regulate behavior according to established norms, though we should not forget that what became 'canon law' was often after debate, compromise, and political dealing. These canonical collections give us invaluable access to the concepts at play in these debates.⁹⁷ Canon law definitely had a broader applicability to the general culture – it was not sequestered only in intellectual circles. Historians such as James Brundage have argued that canon law 'serves as a means of enunciating and defining basic social norms, of establishing and specifying standards of conduct that a community finds acceptable.'⁹⁸ Lawrence Duggan goes even further in arguing that canon law gives us the best insight into the requirements of clergymen. He writes, '[Canon law] is an investigation not of what theologians and others believed the clergy ought to do, but rather of what ecclesiastical laws permitted, required, or forbade them to do.'⁹⁹ Brundage also addresses one of the most problematic aspects of relying on canon law to understand medieval cultural acceptance of clerical warfare: unlike the numerous examples of deposition for simony or marriage, there were relatively few clerics who were degraded for activities in warfare. This calls into question the relative importance placed on canons forbidding armed clerics, as well as the efficacy of those canons at all. He wrote that while laws 'do not necessarily guarantee that every infraction of those norms and standards can or will be punished', even laws that are rarely enforced have a deterrent function, and more importantly, 'laws and regulations serve notice on all of us that society has set certain standards of conduct and that when we ignore or contravene them we are doing

---

⁹⁵ *The Collection in Seventy-Four Titles: A Canon Law Manual of the Gregorian Reform*, trans. and annot. John Gilchrist (Toronto, 1980), 6–7.
⁹⁶ Robert L. Benson, *The Bishop-Elect: A Study in Medieval Ecclesiastical Office* (Princeton, 1968), 13.
⁹⁷ *The Collection in Seventy-Four Titles*, 9.
⁹⁸ James Brundage, 'The Limits of the War-Making Power: The Contribution of the Medieval Canonists', *Peace in a Nuclear Age: The Bishops' Pastoral Letter in Perspective*, ed. Charles J. Reid, Jr. (Washington, D.C., 1986), 71.
⁹⁹ Duggan, *Armsbearing and the Clergy*, 90.

wrong, whether we happen to agree with the rules or not.'[100] This is certainly true. There was always a subset of Christian theologians and canonists who argued and believed that violence was wholly antithetical to the Christian religion, and a comparatively larger group who argued that, while violence itself was a necessary component of the world, it should not be embraced or practiced by clerics. Ultimately, the role of canon law in the question of clerical warfare was as a highly prescriptive exemplar.[101]

Seeing the law as prescriptive gives us a number of salient points to consider. For example, the canons against armed clerics or clerics engaging in warfare did not result in nearly the number of depositions as similar canons against simony or clerical marriage (though it can be argued that much of this disparity could be the result of the relative numbers of clerics involved). Nearly all clerics had the opportunity for simoniac or sexual relationships, but not all would have the opportunity to even choose to engage in warfare. However, when given the opportunity, the evidence suggests that warrior-clerics could be popular. Are we to thus conclude that this canon was anachronistic in its own day, or that it was impossible to enforce? Not necessarily. Canon law was a reformist guide to ideal clerical behavior. It is crucial to understand that canon law was promulgated by segments within the 'church' as a whole, and did not represent a unified and uncontested 'voice of the church'. Unanimity and consensus were oftentimes just as rare at church councils as they are in modern parliaments or congresses. No one would suggest that in order to understand modern political culture, for instance, one need only read the opinions of supporters of successfully enacted legislation. The same holistic approach ought to be utilized for medieval canon law as well. Katherine Allen Smith argues persuasively that even bishops who were engaging in behavior that was condemned by some in the reform movement could themselves be advancing that agenda. She writes, 'as formal or informal supporters of the peace movement, the episcopate might be called on to employ military force in their role as champions of the armed in rural and urban contexts, or to restrain predatory nobles from attacking church property.'[102] Churchmen might utilize warfare when they deemed it necessary, even while advancing arguments that clerics ought to give up the 'knightly' lifestyle and abhor war as a vocation. Engaging in occasional, necessary, and licit warfare was far different than living one's life in a 'knightly' fashion.

Collecting and presenting the various 'laws' of the church was a daunting and difficult task, especially during the period after the fall of the western Roman

---

[100] Brundage, 'The Limits of the War-Making Power', 71–2.
[101] Cushing, 31.
[102] Smith, *War and the Making of Medieval Monastic Culture*, 45–6.

Empire, and before the rise of a centralized, powerful papacy. Consequently, one cannot point to a single tradition of 'canon law' during the Middle Ages, and certainly not during the period from about 500 until 1000. There were a number of collections circulating by 1000, including the influential forgeries termed *Pseudo-Isidore*.[103] However, by the eleventh century, a concerted effort was made to collect and publish the most common laws of the church.[104] Burchard, bishop of Worms produced his *Decretum* sometime between c.1000 and his death in 1025, and probably between c.1012 and 1022.[105] His collection was the 'single most important systematic canon law collection' prior to that of Ivo of Chartres.[106] Over eighty extant copies survive, surpassed only by Ivo's *Panormia* in the period before Gratian, thereby demonstrating the pervasive nature of Burchard's influence over the development of canon law.[107]

In general, Burchard believed war was a sullying activity, and he saw a need for a layman who killed in war to perform penance, even if the war was just, though he made some exception whereby a penitent could bear arms against non-Christians.[108] For clerics, however, Burchard saw no legitimate military role. In his first book of the collection, he reiterated a Carolingian canon that prohibited bishops from accompanying the royal army, unless they were present only in a ministerial capacity.[109] They were certainly not meant to be leading their knightly retinues personally on the field of battle. Burchard also included canons of a more general nature condemning clerics who were involved in warfare. In the second book of his collection Burchard outlined behavioral requirements for clergy.

---

[103] Christof Rolker, *Canon Law and the Letters of Ivo of Chartres* (Cambridge, 2010), 51–60.

[104] This was linked to the reform efforts to target simony and clerical sex for elimination. See Brundage, *Medieval Canon Law*, 35–9; Brundage, *Law, Sex, and Christian Society in Medieval Europe*, 176–416.

[105] For a post-mortem account of Burchard's life, composed by a canon of Worms, soon after his death, see *Vita Burchardi Episcopi*, ed. G. Waitz, *MGH SS* 4 (Hanover, 1841), 829–46. See also Jasonne M. Grabher and Michael H. Hoeflich, 'The Establishment of Normative Legal Texts: The Beginnings of the *Ius commune*', *The History of Medieval Canon Law in the Classical Period, 1140–1234: From Gratian to the Decretals of Pope Gregory IX*, ed. Wilfried Hartmann and Kenneth Pennington (Washington, D.C., 2008), 6–8; Rolker, 60–9.

[106] Rolker, 61.

[107] Ibid. While there are arguments over Burchard's relationship to the 'reform' party, led by men such as Peter Damian, his reiteration of canons against armed clerics moderates the importance of those arguments for this study. See Rolker, 63–9. Rolker also points out that 'the reaction of "reformers" and Gregorian canonists towards Burchard as a whole was neither negative nor had a decisive impact.' Rolker, 68.

[108] Hehl, 'War, Peace and the Christian Order', 186–8.

[109] *Burchardus Wortatiensis Episcopus – Decretorum Libri Viginti*, ed. Migne, *PL* 140: Col 612.

Chapters 211 and 212 specifically dealt with armed clerics and clerics involved in military affairs.[110] Chapter 211 forbade clerics from bearing 'military arms' (*arma militaria*) and it argued that to do so was to profane the sacred canons and the sanctity of the church (*sacrorum canonum contemptores et ecclesiasticae sanctitatis profanatores*). Finally, Burchard closed with the prescription that one could not be both a soldier of God, and of the world (*quia non possunt simul Deo et saeculo militare*). The subsequent canon exhorted clerics to trust in the protection of God, rather than in arms.[111] Burchard was relying on earlier traditions, the councils of Carthage and Orleans respectively, to demonstrate that clerics ought not to be involving themselves in arms or military affairs. Burchard's collection, contemporaneous with the active involvement of the church peace councils of southern France, served to codify the position of those reformers who argued for rejection of secular arms by clerics. Burchard was an 'active participant in regional ecclesiastical reform and attended various provincial councils that passed decrees attempting to enforce tighter discipline. The *Decretum* reflects this commitment.'[112] However, his prescriptive collection was not the final word, though it served as an important baseline for later debates. Even so, Burchard himself was studious in observing the spirit of the law. His biographer noted with great pride that the bishop, when faced with attacks from neighboring nobles around Worms, had

> quickly surrounded his city with a wall on the model of a castle; on the inside, he built a very strong fortification and swiftly raised towers and structures suitable for fighting. Once the castle had been built and strengthened, he bravely resisted the outrageous deeds of the foe and increased hope among his own people; an intrepid man in word and deed, he often terrified even his enemies themselves.[113]

Burchard's own pragmatic application of these canons demonstrates quite clearly the relationship that canon law could have to political reality. The canons served well as an ideal for behavior for those predisposed to adhere to them (i.e. reformers), but even canonists did not always follow them when it was a matter of

---

[110] Ibid., Col 661.

[111] Ibid. 'Omnimodis dicendum est presbyteris et diaconibus ut arma non portent, sed magis confidant in defensione Dei quam in armis.'

[112] *Prefaces to Canon Law Books in Latin Christianity*, trans. Robert Somerville and Bruce C. Brasington (New Haven, 1998), 73.

[113] *Vita Burchardi Episcopi*, 835. Translation by W.L. North. http://www.fordham.edu/halsall/source/1025burchard-vita.html. Accessed December 14, 2015. While there is no mention of Burchard's being armed, he certainly took an active role in defeating his enemies, and did not assume the purely pacifist role envisioned by many reformers.

defending the flock from attack. We should note, as well, the pride with which Burchard's biographer reported his hero's opposition to his secular enemies, remarking that Burchard had 'terrified' his enemies.[114]

Burchard's *Decretum* was the preeminent collection of canon law for the first three quarters of the eleventh century. The last quarter of the century saw a proliferation of additional collections, as the Gregorian popes relied more and more on canon law both to advance their reform agenda and to expand their judicial reach. As representative examples we will consider both the *Decretum* and *Panormia* of Ivo of Chartres.[115] While Ivo considered service in a just war as inherently licit, he generally followed Burchard's precedent by separating clerics from war.[116] He reiterated Burchard's Carolingian canons opposing bishops accompanying the royal army, except in order to hear confessions, perform the Mass, and engage in other expressly spiritual activities.[117] Ivo also promulgated the specific condemnation of clerics bearing arms found in Burchard's *Decretum* 2:211. He likewise included this canon in the shorter, more concise, and more widely read version of his canonical collection, the *Panormia*.[118] He reiterated Burchard's canon exhorting clerics to trust not on the strength of secular arms but, rather, in the strength of God, though he did not see fit to include that in the *Panormia*, only in the *Decretum*. However, taken together the two concepts contained in both Burchard and Ivo, that clerics ought not to be armed nor should they accompany military campaigns in anything other than a spiritual function, demonstrate a clear canonical prescription against clerical involvement in warfare.

In his tenth book of the *Decretum*, however, Ivo introduced a whole variety of canons that sought to demonstrate when killing was permissible. He included many of these in Book VIII of his *Panormia* as well.[119] He argued that there

---

[114] This raises an important psychological point about how clerics saw themselves vis-à-vis the secular, warrior nobility in terms of masculinity. One wonders whether the clerics, not able to normally compete with the knights in feats of manly prowess, thereby used their own positions to downgrade the value and merit of the knightly action, while occasionally relishing the opportunity to engage in such action themselves.

[115] For a good discussion of the reception of these two works and their place in canon law see Rolker, 248–89.

[116] Hehl, 'War, Peace and the Christian Order', 205.

[117] Ivo of Chartres, *Decretum*, Book 5, Cap 332–4.

[118] Some question has been made of whether Ivo was truly the compiler of the *Panormia* by Christof Rolker, cited in Bruce C. Brasington, '"Notes from the Edge": Marginalia and Glosses in Pre-Gratian Canonical Collections', *Bishops, Texts and the Use of Canon Law Around 1000*, 165, n. 1.

[119] James Brundage, 'St. Anselm, Ivo of Chartres and the Ideology of the First Crusade', *Les mutations socio-culturelles au tournant des XIe-XIIe siecles, Colloques internationaux de CNRS, Le Bec-Hellouin, juillet 1982* (Paris, 1984), 181.

were canons which justified violence by judges and kings, and that in the normal execution of their duties shedding blood was necessary: 'The penalties for murder applied to those who slew others out of wrath or hatred, not to those who killed out of zeal for justice.'[120] Ivo then cited authorities, following St. Augustine, who equated lawful coercion with love. It was not 'just' to allow someone to continue in error or evil, thus compulsion and coercion 'for their own good' was legitimate. 'Moreover, bishops and other clerics have both the right and the obligation to encourage the suppression and coercion of heretics and infidels. When Christians undertake war in order to defend themselves and their faith, they are acting justly and the wars that they fight are pleasing to God.'[121] He then cited the example of the pope as the ultimate defender of Christianity, and thus he discussed the examples of popes serving as 'warriors' against the Muslims.[122] Ivo seemed to be trying to create the impression that violence could be acceptable in the right causes, and that the church had the right and obligation to direct this violence towards holy ends, but that clerics were not to wield the secular sword themselves (this follows on the reasoning of popes such as Urban II, as seen above). This would help to explain his decision to include the canon prohibiting clerics from being armed in the *Panormia*, but to leave out the more general canon calling on clerics to trust in the strength of God, rather than secular arms. Ivo's canons, and justifications offered in Book X, would also prove tempting for clerics who wished to take a more active military role against their enemies. While Ivo sought to define the enemies against whom violence was licit as Muslims and heretics, individual bishops, abbots, and clerics could and did make the logical leap that any opponents of the 'church' (as defined by themselves) would be akin to Muslims or heretics, and could therefore be struck with the secular sword. This was a logical step that the Gregorian popes were willing to make.

The canonical collections of Burchard, Ivo, and others were crucial foundations for the development of canon law. That being said, the study, reach, and codification of canon law increased exponentially with the production of the *Decretum* of Gratian in the mid-twelfth century.[123] Gratian's work very quickly came to supersede previous collections of canon law, and while they did not disappear entirely, within a few years the 'papal chancery assumed knowledge

---

[120] Ibid.
[121] Ibid., 181–2.
[122] Ibid., 182. Ironically, Ivo was not enthusiastic about the justification or efficacy of the First Crusade. See page 175.
[123] For an overview of the topic of violence and the church in Gratian particularly, see Stanley Chodorow, *Christian Political Theory and Church Politics in the Mid-Twelfth Century: The Ecclesiology of Gratian's Decretum* (Berkeley, 1972), 223–46.

of the *Decretum* among its correspondents.'[124] Gratian came closer to creating a unified collection of canon law than his predecessors had done, and his achievement fed into and resulted from a strengthening papacy. In the second book of his collection, Gratian compiled a number of canons that illuminated the question of whether clerics ought to be armed or to involve themselves in warfare.

In Causa 23, Gratian compiled canons that posed a variety of questions regarding when warfare was legitimate.[125] In Questio 8, he considered whether or not clerics could be moved to take up arms either by their own authority, the authority of the pope, or the authority of the emperor.[126] His general answer to this question was that clerics were not meant to wield arms, and in order to show this he referred to the scriptural story of Christ telling Peter to put his sword away in the Garden of Gethsemane.[127] He also cited St. Ambrose, who claimed that tears and oration were the weapons of the clergy, not swords. His subsequent thirty-four entries then considered various aspects of this general prohibition. In Capitula 6, Gratian promulgated the canon, found in Burchard and Ivo, that clerics who were found to be armed were to be degraded from their clerical position, and that one could not serve as both a soldier of God and a soldier of the secular world.[128] Gratian also included the stipulation that no offerings could be made for a cleric who was killed in battle, or on the battlefield.[129] In Capitula 19, Gratian offered a broad condemnation of bishops who spent their time engaged in military conflicts. This included guarding the coasts for pirates or even merely keeping watch for them.[130] This was a wide-ranging injunction against any involvement by clerics in warfare or hostilities, even those fought defensively or on behalf of the church.[131]

Gratian also dealt with the legacy of popes who had involved themselves in warfare in the past, and he sought to demonstrate that this view was in keeping

---

[124] *Gratian: The Treatise on Laws with Ordinary Gloss*, trans. Augustine Thompson and James Gordley, intro. Katherine Christensen, *Studies in Medieval and Early Modern Canon Law*, Vol. 2 (Washington, D.C., 1993), xvi.

[125] C.23. See Russell, *Just War*, 55–85. For the role of the church and churchmen in warfare specifically, see 72–85. In commenting on the difficulties in unpacking Gratian's thoughts on the matter, Russell writes on page 72, 'Proper understanding of Gratian's thought here is difficult because he neither discussed these wars separately from the wars and police actions of secular rulers nor satisfactorily analysed the various elements of a Church-related just war.' See also Duggan, *Armsbearing and the Clergy*, 128–30.

[126] C.23 q. 8.

[127] Ibid.; Russell, *Just War*, 76–7. Gerrard, 154–7.

[128] C.23 q. 8 d.p.c. 6.

[129] C.23 q. 8 d.p.c. 4.

[130] C.23 q. 8 d.p.c. 19.

[131] Gerrard, 154.

with the prescriptions of the canons. He explained that it was perfectly acceptable to exhort secular allies to do the will of the church. He also distinguished between clerical lands that owed regalian rights to secular rulers and those that did not owe such obligations. He defended the rights of secular rulers to require military service from clerical lands held by regalia, but presumably if it required the actual cleric to attend the army, it would be in a spiritual role.[132] Clerical lands owing no such regalian rights did not have the same excuse. Gratian asserted 'that a cleric should never accept a church from the hands of a layman.'[133] Gratian argued that the church and other ecclesiastical property was completely at the disposal of the bishop. This, however, refers specifically to the investiture of the bishop with his clerical holdings by a layman, not with lay investiture of temporal regalia. Gratian recognized two types of bishops: those who were content with tithes and offerings, and thus owed no secular service, and those who possessed 'lands, towns, castles, and cities' and thus owed to Caesar his tribute.[134] Gratian certainly felt that the first form of bishop was better, but he considered the other form a legitimate choice for a bishop to make.[135] He later distinguished between two types of ecclesiastical property, with the lands that had secular service requiring the bishop to pay the annual tribute and to 'set off with them to military service when the army is summoned.'[136]

The general condemnations of warrior-clerics found in Gratian formed a starting point for further consideration by glossators and canonists who taught these canons in the universities and schools, and by later ecclesiastical councils and canonical collections.[137] The period from 1150 to 1190, termed by Frederick Russell as the period of the 'decretists', saw a broadening of the argument over licit cleri-

---

[132] C.23 q. 8 d.p.c 20. See also Robert L. Benson, 'The Obligations of Bishops with "Regalia": Canonistic Views from Gratian to the Early Thirteenth Century', *Proceedings of the Second International Congress of Medieval Canon Law*, ed. Stephan Kuttner and Joseph Ryan (Vatican, 1965), 129–31. See also Russell, *Just War*, 78–80. Cf. Hehl, 'War, Peace and the Christian Order', 222.

[133] Benson, 'The Obligations of Bishops', 124.

[134] Ibid., 125.

[135] Ibid.

[136] Ibid. The canonist Sicard, bishop of Cremona, argued in 1180 that this canon meant that bishops owed loyalty to their princes, including their presence on campaign, so that they could exhort their knights to great deeds. See Benson, 'Obligations of Bishops', 128.

[137] For a brief and effective overview of this period, see Kenneth Pennington and Wolfgang P. Muller, 'The Decretalists: The Italian School', *The History of Medieval Canon Law in the Classical Period, 1140–1234: From Gratian to the Decretals of Pope Gregory IX*, 127–59. See also Kenneth Pennington, 'The Decretalists 1190–1234', *The History of Medieval Canon Law in the Classical Period, 1140–1234: From Gratian to the Decretals of Pope Gregory IX*, 211–27. Duggan sees a weakening of the canonical prohibitions in the period of the later twelfth century. Duggan, *Armsbearing and the Clergy*, 128–33.

cal violence. Crusading and anti-heresy operations represented powerful cultural draws for clerics to involve themselves in military affairs. The decretists 'in general maintained Gratian's caution regarding clerical fighting', and though they did argue over 'the conditions that rendered such fighting tolerable on occasion they did agree to deny Christian burial to any cleric who went to war with the intention to fight or who fought for payment or booty or out of hatred.'[138] For Duggan, the period of the decretists saw a loosening of the restriction on clerics fighting in warfare, though at no point was such behavior endorsed or excused completely.[139] As Russell points out, the intention of the clerics was crucial for determining whether their military actions were morally sound. Those who intended to fight had no protection in the canons. Intention was always important, but seems to have become increasingly so in the eleventh and twelfth centuries.[140]

Even when the war was 'just', clerics could support it only with men drawn from their lands and with their prayers and exhortations.[141] This prohibition, recalling as it does the Carolingian prohibitions contained in Burchard, effectively barred clerics from taking active military roles on campaign. Overall, though, the argument was over whether a cleric could fight as a last resort or whether he could use arms to defend Christianity. In crusading warfare, for instance, the greatest canonist of the day, Huguccio of Pisa, allowed clerics to carry weapons and wear armor for self-protection, though it

> was clear that clerics accompanying the crusades to the Holy Land were not armed for the purpose of fighting but to terrify the enemy and to protect themselves from flying arrows. Those clerics who did bear arms with the intention of fighting could not be excused even by papal authority.[142]

Other decretalists, such as Rufinus of Bologna in his *Summa Decretorum* from 1164, allowed for a possible exception in the case of self-defense. Rufinus, after arguing that the canons prohibited clerics from taking up arms, claimed that perhaps, as a

---

[138] Russell, *Just War*, 108. For an excellent overview of the canonical shifts in this period, see Gerrard, 157–68.

[139] Duggan, *Armsbearing and the Clergy*, 131–2.

[140] Helh, 'War, Peace and the Christian Order', 197 and 208.

[141] Russell, *Just War*, 105–12. Cf. Hehl, 'War, Peace and the Christian Order', 223. Helh writes, 'Instead of defending themselves, they were required to submit patiently to injustice; and they were forbidden to shed human blood. The Decretists admitted exceptions only in the case of defence against an attack on one's own life, or for bishops who exercised public and political functions.'

[142] Russell, *Just War*, 108. See also Benjamin Z. Kedar, 'On the Origins of the Earliest Laws of Frankish Jerusalem: The Canons of the Council of Nablus, 1120', *Speculum* 74 (Apr., 1999), 329.

last resort in the case of defending themselves or the faith against pagans, a cleric might do just that.[143] His caveats indicate a deep insecurity regarding clerics taking up arms, but also a recognition that not only were there times when a cleric might be tempted to do so, but also there were times when it was better for a cleric to do so, rather than to abide by the blanket canonical prohibition. Bishop Sicard of Cremona in his own *Summa* from 1179 to 1181 also stated that clerics could potentially take up arms as a last resort in self-defense or in defense of Christianity.[144] Sicard saw war as a morally neutral activity, with the purpose and motivation of the warrior determining whether the war was good or evil.[145]

Gratian, the decretalists, and clerics in general were wrestling with the reality that clerics, especially in the Holy Land, were facing direct bodily threats to the health of Christianity (and Christians) and were perhaps increasingly faced with the problematic nature of a blanket ban on bearing arms. When the biblical realms captured by the Christians in the First Crusade came under threat from Muslim forces, there was a natural desire on the part of some clerics to actively aid the defense of the cities, and at the Council of Nablus in 1120 we have fascinating evidence that this debate penetrated into local canonical arguments.[146] Canon 20 of the council allowed that clerics who helped to defend the walls of the city should not be punished for violating the canons against being armed.[147] This exception flew in the face of the established canonical tradition, as seen above, though it demonstrates that pragmatic reality could influence not only behavior, but also the perception of licitness of that behavior.[148] Even the argument of self-

---

[143] Rufinus of Bologna, *Summa Decretorum*, ed. H. Singer (Paderborn, 1902), 412. 'Cum itaque in canonibus prohibeatur, ne clerici arma ferant, nullusque clericorum ordo inveniatur exceptus, patet quod nullis clericis licet arma movere, nisi forte pro sui defensione vehementissima cogente necessitate, que non habet legem, et nisi contra paganos iussu maioris.'

[144] Kedar, 329. 'nisi forte pro fide tuenda ... nisi forte ubi fides ecclesie periclitaretur.' See page 329, note 87.

[145] Hehl, 'War, Peace and the Christian Order', 223.

[146] The best modern discussion of the Council of Nablus comes in. Kedar, 'On the Origins of the Earliest Laws of Frankish Jerusalem', 310–35. I would like to thank John Giebfried for this citation. Duggan saw the Council of Nablus as representing a 'revolution' in canonical thought regarding clerics and warfare. Duggan, *Armsbearing and the Clergy*, 102–3.

[147] Printed in Kedar, 334. 'Si clericus causa defenssionis [sic] arma detulerit, culpa non teneatur. Si autem milicie aut alicuius curi<a>litatis causa coronam dimiserit, usque ad predictum terminum ecclesie id confessus coronam reddat et deinceps secundum patriarche preceptum se habeat. Si autem amplius celaverit, pro regis et patriarche consilio se contineat.'

[148] Ibid., 324. Kedar writes, 'no matter how widespread clerical recourse to weapons might have been, the church's opposition was unequivocal.'

defense, usually the strongest cultural marker of licit violence, did not persuade popes Nicholas I, Gratian, or Innocent III.[149] However, some, such as Walter the Chancellor, saw a value to armed clerics, especially when fighting the Muslims. In his *Bella Antiochena*, he recounted how clerics and monks were mixed in among Antioch's defenders after the disastrous defeat of June 27, 1119 and the death of Roger of Antioch.[150] Others, such as William, archbishop of Tyre, ignored the canons of Nablus, which could be seen as evidence for his conservatism in the face of these innovations.[151] William also, contra Walter's example of the clerical defenders, reproved a cleric who got himself killed in battle as having justly reaped what he had sown by taking up the sword.

The second half of the canon from Nablus is interesting as well. It stipulates that if a cleric takes on the status of a knight, he must confess his transgression on the first day of Lent and resume his former clerical status. This discourse on status, rather than behavior, brings up a number of interesting implications. The Nablus canon is more lenient than those found in the 'west', which called for excommunication for clerics who became knights, which again indicates an important pragmatic exception due to the circumstances of the Holy Land. Furthermore, this canon reinforces for us the importance of distinguishing between 'worldliness' and engaging in warfare. Contemporaries saw such a distinction, and were often more troubled by clerics who sought to take on other 'professions', or who transgressed into the identity of another *ordo*, than they were by those who engaged in occasional military violence. As we will see in subsequent chapters, this dichotomy was certainly at work in how men such as Philip of Dreux and Odo of Bayeux – men who took on the lifestyles of knights – were portrayed by

---

[149] Ibid. Originals in *Nicolai I epistolae*, ed. Ernest Perels, *MGH Epp.* 6:661, Ep. 142; Gratian D.50 c.6; *PL* 216:45.

[150] Kedar, 325. For the original, see Galterius Cancellarius, *Bella Antiochena* 2.6.7, ed. Heinrich Hagenmeyer (Innsbruck, 1896), 95–6. Walter wrote, 'protectioni Christianitatis necessaria ponerentur et ut singulae turres, quotquot essent, monachis et clericis mixtim cum laicis pro posse et quantitate Christicolarum eminus munirentur huius patris et doctoris prudentissimi omnes una diligenter parent imperio. Munitis itaque turribus intrinseci et extrinseci adhibentur custodes cum custodibus, idemque patriarcha magis precibus quam armis pugnaturus pro salute ac defensione Christiani populi incessanter Deo supplicabat medullitus; nec tamen desiit horis competentibus nocte et die cum armato suo clero et militibus, more pugnatorum portas, moenia et turres murosque circumcirca et ipsorum custodes uicissim uisitare, consolari et incitare, ut uigilanti animo Christianae protectionis curam adhiberent et ab incepto bono nulla hostili perturbatione desisterent. quid singula? clerus cum ceteris fidelibus prouide et strenue, intus et extra, militaris officii uice functus cum Dei uirtute ciuitatem ab hostibus intactam Balduino rege diu optato protegendam reseruauit.'

[151] Kedar, 328–9. Kedar also points out that Fulcher of Chartres completely ignored the council of Nablus.

contemporaries versus those who retained their clerical simplicity, even if they all fought in wars.

In the *Liber Extra*, a vast collection of canon law sponsored by Pope Gregory IX in the 1230s and compiled by Raymond of Penafort, the traditional prohibitions against clerics' bearing arms were reiterated, though there was some mitigation by accepting that clerics who acted in self-defense were not to be subject to the same penalties as those who were aggressors.[152] The most basic condemnation stated that clerics bearing arms (or committing usury) were to be excommunicated.[153] This canon was based on the decrees of an early council of Poitiers, and it clearly linked the bearing of arms with the roundly condemned practice of usury. This canon was glossed, however, by offering an example in which the bearing of arms was licit. A cleric was able to bear arms when passing through dangerous territory in order to scare off potential thieves. However, the gloss went on to state that the cleric bearing arms could not actually strike with them, as they were only a (presumably ineffective) deterrent.[154] While there was some sympathy for clerics who actually did strike to save their lives, the ideal was that thieves would not bother attacking an armed man.[155] The gloss culminated by declaring that, except in the above example, a cleric was not allowed to bear arms. If he did so regardless, he was to be warned three times, and if he failed to desist, he was to be degraded from orders.

This canon and gloss demonstrate the continuing opposition among canonists to clerics who bore arms or engaged actively in military activities. While the canon did not specifically state that leading armies was illicit, it is clearly intended as a prohibition by stating that the only permissible behavior involving weapons was to brandish them, defensively, and only as a last resort. The ordinary cleric could not avoid putting himself in harm's way, whereas a bishop, or abbot, even if he owed military regalian service, could easily engineer a way to be absent from the battlefield. The *Liber Extra* contains a number of canons that illuminate different aspects of this prohibition, and the numerous glosses parse the language and posit examples to further explain it, but at no point does it endorse the actual use of arms in battle by churchmen.[156]

These canonical collections were being compiled against a backdrop of

---

[152] Duggan, *Armsbearing and the Clergy*, 138–40.

[153] X. 3.1.2. 'Clerici armi portantes et usurarii excommunicentur.'

[154] Ordinary gloss to X. 3.1.2. The gloss stated that clerics could bear arms, 'ad terrorem latronum, licet percutere non debeant.'

[155] See X. 5.25.4.

[156] See, for instance, X. 3.3.10, X. 5.24.1, X. 5.25.3. For the basic changes in canon law sources, see Brundage, *Medieval Canon Law*, 53–6. See also Russell, *Just War*, 128–88 for an overview of canonical opinion immediately before and after 1234.

increasing papal efforts to hold ecumenical councils. While there were three ecumenical councils (according to later reckoning) in the twelfth century, the Fourth Lateran Council of 1215 was the first explicitly to comment on the interaction of clerics with warfare and bloodshed, though earlier councils had forbidden clerics to be involved in the shedding of blood in general.[157] Canon 16 regulated the dress of the clergy, proscribing overly showy or ostentatious clothing. 'Let them not indulge in red or green clothes, long sleeves or shoes with embroidery or pointed toes, or in bridles, saddles, breast-plates (pectoralibus) and spurs that are gilded or have other superfluous ornamentation.'[158] The fact that this canon prohibited gilded spurs or breast-plates for clerics would indicate that motivations of worldliness were especially condemnable, alongside active fighting. Canon 18 prevented clerics from issuing sentences that involved the shedding of blood, or from carrying out such a punishment. 'Moreover no cleric may be put in command of mercenaries or crossbowmen or suchlike men of blood.'[159] They also could not practice surgery or bless trials by ordeal or battle. This separation of clerics from shedding blood, coupled with the reference to armor, would tend to support the idea that clerics could participate in campaigns, provided that they did not personally strike a blow in combat. They also could not be involved in matters involving bloodshed, judicial and non-judicial, nor could they 'command companies of mercenaries or crossbowmen'.[160] While the first prohibition would seemingly prevent any clerical involvement in the operational aspects of warfare, the implication of the second part was that clerics could command other sorts of troops in battle, again, provided that they restrained from striking blows themselves. Even the church councils could not offer a perfectly clear statement on the 'proper' role of clerics in warfare. While the prescriptive evidence from canon law and church councils was fairly clear on condemning warrior-clerics, reality saw clerics continuing to be involved in warfare and, furthermore, not being treating as criminals or pariahs.

---

[157] Norman Tanner argues that the decrees of the Fourth Lateran Council represented a broad constituency within the church. See Norman Tanner, 'Pastoral Care: The Fourth Lateran Council of 1215', *A History of Pastoral Care*, ed. G.R. Evans (London, 2000), 112–25.

[158] *Decrees of the Ecumenical Councils*, ed. Norman P. Tanner, Vol. 1: Nicaea I to Lateran V (Washington, D.C., 1990), 243.

[159] *Decrees of the Ecumenical Councils*, I, 244.

[160] Anne J. Duggan, 'Conciliar Law 1123–1215: The Legislation of the Four Lateran Councils', *The History of Medieval Canon Law in the Classical Period, 1140–1234: From Gratian to the Decretals of Pope Gregory IX*, 347.

CHAPTER 3

The Epic Archetype: Evidence from Chivalric Literature

Richard Kaeuper and others have demonstrated convincingly that 'imaginative' chivalric literature was an integral part of the development of the *mentalité* of the elite classes of medieval society and helped to shape and reflect their cultural norms and ideals.[1] This literature, most especially the *chansons de geste* (the 'songs of deeds'), helped to crystallize arguments and debates, and served to illuminate many of the discourses within elite society, especially surrounding how to gain or lose honor. These *chansons*, generally written down in the twelfth and thirteenth centuries (though often deriving orally from earlier materials), were performed in the halls and courts of the wealthy and powerful, and their popularity speaks to the power of their cultural reception. They were not, of course, mirrors of medieval society but, rather, idealized exemplars of desired virtues and inherent tensions within that society. Thus, the heroes are overly strong, brave, and loyal, while the villains are archetypes of perfidy. In general terms, since imaginative literature was often written for the benefit and entertainment of knightly audiences, it often followed familiar tropes. Among these was a focus on the deeds of knights in warfare, and a preference by knights to see their ecclesiastical competitors negatively portrayed as greedy and worldly.

There were exceptions, of course, to this focus on the 'traditional' knights, since the clerics who showed the same virtues possessed by knights – prowess in battle, loyalty, and bravery – are usually praised along with the secular warriors. The most famous of these was Archbishop Turpin of Reims in the cycle of *chansons de geste* focused on Charlemagne. In these epics, Turpin not only matches most of the knightly combatants in warrior skill, he often exceeds all but the best (in fact, it is Turpin who is left alive with Roland after all of the other French knights have fallen). The portrayal and popularity of Turpin could show a desire among

---

[1] See Kaeuper, *Chivalry and Violence in Medieval Europe*, 30–9, 231–72 and Kaeuper, *Holy Warriors*, 1–36 and notes cited therein. Cf. David Crouch, *The Birth of Nobility: Constructing Aristocracy in England and France, 950–1300* (London, 2005); R.C. van Caenegem, 'Chivalrous Ideals and Religious Feeling', *Law, History, the Low Countries and Europe*, ed. Ludo Milis (London, 1994), 145–59; Stephen Jaeger, 'Courtliness and Social Change', *Cultures of Power: Lordship, Status, and Prowess in Twelfth-Century Europe*, ed. Thomas Bisson (Philadelphia, 1995).

the lay elite for clerics to take an active a role in the protection of king and Christ, as demonstrated by Henry II's quotation from 1185 discussed in chapter 2, though other examples from the literature can betray more reticence over the proper clerical roles in battle. Imaginative literature, then, presents a similar dichotomy of tensions and desires as the other evidence from the period. In each case, there is a balance between wanting churchmen to take active roles in the important societal activity of warfare and the desire to see churchmen either absent themselves from worldly actions, or at least leave the fighting to the men for whom it was a profession and source of identity.

Archbishop Turpin was the prototypical crusading archbishop, possessing both the chivalric attributes of the knight and the ideal attributes of a bishop – intense piety and an ability to inspire others to great deeds in defense of the faith. The popularity of Turpin, and the *Song of Roland* in general, was not confined to merely 'lay' or 'ecclesiastical' circles; there was also a commonality of noble culture between those two groups, discussed above in the Introduction, that bears repeating here. Andrew Taylor has made this point clearly in his discussion of the text:

> If soldiers could become clerics and clerics could fight like soldiers, it is scarcely surprising that clerics enjoyed reading or hearing of deeds of arms. Indeed, the interpenetration of chivalric and clerical culture is a commonplace of medieval scholarship – and I would not labor the point were it not that the modern construction of medieval literature has so often tacitly assumed that the two were quite distinct.[2]

The interpenetration of the higher secular and ecclesiastical nobility is most clearly reflected in the chivalric literature surveyed in this chapter. Many of the high-ranking churchmen of medieval Europe came from knightly or noble families, and even those who came from humbler backgrounds could have adopted the dominant ecclesiastical culture, which was set by the higher-ranking ecclesiastics.[3]

We also know that the story had great cultural resonance throughout the period, by the number of copies in various languages that survive, the number of depictions found in art and architecture, and by contemporary references. Among the most celebrated references was that by the Anglo-Norman poet Wace

---

[2] Andrew Taylor, 'Was There a Song of Roland?', *Speculum* 76 (Jan., 2001), 50.
[3] Ibid., 51–2. Taylor argues that it had evolved into a form of saint's life. Cf. D.D.R. Owen, 'The Secular Inspiration of the Song of Roland', *Speculum* 37 (Jul., 1962). Owen argues that the tale was purely about noble values, and that the religious overtones were merely setting, not essential elements of the moral.

in his *Roman de Rou*, who claimed that William I's army sang the deeds of Roland while marching into battle at Hastings.[4] Wace was writing for Henry II, and his interweaving of the Roland tradition with Anglo-Norman history gives us a good indication of the poem's cultural resonance. Henry II, who had complained about clerics who were not willing to suffer the bloody burdens of warfare, would probably have had nothing but admiration for the figure of Turpin hacking and slashing his way through ranks of enemies.

Turpin was also a popular figure of illumination for medieval artists, with an early example coming from the lintel of the tympanum at Angoulême cathedral. In an image that is placed over the first blind doorway to the right of the main entrance, Turpin is shown running Abisme through with his lance. This lintel, dating from around 1120, was the first major effort to render Roland into visual art, and it shows the importance placed on Turpin and his chivalric deeds. Turpin is shown on horseback, mailed, and armed with a lance, striking Abisme and driving him off his horse.[5] The lintel at Angoulême clearly hints at some approval of Turpin's role as a warrior-cleric. It was not, however, the only depiction of Turpin as a knight. In a thirteenth-century miniature, Turpin is depicted visually in the same warrior fashion as he was in literature. In a series of panels highlighting major scenes from the poem, Turpin's warrior nature is clearly illuminated. When Roland is made overlord of Spain by Charlemagne, Turpin is the only knight visible behind him, notable for his wearing the mitre over his clearly visible mail-coif. In a scene depicting the attack of the Christians on the Muslim army, Roland and Turpin, again with the distinguishing mitre, are shown leading the French. The top image shows them with lances, the bottom with swords. Finally, when Roland and Turpin are surrounded by Saracens, Roland is shown blowing his horn, while Turpin brandishes his sword. The bottom scene shows Roland comforting Turpin as he lies dying.[6] Panels from a fifteenth-century *Karl der Grosse* image depicted Turpin not only outfitted as a knight, but also clearly engaging in battle.[7] A Middle English translation of the Pseudo-Turpin chronicle referred to Turpin, alongside Roland, Oliver, and other French knights as a 'worthy warrier'.[8]

---

[4] For a discussion of the implications of his reference to Roland, see Taylor, 'Was There a Song of Roland?', 29.

[5] For the three panels at Angoulême that depict scenes from the Song of Roland, see Rita LeJeune and Jacques Stiennon, *The Legend of Roland in the Middle Ages*, trans. Christine Trollope, Vol. 2 (New York, 1971), panels 14–16.

[6] Ibid., panels 202–4.

[7] Ibid., panels 225 and 228–9.

[8] *Turpine's Story: A Middle English Translation of the Pseudo-Turpin Chronicle*, ed. Stephen H.A. Shepherd (Oxford, 2004), 35. The Chronicle of Turpin was also extremely popular

The *Song of Roland* is based on a highly imaginative version of Charlemagne's expedition into Spain in 788 and focuses on the exploits of the three heroes – Roland, his right-hand man Oliver, and Archbishop Turpin. The poet lavishes praise on them, and immediately focuses attention on Turpin's bravery and courage in the face of danger. Turpin consistently puts himself into positions of danger, with an eye towards loyally serving Charlemagne and winning chivalric glory. Towards the beginning of the poem, Turpin volunteers to serve as an emissary to the Muslim king

> 'Keep your Franks here./ You have been in this land for seven years,/ They have suffered many cares and woes./ Give me the gauntlet and staff, sire,/ And I'll go to the Spanish Saracen,/ So that I can judge him by his looks.'/The Emperor replies with irritation:/ 'Go sit down on that white silk cloth!/ Don't say another word unless I order you to!'[9]

Charlemagne's anger at Turpin for volunteering reflects equally the perceived danger to his emissary, as well as Turpin's bravery. Turpin demonstrates two of the key virtues celebrated in medieval noble society – bravery in the face of danger, and a willingness to die for his king. Turpin, much like many of the figures to be examined later in this book, shows himself to be both brave and loyal. He reinforces these attributes by volunteering for service in the French rearguard protecting Charlemagne's march out of Spain.[10]

Turpin was not merely 'saluting Jerusalem from afar' – he could back up his bravery with prowess in battle. Audiences would have understood that while Roland, Oliver, and Turpin represented larger-than-life depictions of elite figures, they also performed a series of laudable feats worthy of emulation (as well as failures to avoid, such as Roland's pride). While few French knights thought that they could match Roland blow for blow (perhaps unless wine had flowed more heavily than usual in the hall), they certainly could have seen these men as culturally iconic figures of idealized prowess. Even more so than Roland, who was shown to have a very real and human failing (pride), Turpin was presented as a paragon of knightly abilities and clerical spirituality. He suffered from no great failing, but instead seemed to seamlessly unify great piety with prowess. This unity demonstrated how 'muscular Christianity' could be depicted.

on the Continent. It was also known to those who did not read Latin, with five separate French translations being made of it in the thirteenth century alone. See C. Meredith-Jones, 'The Chronicle of Turpin in Saintonge', *Speculum* 13 (Apr., 1938), 160.

[9] *The Song of Roland: An Analytical Edition*, ed. and trans. Gerard J. Brault, Vol. 2. Oxford Text and Translation (University Park, PA, 1978), Laisse 19.

[10] *Roland*, 2, Laisse 64, line 799.

In one of the early battles between the French and Muslims, Roland, Oliver, and Turpin all fight named opponents. Roland fights the Muslim king Marsile's nephew Aelroth, Oliver duels with Marsile's brother Duke Falsaron, while Turpin duels Corsablix, 'a Berber from a foreign land.'[11] After Corsablix mocks the prowess of the French knights, Turpin reacts by engaging him in single combat to defend the honor of French chivalry.

> Archbishop Turpin heard him well,/ There is no one on earth whom he bears greater ill will./ He urges his horse on with his pure gold spurs,/ He went to strike him with great force./ He smashes his shield and rips apart his hauberk,/ He plunges his great spear through his middle,/ He sticks it deeps into him,/ impaling him dead,/ Running him through,/ he throws him dead on the road./ He looks back and sees the wretch lying there,/ He will be through,/ he says, until he speaks to him:/ 'Dirty pagan, you lied!/ My lord Charles is ever our safeguard,/ Our French have no intention of fleeing./ We shall make your companions rest in peace,/ I have news for you: You must suffer death./ Strike, Frenchmen, let none of you forget his duty!/ This first blow is ours, thank God!'/ He cries 'Monjoie!' to hold the field.[12]

Turpin is presented as a glorious knight with golden spurs, and his prowess is ranked alongside that of Roland, Oliver, and the rest of the Twelve Peers. He accomplishes the same feats of strength as Roland and Oliver. His blows destroy the enemy's shield and armor, and still have enough force to kill him immediately. His prowess is directly related to his spiritual concerns as he mocks the dead Saracen as a 'dirty pagan' and oath-breaker. Turpin's victory over Corsablix is equal parts prowess and vengeance. Corsablix had mocked French chivalry, and Turpin had taken up its defense. He had also struck a larger blow in defense of Christendom, and on behalf of his king. Indeed, he invokes the name of Charles, rather than that of Christ, during his combat. Charles would be the safeguard of the French army.

---

[11] *Roland*, 2, Laisse 95.

[12] Ibid. 'Ben l'entendit l'arcevesques Turpin;/ Suz ciel n'at hume que voeillet plus haïr./ Sun cheval brochet des esperuns d'or fin,/ Par grant vertut si l'est alét ferir:/ L'escut li freinst, l'osberc li descumfist,/ Sun grant epsiét parmi le cors li mist,/ Empeint le ben, que tut le fait brandir,/ Pleine sa hanste l'abat mort el chemin./ Guardet a tere, veit le glutun gesir,/ Ne laisserat que n'i parolt, ço dit:/ "Culvert paien, vos i avez mentit:/ Carles, mis sire, nus est guarant tuz dis;/ Nostre Franceis n'unt talent de fuïr./ Voz cumpaignuns feruns trestuz restifs;/ Nuvele mort vos estuvrat susfrir./ Ferez, Franceis, nul de vus ne s'ublit!/ Cist premer colp est nostre, Deu mercit!"/ Munjoie escrïet por le camp retenir.'

Turpin's prowess in battle is presented throughout the poem as evidence of his worthiness. Later in the battle, Turpin engages and defeats the Muslim 'sorcerer' Siglorel, 'And the Archbishop killed Siglorel,/ The sorcerer who was once in Hell,/ Jupiter led him there by sorcery./ Turpin said: "This one did us wrong!"/ Roland replies [seemingly in response to Turpin's blow]: "The scoundrel is vanquished./ Oliver, comrade, such blows are worthy in my eyes!"'[13] Turpin's worth is the partial result of his prowess, and in the eyes of Roland, his prowess is what elevates him to greatness. Turpin's prowess, linked with that of Roland and Oliver, is so great that the poet writes of his raining over a thousand blows on his enemies in the battle.[14] Upon seeing Turpin strike manly blows in the mêlée, Roland comments explicitly on his value as a *knight*. He says to Oliver "'the Archbishop is a very good knight. [*mult bon chevaler*]/ There is no finer one on the face of the earth,/ He is formidable with lance and spear.'"[15] Turpin unifies the role of cleric and knight, and together he, with Roland and Oliver, kill more than four thousand Saracens. Turpin being explicitly called a knight demonstrates a very different conception of the exclusivity of *ordines* as conceived of elsewhere during the period. Despite the highly normative and structurally incompatible ideas of clerical professions versus those of soldiers as expressed by men like Adalbero of Laon, here we have a much more fluid cultural understanding of these roles, and one that allows for significant overlap without criticism.[16] Turpin is presented as an ideal of both fighting and praying, seamlessly mixing the two seemingly distinct *ordines*. Turpin's value as a knight is reinforced by his having a named weapon, 'Almace', alongside Roland's 'Durendal' and Oliver's 'Halteclere'.

> He draws Almace, his sword of burnished steel,/ In the thick of the press, he strikes a thousand blows and more./ Afterward Charles said he spared not a one,/ He finds four hundred of them around his body,/ Some wounded, others pierced through the middle,/ And there were some of them who had lost their heads.[17]

---

[13] Ibid., Laisse 108.
[14] Ibid., Laisse 110.
[15] Ibid., Laisse 127. The use of the term *chevaler* is important. As Brault points out, 'Whenever the term *chevaler* is used in the *Song of Roland* it refers to a fighting man, distinguished by birth and by ownership of expensive heavy armor, weapons, and a war-horse.' See *The Song of Roland*, 1, 15.
[16] Cf. Duby, *The Three Orders*, 13–18.
[17] *Roland*, 2, Laisse 155. 'It trait Almace, s'espee d'acer brun,/ En la grant presse mil colps i fiert e plus./ Puis le dist Carles qu'il n'en esparignat nul:/ tels quatre cenz i troevet entur lui,/ Alquanz nafrez, alquanz parmi ferut,/ S'i out d'icels ki les chefs unt perdut.'

The most glorious of Charlemagne's knights wield weapons made famous enough to deserve names. These swords become synonymous with knightly deeds of honor and violence, and the inclusion of the bishop in this trinity is a further indication of his position as one of the premier knights in Charlemagne's army.

Turpin's prowess was inherently linked to his position as archbishop. The poet does not conceive of Turpin as having two separate roles, one secular and one spiritual, nor does he consider that there has to be any transformation from one to the other for the archbishop. Instead, Turpin performs both his chivalric and his episcopal duties simultaneously and the poet consciously seeks to mix these two natures into one ideal person. This mixing of imagery is evident both in the written poem and in illustrations and depictions based on it. While Turpin is said to be wearing armor in the battle (see Laisse 161), in images he is often depicted with a crozier and mitre 'even in battle'.[18] In the poem itself Turpin's ecclesiastical position is often explicitly cited during his feats of prowess.

> Archbishop Turpin goes through the battlefield./ No tonsured person who ever sang mass was personally responsible for so many meritorious deeds./ He said to the pagan: 'God rain misfortunes on you!/ Your killing this man [Anseis] cuts me to the heart.'/ He made his good horse lunge forward,/ He struck the pagan on his shield made in Toledo,/ Throwing him dead on the green grass.[19]

The poet claims that Turpin's violently chivalric actions are the most 'meritorious' of any 'tonsured' men. Later, after Turpin kills the Saracen giant Abisme, the poet remarks, 'He runs him through from one side to the other,/ Throwing him dead in an empty place. The French say: "Here is a mighty heroic deed! The crozier is quite safe in the Archbishop's hands."'[20] Brault argues that the poet was drawing parallels with Christ's Harrowing of Hell, where he thrust the spear-like tip of His Cross into Leviathan's mouth.[21] If this is true, and Turpin was meant to be emulating Christ in his personal use of military violence to achieve Christian ends,

---

[18] Brault points out his wearing of clerical vestments in battle, 'a notion that did not strike the Brindisi artist or the Conrad illustrator as curious.' See *Roland*, 2, 191. For further evidence of this, see figures 68–70, 102, 104, 114, 116, 203, 204 in Lejeune and Stiennon, *La Legende de Roland dans l'art du moyen age*, second edition, 2 vols. (Brussels, 1967).

[19] *Roland*, 2, Laisse 119. 'Par le camp vait Turpin li arcevesque ;/ Tel coronét ne chantat unches messe/ Ki de sun cors feïst tantes proëcces./ Dist al paien: "Deus tut mal te tramette!/ Tel as ocis dunt al coer me regrette."/ Sun bon ceval i ad fait esdemetre,/ Si l'ad ferut sur l'escut de Tulette/ Que mort l'abat desur cele herbe verte.'

[20] Ibid., Laisse 126. For the whole conflict between Turpin and Abisme, see Laisses 124–6.

[21] Ibid., 209.

this would speak to a far more culturally pervasive acceptance of warrior-clerics.[22] Regardless of the potential allegories with Christ, the text itself unifies Turpin's knightly defense of Charlemagne with his defense of Christ – his prowess protects both his king and the Cross. One is also put into mind of Turpin's dismissive remark in the poem that if men could not fight worthily, they should go off and become monks instead, praying for the well-being of the knights.[23]

Turpin's duality as a spiritual leader and a warrior is reinforced by his death scene.

> He sees the noble warrior lying,/ It is the Archbishop, whom God sent in his name,/ The Archbishop says his confession, he gazes upward,/ He has joined and raised both hands toward heaven,/ And he prays to God to grant him Paradise./ Charles's warrior is dead./ By fighting great battles and preaching many fine sermons,/ He was always a relentless fighter against pagans./ May God grant him his holy blessing![24]

Turpin was a warrior for both God and Charles at the battle, and he served both with bravery and prowess. There is explicit reference to Turpin's 'fighting great battles and preaching many fine sermons'. Each role was crucial to Turpin's position as a warrior-cleric, and each role was pleasing to his earthly and heavenly Lord. Turpin used his prowess to aid his king and God, and because of it he was a better cleric and archbishop. Turpin saw Charlemagne as his lord, and certainly he lamented that he would never see him again, but this loyalty did not

---

[22] This imagining of the cleric as an emulator of Christ would fit well with the creation of an ideology surrounding the Christian knight. See Kaeuper, *Holy Warriors*, 1–36.

[23] *Roland*, 2, Laisse 141. Even monks, however, could get in on the action. In the mid-thirteenth century Norman poem *The Song of Dermot and the Earl*, it was the monk Nichol who slew the traitorous Irish king O'Ryan of Odrone with an arrow in battle. The poem reads, 'And much renown that day/ Was Nichol, a cowled monk;/ For with an arrow he slew that day/ The lord of Odrone:/ By an arrow, as I tell you/ Was O'Ryan slain that day.' Clearly, holding one's own in battle could be seen as laudable, even for a 'cowled monk'. See *The Song of Dermot and the Earl*, ed. and trans.Goddard Henry Orpen (Oxford, 1892), 146–7, lines 2005–10. The original reads, 'E mult esteit le ior preise/ Nichol, vn moine achape;/ Kar de vne sete oscist le ior/ De drone le seygnor:/ De vne sete, cum vus dis,/ Iert orian le ior occis.' For the dating of the poem, see J.F. O'Doherty, 'Historical Criticism of the Song of Dermot and the Earl', *Irish Historical Studies* 1 (Mar., 1938), 4–20, esp. 7.

[24] *Roland*, 2, Laisse 166. 'La veit gesir le nobilie barun,/ C'est l'arcevesque, que Deus mist en sun num,/ Cleimet sa culpe, si reguardet amunt,/ Cuntre le ciel amsdous ses mains ad juinz/ Si prïet Deu que pareïs li duinst./ Morz est Turpin, le guerreier Charlun./ Par granz batailles e par mult bels sermons/ Cuntre paiens fut tuz tens campïuns./ Deus li otreit seinte beneïçun!'

prevent him from faithfully serving Christ.[25] There is no concern in the poem that Turpin is violating his ecclesiastical position by actively embracing the conduct of a knight in battle.

Roland himself comments on Turpin's dual role upon seeing his body, "'Ah, noble man, high-born knight,/ I commend you this day to God in His celestial Glory!/ No man shall ever serve Him more willingly./ There never was such a prophet since the Apostles to keep the Faith and to win men over.'"[26] We should note especially that Roland is saying that Turpin's prowess itself made him a worthier servant of God, and implicitly a better cleric. Turpin was not only exhorting men to great deeds of arms, but in performing these deeds himself, he was showing his worth clearly as a cleric and warrior.[27] The poet ends by praying that Turpin be brought to Heaven, writing 'May your soul not endure any suffering!/ May it find the gate of Paradise open!'[28]

As the *Song of Roland* developed over time, Turpin's role as a warrior continued and, if anything, was expanded in the retelling. We can also examine versions of the Roland text to see if there were measurable changes over time in Turpin's military role and its frequency. Using the Oxford text (O) as a baseline, we can judge later texts by what they included and omitted. This is not to argue that the Oxford text was an actual exemplar for the later texts but, rather, to try to establish a basic understanding of how Turpin's role was portrayed in different regions and periods over time. For instance, three of the versions of the text from the thirteenth century contain a laisse in which Turpin explicitly arms himself before battle, and it is a laisse that did not exist in the Oxford version.[29] In addition to the duels with Corsablix, Malquaint, and Abisme, these same texts also include accounts of a duel between Turpin and a Muslim champion named Roudez.[30] Turpin's increased prowess is also evident in the Paris manuscript, dating from around 1250, in which he turns back a Muslim surge, led by Malprimes de Sartaigne, whom he kills.[31] A similar addition is found in the Venice 7 version of the

---

[25] Ibid., Laisse 162.

[26] Ibid., Laisse 167.

[27] As Andrew Taylor puts it, 'Here the poem [Turpin's sermon at lines 1126–35] presents an exalted vision of those who fight, but it ensures that religious counsel is incorporated into this vision through the figure of Turpin, a prince of the church who is also a mighty warrior and who combines the two roles with absolute moral certainty.' See Taylor, 'Was There a Song of Roland?', 46.

[28] *Roland*, 2, Laisse 167.

[29] *Le Chanson de Roland: The Song of Roland, The French Corpus*, ed. Joseph J. Duggan et al. (Turnhout, 2005), 'C' 107, 'V7' 98, 'P' 7.

[30] Ibid., 'C' 164, 'V7' 155.

[31] Ibid., 'P' 83.

poem, probably written toward the end of the thirteenth century.[32] In this added scene, Turpin slays the Muslim warrior Margo. These various scenes of Turpin's prowess are in addition to those contained in the Oxford text, and demonstrate that Turpin's depiction as a warrior increased.

The *Song of Roland* was the most famous of the French *chansons de geste*, with a wide readership and oft-referenced cultural impact, but it was not the only epic poem to detail the military actions of clerics, or to comment on the proper relationship between clerics and warfare. The *Song of Aspremont*, probably written in Sicily or Calabria during the preparations for the Third Crusade, also characterizes Turpin as both a warrior and a prelate.[33] The poem, one of the longest *chansons* to survive (almost three times the length of *Roland*), and one of the most popular, survives in at least seventeen manuscripts.[34] The poem consistently depicts Archbishop Turpin in highly sympathetic terms. While the poem itself contains both pro-clerical and anti-clerical components, Turpin, according to Michael Newth, 'evokes nothing but admiration for his ready zeal and selfless common sense. His dual role as pastor and fighter, however, is totally bemusing to his superior, Milon the Pope.'[35] This duality, while confusing to the figure of the pope (possibly a reflection of its inconsistency with the increasingly codified canon law), is not a concern for the other characters, nor the poem's author. Turpin's actions on the campaign are lauded, and he delivers some of the strongest invectives against the other clerics, especially Abbot Fromer, for being insufficiently prepared to fight to defend Charlemagne and Christianity.

Turpin excoriates the abbot for caring more about building up wealth, rather than sacrificing for God, and the poem praises Turpin for the exact opposite reason.

> He's loved by all at court and much admired;/ No duke in France, as hard as he might try,/ Could bring to court so great a host to fight;/ He much prefers good destriers to buy/ And noble armor to dub and dress young squires/ Than save his wealth and store it up in piles.[36]

---

[32] *Le Chanson de Roland: The Song of Roland, The French Corpus*, ed. Joseph J. Duggan et al., Vol. 3 (Turnhout, 2005), 17.
[33] *The Song of Aspremont*, trans. Michael A. Newth (New York, 1989), xiii.
[34] Ibid., xxiii.
[35] Ibid., xix.
[36] Ibid., 5, lines 104–10. 'Gentix hom fu et jovenes baceler/ Et a mervelles se fait a cort amer./ N'a duc en France, tant se sace pener,/ Que si grant ost voelle a la cort mener./ Il aime miols cevax a acater/ Et bieles armes por vallés adober/ Que il ne face tresors a amasser.' See *La Chanson d'Aspremont*, ed. Louis Brandin, Vol. I (Paris, 1923), 4.

The praise for Turpin's willingness to use his wealth for laudatory ends is unique, as most major prelates in epic literature are used as foils to the heroic knights. In the early thirteenth-century epic, *The Knights of Narbonne*, Hernault the Red criticizes the papal legate, 'These tonsured thieves have seized the lands of many/ And stolen wealth to make their own selves wealthy;/ Their vestries bulge with gold and silver vestments!/ From here up to Ponthieu these lustful prelates,/ If they live near some honest man, are ready/ To shame his wife and blame him for the error.'[37] The active use of wealth and power to further the muscular defense of king and Christ is in direct contrast with the greedy and useless stockpiling of wealth by prelates. The worldliness and greediness of prelates was a long-standing complaint of the clerical reform movement, as was indicated in the preceding chapters, and was joyously echoed by lay commentators who saw in it the hypocrisy of men who were usually preaching to laymen the importance of sacrifice and poverty. Turpin, as one of the figures delivering this condemnation, represents an idealized version of a prelate, one whose active embrace of violence places him on a similar level with the lay nobility.

Turpin upbraids Fromer for being weak and concerned only with his fortune and easy lifestyle, and then dismissively tells him to '"Begone, sir Abbot! Go sing your matins, please!"'[38] In this derisive tone, the author echoes Turpin's statement in the *Song of Roland* that a knight without prowess was relatively worthless, and ought therefore to become a monk.[39] Active use of arms, whether by knights or clerics, is the proper approach to dealing with enemies. Turpin continues this paean to knightly prowess in his address to the pope, in which he says, '"Father, don't take amiss these words of mine;/ It is our duty to cherish all brave knights;/ For when we clerics sit down to eat at night,/ Or in God's service sing matins at first light,/ These men are fighting for our lands with their lives/"'.[40] We can see in this sentiment the dream of knights that clerics would actually appreciate them for keeping them safe, but it also demonstrates competing desires by knights that clerics were better at the manful activities that knights thought were useful, even if at the same time they thought that most clerics ought to leave fighting in battle to the 'professionals'.

---

[37] *Heroes of the French Epic*, trans. Michael A.H. Newth (Woodbridge, 2005), 559. The original reads, '"Cil ordené ont tot le mont sessy,/ De tot l'avoir do mont sont repleni,/ D'or et d'argent et de robes garny./ N'a si prodome desi que an Ponti,/ Se il estoient menent dejoste lui/ Que tost n'eüssent de sa fame honi."' See *Les Narbonnais*, ed. Hermann Suchier (Paris, 1898), 114, lines 3049–54.

[38] *Song of Aspremont*, 10, line 294.

[39] Ibid., 106, lines 1877–82.

[40] Ibid., 5, lines 117–21. '"Sire apostoles, ne vos en doit peser./ Nos devons molt les chevaliers amer:/ Quant nos seons a nostre halt disner/ Et nos servons de matines canter,/ Il se combatent por la tiere garder"'. *La chanson d'Aspremont*, Vol. 1, 4–5.

During the battle, Pope Milon implores several figures to bear a fragment of the True Cross into the fighting in order to spur on the Christian army and gain God's favor.[41] He is initially rejected by a man named Erengi, who opts instead to bear his weapons, and the pope then offers it to Ysoré, 'a better clerk than you I could not call on', but he is again turned down. Ysoré complains that he has brought his weapons and armor in order to use them. He is there to fight personally, not to sit on the sidelines. He asks Milon, probably rhetorically, '"And why am I set up astride a war-horse/ If I am not allowed to spur it forward?"'[42] Ysoré's complaint would have resonated with militarily minded churchmen, and reinforces the side of the debate which held that active service in war was laudable for clerics as well as knights. Turpin then offers to carry the True Cross himself. He approaches the pope while seated on a warhorse, and he lays out his ecclesiastical service and bona fides in great detail. He had been in holy orders, then became a monk and priest near Rouen, remained a monk for ten years at Jumièges, where he was nearly elected abbot, and he was then ordained and installed by the pope himself as archbishop of Reims. Turpin then agrees to serve, provided that the pope listens to his advice, since he has brought a thousand soldiers with him. He asks the pope to grant him the ability to ride in defense of Charles '"With hauberk girt and helmet laced on tight;/ Yet on the morrow, come back to church and shrine,/ I may resume my offices divine."'[43] Turpin offers his services as the bearer of Christ's Cross with the understanding that he will be a singer of masses and a swinger of swords in equal measure, though his recognition that he must 'resume' his divine office on the morrow indicates some appreciation for the pope's reticence. The pope replies, '"You are strong to advise/ That an archbishop should also be a knight."'[44] Turpin refuses to bear the Cross until Milon agrees, which the pope quickly does.

This exchange between the two clerics demonstrates the contemporary argument over the legitimacy of churchmen directly fighting in war. Pope Milon is initially uncomfortable with the idea of an archbishop actively fighting in the battle, and he sees the ideal role of the cleric as one of support and morale boosting. Turpin, however, represents the position that actively fighting, provided it is in a

---

[41] This scene is very similar to one detailed below from the *Chanson d'Antioche*, where Bishop Adhémar of Le Puy is seeking knights to bear the Holy Lance into battle.

[42] *Song of Aspremont*, 201, lines 8411-12. The French reads, 'Et por qoi sui ge sor cest ceval monté?/ Ja par moi n'iert point ne esperoné.' *La Chanson d'Aspremont*, Vol. 2, 74.

[43] *Song of Aspremont*, 202-3, Laisse 422, lines 8469-71. 'L'auberc vestir et le helme lacier;/ Le matinet, se je vieng al mostier,/ Que je repuisse venir a mon mestier:/ Par tel covent serai cofanonier.' *La Chanson d'Aspremont*, Vol. 2, 76.

[44] *Song of Aspremont*, 203, lines 8472-3. '"Fors ies a consellier/ Que arcevesques doie estre chevalier."' *La Chanson d'Aspremont*, Vol. 2, 76.

worthy cause, is itself worthy and laudable. Turpin's position as an unquestioned hero in the tale, and in similar tales such as *Roland*, indicates where the poet would have come down in this argument, as does Milon's quick acquiescence to Turpin's reasoning. Furthermore, Turpin uses the pope's request that he bear the True Cross as leverage, thereby indicating (in the poet's eyes) where God's favor would have fallen. Before acquiescing to bear the holiest relic in Christendom, thereby denoting Christ's favor, Turpin insists on being allowed to actively fight on Christ's behalf. The fact that this debate was actually happening, however (and was absent from earlier tales such as the *Song of Roland*), could be taken as a sign of the growing awareness, but perhaps not acceptance, of the canonical prohibition on warrior-churchmen, as well as the growing perception on the rigidity of societal *ordines*.[45]

In the heat of the battle, Milon gives an impassioned speech in which he implores the Christian knights to sell their lives dearly. He then promises that he shall die with them, and that their sacrifice will open the way to Heaven. His speech inspires the soldiers to fight on, and inspires Turpin to rejoin the active combat. Turpin says, "'Milon, my lord, pray do not be annoyed!/ I would give back this holy Cross of yours;/ For I've a hauberk and a good horse of war,/ A bright steel helm and at my side a sword;/ I am an archbishop and knight withal;/ I would now show the worth of my employ.'"[46] Turpin's characterization of himself as 'arcevesques sui ge et chevalier' is especially telling. He is personally unifying the two *ordines* – clerical and knightly – and he is taking ownership of the professions belonging to both. This conflating of the two orders, prescriptive ideologies though they may be, causes difficulty for the character of Pope Milon, but he resolves his reticence in favor of embracing the ultimately valuable and laudable goal of defeating the Muslims. Milon also returns the fragment of the True Cross to Turpin so that he may bear it in battle, alongside his weapons.[47] The poet here gives his affirmative answer to the earlier question of whether a cleric could be a warrior while remaining a cleric. The bearing of both weapons – the spiritual in the form of the True Cross and the temporal – represents a powerful endorsement of the Turpin-style of prelate: one who muscularly defends Christianity and his king without worrying about transgressing prescriptive guidelines.

While Turpin is the best example of an idealized warrior-cleric in epic literature, other popular tales discussed these same tensions and anxieties within

---

[45] Kaeuper, *Holy Warriors*, 131–44.
[46] *Song of Aspremont*, 222, lines 9313–18. The French reads, "'Sire apostoles, ne vos doit anuier:/ Or vos revuel la sainte crois ballier,/ Car j'ai hauberc et si ai bon destrier,/ Espee çainte et cler iaume d'achier/ Et arcevesques sui ge et chevalier./ Lors si verrois con je me sai aidier.'" *La Chanson d'Aspremont*, Vol. 2, 102–3.
[47] *Song of Aspremont*, 232, line 9754.

medieval society. Of the many epics based around the character of William of Orange, *Moniage Guillaume*, or *William in the Monastery* (probably composed between 1160 and 1190) clearly discussed the interaction of churchmen with war. His imagined life gave rise to a complete biography, seven epic poems, and seventeen epics regarding his ancestors and relations.[48] His actions in the epics, and the tales that he featured in, give us an excellent opportunity to examine some of the basic debates in medieval society, especially amongst the lay audiences of these stories, over the idealized role of churchmen in warfare.

The mixing of the lay and clerical *ordines* is a prominent feature for discussion in the tale. When Count William of Orange decides to become a monk to atone for his sins he ceremonially divests himself of his earthly weapons, with the obvious intention of relying in future upon only spiritual ones. Katherine Allen Smith argues that former warriors who became monks usually were considered to have done so after they had renounced the use of weapons. She writes, 'The disarming of new monks also emphasized that the transition to monastic life entailed the convert's rebirth as a man of peace, in the image of Christ.'[49] However, William's vow during the ceremony demonstrates that his ultimate loyalty remains to King Louis, rather than his soon-to-be-adopted Order. In the church of St. Julien, he vows to put his shield into the saint's care, but 'if Louis, the son of Charles, has need,/ or my godson, who holds my heritage,/ against pagans, the foul savage race,/ I shall take it again.'[50] William is reserving his primary loyalty to his king, rather than the prescriptive prohibitions of the church. He does not see a conflict between actively serving his king and God; indeed he sees the one necessarily following on the other. His shield, one of the tools with which he defends Louis against his enemies, became a relic to be venerated in the church, alongside the 'club of the noble Rainoart,/ with which he killed many fierce Saracens.'[51]

As a monk, William retains his larger-than-life personality, and he earns the ire of his fellow monks for his appetites (they complain that he leaves little food behind), and his threats to use violence against them if they anger him.[52] As a

---

[48] *Guillaume d'Orange: Four Twelfth-Century Epics*, trans. Joan M. Ferrante (New York, 2001), 1, 16.

[49] Smith, *War and the Making of Medieval Monastic Culture*, 62. Smith also points out that the phenomenon of warriors becoming monks represented an inherent link between the two *ordines*. Smith, 52.

[50] Ferrante, *William in the Monastery*, 283, lines 85–8. 'S'en a mestier Löeys, li fils Charle,/ Et mes filleus qui tient mon iritage,/ Contre paiens, la pute gent salvage,/ Reprendrai le.' See *Les Deux Redactions en Vers du Moniage Guillaume*, ed. Wilhelm Cloetta, Vol. 1 (Paris, 1906), 4–5.

[51] Ferrante, 283, lines 95–6. 'Et le tinel dant Rainuart l'aufage/ Don't il ocist maint Sarrasin salvage.' Cloetta, *Moniage Guillaume*, 5.

[52] Ferrante, 289, lines 278–86.

way to rid themselves of this turbulent man, the monks conspire to send him through thief-infested woods in order to purchase some fish for the monastery. The abbot explains that William must make the trip accompanied only by a single servant, and that he must not use weapons to defend himself or his rich cargo if he is waylaid by robbers. William protests that he must defend himself, at which point the abbot chastises him and responds, "'Silence … don't think of that!/ Since you're a monk blessed and consecrated,/ you cannot wield a fatal weapon.'"[53] The abbot and William then engage in a comedic back-and-forth over what specific items William may fight in defense of, before finally agreeing that if the thieves were to try to take William's pants, he may fight to defend them (since he had to defend his modesty). However, despite the fact that he is allowed to use force in preventing them from taking his pants, he is allowed to use only weapons of flesh and bone.[54] William cleverly engineers a solution to this constraint by investing in a very rich belt guaranteed to elicit the interest of would-be assailants. When they invariably tried to steal it, he would be free to pummel them with reckless abandon and canonical impunity.

As he rides along the road, weighed down with his valuable cargo, he is attacked by a band of ruffians. The robbers relieve him of his various goods, and mock him for his weakness. William, chafing under the restraints upon his prowess imposed by the abbot, is finally left with only his belt and pants. William then purposefully draws attention to the richness of his belt, hoping to entice the leader of the band to try to take it from him. When the leader of the band reaches for it, this frees William from his restrictions, and he commences his counter-attack. 'He raises his fist and strikes the leader;/ he deals such a blow on the front of his face,/ that he breaks the bone of his jaw in two/ and throws him dead to the ground.'[55] In short order he taunts, attacks, and slays six more of the robbers.[56] The remaining thieves recognize his dangerous nature, and they concertedly hurl their spears and javelins at him, but 'God protects him, for he is not touched.'[57] God has made a judgment in this case, and he has judged in William's favor. In the argument between William and the abbot over the utility of righteous violence by churchmen, God's protection of William would seem to weigh the scales in favor of William.

---

[53] Ferrante, 290, lines 313–15. "'Taisiés," dist l'abes, "ne vos vigne en pensé!/ Puis qu'estes mones benëis et sacrés,/ D'arme tranchant nę vos devés meller."' Cloetta, 13.

[54] Ferrante, 291, line 350.

[55] Ibid., 298, lines 596–9. 'Hauce le poig, si vait ferir le maistre;/ Tel cop li done devant en son visage,/ L'os de la goule en deus moitiés li quasse,/ Mort le trebuce a terre.' Cloetta, 24–5.

[56] Ferrante, 298–9, lines 600–22.

[57] Ibid., 299, line 628.

While William did not violate the letter of the abbot's restriction, he certainly violated its spirit by seeking out the battle, and even tearing the haunch off a horse to use as an impromptu club. The poet also seemingly sides with William by referring to the abbot's decision to restrict his use of weapons as a 'sin'.[58] The disparagement of the abbot's restriction, a restriction that itself was more lenient than some of the canons against clerics using arms at all, as inherently unpleasing to God is remarkable. God then further demonstrates his apparent favor for the 'good, and honored' William by restoring the horse's severed haunch to health as a miracle.[59] God's protection on the road leads William to attack the monastery upon his return because it refuses to open the gates to him. In William's calculation, the monks had betrayed him by sending him off to die, and God had saved him. Therefore, he was justified in taking revenge and forcing the monks to forgive him![60]

The justification for William's use of weapons is not merely self-defense, especially since in many ways he brought the conflict on himself, but also that his actions had made a positive difference in the world by freeing the road of thieves. The poet praises William's actions, 'He strikes so hard, the noble, honored count,/ that he kills them all, not one is left standing./ Now William has freed the road of those thieves;/ no poor man will leave his goods there again.'[61] Here we see one of the basic justifications used by warrior-clerics – what they did, they did for the greater good. Upon his return to the monastery, William explains to the abbot what happened on the road (after laying waste to many of the buildings and killing a number of the monks). He explains that he was beset by fifteen robbers, and that he defended himself within the restrictions the abbot had given him. "'I could not find any mercy in them,/ but with flesh and bone I took care of them/ so they will not trouble the road again,/ and no poor man will lose his money there.'"[62] The abbot in response exclaims, "'O God … be praised for this!/ They never loved Jesus in his majesty./ Now may all your sins be forgiven you.'"[63] The laudatory end against which William's violence was directed legitimated the means. Both

---

[58] Ibid., lines 634–7. Further on in this laisse, William complains that he is unable to recover the numerous swords left by the dead thieves, because of the abbot's restrictions.
[59] Ibid., 300, lines 661–8.
[60] Ibid., 302–4, lines 733–819.
[61] Ferrante, 300, lines 655–8. 'Tant i feri li jentix quens proisiés,/ Tous les a mors, n'en remest uns en pié./ Or a Guillaume le cemin aquitié,/ Ja mais povre home n'i laira son marcié.' Cloetta, 27.
[62] Ferrante, 304, lines 807–10. "'Onques merci en aus ne port rover:/ De char et d'os les ai si atorné/ Que li chemins n'en iert mais enconbrés,/ Ne povres hom n'en laira son errer.'" Cloetta, 34.
[63] Ferrante, *William in the Monastery*, 304, lines 811–13. "'Dex … t'en soies aorés!/ Onques n'amerent Jhesu de maïsté./ Tous li pechiés vos en soit pardonés.'" Cloetta, 34.

the abbot and God had praised William for his actions, and he could leave the abbey with a clear conscience and his honor intact and enhanced. For many of the churchmen examined in later parts of this book, we will see a similar intellectual and cultural construction whereby the laudability of the cause legitimates the use of violence and weapons.

Our final example from 'imaginative' literature derives from a slightly different tradition from those discussed above. The *Chanson d'Antioche* relates the events of the First Crusade (largely based on the crusade accounts of Albert of Aachen and Robert the Monk), though the text underwent significant revisions until the middle of the thirteenth century.[64] As such, the *chanson* has great value for understanding how contemporaries in the early thirteenth century might have understood these events, and might have seen them through the lenses of their own experiences and expectations. Included in this depiction is an imagining of religion that is 'quite strikingly militaristic', according to the translators, especially in regards to the primary ecclesiastical figure in the poem – Bishop Adhémar of Le Puy.[65] In actions that could easily mirror Turpin from the *Song of Roland* and *Song of Aspremont*, Adhémar 'is depicted not only encouraging others to fight, and blessing their participation in the battle of Antioch, but orchestrating the whole crusader effort, and even taking the field himself, bearing arms for the first time in his life.'[66] In the scenes examined below, we shall see that Adhémar is made into a figure of debate, as Turpin was before him, though a debate that heavily lauds the militaristic side of his actions.

The comparison with Turpin is apt, though in some ways Adhémar looms larger over the *Chanson d'Antioche* than Turpin does in either *Roland* or *Aspremont*. He serves not only as a paragon of ecclesiastical power and knightly virtue, but also in a variety of military roles, from overall commander, to a commander on the battlefield, to a combatant. In this, he resembles a variety of the figures discussed in the subsequent chapters, from clerics who merely directed war efforts (such as Archbishop Lanfranc of Canterbury) to those who led men in battle (such as Bishop Antony Bek of Durham) and those who physically fought in battle (such as Bishop Peter des Roches of Winchester). In each case, there was a discourse on the licit nature of the cleric's actions, a discourse evident to some extent in the *Chanson d'Antioche*.

---

[64] *The Chanson d'Antioche: An Old French Account of the First Crusade*, trans. Susan B. Edgington and Carol Sweetenham (Farnham, 2011), 3–48. Edgington and Sweetenham argue that while there does seem to be an early vernacular poem regarding the capture of Antioch from around 1110, the existing *chanson de geste* derives largely from the early to mid-thirteenth century.

[65] *Chanson d'Antioche*, 57–8.

[66] Ibid., 58.

In numerous instances Adhémar is mentioned alongside the other commanders, and is shown directing the army in such matters as posting guards and rallying them after a defeat.[67] His overall direction of the crusader army is important for understanding the way that contemporaries could understand the subordination of secular military leaders to an ecclesiastical lord. The late twelfth and early thirteenth centuries were a time of increasing papal authority over crusading, and the portrayal of Adhémar was in keeping with this reality. While Adhémar was often seen in the *chanson* as the overall commander, the poet also drew attention to his prescriptive role as spiritual leader. When the poet recounts a list of the noble leaders of the crusade, Adhémar is listed, but is further distinguished from his colleagues by having his purpose illuminated – he is there 'to preach them a sermon' in addition to his military leadership.[68] This unification of military leader and spiritual father, as we saw earlier with Turpin, was a common formulation in imaginative literature. Had Adhémar remained merely an overall commander of the army, his actions would probably not have elicited much complaint from canonists in the twelfth and thirteenth centuries, since he was not necessarily transgressing the boundaries of his *ordo* (since he was neither armed nor present on the battlefield). Like Turpin, however, Adhémar was depicted as embracing far more knightly activities than overall command.

In numerous laisses Adhémar is shown actively leading men into battle. In laisse 100, Adhémar, with a Christian force, intercepts the fleeing Saracen leader Soliman, 'They fell on the pagans ferociously and overwhelmed them with the force of their attack, killing 4700.'[69] This victory was evidence, according to the poet, of God's favor for the Christian cause. In laisse 209, Soliman of Nicaea explains one of his defeats in battle by remarking that the Christian army had used a 'strange maneuver' of splitting in half, with half commanded by the 'brave-faced Godfrey [of Bouillon]' along with 'a bishop of Le Puy (Mohammed's curse on him!)'.[70] It is interesting that Adhémar has a curse placed upon him, presumably due to his effectiveness against the Muslims. Soliman also says, after naming all of the Christian commanders, that 'all of these fell on us, each with his lance lowered for attack', a group that apparently includes Adhémar, though this would conflict

---

[67] Ibid. See especially laisses 50, 124, 146, 160, and 314 on pages 133, 172, 181–2, 190–1, and 286.

[68] Ibid., Laisse 50, page 133. See also laisse 307, page 282. Footnote 476 on page 282 makes the Turpin comparison explicitly. At numerous times in the text, the poet makes mention of Adhémar's holiness and nobility. See laisses 315, 323 on pages 287 and 292 especially.

[69] Ibid., 159.

[70] Ibid., 224.

to an extent with laisse 306 (discussed below).[71] Later, in a completely invented passage (one that has no grounding in the campaign narrative), Adhémar is seen leading a relieving army to rescue the city of Edessa.[72] The poet has invented an additional opportunity for Adhémar to demonstrate his bravery and devotion to God by leading men into battle against the Saracens. The bishop is instrumental to the military and spiritual well-being of the army, and his actions often lead him into battle, both as a commander and as a combatant.

In a scene referenced above, Adhémar rallies the Christian army after hearing of a defeat in the field. In a scene evocative of Turpin's dismissal of men who cannot fight (they should become monks), the messenger bearing the news insists that Adhémar has no time for sermonizing, and thus the 'bishop leapt into actions. He seized a horn furiously and blew it; the Franks hastened to arm themselves in their barracks and lodgings.'[73] The undermining of traditional ecclesiastical actions in the face of imminent violence is interesting, though perhaps not surprising. Adhémar's response, however, does bear some scrutiny. Throughout the poem, Adhémar is seen balancing his role as commander of the expedition with that of spiritual father to the crusaders. In this most urgent of circumstances, that balance is shown to be very difficult to maintain, and his role as military commander takes precedence.

Adhémar's reaction to imminent and important battle is to become an active combatant. The poet makes clear that Adhémar had tried to avoid becoming embroiled in combat, but with everything on the line now, he needed to become actively involved.

> The bishop of Le Puy was brave and eloquent, determined to serve God to the best of his ability. Ever since the army had entered foreign territories he had never put on armour no matter how grave the situation; now battle was imminent he did not refuse to do so.[74]

After celebrating Mass, Adhémar returned to his tent and put on armor laced with gold, including golden spurs and sword on his left side. He also carried a spear with twin dragons riveted to the haft. His outward transformation from cleric to knight is now complete, a transformation successful to such an extent that Duke Godfrey does not recognize him. Adhémar then gives Godfrey a fairly traditional pre-battle invocation in which he tells the duke to fight hard, and that God will aid

---

[71] Ibid.
[72] Ibid., 232.
[73] Ibid., 191.
[74] Ibid., 282.

them with armies of angels in the field. Godfrey responds, much as Roland would have to Turpin, that he is 'happier to have you bearing arms than if a thousand knights, armed and ready, were to spring up in these fields outside.'[75] The bishop's embrace of the knightly role as combatant is reinforced by Godfrey, and perhaps by God in the favor he shows the crusader army, and Adhémar himself.

This discourse over Adhémar's role in battle mirrors many of those seen elsewhere in this study, in that he is balancing the spiritual with the secular, and the peaceful with the violent. In the case of his abstaining from armor until the crisis-point outside of Antioch, the poet seems to be arguing that it is best if clerics leave actual fighting to knights, except in circumstances of ultimate peril. There is also a reflection of the argument over worldliness, in that contemporaries were more concerned with clerics who became 'knightly' in their love of pomp, wealth, and 'worldly' affairs. Adhémar's golden armor and spurs would seem to indict him for that worldliness, but the poet consciously undermines that impression by later referring to Adhémar specifically as 'a noble cardinal. He says Mass for them [the Christian army] each morning at daybreak. He would rather give battle than go out [hunting] with gerfalcons.'[76] He embraces violence that has purpose, bur abhors meaningless violence – no better balance for a warrior-cleric could be given.

One of Adhémar's most important roles in the *Chanson d'Antioche* is as the custodian of the Holy Lance. In a role reminiscent of that of Pope Milon in the *Song of Aspremont*, Adhémar is entrusted with finding a worthy wielder to carry the Holy Lance into battle against the Muslims. Much as Milon found, no knight wishes to bear the holy relic because he believes that it will inhibit him from actively fighting. After each of the secular lords rejects the Holy Lance in turn, Hugh of Vermandois (the final knight offered the lance) persuades Adhémar to bear it himself. He argues that, as a priest and ordained bishop, Adhémar is the natural choice as lance-bearer, while the knights will fight around him. He says,

> Why don't you stop trying to pester us into doing this? You shall be the one to carry the Lance, armed and on your own warhorse. You will not find anyone else with the temerity to take charge of it … Your job is to ride out in front of us on your armoured warhorse, carrying the Lance by which God was hurt and wounded and tortured on the Holy Cross.[77]

The implication of Hugh's assertion is interesting – Adhémar has a role to play in the battle, namely to ride armed and armored into the fray as the receptacle of

---

[75] Ibid., 283.
[76] Ibid., 293.
[77] Ibid., 285–6. For the refusals from the knights, see 283–5.

God's favor. One of the Muslim leaders, Red Lion, upon seeing him, remarks, '"He carries the Lance like a true leader."'[78] During the battle, the bishop invokes the aid of Blessed Mary, then charges into the fray, encouraging the men.[79] Adhémar will not be striking with the Lance (presumably), and thus his bearing of it will prevent him from striking mortal wounds in battle (despite the sword on his hip). He will thus be in a quasi-canonical position – armed and armored on the battlefield, but not actively shedding blood or causing violence.

The conversation regarding Adhémar's role as warrior on crusade is mirrored by an illustration of clergy fighting later in the *chanson*. Laisse 325 reads, 'The squadron of clergy marched out of the city, wearing their albs tightly belted and tucked in and carrying such arms as they were permitted.'[80] This is an interesting observation regarding what weapons would be 'permitted' to clergy, but more interesting is the reaction from the Muslims. Upon seeing the armed clerics coming forward, Corbaran dismisses them as not a threat, but Amedelis, his advisor, cautions him to take the threat seriously. Despite the fact that 'when they are back home they are not allowed by the Lord to carry arms, neither lance nor spear', he argues that they will fight viciously, since they are defending their lives.[81] With echoes of the Council of Nablus discussed above in chapter 2, we come to a fascinating arrangement, where clergy fighting in defense of God's will (as the First Crusade was seen) have a culturally acceptable opportunity to fight in battle which is denied them in the wars among Christians. The truth of this sentiment is discussed more fully in the chapters to come, but to see this debate in the early thirteenth century is illuminating.

What, then, is the image we get, from imaginative literature, of militarily minded churchmen? While conceding that the *chansons de geste* examined here are only a handful of those produced during the Middle Ages, we can still see some common themes and tropes developing that illuminate important cultural and societal considerations concerning clerical warriors. In each case the clerics who were given the most heroic treatment were those who emulated the lay warriors in their exemplification of prowess and bravery, while those who were given the most opprobrium were those who were greedy, selfish, perfidious, and worldly. Additionally, we can see that in the case of Archbishop Turpin, his heroism was

---

[78] Ibid., 293.

[79] Ibid., 310–11.

[80] Ibid., 294. Footnote 497 explains, 'Clergy were prohibited from shedding blood, and could therefore carry only weapons like maces and staffs. The battalion of clergy is found in BB, but not in other sources. RA refers to the clergy marching out alongside the soldiers though not fighting.' Canon law forbade the bearing of weapons, not simply the shedding of blood.

[81] Ibid.

tied directly to his support of the Christian cause, as well as of Charlemagne himself. His loyalty to his king is in keeping with the examples that will be presented in the subsequent chapters. For English prelates between 1066 and 1240, active warfare in support of the king was almost always justified, whereas warfare for other purposes would generally be treated more circumspectly. Active service for the king was seen in some ways as representing active service to God. The defense of the kingdom against the enemies of the king was a licit cause for the use of force in many theological tracts, from Saint Augustine forward, and clerics, despite the canonical prohibitions on active participation, would perhaps have embraced these conflicts as legitimate and necessary.

PART II

The Debate in Practice

CHAPTER 4

The Norman Conquest: Odo of Bayeux and Geoffrey of Coutances

We now turn our attention to how clerics in Anglo-Norman and Angevin England applied the prescriptive debate to the actual realities of warfare. The Norman invasion of England in 1066 afforded churchmen ample opportunities to take active roles in the conquest and the subsequent pacification of the country. The men surveyed here – Bishop Odo of Bayeux, Bishop Geoffrey of Coutances, and Remigius of Fécamp (later bishop of Lincoln) – benefited from their military service to William the Conqueror. They were among the first to bring together the two traditions of warrior-clerics: the Anglo-Saxon preference for royal service and the Norman reliance of personal loyalty and affinity. Odo and Geoffrey had a close, personal relationship to William, and such personal connections to the ruler gave them the opportunity to rise to lofty heights within the government and elite society. Additionally, they had been raised in households that extolled chivalric virtues and ideology, and were thus comfortable around displays of warfare and personal prowess. While this same background nurtured many bishops and abbots, Odo and Geoffrey relied on their royal connection to place themselves at the highest levels of the ecclesiastical and secular hierarchies. For them, there was a unification of purpose between the chivalry of the high nobility, and success at the highest levels of the ecclesiastical hierarchy. This did not always guarantee that they benefited from direct royal patronage, however, as both men eventually ran afoul of the king. However, these men represent two sides of the same coin: they were both royally connected nobles who accepted the use of warfare in pursuit of their goals.

Odo was among the most famous bishops of the early Norman period of English history. He was the half-brother of William I, and the brother of Count Robert of Mortain. He is often considered the standard example of a warlike, secular bishop in the late eleventh century. He served William loyally, and his participation in government and warfare was not limited to offering advice – he also took an active and vigorous role in the thick of the fighting on the field of battle. Once William became king, Odo served him as a general, and he ran the kingdom during his brother's frequent absences to the Continent. Finally, Odo parlayed his position into personal and independent authority, which allowed him to elevate himself to the highest ranks of ecclesiastical and secular society.

Odo was most probably born around 1030. His father was Herluin, the *vicomte* (ducal representative) of Conteville, while his mother (the same as William's) was Herleva, the favored concubine of William's father, Duke Robert I. Odo's value to Duke William was recognized early, and he was among William's chief advisors and counselors, becoming bishop of Bayeux in either 1049 or 1050.[1] Despite being well under the canonically dictated age of thirty to hold such an office, we have no evidence that William met with major opposition from contemporaries to his elevation of Odo, and this demonstration of ducal authority over the church was reasonably common in eleventh-century Normandy.[2] His appointment recalled that of Hugh, bishop of Bayeux, who himself had been the half-brother to then-duke Richard I, William's grandfather. Odo and Geoffrey were part of a Norman episcopate drawn from the highest ranks of the nobility and that often thought of the well-being of familial dynasties alongside that of the diocese.[3] These clerics did not see a radical difference in their identity versus that of their secular peers; they maintained very similar social outlooks, concerns, and priorities. Although they operated in the specialized world of the ecclesiastical hierarchy, they were not cast entirely outside of the emerging chivalric ethos of secular and courtly society.

Odo's primary loyalty was to William I, rather than to some amorphous notion of 'the church'. While the papacy was actively trying to build itself as the undisputed head of Christendom in the mid- to late eleventh century, this was much more papal desire and propaganda rather than accepted reality. Relative autonomy from the pope was the rule of the day for many clerics in Normandy.[4] The duke was a much closer authority figure for Odo (and other Norman clerics), and Odo's advancement and success in life was directly tied to the patronage of William I. Owing his position and prestige to William's protection and interest, Odo thus repaid him with loyalty and support, at least until 1082. The power of the duke, however, was not the only influence prevalent in Normandy in the mid-

---

[1] William of Poitiers, *Gesta Guillelmi*, ed. and trans. R.H.C. Davis and Marjorie Chibnall (Oxford, 1998), 100–10. For a good overview of Odo's life and career, see David Bates, 'The Character and Career of Odo, Bishop of Bayeux (1049/50–1097)', *Speculum* 50, No. 1 (Jan., 1975).

[2] Ibid., 5.

[3] David Douglas, *William I* (New Haven, 1964; reprint 1999), 118–19. 'Owing their appointment to their dynastic connexions they were naturally concerned to further the fortunes of the families to which they belonged, and as members of the new aristocracy in Normandy, they were deeply committed to the maintenance of that nobility in power.'

[4] Clerical independence from the pope mirrored that of secular nobles from their lords. High-ranking clerics were similar to their secular cousins in the tension that existed between obedience and autonomy.

eleventh century. There was also the power of the reforming ideology emanating from the monastery of Cluny in Burgundy. The reforms were designed to win monastic independence from diocesan bishops, and to try to de-secularize the clergy as much as possible.[5] One would expect that a highly secular and powerful bishop such as Odo would have quickly run afoul of the Cluniacs, but this was not the case.[6] An indication of the pragmatic alliance between bishops such as Odo and the monastic community in Normandy can be seen in the fact that monasteries rarely pushed their rights to independence from episcopal officials. While many Norman monasteries possessed Cluniac-inspired diocesan independence, in actual practice they rarely utilized it. On the other side, many bishops were exceedingly generous with monastic communities in their areas.[7]

Odo's close relationship with Duke William, and his generosity and munificence in endowing monastic holdings with lands and wealth, helped him to gain a positive reputation among some contemporary authors. William of Poitiers (a near-contemporary biographer of William I and his chaplain, and thus not exactly impartial) wrote that Odo was among the greatest prelates in Normandy and that Duke William had done well in elevating him. He took pains to explain that it was Odo's exemplary qualifications, rather than his close relationship with William, that resulted in his elevation, writing, 'from his earliest years the unanimous commendation of the best men rated him among the best. His renown has been carried into the most distant regions; but the zeal and goodness of this most generous and humble man deserve much more.'[8] Since William was writing during a period of papal reform and resurgent idealism, he had to downplay any nepotistic whiffs of simony in Odo's elevation. He was also writing during a period after the battle of Hastings in which Odo was very much in favor with William I, and was arguably the most powerful noble in England and Normandy.

Odo did not just give lands to monasteries; he also gave access to the highest levels of power and education. Odo was known for being a patron of scholars, and his patronage led to the creation of a Bayeux school of later prelates.[9] While ideologically the Cluniacs might not approve of bishops like Odo, they still accepted

---

[5] Indeed, in the *Life of St. William* [of Volpiano] by Rodulfus Glaber, Glaber tells of William's refusing to swear an oath to the local bishop upon becoming a deacon (a 'wickedly usurped custom'). *Rodulfus Glaber*, ed. and trans. John France (Oxford, 1989), 261–3. During his career, however, William worked closely with bishops, but as an equal, rather than subordinate.

[6] Douglas, *William I*, 118.

[7] Ibid., 124; cf. *Gallia Christiana.*, ed. Denis de Sainte-Marthe, Vol. 9, cols. 354, 870 (Paris, 1759).

[8] Douglas, *William I*, 91–3.

[9] Frank Barlow, *William Rufus* (New Haven, 1983; reprint 2000), 19; Douglas, *William I*, 128–30.

them as excellent patrons and protectors. Odo's patronage became famous alongside that of his colleague, Geoffrey of Coutances.[10] Both Odo and Geoffrey were known for their munificence in educational patronage, and Geoffrey's generosity in this area 'became indeed something of a legend'.[11] Odo was mostly responsible for developing the cathedral school at Bayeux, and for overseeing most of the building of the cathedral. Many of their benefactions came after 1066 from the spoils of war. Men like Odo and Geoffrey were lauded, regardless of any warlike exploits, because of their impact on rebuilding the church in Normandy.[12] The rebuilding of the infrastructure of the church, both physically and metaphorically, helped to protect Odo and Geoffrey from criticisms of their other actions. Additionally, there were certainly clerics who *preferred* men like Odo to their more pacifist peers. It would be dangerous to believe that the reform ideology of the Cluniacs and Gregorians was destined to be successful, or in fact was the normative form of Christianity. Men like Odo and Geoffrey were difficult to categorize, even for later clerical authors who had imbibed these reforms, because they were successful in administering their diocese, and they generally left their ecclesiastical affairs in good order.[13] Their personal failings, seen as an embrace of worldliness, could be condemned out of hand, but the reformers also wanted ecclesiastical leaders who were pious as well as successful. It was men such as Odo and Geoffrey who did the heavy lifting of reorganization and reinvigoration of the Norman clergy and diocese structure after the collapse of the tenth century.[14]

Odo was probably involved in patronizing the Bayeux Tapestry, and some have even argued (though more tenuously) that he might have had a hand in the production of the *Song of Roland*.[15] These two texts, taken together, are wonderful examples of the violent and bloody ethos of chivalry and the direct role that the

---

[10] For Odo's patronage, see David Bates, 'Le patronage clerical et intellectual de l'eveque Odon de Bayeux (1049/50–1097)', *Annales de Normandie, Serie des Congres des Sociétés historiques et archéologique de Normandie*, ii (1997), 105–14.

[11] Douglas, *William I*, 128. Among others, some of the prelates who got their starts under Odo's school were: Thurstan, the violent abbot of Glastonbury, Thomas, who became archbishop of York (1070–1100), and Samson, who became bishop of Worcester (1096–1115) (129–30). Samson was the father to Thomas, archbishop of York (1109–19), and Richard, bishop of Bayeux (1108–13).

[12] Douglas, *William I*, 129.

[13] Ibid., 120.

[14] Ibid., 122. The diocese of Bayeux had a long history of bucking ecclesiastical reform trends, including in having married clergy up through the fourteenth century. See David Spear, "The School of Caen Revisited", *HSJ* 4 (1993), 65. Perhaps Odo was less of a 'worldly' outlier, and more of a traditional Bayeux bishop than has been previously thought.

[15] Douglas, *William I*, 129.

church and warrior-churchmen played in those exploits. The Tapestry portrays with great excitement and vigorous precision the various military exploits of Odo's brother, William I, and also shows Odo himself present on the battlefield of Hastings, taking an active role in the direction of the battle. The *Song of Roland* has among its chief heroes the violent and chivalrous Archbishop Turpin (discussed above in chapter 3), who is equally adept at granting absolution, delivering a fiery crusade sermon, and skewering Saracen enemies. The fact that Odo was associated with these texts is not surprising, given his warrior affectations.

Odo's patronage and power made him clearly the most powerful prelate in pre-1066 Normandy, and there is little evidence that his contemporaries bemoaned this reality. When he was not lavishing attention and patronage on his diocese of Bayeux, he was in almost constant attendance at the ducal court of his brother. Here he joined many of his ecclesiastical peers in providing William I with invaluable political, ecclesiastical, and military advice as needed. William of Poitiers remarked on the importance and constancy of the counsel and support given to Duke William by his bishops, abbots, and other clerics, especially on the eve of the invasion of England.[16] Orderic Vitalis, writing a generation later, included Odo and Geoffrey as among the 'brilliant galaxy of bishops' serving William I, men 'of extremely high birth, religious zeal, and every kind of virtue.'[17] The support that Odo consistently gave to his brother William was both a cause and result of William's patronage. Odo had been entrusted with the bishopric of Bayeux because of its strategic location in the defense of the duchy, and thus Odo was, from an early stage, playing a fundamentally important strategic military role in his brother's domain.[18] His vital and centralizing role in the duchy would become more fully displayed in the conquest and subsequent pacification of England.

Odo's role at Hastings is possibly the most well-known example of a warrior bishop on the field of battle, but he also had a vital role in both planning and executing the invasion. Odo's position would have been seemingly precarious from a canonical standpoint, especially in light of the nascent reform movement emanating from Rome which would take form more fully under the subsequent pope, Gregory VII.[19] However, the papacy actually endorsed the invasion, perhaps through the intercessions of Cardinal Hildebrand (the future Gregory VII), and the official story of the conquest included a papal banner sent by Pope Alexander II

---

[16] Poitiers, 100–3.
[17] *The Ecclesiastical History of Orderic Vitalis*, ed. and trans. Marjorie Chibnall, Vol. 2 (Oxford, 1999; reprint 2002), 140–2.
[18] David Bates, 'Character and Career of Odo', 5.
[19] Gregory was himself an advocate of the invasion of England, as he not-so-subtly reminded William I in a letter of May 8, 1080. See *English Historical Documents*, ed. David Douglas and George Greenaway, Vol. 2 (London, 1953), 644–6.

for William's army to bear in the field.[20] An official papal endorsement would have certainly weakened condemnations of warlike behavior by men such as Odo and Geoffrey. Any condemnation was further weakened by the penitential ordinances agreed upon in 1070 by the papal legate Ermenfrid of Sion on his visit to England. The ordinances dealt with clerical violence during the battle separately, and more harshly, from violence committed by laymen, but they did not call for the degradation from orders for offending clerics, but rather a series of penances. In any case, it was unlikely that men such as Odo, Geoffrey, or Remigius of Fécamp (who later became bishop of Dorcester/Lincoln) were touched by the penances at all.

While much of our understanding of Odo's role comes from its vivid depiction on the Bayeux Tapestry, other contemporaries also commented on his participation in the battle. Accounts of the battle itself appeared in almost every contemporary and near-contemporary source, both Anglo-Saxon and Norman; however, the Anglo-Saxon sources, while invaluable for their treatment of King Harold's motivations and aspects of the campaign not found elsewhere, do not remark upon the role played by individual Normans. For Odo's role we need to rely on exclusively Norman sources. The Norman sources that are considered roughly contemporaneous are the *Gesta Normannorum Ducum* written by William of Jumièges, the *Gesta Guillelmi* by William of Poitiers, the Bayeux Tapestry, and the *Carmen de Hastingae Proelio* by Bishop Guy of Amiens.[21]

The most valuable Norman sources for details of Odo and Geoffrey's participation in the battle are the *Gesta Guillelmi* and the Bayeux Tapestry. William of Poitiers was especially well suited to discuss the military roles of the two prelates because, as Orderic Vitalis two generations later explained, he had been 'trained as a knight and fought for a time in secular warfare'.[22] William's background as a knight gave him a singular insight into military affairs and allowed him a certain authority and authenticity when recounting military campaigns. While he had rejected the life of temporal warfare, he still exhibited and retained an appreciation of the value and efficacy of violence and warfare, provided that they were cast in defense of the right cause. In William's view there were few more righteous and

---

[20] For questions about the veracity of the papal banner story, see David Bates, *Normandy Before 1066* (London, 1982), 202; cf. Catherine Morton, 'Pope Alexander II and the Norman Conquest', *Latomus: Revue d'etudes latines*, xxxiv (1975), 362–82.

[21] For an overview of materials on the battle, see Stephen Morillo, *The Battle of Hastings: Sources and Interpretations* (Woodbridge, 1996); for the discussion over the dating of the Carmen see *Carmen de Hastingae Proelio of Guy, bishop of Amiens*, ed. Catherine Morton and Hope Muntz (Oxford, 1972) and *The Carmen de Hastingae Proelio of Guy Bishop of Amiens*, ed. Frank Barlow (Oxford, 1999); cf. R.H.C. Davis, 'The Carmen de Hastingae Proelio', *EHR* 93 (1978), 241–61.

[22] Poitiers, xv.

proper campaigns than Duke William's conquest of England. William also wrote approvingly of the Conqueror's aggressive policy for pacifying England, though since he was writing after the penitential ordinance of Ermenfrid of Sion imposed penance on those guilty of bloodshed, he had to tread carefully.[23]

William of Poitiers had probably accompanied Duke William on some of his military campaigns, though not to Hastings. These experiences gave him a first-hand view of the duke's military abilities, and helped to foster in William an appreciation for the value of violence. They also gave him an appreciation of Dukes William's military abilities, which were to be glorified and defended as those of a latter-day Christian Caesar.[24] William's closeness and familiarity with Duke William also led to an association later in life with Bishop Odo.[25] As will be seen below, William took pains to glorify the contribution to the campaign made by Bishop Odo, but to do so in a way that would have been uncontroversial to the clerical reformer movement. His chronicle is an excellent example of the tensions and concerns inherent in two competing cultural traditions in medieval society. On the one hand, William was writing during the ascendancy of a reform ideology that took a dim view of overt and active warfare by clerics; on the other hand, he was a product of a society that respected and celebrated prowess and glorious displays of bravery and audacity in pursuit of noble causes. Furthermore, the late eleventh century, as discussed in chapter 2, was also on the cusp of drawing together the notions of just war with holy war, and thus the papal imprimatur of the Norman invasion of England could render the campaign holy and just.

The second half of the *Gesta Guillelmi* is devoted to the campaign against England and its aftermath. After learning that King Harold had seized the throne (in apparent violation of the oath he was said to have sworn to Duke William), and had gained 'an impious consecration from Stigand, who had been deprived of his priestly office by the just zeal and anathema of the pope', William took counsel with his advisors.[26] By ignoring the fact that Edward had named Harold as his heir on his deathbed, and by attributing the consecration to the disgraced Stigand, archbishop of Canterbury, despite contemporary Anglo-Saxon evidence that it was actually Aldred, archbishop of York, who had performed the ceremony, William of Poitiers sought to de-legitimize Harold and thus justify Duke William's war against an anointed Christian king.[27] While Harold's status as a

---

[23] Ibid., xxiii.
[24] For an overt comparison of William to the great warriors of the Classical world, see Poitiers, 154–7.
[25] Ibid., xxxi.
[26] Ibid., 100–1.
[27] For the Anglo-Saxon account of what happened with Harold's ascension, see *The Anglo-Saxon Chronicles*, ed. and trans. Michael Swanton (London, 1996; Reprint 2000),

consecrated and anointed king needed to be impugned in order to provide justification for the invasion, this also served to protect from condemnation those clerics (including Pope Alexander II, Odo, and Geoffrey) who were involved in the invasion. William used the overt papal support for the invasion as a means to isolate his hero from criticism regarding the attack on a Christian kingdom. He considered the papal banner borne by the Norman army to be 'the approval of St Peter, by following which he might attack the enemy with greater confidence and safety.'[28] The fact that William claimed a papal banner for the invasion is interesting, since it denoted clear papal support, and could thus be seen as support for the invasion from the 'official' church hierarchy.

William of Poitiers walked a tightrope between glorification and over-justification in his description of the actions of Odo and Geoffrey at Hastings. He wanted to give them credit for doing manly deeds on behalf of Duke William, and in a war fought under a papal banner, but also to protect them from any criticism for overtly warlike behavior. In recounting the moments right before the battle began, William placed the clerics in a canonically correct supporting role. He wrote, 'Two bishops who had accompanied him [Duke William] from Normandy, Odo of Bayeux and Geoffrey of Coutances, were in his company, together with numerous clerks and not a few monks. This clerical body prepared for the combat with prayers.'[29] Odo and Geoffrey were threading the needle here, in that they were present at the battle and on the battlefield, but they were behaving only in a supporting role, rather than as active warriors.[30] Despite William's claims, both bishops were known to be experienced in leading men into battle, and thus he might have been overtly trying to cast their role as that of noncombat-

---

192–200. Aldred also later consecrated William as king, thus he had to be 'replaced' in the narrative by the disgraced Stigand in order to invalidate Harold's kingship.

[28] Poitiers, 105.

[29] Ibid., 125. 'Aderant comitati e Normannia duo pontifices, Odo Baoicensis et Goisfredus Constantinus, una multus clerus et monachi nonnulli. Id collegium precibus pugnare disponitur.'

[30] Ibid., 124, n. 3. In her note glossing the text, Marjorie Chibnall drew attention to Duke William's perceived piety and to 'the canonically correct noncombatant role of the two bishops ... both of whom were capable of leading troops in battle. In a similar vein, Odo is shown in the Bayeux Tapestry, dressed in a padded tunic, not a hauberk, and encouraging the troops with a mace, not a sword.' Elsewhere, she speculates that Geoffrey had received military training as a youth, and she equates this experience with that which was given to men to such as William of Poitiers and Raoul, son of Giroie. Marjorie Chibnall, 'La Carriere de Geoffroi de Montbray', *Les évèques normands du XI siecle*, ed. Pierre Boulet et François Neveux, Colloque de Cerisy-la-Salle, 30 Septembre–3 octobre 1993 (Caen 1995), 281. David Bachrach also portrays the role of Odo and Geoffrey as one of support. See Bachrach, *Religion and the Conduct of War*, 84–5. For an image of a more active military role for Odo, see Gerrard, 36–8.

ants in order to draw a contrast with their prior behavior. We know that clerics fought in the battle, both from the experiences of Remigius of Fécamp (see below) and from the penitential ordinances of 1070. It is thus unlikely that in a battle in which clerics of varying ranks fought, the most prestigious and powerful ecclesiastical lords chose not to, especially since they never shied away from doing so either before or after the Conquest.

The best evidence we have regarding Odo's actual behavior during the battle is the famous scene from the Bayeux Tapestry mentioned by Chibnall above, which was probably made less than a decade after the battle, perhaps around 1075.[31] In panel 72, Odo is shown horsed, at full gallop, among soldiers, wielding a mace on the battlefield.[32] It has proven to be a very difficult panel to decipher, despite its relatively straightforward subject and caption. He is attempting to rally the Norman army after it was (wrongfully) reported that Duke William had been slain, and above his image is the caption, 'HIC ODO EPS BACULU TENENS CONFORTAT PUEROS', or 'Bishop Odo holding a mace encourages the young men'. Odo's role is that of military leader; as Stephen Morillo has shown, medieval armies were especially prone to fragmentation and disintegration, and thus strong, effective leadership was necessary to keep the army together and focused on the enemy.[33] The Tapestry shows Odo in this role as commander, intervening on behalf of Duke William, and personally saving the duke's army from disaster, despite the purely supporting role presented by William of Poitiers and the later medieval author Wace.[34]

The Bayeux Tapestry promotes Odo's importance to the invasion beyond just the battle of Hastings. For instance, it is Odo's castle at Bayeux that is the scene of Harold's supposedly perjured oaths. Odo also is placed prominently to William's right when the duke orders the assembly of the fleet to invade England. In fact, Odo is seated higher than the future king. He, rather than William, gestures his

---

[31] H.E.J. Cowdrey, 'Towards an Interpretation of the Bayeux Tapestry', *Anglo-Norman Studies* 10 (Woodbridge, 1988), 63. For a current overview of the various arguments about who commissioned the Tapestry, where it was made, and when, see R. Howard Bloch, *A Needle in the Right Hand of God: The Norman Conquest of 1066 and the Making and Meaning of the Bayeux Tapestry* (New York, 2006), 42–6. For an interesting, though highly speculative, argument against Odo's patronage see Andrew Bridgeford, *1066: The Hidden History of the Bayeux Tapestry* (New York, 2005), 162–72.
[32] *English Historical Documents*, 2, 274.
[33] Stephen Morillo, *Warfare under the Anglo-Norman Kings 1066–1135* (Woodbridge, 1994), 146–7.
[34] *Maister Wace's Roman de Rou*, ed. Hugo Andresen, Vol. 2 (Heilbronn, 1877), 352–3. For Bates' and Freeman's views, see Bates, 'The Character and Career of Odo', 6. See also Duggan, *Armsbearing and the Clergy*, 15. Cf. Douglas, *William I*, 200.

hand towards the fleet. The shipwright even looks to him for instruction.[35] Odo also appears at the council of war with William, and their other brother Count Robert of Mortain. All three brothers are on the same bench, to reinforce their importance in the invasion.[36] Odo finally appears at the battle of Hastings, where he is depicted 'on horseback and at full gallop', wielding a staff or mace.[37]

It is not my intention to argue that Odo must have been at the forefront of battle, must have been wearing exactly the same style of chainmail as the secular knights (though there is evidence he was wearing the same sort of armor as Duke William), and must have been wielding a 'traditional' weapon.[38] However, let us focus on what we do know. We know that Odo was present in the thick of the battle. We know that he was horsed and was galloping, and we know that he was wearing some form of protective covering.[39] Finally, we know that he was holding a large, heavy object which was held in an aggressive pose. Odo was

---

[35] Cowdrey, 'Towards an Interpretation of the Bayeux Tapestry', 50. Gale Owen-Crocker argues that Odo, given his probable status as patron of the tapestry, wanted his role as a planner and director of the invasion to be emphasized. Gale R. Owen-Crocker, "The Interpretation of Gesture in the Bayeux Tapestry", *Anglo-Norman Studies* 29, ed. C.P. Lewis (Woodbridge, 2007), 170.

[36] Ibid., 51.

[37] Ibid. Cowdrey translates *baculum* as 'staff', and has a footnote to explain why calling it a 'mace' would be wrong. '*Baculum* is translated "staff" not "mace" because the two should be distinguished. In the Tapestry, the *baculum* is a symbol of authority rather than an offensive weapon (21, 56, 59, 68). Cowdrey, 'Towards an Interpretation of the Bayeux Tapestry', 51, n. 6. Cowdrey argues that Odo was shown with this same staff, rather than a sword, on the obverse of one of his seals, though he is depicted in armor and on horseback. However, he is possibly incorrect in this assessment, as the evidence from the seal is, at best, inconclusive; since it was patterned directly on that of William I, Odo was probably depicted with a sword. See *A Guide to British Medieval Seals*, ed. P.D.A. Harvey and Andrew McGuinness (Toronto: University of Toronto Press, 1996), 63.

[38] Gerrard does an excellent job of laying out the historiography of this argument. See Gerrard, 243-6. For a discussion of Odo's armor, see Michael John Lewis, 'Identity and Status in the Bayeux Tapestry: The Iconographic and Artefactual Evidence', *Anglo-Norman Studies* 29, ed. C.P. Lewis (Woodbridge, 2007), 105 and 113. Lewis theorizes that Odo's armor, like that of Duke William and Guy of Ponthieu, could denote a higher quality of chainmail, due to his higher status. For a general discussion of eleventh-century arms and armor, see Ian Pierce, 'Arms, Armour and Warfare in the Eleventh Century', *Anglo-Norman Studies* 10 (Woodbridge, 1988), 237-57.

[39] Contrast Odo's 'padded tunic' (according to Chibnall) with other non-combatant clothing depicting in the Tapestry. While Odo's armor is not completely the same as that worn by the soldiers, it is far closer than that worn by those in non-combat roles. He is clearly not depicted in vestments of any kind, as can be seen by contrasting him with Archbishop Stigand and archɛbishop Aldred. See panels 39, 72, 80, and 113 for evidence of clerical clothing.

behaving as a soldier or commander, and was living up to the chivalric language popular among elites.[40] In addition to the cultural importance, Odo's role might well have been crucial. The Normans launched an attack up the hill against the Saxon shieldwall, but they were repulsed and retreating in disorder. There was a danger that the Norman force would dissolve, and it is here that the Bayeux Tapestry shows Odo seeking to rally the troops.[41] Whether this assessment was accurate or not – and David Bates sees evidence that Odo was trying to exaggerate his role in the Conquest – it would indicate a desire to have people associate him with a crucial and valiant role in the battle.[42] Indeed, Odo is one of only a few characters in the Tapestry to be portrayed full-face, which was an established artistic device used to denote 'both spiritual and worldly sovereignty.'[43] Whether this depiction would have given an observer the idea that Odo was manfully helping his brother to conquer England can be debated. The plain meaning of the scene seems to be that Odo was an active participant in the battle, and that he took an active role in the victory over the English, which God had endorsed, as denoted by the papal banner.

Odo was not the only major churchman to take an active role in the battle, as he was joined by Geoffrey of Coutances (among others). Geoffrey, while not depicted in the Tapestry, gave sufficient service to William at Hastings that he was afforded a prominent role at the new king's coronation.[44] Geoffrey was also handsomely rewarded by William I with lands in England, and his rewards were as rich and magnificent as those of the other major secular nobles who had led retinues in the campaign.[45] When lands were given out after the conquest of England, defense was one of the chief considerations and interests that William had in mind. Geoffrey's share of the lands reflected not only his importance in the conquest itself, but his continuing military abilities and acumen. Chibnall points out that the distribution of fiefs indicated that Geoffrey's role in the defense of the kingdom was important, as he showed with his command of soldiers in 1069.[46] William I utilized Geoffrey to maintain security and order within England,

---

[40] Cowdrey, 51.
[41] Douglas, *William I*, 200. See also Bloch, 37–8.
[42] Bates, 'The Character and Career of Odo', 6.
[43] Bloch, 129. The other two men so portrayed were the anointed King Harold and the worldly prelate Stigand. William himself was probably also portrayed this way, in conscious reflection of Harold, in the lost ending section to the Tapestry, which probably showed his own consecration. See pp. 130–2 for more discussion of the importance of this style and the idea that the Tapestry was designed to unify the various peoples affected by the Conquest.
[44] Bishop Guy of Amiens, *Carmen de Hastingae Proelio*, Morton and Muntz, 53.
[45] Marjorie Chibnall, 'La Carriere de Geoffroi de Montbray', 286–7.
[46] Ibid., 287.

especially in the vital and untamed western counties near to Wales, and indeed over 60 percent of Geoffrey's lands were concentrated in the southwestern counties of Devon and Somerset, where he helped to enforce the Conqueror's rule.[47]

For Remigius, a monk from the Norman abbey of Fécamp, Hastings was the opportunity to actually win a bishopric through service in battle. He came over to England 'with duke William's expeditionary force and in 1067 was given the bishopric of Dorchester by the new king in succession to the English Wulfwig.'[48] His elevation was due to the important military role that he had played in the invasion in providing troops (apparently one ship and between ten and twenty knights) from the abbey of Fécamp, and personally leading them into battle at Hastings.[49] Remigius's overt aid of William's invasion and then quick elevation led to accusations of simony.[50] He also suffered by having been elevated to the bishopric in 1067 (being the first Norman to gain an ecclesiastical post in post-Conquest England) and thus doing his profession of obedience to Stigand, the disgraced archbishop of Canterbury.[51] As Stigand was eventually deposed on April 11, 1070, the legitimacy of Remigius's consecration was called into question. These two issues necessitated Remigius traveling to Rome in 1071 accompanied by Archbishop Lanfranc of Canterbury, and Archbishop Thomas of York, a trip recounted by Eadmer, the twelfth-century historian and biographer of Archbishop Anselm of Canterbury.

The pope suspended Remigius because of the accusations of simony and for receiving consecration at the hands of an already-suspended archbishop – not for actions on the battlefield, except in so far as they were seen as a 'payment' for his bishopric. In fact, his clear violation of the existing canons regarding military activities by clerics was never brought against him, and at Archbishop Lanfranc's insistence he was reinstated as bishop. Lanfranc argued that Remigius and Thomas were both wise in a wide range of things, that they were necessary to the disposition of the kingdom, and that they were outstanding in the art of oratory. When given the choice by the pope, he immediately reinvested them with their pastoral staves.[52] Remigius faced ecclesiastical censure only when legates arrived in 1070 to depose Stigand, further demonstrating that it was his association with the disgraced archbishop, rather than his leading men in battle, which led to his own legal troubles. Bates has argued that Remigius escaped permanent

---

[47] Ibid., 288–9.
[48] *English Episcopal Acta I: Lincoln 1067–1185*, , ed. David M. Smith (Oxford, 1980), xxxi.
[49] David Bates, *Bishop Remigius of Lincoln 1067–1092* (Lincoln, 1992), 6.
[50] Eadmer of Canterbury, *History of Recent Events in England*, trans. Geoffrey Bosanquet (London, 1964), 11.
[51] Bates, *Remigius*, 1.
[52] Eadmer, *History of Recent Events in England*, 12.

deposition only through his very close contacts with the Anglo-Norman elite, and that, while reformers would probably have cringed at his warlike abilities, William would have seen it as indicative of 'the sort of man who would be very useful in the often desperate conditions which prevailed in England after 1066.'[53] Lanfranc's fervent support of him was also vital to Remigius's success, and we shall see in the next chapter that Lanfranc saw a valuable utility in clerics who firmly (including in warfare) supported their king.

Remigius's career should be considered successful by almost any measure. He oversaw the translation of his see from Dorchester to Lincoln, persistently served the king and received numerous rewards for doing so, and a century after his death Gerald of Wales wrote a hagiographical *Vita* for him in an attempt to get him canonized. Until his death in 1092, he was a stolid and revered royal servant, and he was one of the commissioners who compiled Domesday Book.[54] In the early and confused days of William Rufus's reign, Lanfranc himself vouched for Remigius's loyalty to the new king, which he showed when he accompanied William Rufus on his 1091 campaign against his brother Duke Robert of Normandy.[55] He also oversaw the rebuilding of the cathedral at Lincoln, and he incorporated a number of architectural elements from the White Tower in London and the existing castle in Lincoln.[56] As we saw previously with men such as Odo of Bayeux and Geoffrey of Coutances, patronage of this sort could earn a cleric a well-spring of positive feelings, and could smooth over other, less savory aspects of their character or actions. However, later historians have interpreted his career through the prescriptive lens of reformers who condemned warrior-clerics, with one modern historian giving him credit for being 'an extremely good bishop' even 'in spite of the blemishes on his career such as his role at the battle of Hastings.'[57]

These 'blemishes' did not prevent Gerald of Wales, over a century after Remigius's death, from spearheading an attempt to have him canonized. Gerald spent 1196–99 at Lincoln, and while there he wrote a *Life* of the long-dead

---

[53] Bates, *Remigius*, 6. He writes that Remigius's military actions 'brought him a set of problems which were subsequently compounded by his having made a profession of obedience to the English archbishop of Canterbury, Stigand, whose archiepiscopal status was questionable, and who was eventually deposed by papal legates in 1070 … His earliest difficulties – which were perhaps not as great as they appear – stemmed from an over-close, and perhaps over-ambitious, association with a war of conquest.' Pages 4–5.

[54] Ibid., 13.

[55] Ibid., 14–15.

[56] Ibid., 17–19. Bates cautions, however, 'It seems to me important only to observe that there are dangers in moving too sharply away from a stylistic approach to buildings to a functional one. We must distinguish between a building which might itself include features typical of fortifications and one which was itself fortified.'

[57] Ibid., 36–7.

bishop.[58] He drew heavily on an existing record of miracles at Remigius's tomb, and when that failed him, he invented a fair number of his own. He revised his work between 1210 and 1214 into a second edition, which he presented to Archbishop Stephen Langton of Canterbury. While Gerald did not whitewash Remigius's role at Hastings, he did reduce the number of knights he led from twenty to ten.[59] He also claimed that Remigius had gained consecration at the hands of Lanfranc (rather than the disgraced Stigand). That Gerald would seek to get him canonized speaks to Remigius's popularity and perceived worthiness in the eyes of later twelfth-century clerics. What is striking is that Gerald did not ignore Remigius's role in battle; he retold it as part of the story why Remigius deserved canonization, despite having tried to smooth over other aspects of his reputation (such as his consecration by Stigand). It is important for us to understand that Gerald and his contemporaries at Lincoln saw Remigius as the best of St. Hugh's predecessors.[60] However, the very fact that he tried and that he did not overtly cover up Remigius's military actions demonstrates a reasonable expectation that it would not be seen as disqualifying.[61]

To return to the late eleventh and early twelfth centuries, we know that the actions of clerics at Hastings caused serious reflection among contemporaries on the tensions between the glorification of violence and the condemnation of worldliness. Orderic Vitalis in Book 3 of his *Historia Ecclesiastica*, written between 1114 and 1123, followed William of Poitiers' account of Hastings very closely, and sought to minimize clerical actions in battle even further.[62] While Orderic men-

[58] Gerald of Wales, *Vita Sancti Remigii*, Vol. 7, ed. James Dimock (London, 1877), xi.
[59] Ibid., 14. 'puta qui cum ipso in regnum venerat, et decem militibus, quos in eius auxilium et obsequium abbas eius miserat, quasi decurio nobilis in necessariorum ministratione praefectus.' Bates saw Gerald's reporting of the number of knights Remigius led as ten, rather than twenty, as a clear demonstration that he was trying to 'smooth over the less laudable features of Remigius' career.' See Bates, *Remigius*, 6 and 35. Since leading ten knights into battle was not half as bad as leading twenty, it could have been simply an innocent mistake. Were Gerald truly concerned about it or were he trying to 'smooth [it] over', he would have either eliminated the story altogether, or transformed Remigius into a noncombatant.
[60] Bates, *Remigius*, 35.
[61] Admittedly, considering that Remigius was not actually canonized, one could argue that Gerald's gambit failed. However, it is far more likely that the very weak evidence of Remigius's miracles contributed far more to the unsuccessful attempt. See Bates, *Remigius*, 36.
[62] Orderic Vitalis, 1, 46. Book III was the first book of the *Ecclesiastical History* to be written. For a closer examination of Orderic's portrayal of Odo, see Bates, 'The Character and Career of Odo'. Interestingly, Orderic praised William of Poitiers as a modern-day Sallust, as well as his service as an archdeacon on behalf of the bishops of Lisieux. He also praised his former career as a soldier. Orderic wrote, 'He had been a brave soldier

tioned clerical aid in assembling the fleet to sail against England, he does not glorify clerical actions in battle.[63] When discussing Hastings, Orderic mentioned that there were two bishops who accompanied the army, Odo and Geoffrey, and that they came with many monks and clerks, but he was careful to sanitize their activities by saying it was their 'duty ... to support the fight with their prayers and counsel.'[64] Orderic tells the story of William rallying his troops when they thought that he had been slain, but he omits any reference to Odo's help in this, contrary to the image in the Bayeux Tapestry.

Orderic's reticence should be read as reaction to the First Crusade, which had glorified violence on behalf of Christ and had illuminated these competing tensions. That campaign had as one of its military leaders Adhémar, bishop of Le Puy. Even prior to the preaching of the crusade, in fact, there was an acceptance of violence led by the church, provided that it was for the 'right' ends. One may see this by reading Gregory VII's calls for an expedition to the Holy Land – which he would lead himself – or his calls to action against his foes in Italy. William gained papal support for the invasion of England, due to his promise to reform the English church, to remove Archbishop Stigand specifically, and to support the 'reform papacy' in general.[65] However, William elevated men like Odo, Geoffrey, and Remigius to positions of authority as a reward for their support (military and otherwise). This tells us that active service in warfare, as exemplified by these men, was not *ipso facto* antithetical to reform, and was not always a top priority for papal reformers. It also shows that the papacy was willing to work with warrior-clerics to achieve broader aims, and did not even do so while holding its nose. Warfare could not be condemned entirely, but for men like Orderic there was still something very wrong and very unseemly about worldly bishops such as Odo.[66]

As will be seen below, Orderic consistently criticized Odo for his secularity and worldliness; however, he did not specifically condemn his actions in warfare. For Orderic, Odo was far too interested in worldly, rather than spiritual, pursuits. Indeed, when William I left England in 1067 to attend to affairs in Normandy, he left the government in the hands of Odo and William fitzOsbern (the king's

---

before entering the church, and had fought with warlike weapons for his earthly prince, so that he was all the better to describe the battles he had seen through having himself some experience of the dire perils of war.' See Orderic Vitalis, 2, 259.
[63] Orderic Vitalis, 2, 144, n. 1.
[64] Ibid., 173.
[65] Douglas, *William I*, 187.
[66] Christopher Holdsworth theorizes that, while armed clerics were not acceptable by Orderic's time, he was more concerned with married clergy than warrior ones. See Christopher J. Holdsworth, 'Ideas and Reality: Some Attempts to Control and Defuse War in the Twelfth Century', *The Church and War*, ed. W.J. Sheils, *Studies in Church History* 20 (London, 1983), 62–4.

cousin). Orderic wrote that Odo was 'a man conspicuous for his magnificence and activity in secular affairs'.[67] One need only contrast Orderic's treatment of Odo with his treatment of men like Wulfstan of Worcester, Lanfranc of Canterbury, and even Geoffrey of Coutances, all of whom conducted military activities, but did so without transgressing that cultural line into becoming 'worldly', nor seeking to rule as 'second kings', to quote Orderic's complaint about Odo. Odo was a knightly bishop; Wulfstan, Lanfranc, and Anselm remained 'clerical', even when active in military affairs.

Orderic offered summary judgments on both Odo and Geoffrey in regards to their secularity and actions in warfare. For Odo he wrote,

> What shall I say of Odo, bishop of Bayeux, who was an earl palatine dreaded by Englishmen everywhere, and able to dispense justice like a second king? He had authority greater than all earls and other magnates in the kingdom, and gained much ancient treasure, as well as holding Kent.[68]

This underscored Odo's importance as a nobleman, royal administrator, and defender of the kingdom. While Orderic probably exaggerated Odo's authority, it certainly served to highlight his power.[69] He acted as a second king in all things, and Orderic condemned him for relishing secular authority. This account of Odo's power was followed by Orderic's judgment on his suitability as a cleric. In Odo 'vices were mingled with virtues, but he was more given to worldly affairs than to spiritual contemplation. Holy monasteries had good cause to complain that Odo was doing great harm to them, and violently and unjustly robbing them of the ancient endowments given them by pious Englishmen.'[70] In Orderic's eyes, Odo's greatest sin was basing his identity on his loyalty to his king, rather than God.

Orderic later offered a more balanced portrayal of Geoffrey of Coutance's military actions when he wrote about his role in suppressing the rebellions and Danish incursion of 1069. In the western shires of Dorset and Somerset, remnants of the Anglo-Saxon power base attacked Montacute, one of Robert of Mortain's castles (and near to some of Geoffrey's own lands). Geoffrey, leading soldiers from Winchester, London, and Salisbury, defeated these 'West Saxons'.[71] He 'marched

---

[67] Orderic Vitalis, 2, 197.
[68] Ibid., 265–7.
[69] David Bates makes an interesting point regarding how English and Norman sources saw Odo's power. English sources were more interested in what Odo did as an administrator, whereas Norman sources were more interested in his legal rights to do so. See Bates, 'The Character and Career of Odo', 8.
[70] Orderic Vitalis, 2, 267.
[71] Orderic Vitalis, 2, 229.

against them, killed some, captured and mutilated others, and put the rest to flight.'⁷² There were further risings to the west, but the rebels gained no foothold, even in Devon and Cornwall. However, if Geoffrey had been unsuccessful, it would have made the Norman position that much more difficult and could have undermined Norman rule throughout this region.⁷³ Orderic gave Geoffrey clear credit for leading the troops; no secular lord was mentioned as playing a significant role. Furthermore, Geoffrey was said to have overseen the killing and mutilation of his enemies, further demonstrating the lack of behavioral distinctions between armies led by ecclesiastical lords and those led by secular lords. Even in light of this behavior by the troops, Orderic did not condemn Geoffrey's behavior as unbecoming of a cleric.

Orderic then went on to discuss Geoffrey in more general terms. He wrote, 'Then there was Geoffrey bishop of Coutances, of noble Norman stock, who had fought (*certamini*) in the battle of Senlac as well as offering up prayers, and had led his knights in various other battles between English and invaders.'⁷⁴ This is a remarkable passage for a variety of reasons, not the least of which being that Orderic felt that the best eulogy (of sorts) for Geoffrey was to describe his military exploits on behalf of William I. He overtly claimed that Geoffrey had fought at Hastings, and that this was distinguished from praying, because he did that as well. He also reinforced this image by discussing Geoffrey's later military exploits. In fact, Marjorie Chibnall saw Orderic's comment as more a simple statement of fact, rather than a criticism. She explains Orderic's famous statement that Geoffrey understood the affairs of knights and combat better than he did the affairs of clerics as simply reflective of the period.⁷⁵ Geoffrey certainly fit the mold of an eleventh-century prelate from a high-status family, but we also need to

---

⁷² Ibid. Cf. J.H. Bettey, *Wessex from AD 1000* (London, 1986), 11–12.

⁷³ For some discussion of the strategic importance of Geoffrey's actions, see Douglas, *William I*, 219. Douglas put it thus, 'The whole Norman venture in England had thus been placed in peril, for at last the resistance to William was assuming a coherence which it had hitherto lacked.' This large-scale Scandinavian invasion and northern rebellion gave birth to other uprisings throughout the country, most especially in the southwest and western counties. William had to act quickly and comprehensively to stifle the budding rebellions. He initially headed north, causing the Danes to fall back, and then struck out west to pacify the regions bordering on Wales. Afterwards he headed north to Lincolnshire, but he delegated Geoffrey, bishop of Coutances to suppress a rebellion in Dorset 'that was threatening the newly constructed castle of Montacute', and with it Norman control over the region. Geoffrey was successful in this, and the king was able to focus entirely on his northern campaign, which saw him recapture the burned-out city of York just before Christmas. See pages 219–20.

⁷⁴ Orderic Vitalis, 2, 267.

⁷⁵ Marjorie Chibnall, 'La Carrière de Geoffroi de Montbray', 292. 'savait mieux apprendre aux chevaliers à combattre qu'aux clercs à chanter'.

recall the fact that the Gregorian reforms were primarily concerned with stamping out simony and secular control of clerics, rather than clerical involvement in warfare.[76] In fact, many reformers saw the crusades as the ultimate expression of piety, and could very easily be seen as endorsing military involvement among the clergy in some form or another. Furthermore, Geoffrey had been a committed reformer in modernizing Norman monasticism and in securing patronage for Coutances, two factors that could have spoken well in his favor in the minds of reformers.[77]

In the dispensation of titles and lands after Hastings, both Odo and Geoffrey fared well – Odo was created earl of Kent in early 1067 and he served as justiciar alongside William fitzOsbern during William's absences. Odo was the most wealthy and powerful of the Norman aristocrats after his enfranchisement with the earldom and numerous manors throughout England, though his power was strongest in the southeast.[78] He used his wealth, influence, and his reputation to expand his holdings and his power. He even adopted a hybrid seal to represent his two-fold power. He amended his brother's seal, which featured the king in an equestrian pose wielding a sword, by featuring images of himself in his clerical vestments on one side, and horsed with either a sword or staff on the other. Equestrian seals had grown in popularity among the nobility during the eleventh century, and in this regard Odo was no different. In their guide to British medieval seals, Harvey and McGuinness write of them, 'Like the king's great seal, these equestrian seals were a personification of their owners, a powerful image of their social standing and military skills.'[79] Odo would have been attracted to the symbolic linking of his seal to that of the king, and also to the personification of military power inherent in the design. Odo's seal represented a major shift for the seals of an ecclesiastical personage, since most others depicted the clerics in a pose designed to reinforce their clerical nature. Thus, they are almost always shown in their vestments, holding their crozier, and prepared to celebrate Mass. Odo's role as earl of Kent led him to adopt the dualist seal that wedded his clerical nature

[76] Cf. Jean le Patourel, 'Geoffrey of Montbray, Bishop of Coutances, 1049–1093', *EHR* 59 (May 1944), 157.
[77] Ibid., 138–43. Patourel also raised the question of clerical attitudes towards warrior-clerics, though he did not venture an answer. He asked, 'It would be interesting to know what was, precisely, the attitude of the eleventh century to ecclesiastics who took on an active part in military operations.... No doubt the ecclesiastical aversion to the shedding of blood was not offended provided the priest himself did not wield the sword; but even in his own day, Geoffrey's military proclivities were commented upon.' Ibid., 151.
[78] Bates, 'The Character and Career of Odo', 2. For his holdings in the southeast specifically, see Robin Fleming, *Kings and Lords in Conquest England* (Cambridge, 1991), 114, 152, 189–91.
[79] Harvey and McGuinness, 43.

to his secular nature.[80] He thus created symbolically a reflection of his dualistic status in the world.

Ironically, despite his reticence about Odo's role at Hastings, William of Poitiers repeatedly praised him for his military actions after the Conquest. William related how Odo was entrusted with the strategically vital castle of Dover, and he praised his ability to excel in ecclesiastical and secular business.[81] Due to his good counsel and dignity he was 'useful to the whole of Normandy, and a great ornament to it.'[82] William then offered an odd, and not very convincing, account of Odo's devotion to justice.

> He never took up arms, and never wished to do so; nevertheless he was greatly feared by men at arms, for when need arose he helped in war by his most practical counsels as far as his religion allowed. He was singularly and most steadfastly loyal to the king, his uterine brother, whom he cherished with so great a love that he would not willingly be separated from him even on the battlefield, and from whom he had received great honours and expected to receive still more.[83]

This is an excellent example of an assessment being both true and misleading. It is possible that William is quite correct here, and that Odo never personally took up a sword, but he also lends support to Odo's military role when he writes that Odo would 'not willingly be separated from [King William] even on the battlefield'. William tried to thread the needle here – cover Odo with glory for manfully serving his brother and king, while also protecting him from accusations of engaging in personal violence. William's descriptions of Odo's activities demonstrate the gray areas in the argument over warrior-clerics. Odo was someone who was 'singularly and most steadfastly loyal' to the king to the extent that he could not be separated from him, even on the battlefield, but he never 'took up arms', despite his constant appearances as a royal general. William wanted to glorify Odo as a warrior, but also inoculate him from attacks by reformers who would be offended by his embrace of military actions.

As mentioned earlier, Odo took on the governance of England after the

---

[80] Ibid., 63.
[81] Poitiers, 165.
[82] Ibid., 167.
[83] Ibid. 'Arma neque mouit unquam, neque uoluit moueri: ualde tamen timendus armatis. Bellum namque utilissimo consilio, cum necessitas postularet, iuuabat, quantum potuit religione salua. Regi, cuius frater erat uterinus, quem tanto amplectabatur amore ut nec inter arma uellet ab illo separari, a quo magnos acceperat atque sperabat honores, unice constantissimeque fidelis fuit.'

Conquest. William took many of the former leaders of the English – including Edgar, the great-nephew of Edward the Confessor and grandson of Edmund 'Ironside', the brothers Earl Edwin of Mercia and Earl Morkar of Northumbria, and Stigand, archbishop of Canterbury – with him to Normandy.[84] Soon after the king left, a plot was hatched to entice Eustace, count of Bolougne and recent hero of Hastings, to come to England to try for the throne. Orderic attributed this mini-invasion to the overly harsh and prideful manner in which Odo and his fellow vice-regent, William fitzOsbern, handled affairs of the English government. Eustace arrived in Kent and laid siege to Dover castle while Odo and Hugh de Monfort were away 'on the other side of the Thames' with most of the garrison.[85] The assault was unsuccessful, and as the invaders retired the garrison counter-attacked. Orderic then wrote, 'The fugitives, imagining that the bishop of Bayeux had suddenly arrived on the scene with a strong force, lost their heads, and in panic went rushing down the precipice of the trackless cliffs.'[86] The invaders thought that the relief force was under the command of Bishop Odo himself and his reputation as a war leader was sufficiently respected that at the mere thought of facing him, potential enemies were panicked. While Orderic might have been exaggerating Odo's military prowess we should remember that Eustace had served alongside Odo on the Hastings campaign, and thus would have gained first-hand knowledge of his strengths or deficiencies as a military commander. Clearly, the bishop had a reputation for military prowess, and even if Orderic was inflating Odo's military reputation, the fact that he was doing so further underscores the potentially laudatory aspect of clerics' militarily supporting their rulers.

Odo, as earl of Kent, was expected to take an active role in administering and defending the kingdom. The office of 'earl' changed greatly after the Conquest. It shifted from being a Danish-inspired *jarl*, or major, semi-autonomous noble landowner, to more closely approximate the Norman *comes* (count).[87] Indeed, it was no accident that Latin authors writing of English earls consistently referred to them as *comites*, in exactly the same fashion as their continental cousins. Before 1066 almost all land in England was held in earldoms by two great families, the Godwines and the house of Leofric. This enabled them to build up extremely powerful independent systems of wealth for their entire families, most famously exploited by the Godwines, who before Tostig's expulsion controlled every earldom of England with the exception of Mercia. William's post-1066

---

[84] Orderic Vitalis, 2, 196–7.
[85] Ibid., 205.
[86] Ibid.
[87] Douglas, *William I*, 295.

earldoms were smaller, and more focused on defensive measures. Thus, they were created in areas needing special defense: Kent, East Anglia, and the Welsh borders.

Odo and Geoffrey's value to the kingdom's defense was further showcased in 1075. Roger, earl of Hereford and Ralph, earl of East Anglia, took advantage of the king's absence (he was busy leading Norman and levied English troops against enemies in Normandy) and formed a conspiracy against his rule.[88] They also drew one of the last remaining English noblemen, Waltheof, earl of Northumbria, into the cabal of rebels. It was Waltheof, supposedly repenting of even his unwilling participation, who confessed the evidence of the rebellion to Lanfranc, archbishop of Canterbury.[89] Lanfranc managed the royal response nationwide; Wulfstan, bishop of Worcester, dealt with Roger, while Odo and Geoffrey led a force against Ralph's forces near Cambridge.[90] John, monk of Worcester and Symeon of Durham (who based his account on John), both gave credit to the two prelates for playing active roles in the campaign (whereas Orderic credited secular rulers).[91] John wrote that Geoffrey and Odo' led the defense, alongside Wulfstan of Worcester, and Æthewig, abbot of Evesham; the two bishops 'assembled a force of English and Normans and prepared for battle' against Earl Ralph of East Anglia around Cambridge.[92] The chroniclers noted that the bishops raised a force that consisted of both Englishmen and Normans, thus indicating that they were probably able to utilize the surviving system of the fyrd, in addition to the new military recruitment system based on William's retainers. Odo was thus acting on behalf of the king in his defense of the kingdom and he used the institutions of royal government. The battle was a huge victory for the royalists, and the

---

[88] John of Worcester, 3, 22–3. See also *ASC*, 208–9. This rebellion is discussed more fully in chapter 5.

[89] John of Worcester, 3, 24–5. William Kapelle has argued for a more active role by Waltheof. He portrays him as far more of a ringleader and instigator of the revolt, rather than an unwilling participant. William Kapelle, *The Norman Conquest of the North: The Region and Its Transformation, 1000–1135* (Chapel Hill, 1979), 133–7.

[90] John of Worcester, 3, 24–5. Contrast John's account with Orderic's. See Orderic Vitalis, 2, 316–17.

[91] The differing accounts of this battle between Orderic, John, and Symeon can certainly be explained by reference to their different sources for the account. However, if Orderic's decision to ignore the roles played by Odo and Geoffrey was intentional, it demonstrates the debate that existed between chroniclers such as himself, and men such as John and Symeon, who were more comfortable relating the military activities of the bishops. For a good discussion on the incorporation of one text into another by chroniclers, see Gerrard, 169–70. I would argue, however, that we can derive some insight into the copying chronicler's subjective judgment from which materials he chose to either copy or ignore.

[92] John of Worcester, 3, 25.

defeated enemy fled back towards East Anglia. Archbishop Lanfranc, in his letters to William I regarding the siege and subsequent capture of the rebel-held castle of Norwich, commented favorably upon Geoffrey's effective generalship.[93] As in 1069, having a cleric leading the royal army did not prevent the corporal punishment of those captured. When Ralph fled to Brittany, 'His enemies pursued him as he fled and either put to death or mutilated in various ways all those they were able to capture.'[94] Neither John nor Symeon condemn this mutilation, despite its occurring during a conflict between two Christian forces and under the command of ecclesiastical generals – the ecclesiastical generals were defending the king, and thus they were given significant latitude (political and cultural) in dealing with the threat.

The defeat of the 1075 rebellion led directly to another opportunity for Odo to show off his military abilities. With the trial and execution of Earl Waltheof, Walcher, bishop of Durham, was elevated to the earldom of Northumbria, and entrusted with the defense of the north. His dual appointment of Earl of Northumbria and bishop of Durham did not last very long. In 1080 he was murdered by an angry mob regarding a local dispute.[95] In response, King William dispatched a royal force under Odo to restore order and seek vengeance for the murder. Symeon of Durham recorded the events,

> When news of what had been done spread far and wide, Bishop Odo of Bayeux, who was then second only to the king, came to Durham with many of the leading men of the kingdom and large force of armed men; and in avenging the death of the bishop virtually laid the land waste.[96]

Odo again reprised his role as one of the chief military leaders available to the king. His use in this extremely delicate situation underscores the value that William I placed on him and his contribution to defending the throne. Odo is the only royal military commander mentioned on this expedition, and is mentioned only by Symeon, who obviously had much closer knowledge of the campaign,

---

[93] Lanfranc, #34–5, 126–7.
[94] John of Worcester, 3, 27.
[95] *Symeon of Durham: Libellus de Exordio atque Procursu Istius, Hoc Est Dunhelmensis, Ecclesie*, ed. and trans. David Rollason (Oxford, 2000), 218–19. See also John of Worcester, 3, 32–7, though John does not name Odo, or anyone else, as the commander of the force.
[96] Symeon, Rollason, 218–19. 'Nec mora ea que gesta fuerant fama ubique diuulgante, Odo Baiocensis episcopus, qui tunc a rege secundus fuerat, et multi cum eo primates regni cum multa armatorum manu Dunhelmum uenerunt, et dum mortem episcopi ulciscerentur terram pene totam in solitudinem redegerunt.'

and who offered no condemnation of Odo for his actions.[97] Odo's actions were doubly justified – he was avenging the murder of one of God's ministers, as well as a royal official. Symeon's language was very much chosen to reinforce Odo's secular power, in referring to him as being second only to the king and leading the most powerful nobles, and referring also to his righteousness by speaking of his mission as seeking vengeance. What is perhaps most interesting is that Odo was not condemned, even for overseeing the traditional medieval military practice of 'laying waste' to a region during a campaign. In this case it included beheading those responsible for the murder, or mutilating them by amputating their limbs. Lastly, Odo 'also took away certain ornaments from the church, including a pastoral staff of wonderful substance and workmanship (for it was made of sapphire). This was put in the castle under the guard of the soldiers and soon disappeared.'[98] We see Odo behaving here exactly as a secular lord, right down to the pillaging of the church. Yet, there is no condemnation forthcoming from any of Symeon, John of Worcester, or even his old critic, Orderic.

Our brief look at Odo's career to 1080 enables us to contextualize his arrest and imprisonment in 1082. As often is the case with contemporary observers, a remarkably important and telling incident elicits only the most cursory of mention. The two sources best situated to comment on Odo's arrest and imprisonment are also the pithiest. The Anglo-Saxon Chronicle entry for 1082 reads only, 'Here the king seized Bishop Odo; and here there was a great famine.'[99] There was neither discussion as to why Odo was seized, nor any further mention of him until 1088. John of Worcester, who based his own work on the Anglo-Saxon Chronicle, wrote only, 'King William placed his brother Odo, bishop of Bayeux, in custody in Normandy.'[100] John, while following the earlier chronicle closely, at least informs us that Odo was imprisoned in Normandy, away from his center of power in Kent, and out of the kingdom altogether. This supports the idea that Odo had become more powerful in England than he was in Normandy, and that most of his partisans and adherents were primarily in England.

It is not until the writings of William of Malmesbury and Orderic Vitalis in the first third of the twelfth century that we begin to get a more in-depth story about

---

[97] For a discussion of how Norman historians integrated into the Anglo-Saxon community of Durham, see Theodore Johnson-South, 'The Norman Conquest of Durham: Norman Historians and the Anglo-Saxon Community of St. Cuthbert', *HSJ* 4 (1993), 85–95.

[98] *Symeon*, Rollason, 220–1. 'Quedam etiam ex ornamentis ecclesie, inter que et baculum pastoralem materia et arte mirandam (erat enim de saphiro factus), prefatus episcopus abstulit, qui posito in castello militum presidio protinus abscessit.'

[99] *ASC*, 214. There is no indication that the arrest of Odo was connected to the famine. Odo, however, might have disagreed.

[100] John of Worcester, 3, 39.

why Odo was suddenly imprisoned.[101] The story that emerged in the 1120s was that Odo was arrested for trying to buy or win the office of pope. He apparently enticed a number of William's retainers and knights to join him on this Italian adventure, and when he was close to launching the campaign, he was arrested and imprisoned. Orderic claimed that Odo 'with his brother King William ruled the Normans and English.'[102] From this exalted (and exaggerated) position, Odo decided that he wanted to achieve singular greatness within the ecclesiastical sphere by making a bid for the papacy. He therefore attracted nobles and knights, including the powerful Hugh, earl of Chester, to his retinue in order to lead a military endeavor to Italy essentially to conquer Rome. For contemporaries, the most famous element of this episode was that Odo was imprisoned as an earl, not a bishop. Since the imprisonment of a bishop by a secular lord usually led to an outcry by ecclesiastical authorities, accommodation had to be made in order to get around this problem. His arrest precipitated a trial in which Orderic creates a speech for the king in which he justified his actions of seizing a bishop. He began by recounting that he had entrusted the government of England to Odo, but that Odo had cruelly oppressed the kingdom

> robbing churches of their estates and revenues, stripping them of the ornaments given by his predecessors and misleading my knights, whose duty was to guard England against Danes and Irishmen and others enemies who hate me, and planning to lead them to foreign kingdoms beyond the Alps, regardless of my interests.[103]

William then went on to bemoan the loss of treasures given to the churches of England by his predecessor, "'my brother, to whom I entrusted the regency of the whole realm, violently seized the riches, cruelly oppressed the poor, just now suborned the knights with empty hope and tormented the whole kingdom, shaking it to its foundations with unjust exaction.'"[104] When no one would seize Odo, William did it himself, thus causing Odo to protest his ecclesiastical status. William responded, "'I condemn neither a clerk nor a bishop, but arrest my earl, whom I have made viceroy in my kingdom, desiring to hear an account of the stewardship entrusted to him.'"[105]

---

[101] There are, of course, requisite dangers with relying on fifty-year-old evidence. See Orderic Vitalis, 4, xxvii–xxx. There remains, of course, the possibility that this length of time allowed further evidence to come to light.
[102] Ibid., 39.
[103] Ibid., 43.
[104] Ibid.
[105] Ibid.

Why was Orderic consciously creating a justification for William's actions? We will start with the idea that Odo was raping and pillaging the English churches, a claim designed to elicit condemnation from his clerical peers. The charge of stripping churches of their ornamentation is especially damning, since we have first-hand accounts of Odo doing just this from Symeon of Durham, during the 1080 campaign. Interestingly, Odo was not condemned by those writing about the 1080 campaign directly, perhaps because he was acting as an avenging instrument of God's will, sent to destroy those who had committed one of the worst crimes against the church that was possible, the murder of a bishop. Furthermore, Odo's ability to gain valuable and impressive church ornaments was of a definite benefit to those who enjoyed his patronage, as was discussed earlier. Many of these ornaments were used to beautify churches and monasteries in Normandy and England under his protection.[106] Thus, Orderic's attempt to condemn Odo's rapacity would have been met with far different reactions from those who did not benefit from his largesse than it would have been from those who did.

Orderic was probably not in favor, however, of secular lords imprisoning clerics. Clerical immunity was something near and dear to virtually all clerics. It is certainly an anomaly, on the face of it, to see a clerical author, especially one writing in the heyday of the reform movement, craft justifications for the violation of this principle. However, it was the prisoner, not the jailor, who caused this reaction. Orderic saw Odo as a worldly, secular cleric, and in this case he was working against King William's interests. Orderic, himself a determined royalist, accepted Odo's imprisonment at the king's hands, much as he probably would have accepted the imprisonment of any noble by the king for similar crimes, Odo's clerical status notwithstanding.[107] Orderic, however, was not alone in being unmoved by Odo's arrest. There is little evidence that Odo's arrest caused much of an uproar in ecclesiastical circles, though the lack of contrary arguments could easily be attributed to the lack of contemporary accounts of the trial, and the biases of the next generation of observers. In any case, William of Malmesbury dealt with the arrest only tangentially, and without Orderic's rhetorical flourishes. In his *Gesta Regum*, he mentioned Odo's scheme when recounting his elevation to the bishopric of Bayeux. In Book III, Section 277, he wrote,

> he almost succeeded in buying the see of Rome from the citizens in his own absence, by stuffing the wallets of pilgrims with letters and coin. When rival

---

[106] Bates, 'The Character and Career of Odo', 11 refers to Odo's use of post-Conquest spoils to buy loyalty, though Bates specifically is referring to lands.

[107] Holdsworth comments that Orderic condemned Odo for rebelling against the king, not for bearing arms. Holdsworth, 64.

throngs of knights from the whole kingdom hastened to join him on hearing of the journey he was planning, the king was furious and put him in chains, having explained that his fetters were not for the bishop of Bayeux but for the earl of Kent.[108]

Malmesbury went on to explain that incalculable treasures were unearthed from secret hiding places after Odo's arrest, treasures that were no doubt earmarked for bribes and wages in his quest to be made pope. In his *Gesta Pontificum Anglorum*, William had likened Odo to a modern-day Proteus, and praised Lanfranc for being able to use the royal courts to prevent Odo from despoiling Canterbury's estates.[109]

Malmesbury also introduced the fact that it was Lanfranc, not King William, who had formulated the elegant and scholastic notion that it was not the bishop being imprisoned but, rather, the earl. When writing about the 1088 rebellion (to be discussed below), Malmesbury recounted an earlier discussion between King William and Lanfranc in which the king was complaining about Odo. When Lanfranc suggested that William should simply lock up Odo, the king balked because Odo had the benefit of clergy. Lanfranc responded, laughing, "'No … you will not be arresting the bishop of Bayeux, you will be taking into custody the earl of Kent.'"[110] It is quite telling that it was Lanfranc, a respected canonist and scholar, who not only acquiesced to Odo's arrest, but actively advocated it.[111]

---

[108] William of Malmesbury, *Gesta Regum Anglorum*, ed. and trans. R.A.B. Mynors, R.M. Thomson, and M. Winterbottom, Vol. 1 (Oxford, 1998), 509. 'Itaque in aggerandis thesauris mirus, tergiversari mirae astutiae, pene papatum Romanum absens a civibus mercatus fuerat; peras peregrinorum epistolis et nummis infarciens. Cujus futuri itineris opinione cum certatim ex toto regno ad eum milites concurrerent, rex indigne ferens, compedibus irretivit; praefatus non se Baiocarum episcopum, sed comitem Cantiae prendere.' William of Malmesbury, *Gesta Regum Anglorum*, Vol. 2, ed. Thomas Duffy Hardy (London, 1840), 457.

[109] William of Malmesbury, *Gesta Pontificum Anglorum: The History of the English Bishops*, ed. and trans. Michael Winterbottom, Vol. 1 (Oxford, 2007), 102–3. Proteus was an early Greek sea-god, known for being changeable, malleable, and untrustworthy. He lent his name to the adjective 'protean', meaning multifarious and overly concerned with worldly things.

[110] Malmesbury, *Gesta Regum*, 545. This is all the more remarkable considering Lanfranc's reputation as a canonist. '"Non" (dixit) "episcopum Baiocarum capies, sed comitem Cantiae custodies."' William of Malmesbury, ed. Duffy, 488.

[111] Orderic Vitalis, 4, xxx. See also Douglas, *William I*, 243, Barlow, *William Rufus*, 38, and Bates, "The Character and Career of Odo", 15–16 for modern assessments of this episode. Douglas particularly does not seem willing to concede that Odo had planned to use military power to gain the Holy See, whereas an examination of his career to date would indicate that this was perfectly in keeping with his past endeavors. Barlow is

Ecclesiastical immunity was something that the reform papacy had championed, and thus Gregory VII wrote a letter to the king on Odo's behalf, though it was weak and doomed to failure. He wrote that the king had "'acted unworthily, putting worldly considerations before the law of God and having insufficient regard for the honour due to a priest.'"[112] The pope, however, failed to take additional steps against King William. We can explain, perhaps, Gregory's effective abandonment of Odo by referring to facts on the ground facing the pope. After 1080 he was under increasing military pressure from Emperor Henry IV, and he could not afford to spoil his relationship with the Normans of Sicily and Italy, to whom King William was a hero. Gregory also needed to keep England in his court in the papal schism, or at least out of the court of his rival, Clement III.[113] Indeed, the English kings would use the threat of embracing the anti-pope repeatedly during this period. Finally, we must not forget that Odo was arrested for plotting to seize the papacy, which probably would not have gone down well for the current occupant of the Holy See. Odo was not, however, being abandoned for his warrior abilities, as Orderic would have had us believe but, rather, because his jailor was too important for the pope to offend.

While Odo's arrest took him out of active governance of England and prevented him from furthering his career, it did not render him impotent or poor. Importantly, he was not dispossessed of his estates in England or Normandy. This enabled him to regain much of his power upon his release on the death of William I in 1087.[114] William Rufus's Christmas court was held in London, and most of the prelates of England and Normandy were there, including the recently released Odo.[115] Odo's ability to re-establish himself in his old lands, titles, and power bases speaks to his political acumen and his perceived value to the new administration. Within four months of his release he had regained his lands and honors almost entirely. He also began to cultivate a new relationship with Lanfranc, probably in order to ingratiate himself with the new king, to whom Lanfranc was a devoted servant. The two old men did not much like one another, and, as Lanfranc had a hand in Odo's arrest and imprisonment, this new détente probably struck

---

especially helpful for keeping in mind the rivalry that existed between Lanfranc, Odo, and Geoffrey of Coutances. Bates makes interesting suggestions as to why Odo would have wanted to become pope.

[112] Margaret Gibson, *Lanfranc of Bec* (Oxford, 1978), 136.

[113] See ibid., 134–7 for an overview of this affair.

[114] It should be noted that William was apparently unwilling to release Odo even as his death loomed, but finally acquiesced to the advice of his barons. This could indicate that Odo's offense was worse than previously thought, or it could be retroactive justification to bolster William's legacy, considering Odo's future role in rebellions.

[115] Barlow, *William Rufus*, 67.

contemporaries as equally odd. The new king welcomed Odo back, albeit grudgingly, as Odo showed himself to be a contrite and humbled servant.[116]

Soon after William Rufus became king, however, his brother Duke Robert of Normandy began a campaign to unseat him, with Odo right in the thick of the fighting.[117] Odo's generalship during the rebellion earned him no specialized condemnation for being a cleric on a battlefield; rather, he was condemned only for his perfidy and untrustworthiness. The chroniclers, who endorsed the legitimacy of William Rufus as king, took a dim view of this rebellion for a variety of reasons, not the least of which was the almost instinctual support clerics had for monarchs over rebels, and the fact that their own lord was Henry, king of England and duke of Normandy, whose claim had also been contested by his brother Robert.

Odo became one of Duke Robert's chief advisors, and between 1088 and 1095 the aged bishop was one of the duke's closest confidants. Contemporary observers in England saw Odo as the prime mover of the rebellion, and the chief commander of its most important military contingents.[118] He was a progenitor of the hostilities, not a mere follower or opportunistic noble lord seeking to enhance his position during the instability. Many of his confederates were members of the 'old guard' who had stood with William I, some of whom had helped him win the kingdom at Hastings.[119] Only a small part of the Norman nobility supported William Rufus, those from whom he garnered support being the native English power structure (a fact which the Anglo-Saxon Chronicle took as a point of pride) and the ecclesiastical leaders of England, with the exception of William, bishop of Durham.[120]

Once Easter came, the three bishops (Odo, Geoffrey of Coutances, and William) and their secular allies led armies throughout the countryside burning and pillaging, and then 'each traveled to his castle and manned and provisioned it as best they could.'[121] In the case of Odo, this meant making his base in the castle

---

[116] Ibid. Barlow suggests that Odo might have been genuine in his initially favorable reaction to William Rufus, but that he soured towards the new king when he elevated William, bishop of Durham, to be his chief advisor instead of Odo. The fact that William of St. Calais had been a protégé of Odo's would have galled him even further.

[117] See Barlow, *William Rufus*, 70–83 for a good summary of the campaign.

[118] *ASC*, 222–3. Odo, Geoffrey of Coutances, and William of St. Calais are the three main rebels listed.

[119] The Anglo-Saxon Chronicler stressed the 'French' (or, more importantly, not 'English') nature of the rebels. This was probably a matter of ethnic pride, as at another point the chronicler pointed out that the English always stood by their princes. See *ASC*, 222–3. See these same pages for a list of the conspirators. See also John of Worcester, 3, 49; cf. Orderic Vitalis, 4, 125.

[120] John of Worcester, 3, 49.

[121] *ASC*, 223. 'Sona swa hit com to þam Eastron. þa ferdon hi 7 hergodon 7 bærndon 7 aweston þæs cynges feorme hames. 7 eallra þæra manna land hi fordydon þe wæron

of Rochester. It was situated at the bridge over the Medway on Watling Street, the major Roman road that linked Dover to London by way of Canterbury. Rochester was walled, and had a motte-and-bailey castle guarding the south entrance to the city and the bridge. Odo controlled both the city and the castle. The choice of Rochester made great strategic sense, since it bisected the route from London to Canterbury and could be re-supplied and reinforced by sea. The primary target of Odo's plundering was the estates belonging to Lanfranc. Odo was killing two birds with one stone – he was depriving one of King William's major allies of his livelihood, and also getting cathartic vengeance on Lanfranc for his years of opposition and his complicity in Odo's imprisonment.

Once Odo was ensconced in Rochester, he received reinforcements from Duke Robert – five hundred knights, according to Orderic Vitalis.[122] These men were directly under Odo's command, and he placed them as a garrison in Rochester, probably until he could build a larger force around them to contend with William II. Odo and his allies hoped to convince various garrisons around the southeast to declare for Robert, and to use the disorders elsewhere in the kingdom as a diversion until they could build up their position. By holding Kent and Sussex, they could also control the flow of reinforcements into England.[123] While this made sense under the circumstances, it turned out to be a strategic blunder. King William had recognized very quickly that Odo was the linch pin and guiding force of the rebellion, and thus made destroying him his primary consideration. William was able to focus on a single target, since most of the conspirators were with Odo. The king set about reducing Odo's hold on Kent, before trying to tackle Rochester. William captured Tonbridge, and then invested Pevensey in an attempt to gain control of the coast and, hopefully, to capture Odo, as Odo had gone there personally to oversee its defenses. William, along with Archbishop Lanfranc, besieged Pevensey for six weeks. The port-city finally surrendered in early June. Odo was captured, and promised to go into exile after securing the surrender of Rochester. This he did, though not without controversy. While he was negotiating the surrender of the castle, he was 'seized' by the garrison, thus necessitating a siege by King William, which was successful and effectively ended the rebellion.

Orderic Vitalis provided the best evidence for the surrender of Rochester, and it will serve to underscore Odo's 'worldly' demeanor. After Rochester had surrendered (the second time), Orderic invented another debate as to what to do

innan þæs cynges holdscipe. 7 heora ælc ferde to his castele. 7 þone mannoden 7 metsoden swa hig betst mihton.'
[122] Orderic Vitalis, 4, 125; cf. John of Worcester, 3, 51.
[123] Barlow, *William Rufus*, 71.

with the defeated garrison and their episcopal commander. Odo initially asked for a confirmation of his fiefs, and promised to faithfully serve the king thereafter, to which the king, in anger, made a counter-offer of hanging the garrison on gibbets, or similarly removing them from the face of the earth.[124] Odo's concern was for his territories and titles, and his proffered service would have been based on these. After this exchange the other leading men serving the king pressed the king to be lenient. They supposedly argued, 'It is most proper that, just as you conquered them in their pride and folly by your strength, you should by your graciousness spare them now that they are humbled and penitent.'[125] The two sides then exchanged biblical support for their respective positions. The final argument designed to sway the king was that 'Odo of Bayeux is your uncle, and is a consecrated bishop. He helped your father dominate the English and stood by him in many dangers and anxieties … God forbid that you should lay hands on a priest of the Lord, or shed his blood.'[126] While Odo argued for leniency based in traditional chivalric terms, the magnates argued that it was both his status as a consecrated bishop that offered him protection against the king's vengeance, and also his earlier military actions and loyalty to William I. There is no indication that the English bishops in the king's camp, including Lanfranc, offered a refutation of this characterization. The utility of well-directed warfare was still appealing.

Odo's 'worldly' outlook was on further display when he asked the king not to have trumpets sounded as the garrison left.[127] This was a traditional action when a castle was taken by force, but was also seen as a humiliation to the dignity of the men leaving. There is quite the element of noble pride in this request. This is further evidence of the cultural milieu that formed Odo. He was part and parcel of the high nobility, and his clerical status did not change his sensibilities. Odo and his men had to leave while the English taunted them and called for their deaths. Orderic concluded, 'In this way the worldly bishop was banished from England, and stripped of his vast possessions.'[128] He had previously referred to Odo's 'magnificence', and had criticized his secular interests, and his criticisms here follow that same mold – Odo was a 'worldly' bishop whose ambition, arrogance, and secularity had led him to ruin.

Geoffrey of Coutances's actions during the 1088 rebellion did not elicit nearly as much comment as did those of Odo, and we rely on John of Worcester for our understanding of his role. John paired him with his brother Robert de Montbray,

---

[124] Orderic Vitalis, 4, 129.
[125] Ibid., 131.
[126] Ibid., 133.
[127] Ibid.
[128] Orderic Vitalis, 4, 135; cf. Barlow, *William Rufus*, 156–60.

and wrote that these two men, from their base at Bristol, plundered and destroyed the city of Bath. They then pushed on to Gloucester and besieged it, though this element of the campaign was apparently directed by Robert. John claimed that during their campaign they were 'sacking townships and slaughtering a multitude'.[129] What is especially interesting is that even though John was politically opposed to Geoffrey, and Geoffrey and Robert's campaigns involved the wholesale slaughter of fellow Christians, John never once cited against Geoffrey his ecclesiastical status as a general and rebel. We can reasonably presume that if Geoffrey's being an episcopal general was truly offensive, John would have made use of it against him.

When we examine the last stages of Odo and Geoffrey's careers, we can see the tensions inherent in their prior experiences. Odo's defeat in 1088 forced him to focus his attentions on Normandy full time, and caused him to show more interest in his ecclesiastical establishments and responsibilities. He quickly became his nephew Duke Robert's chief councilor and advisor, and was credited by later men such as Orderic for helping to stiffen the notoriously weak spine of the duke. In one very famous example, Orderic recorded an invigorating speech by Odo that called upon Robert to pluck up his courage and use his power to put an end to the lawlessness ravaging Normandy and to defend his subjects. He likened the duke's enemies to pagans, and he implored the duke to act on behalf of the widows and monks crying out to him for protection.[130] He then gave an accounting of historical personages designed for Robert to emulate, which included King David, Alexander the Great, Julius Caesar, Hannibal, Rollo, William Longsword, and even his father William I of England.[131] Odo argued that bold, courageous action was needed to destroy the duke's enemies, such as the Bellêmes, as well as to expand the duke's power and authority, and finally to protect the interests of the church. Odo's advice is highly dependent on and deferential to military power, and extols the manly use of the sword and the importance of displays of prowess to achieve beneficial ends. While all of these speeches are probably imaginary, it is important that this was how Orderic imagined Odo would and should have argued, given the opportunity.

Robert took his advice and launched a campaign into the turbulent county of Maine, with Odo as one of his featured military commanders. Odo was given pride of place in the list of ducal commanders, and was clearly a part of this group of men whom Orderic referred to 'warriors of conspicuous courage.'[132] This is a

---

[129] John of Worcester, 3, 53.
[130] Orderic Vitalis, 4, 151.
[131] Ibid.
[132] Ibid., 155. Despite the success of his campaign, Robert made a truce with his enemies that failed to solve the problems plaguing the duchy.

clear recognition of Odo's military value and his military reputation. His bravery, courage, and prowess were never in question, and even at his advanced age his chivalric abilities still caused some awe and respect from men such as Orderic. Thus, it was not Odo's warlike prowess that caused his downfall or condemnation, it was his secularity and worldliness; when he fought for 'noble' causes (such as bringing stability to Normandy), he elicited more sympathetic treatment in the sources.

Ultimately, using Orderic as our guide, we can see that Odo's activities were very much a mixed bag for his contemporaries and his near-contemporary observers. In a summary judgment on his career, Orderic wrote, 'He was a man of eloquence and statesmanship, bountiful and most active in worldly business. He held men of religion in great respect, readily defended his clergy by words and arms, and enriched his church in every way with gifts of precious ornaments.'[133] Here is explicit reference to Odo's use of military power, and it is cast in a very personal sense, in that he used a sword and words to defend his clergy. His motivations are laudable, in that his use of prowess was for his clerical subordinates. There is no condemnation in Orderic's passage, and ultimately Orderic claimed that Odo had done both good and evil during his fifty-year reign. Sometimes the spirit triumphed, and other times worldly concerns did.

Orderic also wrote of Odo's patronage and his value to his churches. He wrote that, despite being 'a slave to worldly trivialities, externally he brought about many improvements in the church's welfare.'[134] Odo was a bishop overly concerned with secular and worldly things, but his secularity and worldliness benefited the infrastructure of his church, and the church in Normandy in general. For all of his faults, his actions often benefited the clergy and the fabric of the church. For instance, when Odo was imprisoned, his newly founded monastery of St. Vigor was dispersed. The abbot, whom Orderic considered 'a learned and pious man', went into exile in Rome and the house disbanded. Thus, without Odo's patronage and protection, this worthy house of God fell apart. Contemporaries would not have missed the irony in that the cause of the Spirit's being set back was the imprisonment of this most worldly of bishops. Once Odo was released, he re-established the house under Gerento, abbot of Dijon, and the monastery flourished. Ultimately, Orderic criticized Odo for being worldly, but what he meant was a lust for wealth and power, and even these Odo often bestowed on his churches and clergy. Critiques of his concern with secular affairs did not necessarily include his military activities. While some observers clearly sought to minimize his active role in combat and military affairs, this was not always because of devotion to

[133] Ibid., 115–17.
[134] Ibid., 117.

pacifism or a desire to take the clergy out of warfare but, rather, because Odo was seen as utilizing military force in pursuit of worldly, rather than spiritual aims.[135] We can see throughout the careers of Odo, Geoffrey, and others, that military service was not, in and of itself, a condemnable behavior; rather, it was the manner in which a cleric fought, and in what cause. A noble cause (defending the king, pacifying the realm), fought without ostentation, would be treated very differently than fighting to expand one's own power or unseat legitimate authority.

---

[135] David Bates argues that Odo was not as remarkable as we often think, and that he was very similar to other prelates of his day. See Bates, 'The Character and Career of Odo', 20. I tend to agree with him, and it further underscores the argument of this chapter that Odo was not a pariah for being a warrior bishop. Odo was criticized for taking on the trappings of a worldly prelate. His knightliness transgressed the prescriptive boundaries between clerics and knights, and offended chroniclers.

CHAPTER 5

Negotiating a New Anglo-Norman Reality

WHILE King William I brought a number of men from Normandy to administer England, he also utilized others from further afield and from within the conquered kingdom. These included the Italian Lanfranc, who became archbishop of Canterbury, and Wulfstan, the Anglo-Saxon bishop of Worcester. These men served as a core of loyal royal servants who were intimately involved in William's government and his military endeavors. His son William elevated Anselm of Bec (from the French/Italian borderlands) to become archbishop of Canterbury upon Lanfranc's death. Lanfranc was a closer partner to William I in royal government than Anselm was to either William II or Henry I, but both served in warfare to one extent or another on behalf of their king. Despite this military service, their avoidance of a knightly lifestyle and worldly interests allowed them to avoid criticism (unlike Odo of Bayeux). This chapter examines their roles and reputations, and then contrasts them with the example of Bishop Gaudry of Laon, who was one of the most controversial ecclesiastical figures during the same period. There was a broad spectrum of possible clerical actions in military activities, and Anselm and Lanfranc represent one end of this spectrum – they did not charge into battle in full armor alongside their knights – but were still directing troops, defenses, and royal campaigns. This acceptance is especially important for our purposes precisely because of the leading theological and ecclesiastical roles that some these men played. Lanfranc and Anselm were both respected archbishops of Canterbury, while Wulfstan was a nearly saintly paragon of episcopal spirituality. Gaudry, on the other hand, represents the polar opposite. Like Remigius of Fécamp, who became bishop of Dorchester in return for his service at Hastings, Gaudry became bishop of Laon after his military service at the battle of Tinchebrai in 1106. Unlike Remigius, controversy surrounded Gaudry from the time of his elevation and subsequent murder, and this underscores the debatable nature of the legitimate role of clerics in warfare.

We have already discussed Lanfranc of Canterbury's coordination of the royal response to the rebellion of 1075, but we should consider it more deeply. The existing sources make it very clear that Lanfranc served as the overall head of the royal war effort against the rebels. The simultaneous revolt of major landowners and military lords in the West Country, East Anglia, and Northumbria threatened to overwhelm royal forces in the king's absence. Archbishop Lanfranc, serving as the king's justiciar, immediately took action to deal with the rebellion. He was dedicated to preserving peace in the kingdom and driven by his personal loyalty to William I. William probably had chosen Lanfranc for a variety of reasons, including his sterling ecclesiastical reputation, but also because Lanfranc did not have many powerful friends in England and would thus be dependent on the king for support and protection.[1] While some have argued that Lanfranc's comfort with secular service was because he was an 'old-fashioned', Carolingian-style traditionalist, it seems likelier that Lanfranc's vision for himself as a co-author of royal action was a reflection of his affinity to the early reform popes – Nicholas II, Leo IX, and Alexander II.[2] He made multiple trips to Rome prior to 1073, and he had affection for some of the chief reformers at the papal court.[3] Lanfranc was not, therefore, an ecclesiastical or ideological outlier in the later eleventh century but was, rather, representative of a sizeable number of ecclesiastics who saw no conflict between the ideals of the reform papacy and the exercise of secular power.

Eadmer, Anselm's biographer, remarked that Lanfranc was William I's chief advisor and counselor during this period.[4] According to Milo Crispin, who wrote the *Vita Lanfranci* a couple of generations later, during the 1075 rebellion Lanfranc was called *princeps et custos Angliae*, or the 'prince and protector of England', and it was a role at which he excelled.[5] All of these factors are consistent

---

[1] Gibson, *Lanfranc of Bec*, 156. For an overview of how Lanfranc and Anselm saw their roles as royal advisors and archbishops, see Jean Truax, *Archbishops Ralph d'Escures, William of Corbeil, and Theobald of Bec: Heirs of Anselm and Ancestors of Becket* (Farnham, 2012), 10–26.

[2] Ibid., 191; cf. H.E.J. Cowdrey, 'The Enigma of Archbishop Lanfranc', *HSJ* 6 (Woodbridge, 1995), 132–9. Lanfranc combined a 'zeal for canon law' with a willingness and aptitude to serve secular powers. See Gibson, *Lanfranc of Bec*, 139. Lanfranc's zeal was demonstrative in the fact that he brought his canon law collection into England and disseminated it. Ironically, it was from Lanfranc's own collection that William of St. Calais cited canonical precedents at his trial of 1088, a trial in which he was opposed by Lanfranc. Lanfranc also relied on the Pseudo-Isidorian Decretals to support William Rufus during the succession crisis of 1087–88. See Neil Strevett, 'The Anglo-Norman Civil War of 1101 Reconsidered', *Anglo-Norman Studies* 24, ed. John Gillingham (Woodbridge, 2002), 170–1. For a broader discussion of both Lanfranc and Anselm's intellectual approach and background, see Suzanne J. Nelis, 'What Lanfranc Taught, What Anselm Learned', *HSJ* 2, ed. Robert Patterson (Woodbridge, 1990), 75–82. See also Sally Vaughn's excellent volume on Anselm, *Archbishop Anselm 1093–1109: Bec Missionary, Canterbury Primate, Patriarch of Another World* (Farnham, 2012), esp. 23–48.

[3] Cowdrey, 'Archbishop Lanfranc', 133–6.

[4] Eadmer, *History of Recent Events in England*, trans. Geoffrey Bosanquet (London, 1964), 12.

[5] Milo Crispin, *Vita Lanfranci*, ed. D'Achery, *Lanfranci Opera (ut supra)*, ed. Migne (1854), Cap. 15. The full sentence reads, 'Quando gloriosus rex Vuillelmus morabatur

with the ideals of the reform papacy, which sought to empower clerics in their relations with secular powers, but to not disassociate them from secular power. The ideal of faithfully serving the church while working with the king (including in military service) was not something that was anathema to many late eleventh-century prelates (nor those of later periods), and to construct a conformist ideology to the contrary unfairly characterizes one group as normative and somehow more 'legitimate' than another. We are able to gain an insight into how Lanfranc himself saw his actions because some of his letters have survived, and they do not contain any sense that he was behaving improperly by actively directing royal military campaigns.

Lanfranc's letters to the king discussing the campaign against the rebels are couched in questions of honor and reputation, chivalric concerns not unlike those of a secular noble. We cannot separate these men from the cultural milieu of their times, and Lanfranc was no exception. He wrote to Earl Roger of Hereford asking that the earl 'imitate the loyalty of his father, Earl William' and turn away from rebellion.[6] This initial letter did not sway the earl, and as the rebellion gathered steam Lanfranc was forced to write again, appealing to the earl as a father would to a son (as befit his pastoral duty),

> I grieve more than I can say at the unwelcome news I hear of you. It would not be right that a son of Earl William – a man whose sagacity and integrity and loyalty to his lord and all his friends is renowned in many lands – should be called faithless and be exposed to the slur of perjury or any kind of deceit … I therefore beg you, as a son whom I cherish and the dearest of friends … if you are guilty of such conduct to return to your senses; and if you are not, to demonstrate this by the clearest possible evidence.[7]

---

in Normannia, Lanfrancus erat princeps et custos Angliae, subjectus sibi omnibus principibus, et juvantibus in his quae ad defensionem, et dispositionem, vel pacem pertinebant regni, secundum leges patriae.' See also Sally N. Vaughn, *Anselm of Bec and Robert of Meulan: The Innocence of the Dove and the Wisdom of the Serpent* (Berkeley, 1987), 156–7.

[6] *Regesta Regum Anglo-Normannorum*, ed. H.W.C. Davis, Vol. I (Oxford, 1913), 20–1, #78.

[7] *The Letters of Lanfranc Archbishop of Canterbury*, ed. and trans. Helen Clover and Margaret Gibson, Vol. 1 (Oxford, 1979), 120–1, #32. The Latin reads, 'Auditis de te quae audire nollem, doleo quantum dicere non possum. Neque enim deceret ut filius Willelmi comitis – cuius prudentia et bonitas et erga dominum suum et omnes amicos suos fidelitas multis terris innotuit – infidelis diceretur, et de periurio vel faude aliqua infamiam pateretur … Propterea rogo te dulcissimie fili et carissime amice … si culpam de tali re habes, resipiscas; si vero non habes, manifestissimis documentis te non habere ostendas.'

Lanfranc embraced his role as a paternal spiritual advisor looking out for the well-being of the rebellious earl, as would a caring father. He was utilizing his role as prelate while also actively directing the war effort against Roger and his conspirators. His use of the spiritual capital of the archbishopric in the fighting of a rebellion against the king neatly demonstrates the unity of the spiritual and the military in royal service that Lanfranc saw as his duty. These letters came to naught, and a final letter from Lanfranc indicated the futility of further attempts at negotiation. In the last letter that he sent to Earl Roger, Lanfranc made clear that his patience was at an end. He wrote,

> But because the devil's prompting and the advice of evil men have led you into an enterprise which under no circumstances should you have attempted, necessity has forced me to change my attitude and turn my affection not so much into hate as into bitterness and the severity of justice ... Therefore I have cursed and excommunicated you and all your adherents by my authority as archbishop; I have cut you off from the holy precincts of the Church and the assembly of the faithful, and by my pastoral authority I have commanded this to take effect throughout the whole land of England.[8]

Lanfranc was speaking in this instance in his capacity as the ecclesiastical head of the English church. His excommunication of the rebels freed their vassals from their oaths of loyalty and it placed the rebels' souls in jeopardy. Lanfranc did not, however, limit his response to the rebellion to the spiritual realm. Royal forces were also busy making successful inroads into rebel-held areas. These forces were commanded by Bishop Wulfstan of Worcester, Abbot Æthelwig of Evesham, William of Warenne, and Richard de Clare; they prevented Earl Roger and Earl Ralph from linking their forces at the river Severn.[9] William I had entrusted Æthelwig, also a native Englishman, with control over much of the western Midlands.[10] The

---

[8] Lanfranc, 122–3, #33A. 'Sed quia instinctu demonis et consilio prauorum hominum ea molitus es quae te moliri minime oportuerat, necessitate coactus mentem mutaui, et dilectionem non in odium tantam quantum in rancorem mentis et iustuam seueritatem conuerti ... Canonica igitur auctoritate te et omnes adiutores tuos maledixi et excommunicaui atque a liminibus sanctae aecclesiae et consortio fidelium separaui, et per totam Anglicam terram hoc idem pastorali auctoritate fieri imperaui.'

[9] *The Chronicle of John of Worcester*, ed. and trans. P. McGurk, Vol. 3 (Oxford, 1998), 24–5. Gibson comments on this, 'In William's absence abroad it was Lanfranc who had the overall direction of Wulfstan and Aethelwig holding the line of the Severn and the bishops of Bayeux and Coutances with Richard fitz Gilbert and William of Warenne containing the eastern rebels within Norfolk and Cambridgeshire.' Gibson, *Lanfranc of Bec*, 156.

[10] R.R. Darlington, 'Æthelwig, abbot of Evesham', *EHR* 48 (1933), 11–18. For the original, see *Chronicon Abbatiæ de Evesham*, ed. William D. Macray, RS 29 (London, 1863), 89.

abbot also had a history of seeking to ameliorate the suffering caused by war and thus probably felt compelled to protect his region from destructive rebellion.[11]

With this defeat (at the battle of Fagaduna, according to John of Worcester), Earl Ralph fled back to his castle at Norwich with the royal forces in hot pursuit. They besieged his castle for three months, during which time Lanfranc wrote to William I and begged him not to return to England until the rebellion had been subdued. This was not because of any danger to the king's person, but rather because the king 'would be offering us a grave insult were you to come to our assistance in subduing such perjured brigands.'[12] Lanfranc was taking pride in the undertaking, and had linked his honor to its successful prosecution. He had not shirked his duty to direct the campaign, nor did he turn it over to a secular noble; he was actively investing his own honor into the proceedings and he saw its successful prosecution as a reflection of his efficacy as justiciar, and perhaps as archbishop as well. After a siege of three months the castle surrendered, though Earl Ralph escaped to Brittany. Lanfranc sent word of the victory at Norwich to William I, writing,

> Glory be to God on high, by whose mercy your kingdom has been purged of its Breton dung. Norwich castle has been surrendered and those Bretons in it who held lands in England have been granted their lives and spared mutilation ... Bishop Geoffrey [of Coutances], William of Warenne and Robert Malet have remained in the castle itself with three hundred heavily-armed soldiers, supported by a large force of slingers and siege engineers.[13]

The fall of Norwich and the flight of Ralph essentially ended the rebellion. Earl Waltheof was already in William's custody and Earl Roger had been unable to recover his strategic position after his defeat at the Severn.[14] One final action

---

[11] Æthelwig had earlier gained accolades for aiding the refugees from William's earlier destructive campaigns in the North. See Macray, *Chronicon Abbatiæ de Evesham*, 90. See also R.R. Darlington, 'Æthelwig, abbot of Evesham (Continued)', *EHR* 48 (1933), 177–85. Unfortunately, the *Chronicon* is silent on Æthelwig's actions during the 1075 rebellion. See Darlington, 'Æthelwig, abbot of Evesham', 4–5.

[12] Lanfranc, 124–5, #34. 'quia magnum dedecus nobis faceretis si pro talibus periuris et latronibus uincendis ad nos ueniretis.'

[13] Lanfranc, 124–7, #35. 'Glorio in excelsis Deo cuius misercordia regnum uestrum purgatum est spurcicia Britonum. Castrum Noruuich redditum est, et Britones qui in eo erant et terras in Anglica terra habebant, concessa eis vita cum menbris ... In ipson castro remanserunt episcopus Gausfridus, W. de Warenna, Rob. Malet et trecenti loricati cum eis, cum balistariis et artificibus machinarum multis.'

[14] After the end of the rebellion Roger obeyed a summons of the king where he was judged guilty of rebellion. He was stripped of his holdings and condemned to a life of perpetual imprisonment. He later died in prison. See Orderic Vitalis, 2, 318–19.

remained to be taken, though, and this was in response to a feared Danish invasion of the northern parts of the country that the rebels had attempted to arrange. Royal forces in the North were placed under the control of Bishop Walcher of Durham. With Waltheof implicated in the rebellion, Walcher represented the chief royal figure north of York. It was left to him to defend this vital area against rebellion, possible invasion from Scotland, and possible invasion from Denmark. Lanfranc wrote to him after the fall of Norwich castle with the intention of securing the defense of the North, 'The Danes are indeed coming, as the king told us. So fortify your castle with men, weapons and stores: be ready.'[15] As it turned out, the king had faulty intelligence and the Danes were unable to invade; the North was secure. When Waltheof was executed by William I upon his return to England, Bishop Walcher was made earl of Northumbria.[16]

Lanfranc's successor as archbishop, Anselm of Bec (r. 1093–1109), was also involved in military affairs in England during his period in office. While his military activities featured more personal involvement than had Lanfranc's, he had less actual direct oversight of military operations (due to the presence of the king in England, unlike in 1075). Anselm saw a role for clerics in secular affairs when he deemed it necessary in the service of a greater good, and provided that they did not fall victims to worldliness in the course of their secular duties. He argued that a monk could perform secular service if ordered by his abbot, and that he could avoid sin by

> doing nothing for vainglory; by doing nothing that God forbids because of any hope of gain; by so carrying out the task enjoined on his obedience that he both protects and preserves the goods of the church manfully and justly against all men, and yet tries to bring nothing belonging to another into his church's possession by injustice.[17]

Eadmer, who discussed Anselm's actions in both his *Historia Novorum* (ending in 1122) as well as in his *Vita Anselmi* (written c.1124), portrayed Anselm as believing that worldliness and personal pride were to be condemned, but that secular service was not, in and of itself, a terrible thing. A cleric was to protect his church

---

[15] Lanfranc, 126–7, #36. 'Dani ut rex nobis mandauit reuera ueniunt. Castrum itaque uestrum et hominibus et armis et aliementis uigilanti cura muniri facite.'

[16] *Symeon*, Rollason, 212–13.

[17] Eadmer, *The Life of Saint Anselm*, ed. and trans. R.W. Southern (Oxford, 1962), 76. 'Nichil per inanem iactantiam agat, nichil quod Deus prohibet cuiuslibet lucri gratia faciat. Oboedientiae quae sibi iniuncta est ita studeat, ut et res aecclesiae contra omnes viriliter iusteque tueatur et protegat, et de alieno per iniustitiam sub dominium aecclesiae nil redigere satagat.'

vigorously and with justice, but he should never seek out personal gain, nor the gain of his church through illicit means.[18]

Eadmer, as both a biographer of Anselm and also a historian of contemporary England, gives us a unique insight into how Anselm saw the world and his role as an archbishop. Eadmer was an intimate of Anselm's, and thus his portrait of the archbishop is personal.[19] Anselm, who was later sanctified, was a controversial figure for contemporaries – not for his actions in warfare but, rather, for his self-imposed exile from England in a dispute with the king over ecclesiastical liberties (this was during the height of the Investiture Controversy). Eadmer tried to show Anselm as saintly from the earliest examples of his life and career, and this casts Anselm's actions in an even more intriguing light, since Eadmer was using Anselm's career as an example of sanctity, and while he certainly reinforced Anselm's rejection of the secular and worldly as evidence for his holiness, Eadmer did not extend that paradigm to his military activities.[20] Eadmer likened the relationship of Lanfranc and Anselm to the king as similar to the ideal example demonstrated by the relationship between Dunstan and King Edgar, where archbishop and king worked hand in hand to govern England.[21]

Anselm's priorities were the protection of the perquisites of Canterbury, even above the controversy over lay investiture, and the avoidance of simony.[22] These priorities could lead to famous breaches with the king, as when Anselm voluntarily went into exile during the later years of William II's reign, but they could also lead to close cooperation between the archbishop and king, including in military affairs. In general, however, Anselm was personally disinterested in secular affairs, and his involvement in warfare should be seen primarily as a result of his loyalty to the king and as his basic acceptance of his role as defender of Canterbury. Eadmer explained that, in secular affairs, Anselm always 'delegated the business of the monastery to the care and attention of brethren in whose uprightness and energy

---

[18] Vaughn gives an excellent overview of the changing images of Anselm the politician, from Southern's conception of him as a naïve churchman buffeted by political forces, Cantor's image of him as a political supporter of papal authority in the investiture controversy, or her own conception that he was an independent political actor navigating both sides. See Vaughn, *Archbishop Anselm 1093–1109*, 3–22.

[19] Michael Staunton, 'Eadmer's *Vita Anselmi*: A reinterpretation', *Journal of Medieval History* 23, No. 1 (1997), 1–2.

[20] Ibid., 3. Richard Southern believed, however, that the *Vita Anselmi* only later was used as the basis for a hagiography. See Staunton, *Vita Anselmi*, 2.

[21] Eadmer, *History of Recent Events in England*, 3. See also Eadmer's *Vita Sancti Dunstani* in *Memorials of Saint Dunstan, archbishop of Canterbury*, ed. William Stubbs (London, 1874), 162–222.

[22] Vaughn, *Anselm of Bec and Robert of Meulan*, 149. See also Vaughn, *Archbishop Anselm 1093–1109*, 136.

he had confidence, and he gave himself up continually to the contemplation of God, and to the instruction, admonishment and correction of the monks.'[23] If something came up that he had to deal with, he did so 'as justice required, according to the circumstances and nature of the case.'[24] Eadmer portrayed Anselm as not seeking out secular service, but also not shirking his responsibilities to his king and diocese. Since we know that Anselm took an active military role in both 1095 and 1101, we can conclude that he saw these activities as necessary and that it would have been unjust for him to refuse. Anselm was neither a strict canonist nor a reformer who saw secular service as inherently evil but, was, rather, one who simply had little interest in it. He was a deeply spiritual leader, but he was not overtly ideological. Eadmer commented on Anselm's disinterest in secularity later in his biography when he wrote that 'Secular business ... was something which he could not patiently abide, and he used every pretext to withdraw himself from it so far as he could.'[25] So, given Anselm's obvious distaste for and disinterest in secular affairs, how do we account for his embrace of a military role during his archiepiscopate? Was it purely the result of his obligations as archbishop, or did he see a licit role for himself beyond that expected of him? Anselm's support of William II in 1095 and of Henry I in 1101 indicates that he did not equate engaging in warfare when times were dire with the more general secular service that he warned against. Defending the king during a war, or protecting one's city, was not the same as throwing oneself fully into a courtly life to the detriment of one's spiritual well-being. Anselm's actions also reinforce the argument made throughout this book, that avoidance of worldliness was a more important concern for most churchmen than rejecting military power.

Eadmer may have been overselling Anselm's opposition to and interaction with secular affairs in general and military affairs in particular. During the baronial rebellion of Robert de Montbray in 1095, Eadmer recorded the conflict over the obtaining of the pallium and the recognition of Urban II, but completely

---

[23] Eadmer, *The Life of Saint Anselm*, 45. 'Delegatis itaque monasterii causis curae ac sollicitunidini fratrum de quorum vita et strenuitate certus erat, ipse Dei contemplationi, monachorum eruditioni, admonitioni, correctioni iugister insistebat.'

[24] Ibid.

[25] Ibid., 80. 'Secularia vero negotia aequanimiter ferre nequibat, sed pro posse suo modis omnibus suam eis praesentiam subtrahebat.' R.W. Southern endorses Eadmer's view, arguing that Anselm had 'turned his back on the world' as a monk and that so 'far as we can judge, this general attitude of abhorrence overpowered all other thoughts about practical questions, even questions like the defence of the eastern empire, the Crusade, or the reduction of freemen to servitude, which have obvious spiritual implications.' R.W. Southern, *Saint Anselm and his Biographer: A Study of Monastic Life and Thought 1059–c.1130* (Cambridge, 1966), 122.

ignored Anselm's involvement in defending Canterbury on behalf of the king.[26] For Anselm's involvement, and his view of his role, we must rely on his own letters. Southern argues that Anselm was seemingly untouched by the reform of the papacy under Gregory, and that his 'desire was for royal co-operation, and he persisted in this course despite all Rufus' delays.'[27] This cooperation extended to military affairs as well; Anselm himself noted approvingly that when William took his army into Scotland, the king left him with the serious business of guarding Canterbury. He was so earnest about this duty that he put off meeting the papal legate who had brought his pallium. We must recall that Kent was not necessarily a secure area of royal power, and that only seven years earlier, under the control of Odo of Bayeux, it had been one of the centers of resistance against William II. Thus, the military defense of Canterbury, especially with the king taking the chief royal army to the other end of the country, was an important military command.[28]

In June of 1095, Anselm wrote to Bishop Walter of Albano, the papal legate, informing him that he would be unable to meet with him to discuss reforming the English church because he was busy defending Canterbury while William II was in the North. He wrote that he dared

> not move from Canterbury at all because we are daily expecting enemies from across the sea to invade England through those ports which are close to Canterbury. For this reason my lord the King himself commanded me ... to guard Canterbury and always to be prepared, so that at whatever hour I receive a message from those guarding the coast for that purpose, I should command the knights and foot-soldiers to be summoned from all quarters and to hasten to resist the violent attacks of the enemies. That is why I dare not leave Canterbury, except [to go to] those areas where we expect the arrival of the enemies.[29]

Anselm prioritized both his personal defense of Canterbury against attack and his loyalty to William II over the opportunity to discuss ecclesiastical reform.[30] He

---

[26] Barlow, *William Rufus*, 349. However, Eadmer's later reporting of Anselm's active role in suppressing the 1101 noble rebellion undermines this interpretation. I suspect that Eadmer did not include the 1095 episode because it came to nothing, rather than because of some basic opposition to Anselm's role. Eadmer's inclusion of Anselm's 1101 military role, and probably exaggeration of it, indicates that he was proud of Anselm's service.
[27] R.W. Southern, *Saint Anselm: A Portrait in a Landscape* (Cambridge, 1990), 252. For originals, see Anselm, *Letters*, #191 and 192.
[28] Barlow, *William Rufus*, 349.
[29] Anselm of Canterbury, *Letters*, trans. Walter Fröhlich, Vol. 2 (Kalamazoo, 1994), 115.
[30] In addition to his duties in serving as the defender of Canterbury, Anselm was also not enthralled with the idea of enfranchising papal legates with greater authority, as a strong papal voice could certainly curtail episcopal independence. See Southern, *Saint*

also demonstrated a willingness and comfort with taking a personal role in the defense, both as the overall strategic commander and as a direct participant in the campaign. He made clear that he would leave Canterbury only to go to 'those areas where we expect the arrival of the enemies.'[31] Beyond just sending the knights in the command of someone else, he was prepared to go with them personally into the field. A subsequent letter reinforced the importance of Anselm's mission to defend Canterbury, stressing that William had instructed him to defend the region 'carefully' and to be daily prepared to resist the enemy.[32] Anselm explicitly stated that this excuse was 'reasonable and acceptable', thus demonstrating his belief that serving the king militarily was acceptable and exculpatory, and could even take priority over ecclesiastical duties. As Frank Barlow points out, Anselm seemed to embrace this military role 'almost, it would seem, with relish', and his tone betrayed a certain patriotism.[33] Anselm certainly served as a defender of the kingdom, though since he had done homage to William II for his Canterbury properties it could be said that he was obliged to offer such service to the king. Questions such as this precipitated Anselm's decision to enter voluntary exile in 1097, where he remained for three years.

After William Rufus's death in 1100, and the accession of Henry I, Anselm returned from exile and began promoting the interests of the new king. This included supporting Henry against his elder brother Duke Robert of Normandy. In 1101, many of the English nobles, including such powerful figures as Robert of Bellême, rebelled against Henry. Anselm again, according to Eadmer, came to the defense of his king. Eadmer wrote ('proudly' according to C. Warren Hollister), 'Father Anselm, loyally supporting the King, camped with his men in the field.'[34]

Anselm and His Biographer, 253–5. Anselm's relative independence from the papal centralization tendencies of the Gregorian reforms can also be seen in his general use of 'common sense' in resolving conflicts, rather than strict reliance on canon law. Anselm relied on 'general principles' to argue his positions, much more than 'canon law'. He even exhibited some annoyance with those '"who would not be persuaded by any other argument than authority."' See Southern, *Saint Anselm and His Biographer*, 255–6. See also Anselm, *Letters*, 2, 56. n. 3.

[31] Anselm, *Letters*, 2, 115.
[32] Ibid., 118.
[33] Barlow, *William Rufus*, 349.
[34] Eadmer, *History of Recent Events in England*, 132. For the original, see Eadmer, *Historia Novorum in Anglia*, ed. M. Rule (London, 1884), 127. 'Exercitus vero grandis erat atque robustus, et circa regem fideliter cum suis in expeditione excubabat pater Anselmus.' Anselm's role in defense of Henry's interest is similar to what Eadmer claimed he had done with Pope Urban II during his exile. Anselm and the pope traveled to the siege of Capua, which was being conducted by Roger of Apulia, and they camped in the field with the armies. See Eadmer, *History of Recent Events in England*, 101. For Hollister's characterization, see C. Warren Hollister, *Henry I* (Yale, 2001), 137.

Eadmer was notably proud of Anselm's support of Henry I, and he probably was inflating the archbishop's importance to the royal cause. For instance, once Robert had landed and the nobles prepared to desert Henry, Anselm took a leading role in seeking to craft a peace in order to avoid war.[35] Anselm's loyalty to Henry is noteworthy, and serves as an important contrast with the actions of men such as Odo of Bayeux and Geoffrey of Coutances in 1088. In that instance they had actively supported Robert against William Rufus, and were excoriated by chroniclers for that support.[36] In this case, Anselm was supporting the anointed king against his elder brother, and his support was both praised by contemporaries and reciprocated by Henry. Eadmer wrote, 'The King himself, apprehensive not only of losing his kingdom but even for his life, could not believe anyone or trust anyone except Anselm.'[37] Eadmer went so far as openly to state that without Anselm, Henry would have lost the throne.[38] If Anselm did not play as crucial a role as Eadmer suggested, the latter's exaggeration shows the cultural value of claiming Anselm's loyal and vital support for the king. Eadmer clearly saw an advantage in painting Anselm as a loyal supporter of Henry I, and he did so in such a way as to draw attention to Anselm's military service. While there is no indication that Anselm served in an overtly violent fashion, his willingness to involve himself in military affairs is noteworthy and did not equate to embracing secularity or undermining the rights and independence of Canterbury. As we saw in chapter 4, criticism of prelates in this period was often based on their overt worldliness, rather than on military service. As Anselm was indifferent, if not hostile, to most secular activities, his activities in war were not generally used to criticize him.

---

[35] Eadmer, *History of Recent Events in England*, 133. 'Quod sic esse Anselmus certu relatu agnoscens, doluit, coque magis nequid adversi regi accideret intendere coepit.' Eadmer, *Historia Novorum in Anglia*, 127.

[36] Neil Strevett points out that there were no threats of excommunication for the losing side in 1088 or 1101, unlike in 1075. This could mean that churchmen did not see the 1088 and 1101 wars as rebellions in the same fashion as 1075. See Strevett, 171–2.

[37] Ibid. 'Rex ipse non modo de regni admissione, sed et de vita sua suspectus, nulli credere, in nullo, excepto Anselmo, fidere valebat.' Anselm's role as ecclesiastical supporter of Henry I was mirrored by that of Robert Bloet, bishop of Lincoln. During the rebellion of Robert of Bellême in 1102, Henry sent Bishop Robert to Tickhill to lead the siege of the castle there. Robert's role is neither praised nor condemned by John of Worcester, who reported it. He was referred to in the same manner as a secular lord would have been. See John of Worcester, 3, 101. For a useful discussion of this campaign, see C.W. Hollister, 'The Campaign in 1102 against Robert of Bellême,' *Studies in Medieval History Presented to R. Allen Brown*, ed. C. Harper-Bill, C. Holdsworth, and J.L. Nelson (Woodbridge, 1989).

[38] Eadmer, *History of Recent Events in England*, 133. Vaughn, *Anselm of Bec and Robert of Meulan*, 234. Strevett also believes that Anselm's support of the king was important. See Strevett, 161.

Like Anselm and Lanfranc, Bishop Wulfstan (c. 1008–1095) of Worcester earned positive treatment by chroniclers for his stout defense of his region and royal interests. Wulfstan was one of the most prominent of the Anglo-Saxon bishops to survive the Norman Conquest of 1066, and he was the last among them to die. Among our best sources for Wulfstan's actions is the *Life of Wulfstan*, written by his former chancellor, Coleman, and designed to show Wulfstan's spiritual purity. William of Malmesbury translated this text, originally written in English, into Latin for a wider readership. According to this text, Wulfstan embraced the monastic life after a divinely inspired dream whereby a cloud descended from the heavens and stripped him of his worldly desires. As a monk, Wulfstan quickly developed a reputation for austerity and holiness. He rose in the ranks of the monastery, and in 1061 he was chosen as the new bishop of Worcester, where his humility and spirituality were interpreted by some as signs of saintliness, and his fame as a holy and ascetic churchman spread throughout the British Isles. He, like Archbishop Anselm, was venerated as a living saint by many of his contemporaries – he was seen as humble, pious, holy, and ascetic, but also wise, shrewd, loyal, and an able administrator.

Wulfstan showed that, despite being a monastic bishop who had turned from the temptations of the world, he could and would still be active in warfare to achieve salutary ends. He was actively involved in the military affairs of England on at least three separate occasions between 1066 and 1088, taking leading roles in directing military campaigns within England at the behest of or in support of the king (or the king's interests). His military actions garnered him acclaim from contemporary chroniclers, who saw him as a steadfast supporter of the king and a warrior against disorder. His active role did nothing to undermine the adulatory treatment he received, nor did it stem the tide of stories of his miracles. The tales of his miraculous intercessions finally resulted in his canonization by Innocent III in 1203.

Wulfstan utilized his office to support his kings at several pivotal moments in late Anglo-Saxon and early Anglo-Norman England. His support for the royal office was not predicated on being a partisan of either the Anglo-Saxon or Norman rulers; rather, Wulfstan was a steadfast supporter of the crown as a means to ensuring peace and stability within England. As with the other men profiled in this chapter, Wulfstan's active use of military power in support of the king was a manifestation of his loyalty as well as of his desire to defend his flock from violence. In 1066 he supported Harold Godwineson against the uprisings in the North perpetrated by his brother Tostig and King Harald of Norway; in 1075 he supported William I against a baronial uprising; and in 1088 he supported William II against an invasion led by Duke Robert of Normandy (an invasion that was actively aided and abetted by his episcopal colleagues Odo of Bayeux,

Geoffrey of Coutances, and Bishop William of Durham). In each case Wulfstan took a position as a military leader to defend the interests of his king, and his supporters couched these actions not as detracting from his spiritual role but, rather, as the necessary outcomes of his holiness, wisdom, and bravery.

We begin with Wulfstan's clearest military action – his support of William I during the 1075 rebellion. As discussed before, the 1075 rebellion pitted three earls against the absent king. As the king was away, the royal administration was bereft of its primary leadership, and that position was ably filled by Lanfranc. However, John of Worcester, the twelfth-century monk who served as one of the primary sources for the rebellion, recorded that Wulfstan took some of the first steps against the earls' perfidious actions. After swearing allegiances to each other, the rebellious earls retreated to their castles to make preparations for the coming war. Bishop Wulfstan

> with a great force and Æthelwig, abbot of Evesham, with his, and with the assistance of Urse, sheriff of Worcester, and Walter de Lacy with huge forces and a great multitude of people, prepared to oppose the earl of Hereford's crossing of the Severn and his meeting with Earl Ralph and his army at the agreed place.[39]

John, relying on the Worcester house tradition, portrayed Wulfstan as being stalwart in opposing the earls' rebellion. We can contrast John's highlighting of Wulfstan's military role with the complete lack of treatment of his actions in the Anglo-Saxon Chronicle (even in the Worcester manuscript) or the *Vita Wulfstani* of William of Malmesbury.[40] We must be careful of attributing too much importance to the Chronicle's silence, though it is notable that Wulfstan's actions are absent, given John's general reliance upon it for information. This possible ambivalence about Wulfstan's military role on the part of the anonymous chronicler of the Anglo-Saxon Chronicle and the *Vita Wulfstani* could be evidence for a range of opinions regarding direct uses of violence in legitimate causes by churchmen, a point argued by Ann Williams regarding the 1088 campaign (discussed below) between William Rufus and Odo of Bayeux.[41]

---

[39] John of Worcester, 3, 24–5. 'Sed Herefordensi comiti, ne, Sabrina transuadato, Rodulfi comiti ad locum destinatum cum suo exercitu occurreret, restitit Wlstanus Wigornensis episcopus cum magna militari manu, et Aegeluuius Eoueshamnensis abbas cum suis, assicitis sibi in adiutorium Vrsone uicecomite Wigorne, et Waltero de Laceio, cum copiis suis, et cereta multitudine plebis.' Emma Mason presents Æthelwig as a 'complex' figure who was astute in politics and knew how to navigate the channels of power. See Mason, *Saint Wulfstan of Worcester, c.1008–1095* (Oxford, 1990), 125–7.

[40] See *ASC*, 110–12.

[41] Williams, 'The Cunning of the Dove: Wulfstan and the Politics of Accommodation', *St. Wulfstan and His World*, 24.

John of Worcester draws further attention to Wulfstan's central role, along with that of Abbot Æthelwig, by placing him first among the commanders. John also claimed that Urse, sheriff of Worcester, rendered them 'assistance' (*adiutorium*), perhaps indicating that the clergymen were in charge of the expedition.[42] Wulfstan is also credited with the overall strategy of fortifying the crossing-place of the Severn. Not did only this prevent the linking up of the two enemy forces; as a naturally defensible position, it could be held by a small number of troops. The lack of an actual engagement between the armies meant that neither Wulfstan nor Æthelwig had to actually ride into battle, and thus neither was in danger of personally shedding blood. So, while Wulfstan's actions as a military commander would not have been as egregious to reformers as those of his contemporaries Bishop Odo of Bayeux or Geoffrey of Coutances, they still could have represented, from the perspective of reformers, an unhealthy involvement in warfare.

As we saw with Eadmer possibly inflating Anselm's role in 1101, whether or not Wulfstan was actually directing the defense is not as important as the fact that John was clearly putting him in that position. John illuminated Wulfstan's active and direct role as commander, and he probably did so out of pride for Wulfstan's actions, since his account was adulatory, rather than critical. For John, Wulfstan was quite rightly taking active steps to defend his flock and his king from the perfidious attacks of rebellious and rapacious nobles.[43] In John's telling, Wulfstan well-nigh saved the kingdom, since he went out of his way to explain that the conspiracy of Roger and Ralph was 'large' and 'had the agreement of many.'[44] Again, we see shades of Eadmer's presentation of Anselm's importance to Henry I; John was subtly demonstrating that without Wulfstan's active role, the kingdom could have been torn asunder by this conspiracy. John's treatment of these events was echoed by the Durham chronicler, Symeon. In following John's interpretation and presentation, Symeon reinforced the importance of Wulfstan's military actions, and the implicit acceptability of those actions to many contemporaries. There is no condemnation of Wulfstan for leading soldiers onto a potential battlefield, since John and Symeon deemed his cause (the defense of his region and his king) to be licit.

In further demonstration of John's acceptance of Wulfstan's role and the roles of the other clerics involved – Odo of Bayeux, Geoffrey of Coutances, and

---

[42] Emma Mason argues that Wulfstan's role was probably advisory, due in part to his relatively advanced age (he was around 67 years old in 1075) and because of the canonical prohibitions on clerics being warriors. Mason, 141.

[43] Ibid. Mason makes this point as well regarding the motivations of Wulfstan and Æthelwig.

[44] John of Worcester, 3, 24–5. 'magnam coniurationem plurimis assentientibus, contra regem Willelmum ibi fecerunt'.

Æthelwig – the very next section of his chronicle discussed Pope Gregory VII's attempts to prevent married clerics from performing Mass. This move was part of Gregory's broader attempt to 'purify' the clergy, and involved cracking down on married clergy, clergy who maintained concubines, and simoniacs. The juxtaposition within John of Worcester's text is quite interesting. John had just finished regaling his readers with the manful tale of Wulfstan's bravery and dedication in leading a military campaign, and his immediate pivot into the efforts of the papacy to correct the behavior of worldly clerics demonstrates that, in John's view, there was nothing 'worldly' about what Wulfstan and his ecclesiastical colleagues had done in fighting on behalf of the king. Wulfstan himself was an ascetic devoted to stamping out the 'sin' of sex and marriage among the clergy, despite (or perhaps because of) his own father's having been a married cleric.[45] Wulfstan's position on clerical marriage and sex was matched by that of his contemporary, Archbishop Lanfranc (as seen above). As demonstrated in Part I above, ecclesiastical reformers in the eleventh century focused on stamping out sexual and monetary corruption among the clergy, with a lesser effort directed against armed and militarily active clerics. Violence had utility when correctly directed against legitimate threats, as demonstrated by the defense of the kingdom in 1075, whereas the same could not be said of simony and sex.

Wulfstan's engagement with national politics began almost as soon as he was made a bishop in 1062. His rise to the highest ranks of the political circles was meteoric, despite (or because of) his reported disinterest in secular affairs.[46] Within four years of being elevated to the bishopric he was giving advice to the king on major issues of state and taking part in royal campaigns designed to forestall rebellion. His acceptance of a political life was perfectly in keeping with his understanding of his proper role as both a spiritual and a secular leader. He was trained to be a loyal servant of the king, and this training was inherent in the eleventh-century monastic tradition as laid out by the *Regularis Concordia*, a document prepared by Bishop Æthewold of Winchester in 970. This document involved an '[u]nhesitating obedience to the anointed king' and the belief that the king ought to be supported by his clerics.[47] For Wulfstan, supporting the properly consecrated king was fundamental to being a good shepherd of his flock. Rebellion against the king brought war, pillage, and destruction to the countryside, so a strong episcopal leader should actively support the king as a

---

[45] Mason, 162–4.
[46] Morris references the tale from William of Malmesbury that Wulfstan was known to nod off during discussions of secular affairs. See Colin Morris, 'William I and the Church Courts', *EHR* 82 (July, 1967), 449–63.
[47] Ibid., 92.

way of ensuring peace and stability. Thus, supporting a rebellion against the king constituted a 'major sin', whereas those who opposed rebels would be supporting both God and king.[48]

With the death of King Edward in 1066, Harold Godwineson was chosen as king and immediately faced challenges from Duke William of Normandy, Harald Haardrada of Norway, and his own younger brother, Tostig, the recently deposed earl of Northumbria. There was opposition to Harold's rule in northern England, and this followed long-standing difficulties that English kings had in controlling Northumbria and Yorkshire. There was a sizeable Danish population in the North, and the region was 'ground-zero' for opponents of the monopolization of political power by the Godwin family. Tostig had fanned the flames of social unrest by increasing the tax burden on his people far above historical levels.[49] When the inhabitants of Northumbria threw off Tostig's rule in 1065, they turned to Morcar, brother to Earl Edwin of Mercia, as their new earl. Harold Godwineson, then the earl of Wessex and the right-hand man of King Edward, was sent to deal with the rebels, and he eventually acquiesced in their decision to expel Tostig. He recognized Morcar as earl, and he 'renewed the "Law of Cnut", that is, the preferentially low rate of taxation due from Northumbria.'[50] However, when he became king upon Edward's death, the people of the North feared, perhaps rightly, that he would now take vengeance upon them, reinstall his brother, and rescind the favorable tax rates that he had promised them.[51]

Harold had to decide whether or not to launch a military campaign against Edwin and Morcar to bring the Northerners to his side. He was constrained by the realization that William of Normandy was preparing to invade, and that Tostig was still a dangerous wild-card (as he was actively seeking support from Flanders, Scotland, and Norway). Harold also recognized the military problems inherent in trying to win supporters to his cause by invading the North, and so he turned to Bishop Wulfstan as an intermediary who could potentially convince the Northerners to willingly cast their lot in with the Godwineson king. In an interesting juxtaposition with the case of 1075, Wulfstan's actions for the king in 1066 are discussed only in the hagiographical *Vita Wulfstani*, and not at all by John of Worcester. According to William of Malmesbury in the *Vita*, the North 'a great and turbulent folk' (*magnum et gentile tumentes*), refused to 'submit to the feeble South.'[52] William claimed that Harold had summoned Wulfstan to aid him

---

[48] Ibid., 104.
[49] Ibid., 99; Kapelle, *The Norman Conquest of the North*, 94–8.
[50] Mason, 99. cf. Douglas, *William I*, 183.
[51] Mason, 99.
[52] William of Malmesbury, *Life of Saint Wulfstan*, trans. J.H.F. Peile (Felinfach, 1934), 33. For the Latin, see *Vita Wulfstani*, ed. R.R. Darlington (London, 1928), 22.

because the bishop's reputation for holiness was widespread. He wrote, 'For the fame of his holiness had so found a way to the remotest tribes, that it was believed that he could quell the most stubborn insolence.'[53] Wulfstan's humility and holiness was directly proportional to his influence over political affairs and his persuasiveness to the Northerners. Mason believes that he had added cachet with the Northerners, due to his ability to evoke the lifestyle and mannerisms of the Northumbrian saints. Upon reaching the North, Wulfstan did not speak 'smooth words' to the recalcitrant Northumbrians but, rather, 'rebuked their vices, and threatened them with evil to come. If they were still rebellious, he warned them plainly, they should pay the penalty in suffering.'[54] For Wulfstan, defending the legitimate king trumped any other political or ideological considerations, and it mattered little whether the king was a Norman or an Englishman.[55]

Wulfstan's forceful and forthright actions in defense of the king, and his own region, were again on display during the contested succession after the death of William I in 1087. The rebellion of 1088 has already been discussed, but Wulfstan's role deserves to be discussed in the light of his other episcopal actions on behalf of his rulers. The 1088 rebellion was the result of William the Conqueror's decision to partition his landed holdings between his two oldest sons. To his eldest son, Robert, he gave, albeit reluctantly, rule over Normandy, while he gave England to his second son and namesake, William.[56] When William I died, the resulting tensions led to an attempt to reconnect the divided empire under the ultimate control of Robert. While Robert was in Normandy, his cause was adopted by a large number of the strongest and wealthiest nobles in England. These included his uncle Odo of Bayeux, Geoffrey of Coutances, Roger Bigod, and Earl Roger of Shrewsbury. There were rebels in all parts of the country, from Kent (Odo), to the Welsh marches (Roger of Shrewsbury), and from East Anglia (Roger Bigod), to Northumbria (Robert de Mowbray). This rebellion dwarfed that of 1075 in terms of the strength of the rebels and their potential for success. William Rufus was newly crowned, he faced an enemy well regarded and well positioned for success in his brother Robert, and he had lost the support of most of the strongest nobles in the kingdom.

---

[53] *Life of Saint Wulfstan*, 34. 'Sic enim fama sanctitatis eius etiam abditissimas penetrauerat gentes'. See *Vita Wulfstani*, 22–3.

[54] *Life of Saint Wulfstan*, 34. 'Sane licet esset pontifex bonus mansuetus et lenis; non tamen ad improbos indulgebat blandiciis; sed uicia corum arguens, minacibus infrendebat uerbis. Sin id procederet; aperto eis preconabatur uaticinio; quanto multandi essent supplicio.' *Vita Wulfstani*, 23.

[55] Brooks, *Saint Wulfstan and His World*, 2.

[56] For an excellent overview of this rebellion, see Barlow, *William Rufus* (New Haven, 2000), 68–93.

With these dire circumstances laid out, it becomes clear why a chronicler such as John of Worcester proudly extolled Wulfstan's forthright actions in defense of William II. When the rebels in the West Country, led by Earl Roger and Roger de Lacy, targeted Worcester because of Wulfstan's support for the king, John recounted how the aged bishop (now nearly eighty) stood firm in defiance of them.

> When he learnt this, the bishop of Worcester, Wulfstan, a man of great piety and dove-like simplicity [*uir magne pietatis et columbine simplicitatis*], cherished in every way by God and by the people over whom he ruled, utterly faithful to the king, his earthly lord, was very troubled, but drawing on God's compassion, like a second Moses, got ready to defend vigorously his flock and his city.[57]

John was reinforcing Wulfstan's monastic ideal of mildness, humility, simplicity, and piety, but at the same time highlighting his courage and bravery in facing down the marauding rebels. He was 'utterly faithful' to his king, and he defended his flock 'vigorously'. He was, as John says, a 'second Moses', ready to lead his people both spiritually and physically against their enemies. Wulfstan's faithfulness to his king and people made him an ideal bishop, and these qualities dovetailed with his piety.

His Norman military advisors counseled him to retire to the castle for protection, temporary though it may be, were the city to fall, and Wulfstan acquiesced. John took this opportunity once again to reinforce Wulfstan's salutary qualities. Even his decision to withdraw to the castle was 'because he was of a wonderful sweetness, and because of his loyalty to the king and of his love for his flock.'[58] After the bishop retired, his household and the stoutest of the townsmen assembled with the intention of counter-attacking the invading forces, provided they had the bishop's permission. John twice mentioned that the soldiers and militia sought the bishop's permission, perhaps indicating that Wulfstan was militarily

---

[57] John of Worcester, 3, 53–5. 'His auditis, uir magne pietatis et columbine simplicitatis, Deo populoque quem regebat in omnibus amabilis, regi, ut terreno domno, per omnia fidelis, pater reuerendus Wlstanus, Wigornensis episcopus, magna turbatur molestia, sed Dei respirans misercordia, iam quodammodo alter Moyses parat se uiriliter staturus pro populo et ciuitate sua.' The author of the Anglo-Saxon Chronicle also credited Wulfstan's 'merits' and 'God's mercy' for the victory at Worcester. See *ASC*, 223. See also Mason, 142–4. Mason points out that it is likely that John himself witnessed the events of 1088 as a young man or an oblate.

[58] John of Worcester, 3, 54–5. 'Ipse autem, ut erat mire mansuetudinis, et pro regis fidelitate, et pro eorum dilectione, petitioni eorum adquieuit.'

directing affairs within the city.⁵⁹ He gave his permission gladly, and he lent the potential soldiers the power of his faith. John reported that he said, "'go forth assured by God's blessing and by mine. With trust in God, I assure you that this day the sword will not hurt you, nor will any adversity nor any adversary. Remain firm in your loyalty to the king, fight vigorously for the citizens of Worcester.'"⁶⁰ Wulfstan's purported speech had crusader imagery in it, as John was writing after the period of the successful crusades, and it invoked the trust of God as a shield against his enemies. Wulfstan and his people were supported by God because of his piety, and because he was defending his king against illegitimate rebellion.

Wulfstan then went even further, taking an active, albeit spiritually violent, role in the battle. He worked a miracle by afflicting the limbs and eyes of his enemies so that they were unable to either flee or defend themselves, and thus were easily crushed by his forces. With the enemy thus hobbled, Wulfstan's army showed little mercy. 'The footsoldiers were killed, the knights, Normans and English as well as Welsh, were captured, the rest barely escaped in a wretched flight.'⁶¹ His own men returned without any losses, and thanked him for his 'beneficial counsel', thereby further underscoring his active role in the defense of the town, and his role in apparently making his (Christian) enemies that much easier to slaughter. For John, Wulfstan's actions in defense of his town, including his marshaling of the defenders, his directing them against the enemy, and his use of God's power to aid them in battle, modeled that of a perfect episcopal defender. Furthermore, God had clearly lent aid to Wulfstan's cause, as he would in licit engagements against unbelievers abroad. God's endorsement of Wulfstan's actions served as a powerful reminder that Wulfstan was in the right, and the rebellious forces were in the wrong.

John of Worcester and the *Vita Wulfstani* devoted the most attention among contemporaries to the actions of Bishop Wulfstan. Each source, however, had a very different approach to demonstrating Wulfstan's sanctity and holiness. Whereas John focused on Wulfstan's secular actions as demonstrative of his spiritual strength, the *Vita* followed the traditional hagiographical route of discussing his ascetic devotion, his miraculous interventions, and his abstention (usually)

---

[59] Ibid.
[60] Ibid. '"Ite"', inquit, '"filii, ite in pace, ite securi, cum Dei et nostra benedictione. Confidens ego in Domino, spondeo uobis, non hodie nocebit uobis gladius, non quicquam infortunii, non quicquam aduersarius. State in regis fidelitate, uiriliter agentes pro populi urbisque salute."'
[61] Ibid. 'Ceduntur pedites, capiuntur milites, cum Normannis tam Angli quam Walenses, ceteris uero uix debili elapsis fuga.'

from secular affairs.⁶² John discussed at great length Wulfstan's actions in defense of the king in 1075 and 1088, but ignored his actions on behalf of Harold in convincing the northerners to join the newly crowned Godwineson. The *Vita* did the opposite, highlighting Wulfstan's aid to Harold, but ignoring his actions in 1075 and 1088, perhaps showing his uneasiness with Wulfstan's military actions.⁶³ This argument reinforces the idea of a debate existing among contemporaries over whether active military actions for licit purposes would enhance or detract from a churchman's being considered holy and spiritually pure. The evidence from John is that these actions did, in fact, make a man such as Wulfstan a better and more faithful pastor and shepherd for his flock. There was a basic disagreement, it would seem, between John and Coleman about what constituted proper military behavior from a saintly bishop, or over which king should have benefited from the bishop's loyalty.⁶⁴ John was certainly using Wulfstan's military actions as evidence of his piety and sanctity, especially regarding his actions in 1088, whereas the *Vita* ignored them. Coleman might have not seen Wulfstan's actions in defense of the Norman rulers as particularly praiseworthy, unlike his actions on behalf of the Englishman Harold. We cannot know whether this ethnic pride played much of a role, but it cannot be discounted, especially since Coleman chose to write in English.

Upon Wulfstan's death in 1095, he was eulogized by contemporaries in terms appropriate for a saintly figure. John of Worcester began his entry for 1095 with the news of Wulfstan's death. He wrote that the bishop, 'revered and admirable', had devoted himself to God's service since adolescence, and that he had sought to serve God 'with great reverence and humility of spirit'.⁶⁵ He then proceeded to date Wulfstan's death according to a variety of chronological reckonings. Immediately thereafter he told of a miraculous appearance by the recently deceased Wulfstan to Bishop Robert of Hereford in the hour of his death, and then again thirty days later.⁶⁶ The *Vita Wulfstani* also recorded a number of miraculous occurrences at his death, including Wulfstan's appearance to the brothers of the cloister, to whom he continued to give correction and guidance.⁶⁷ Eadmer, in his *Historia Novorum*, wrote that Wulfstan was of 'blessed memory' and that he

---

⁶² See Williams, 24. In pointing out that John took a more holistic view of Wulfstan's achievements than Coleman, Williams writes in reference to his actions during the 1088 rebellion, 'John of Worcester praises not only Wulfstan's devotion to religion but also his inspirational leadership of the church's military tenants in battle.'
⁶³ Brooks, *St. Wulfstan and His World*, 10.
⁶⁴ Ibid.
⁶⁵ John of Worcester, 3, 74–5.
⁶⁶ Ibid., 74–7.
⁶⁷ *Vita Wulfstani*, 62–4.

was 'a man eminent in all the religious life and unrivaled in his knowledge of the ancient customs of England.'[68] This treatment of Wulfstan was in keeping with his reputation as a living saint towards the end of his life.[69]

The efforts to canonize Wulfstan began almost as soon as he had died. Canonization was not entirely dependent on papal approval at the end of the eleventh century, though momentum was clearly moving in that direction. John Crook argues that the 'fact that Coleman wrote so soon after Wulfstan's death may indicate that the Worcester community – certainly Coleman himself – already entertained hopes that the bishop would be regarded as a saint.'[70] Despite Coleman's efforts, the cult of Wulfstan was not widespread in 1095, perhaps because he was too much an ascetic monastic figure.[71] Wulfstan had not been successful in defending Worcester's lands from encroachment by neighboring nobles, nor had he provided astute political advice or decisive military assistance to the Norman kings, at least, not according to Coleman's *Vita Wulfstani*. Furthermore, a bishop's spirituality was thought to be reflected in the benefits he could bring to his house, and since Wulfstan was too ascetically spiritual, he had not been successful in increasing the power of his monks and priests.[72] It is ironic to consider that Coleman's efforts to focus on Wulfstan's non-political and non-military achievements might have hamstrung his goal of getting recognition for Wulfstan's cult. John of Worcester seemingly understood this reality much better when he was writing in the 1120s and 1130s.

The efforts to gain papal support for the nascent cult developing around Wulfstan's tomb gained impetus in 1113 when Worcester cathedral burned down, but Wulfstan's tomb not only survived, but suffered no appreciable damage. This occurrence was reckoned a miracle, and the cult gained a further boost when William of Malmesbury chose to translate Coleman's *Vita Wulfstani* into Latin, and thus garner for it a larger readership and give it greater respectability among the educated elites of England and elsewhere.[73] By 1131, Archdeacon Henry of Huntingdon was referring to Wulfstan as 'sanctus' in his *Historia Anglorum*.[74] Wulfstan had achieved a cultural acceptance as a saint, but he still lacked formal

---

[68] Eadmer, *History of Recent Events in England*, 46.
[69] Williams, 23. Williams makes the further point that notions of sanctity ran through all of the major sources for Wulfstan's life, not just the *Vita Wulfstani*.
[70] Crook, 'The Physical Setting of the Cult of St. Wulfstan', *St. Wulfstan and His World*, 201. Crook further argues that the nature of the miracles attributed to Wulfstan indicates a 'spontaneous, popular cult rather than one that was strictly orchestrated by the monks of the cathedral priory'. See page 207.
[71] Mason, 271.
[72] Ibid.
[73] Ibid., 272–5.
[74] Ibid.

canonization at the hands of the pope. The murder and subsequent canonization of Archbishop Thomas Becket in 1170 rekindled interest in the promotion of local saints, and Bishop Robert of Worcester (a cousin to Henry II's) began to build interest in the cult of Wulfstan. However, his initiative was not taken up by any of the next four bishops of Worcester, and it was not until the episcopate of John of Coutances (1196–98) that broader efforts were made to gain papal approval.[75] Bishop John, responding to numerous reports of visitations from Wulfstan, but without papal leave, ordered Wulfstan's body exhumed and moved into a shrine. His death three weeks later was deemed sufficient evidence that he was impudent in not waiting for papal action.[76] His successor, Bishop Mauger, replaced Wulfstan in his tomb, and then petitioned the pope for sainthood for Wulfstan. Pope Innocent III appointed a commission to look into the matter, comprised of Archbishop Hubert Walter of Canterbury, Bishop Eustace of Ely, Abbot Samson of Bury St. Edmunds, and Abbot Peter of Woburn. They arrived in Worcester in September of 1202 and determined that the miracles were genuine. On April 23, 1203, Wulfstan was canonized.[77] According to Roger of Wendover, King John, at the end of his life, commended his body and soul to God and Saint Wulfstan, and he was buried near to Wulfstan's shrine at Worcester.[78] Wulfstan's zealousness in defense of his flock, and his active support for the king, were part and parcel of his spirituality, and were endorsed, even if only implicitly, by his canonization at the hands of the papacy.

If the previous clerics were considered almost uniformly praiseworthy, and almost saintly, the final cleric examined in this chapter was quite the opposite. Bishop Gaudry of Laon, was one of the most controversial clerical figures of his day. His elevation to episcopal office was not so much a direct reward for service but, rather, came after his military exploits in battle, and can thus show the intense passions elicited by warrior-clerics. He was elected to the bishopric of Laon after he captured Duke Robert of Normandy at the battle of Tinchebrai on September 28, 1106. Guibert of Nogent and Orderic Vitalis both discussed Gaudry at some length, though mostly because of the later rebellion of the commune in Laon, in which he was killed. Following the vacancy of the episcopal see from 1104-6, King Philip I of France and the clergy agreed on Gaudry, who was King Henry I of England's chancellor, and was reputed to be extremely wealthy.[79] While the

---

[75] Peter Draper, 'King John and Saint Wulfstan', *Journal of Medieval History* 10, No. 1 (1984), 44–5.
[76] Mason, 277–8.
[77] Ibid., 280.
[78] Draper, 41–2. Draper interprets John's association with Wulfstan early in his reign to political considerations of Wulfstan's popularity. See 49–50.
[79] H.W.C. Davis, 'Waldric, the Chancellor of Henry I', *English Historical Review* 26 (Jan., 1911), 88.

early twentieth-century historian H.W.C. Davis attributes Gaudry's election to his wealth, Gaudry's twelfth-century contemporary Orderic Vitalis explicitly attributed his elevation to his valorous deeds at Tinchebrai.[80]

Prior to his election, both archdeacons of Laon, Gautier and Ebal, had sought the position, but neither was qualified, according to Guibert de Nogent. Gautier 'had always behaved more like a soldier than a churchman, while Ebal was more than the average womanizer.'[81] Gaudry was sought at the court of Henry I, where he was serving as a royal clerk. When he heard of his election, he 'used his influence to be ordained a subdeacon immediately and to receive a canon's stall in the church of Rouen, though until this time he had been nothing more than a soldier.'[82] It was during his time in minor orders that he had been serving as a soldier for Henry I and had thus captured Duke Robert. Guibert mentioned, grudgingly, that Gaudry's election was lauded and praised by everyone in the chapter and city except for Master Anselm, dean and chancellor of the cathedral of Laon, who had become archdeacon in 1106 after Gautier died. Guibert claimed that there were those among them who opposed the election, presumably himself, but who were cowed by their peers.[83] However, Guibert did accompany the bishop, and two other abbots, to Rome. He was questioned as to Gaudry's qualifications, and admitted that they had elected him without knowing too much about him. Pope Paschal II approved Gaudry's election, and sought to get Gaudry to support him in his quarrel with Emperor Henry V, a request that horrified Guibert for its brazenly political nature.[84]

What comes across most clearly in Gaudry's election and elevation is that a man such as Paschal II represented a very different understanding of proper and acceptable clerical behavior than a writer such as Guibert de Nogent. Paschal was clearly not overwrought by Gaudry's character or his actions at Tinchebrai, and if he was at all concerned about it he quickly sublimated that concern in favor of his

---

[80] Guibert de Nogent, *Memoirs, A Monk's Confession: The Memoirs of Guibert de Nogent*, trans. Paul J. Archambault (University Park, 1996), 129, n. 21. Even if the link between Gaudry's prowess and his election was not as clear as Orderic indicated, it is especially interesting that Gaudry was elected at all, as Laon fell outside of Henry I's power.

[81] Guibert, *Memoirs*, 129. 'Galterius enim non clericum, sed militarem se simper exhibuerat; alter mulierum plus æquo incontinens erat.' See *Guibert de Nogent: Histoire de sa Vie (1053–1124)*, ed. Georges Bourgin (Paris, 1907), 138.

[82] Guibert, *Memoirs*, 130. 'Qui nequaquam huius electionis incertus, quod sub nullius ecclesiae titulo erat, nec quippiam sacri ordinis praeter clericatum exceperat, factione egit, ut e vestigio subdiaconus fieret et canoicam in ecclesia Rothomagensi susciperet, cum hactenus sese omnino militariter habuisset.' Bourgin, 138–9. Cf. Taylor, 'Was There a Song of Roland?', 50.

[83] Guibert, *Memoirs*, 130.

[84] Ibid., 133–4.

political interests. Guibert, who had no such political concerns, offered a forceful condemnation of Gaudry because of his perceived worldliness. He wrote, 'In his speech, as well as his behavior, Gaudry proved remarkably unstable and shallow. He loved talking about military matters, dogs, and hawks, as he had learned to do while in England.'[85] These interests were not suitable for a cleric, in the mind of a monastic reformer like Guibert, as they smacked of worldliness. Immediately afterwards, Guibert offered an even clearer example of Gaudry's worldly interests. He wrote,

> One day he was on his way to dedicating a church, and I was riding with him with another cleric, a pleasant young man. All of a sudden the bishop caught sight of peasant holding a lance; and while he was still wearing the mitre he had worn for the consecration he snatched the lance from the peasant's hands, gave his horse the spurs and went charging at some imaginary target. The cleric and I cried out (he in French and I in Latin verse): 'The mitre and the lance do not sit well together.'[86]

Guibert was giving life to the common complaint about secular clerks, namely that their time around royal and noble courts had given them interests and affectations that were unbecoming of clerics. Learning to joust was not an easy thing, and even if Gaudry was only doing so in jest, it is a reasonable assumption to make that he had wielded a lance before. Guibert's reaction to a man like Gaudry tends to become inflated in our eyes because he wrote about it. As was discussed in the Introduction, the sort of cleric who wrote about events such as Tinchebrai was not usually the sort of cleric who actually took part in such events, and thus we tend to inflate the influence of the prescriptive side of the debate.

In fact, we can see evidence of Guibert's internal debate by briefly examining his account of Gaudry's murder at the hands of the commune of Laon. The commune came to believe that Gaudry sought to destroy them, despite the fact

---

[85] Ibid., 135. 'In verbo namque et habitu, mire instabilis, mire levis extiterat. De rebus nempe militaribus, cannibus et accipitribus loqui gratum habuerat, quod apud Anglos didicerat.' Bourgin, 143.

[86] Guibert, *Memoirs*, 135. Unde quodam tempore, cum quondam dedicavisset ecclesiam, et ego cum quodam bonæ indolis iuvene cleric ei adequitaremus, rusticum cum lancea reperit. Qua pontifex, tiara, quam inter sacra habuerat, habens in capite, mox sublata, equum calcaribus urgens acsi aliquem percussurus intendit. Cui ego et clericus, ipse vulgariter, ego poetice: Non bene convenient, nec in sede morantur, Cidaris et lancea. Bourgin, 143-4. The classical reference is adapted from Ovid on the incompatibility of royal authority and love in the *Metamorphoses*, 2, lines 846-7. The specific section of the *Metamorphoses* referred to Jove taking on the form of a bull to bear Europa to Crete. See Ovid, *Metamorphoses*, trans. Allen Mandelbaum (London, 1993), 71-3.

that he had been instrumental in getting it established. Through Gaudry's machinations the commune's charter was revoked and the two sides began to plan for violence.[87] Despite being warned about the possible violence, Gaudry haughtily replied "'Nonsense, am I going to die at the hands of people like this?'"[88] He did, however, have his guards follow him in the clerical procession with swords under their robes, and afterwards he 'summoned a great number of peasants from the episcopal manors and manned the towers of the cathedral and ordered them to guard his palace.'[89] The following Thursday the burghers attacked the episcopal palace, streaming through the cathedral doors armed with axes, clubs, swords, bows, and spears. Guibert then recounted how the bishop fought on his own behalf,

> Now the insolent mob, which had been screaming before the walls of the palace, attacked the bishop. Gaudry, along with those who had come to his aid, kept the enemy at bay by throwing stones and shooting arrows. In this as in other moments Gaudry showed the fierceness in battle that had always been his hallmark; but because he had unjustly and wrongly taken up that other sword, he perished by the sword.[90]

When he was finally found, he begged for his life and offered the burghers riches and to renounce his office. They slew him, and then mutilated the corpse to such an extent that they could recognize him only from a scar that he had gained in jousting. His chamberlain Guillaume bemoaned that the bishop was too interested in military affairs, and he recalled a conversation where Gaudry had boasted of having wounded a knight in the neck during a joust.[91] Guibert clearly thought that Gaudry got what was coming to him for his desire to embrace the secular sword rather than staying content with the spiritual one. Guibert was torn, however, because he despised the commune itself even more than he did Gaudry, writing that Laon and its citizens accumulated crimes greater than anywhere else in France.[92] Nevertheless, Guibert saw Gaudry's death as coming, much as Christ

---

[87] Guibert, *Memoirs*, 151–2.
[88] Ibid.
[89] Ibid., 152–3.
[90] Ibid., 155. Porro episcopum insolens vulgus aggrediens, cum pro moenibus aulæ prostreperet, episcopus cum quibusdam qui sibi opitulabantur, iactibus lapidum sagittarumque ictibus, quoad potuit, repugnavit. Plurimam enim suam semper in armis acrimoniam, uti quondam, et nunc quoque promebat. Sed quia indebite et frustra alium acceperat gladium, gladio periit. Bourgin, 166.
[91] Ibid., 162.
[92] Ibid., 171.

had foretold in the Garden of Gethsemane, namely, that he who lives by the sword dies by the sword. Guibert's condemnation of Gaudry, however vociferous, has to be set against his elevation, which was met with the acclaim of most, and his confirmation as bishop by the pope himself. Gaudry was not consecrated by the pope because of his military actions, but neither was he elevated in spite of them. The warlike achievements that had earned him favor and acclaim were at worst morally neutral, and at best a demonstration of his bravery and loyal service to his king.

Overall, this chapter has presented us with a number of contrasts. While men such as Lanfranc, Anselm, and Wulfstan were very highly respected members of the ecclesiastical hierarchy, and two of them were eventually canonized by the pope, they existed alongside clerics such as Gaudry, whose reputations were much more circumspect. Lanfranc, Anselm, and Wulfstan all successfully engaged in warfare, and avoided censure, on behalf of their kings and in defense of their flocks. Gaudry, on the other hand, fought for himself, and embraced the knightly lifestyle so abhorrent to clerical reformers. Lanfranc, Anselm, and Wulfstan were more reluctant to serve, and did not indulge in displays of worldly wealth. For contemporaries, the determinant of whether a cleric's behavior was praiseworthy or condemnable was whether he was fighting on behalf of a legitimate cause, usually his king, and whether he was fighting without embracing the worldly aspects of a knightly lifestyle. Most observers were more horrified by a cleric who looked and acted like a knight during peacetime than they were by one who manfully defended his king during war, but who otherwise was a conventional member of the ecclesiastical *ordo*.

CHAPTER 6

The Civil War between Stephen and Matilda

AFTER the long peace of Henry I's reign (in England, at least), the civil war between Stephen and Matilda brought active warfare to England for the first time in a generation. For nearly twenty years, the country was torn apart by warfare between partisans of Henry's nephew Count Stephen of Boulogne (who became king in 1135) and those of his daughter Matilda, to whom Henry had made his chief nobles swear allegiance before her marriage to Count Geoffrey of Anjou. The war ended in 1153, when Stephen recognized Matilda's son Henry (the future Henry II) as his heir. Stephen then died in 1154. The unsettled nature of the legitimate succession muddied the waters for contemporaries judging clerical military actions through the scope of royal service – partisans on each side could argue that they were supporting the legitimate ruler. This chapter examines the arguments and actions of churchmen who actively participated in the war, primarily Stephen's brother Henry of Blois, abbot of Glastonbury (1126–71), bishop of Winchester (1129–71), and papal legate (1139–43).[1] In addition to Henry, there were other clerics who fought on behalf of either side as well as to defend their local interests, such as Thurstan, the aged archbishop of York, who defended the North from Scottish invasion in 1138. While Thurstan garnered universal acclaim for his actions, Henry was a much more controversial figure, probably due to his 'knightly' demeanor and overtly political lifestyle.

If the image of the warrior-cleric was of a man descended from an elite lineage, with the finest education and close affinities with noble and royal families, then Henry of Blois had impeccable credentials. His family lineage was the bluest of the blue; he was the nephew of two English kings, William Rufus and Henry I, he was the grandson of William the Conqueror, and brother to King Stephen. His

---

[1] Henry has been the subject of a few scholarly treatments. Lena Voss, *Heinrich von Blois, Bischof von Winchester, 1129–1171* (Berlin, 1932); Douglas Senette, 'A Cluniac Prelate: Henry of Blois, Bishop of Winchester (1129–1171)' (Ph.D. diss., Tulane University, 1991). For a more recent biography of Henry see Michael R. Davis, *Henry of Blois: Prince Bishop of the Twelfth Century Renaissance* (Baltimore, 2009). A forthcoming volume edited by John Munns and Will Kynan-Wilson (to which I have contributed an article derived from this chapter discussing Henry as a general) will help to address this deficiency.

father was Count Stephen of Blois, who had gained a not-so-sterling reputation as a crusader (by fleeing the siege of Antioch), and his mother was Adela, daughter of William I. His ecclesiastical lineage was almost as impressive. He was an avowed Cluniac. Cluny was still a powerful ideological institution, which in Henry's youth was under the control of St. Hugh, and later Peter the Venerable. Henry circulated in the stratified air of noble and ecclesiastical excellence and this makes his overt embrace of military violence as an acceptable means to an end all the more interesting. He was not a chiefly secular man thrust into ecclesiastical office purely because he was related to the ruler; he was a 'traditional' noble ecclesiastic. While Henry's royal connections certainly paved the way for him to excel in the church, he was also a *bona fide* adherent to church reform and he spent his time and energy primarily on ecclesiastical concerns.

Stephen's reign is well represented in contemporary writings, including those by William of Malmesbury, John of Worcester, Henry of Huntingdon, and the anonymous author of the *Gesta Stephani*.[2] Henry of Winchester featured prominently in all of these chronicles and histories, and his activities excited the pens of almost all of his contemporaries. Henry's major military activities occurred, not surprisingly, during his brother's troubled reign. He was an active participant in the warfare of the period, and he certainly elicited fierce passions in his defenders and detractors. He was a controversial figure, and while his activity in war played a role in this, it was not the primary cause. Henry was not criticized for fighting in war but, rather, for acting like a knight.

We can see Henry's elevation as Innocent II's legate in 1139 in this light too. He was an active military leader prior to, during, and after becoming legate, and it would be difficult to imagine such an appointment being given to an outright simoniac or openly married bishop. The utility of military violence and the social power associated with prowess partially insulated him from the criticism that came from his military actions, if not his chivalric display. He was also successful in getting an archbishopric for himself in western England, which failed to materialize only because of the untimely death of Pope Lucius II, and, finally, after the death of Stephen, Henry became a well-respected elder member of the church hierarchy. His avoidance of negative repercussions (though not criticism) from his warrior activities is important in its own right, but more interesting was the paradoxical treatment of his activities by contemporary authors. He was

---

[2] The author of *Gesta* was most probably either Robert of Lewes, bishop of Bath, or a secular clerk writing in two phases (c. 1148 and after 1153). For the arguments in favor of Robert of Lewes, see *Gesta Stephani*, ed. and tr. by K.R. Potter, intro. by R.H.W. Davis (Oxford, 1976), xxxiv–xxxviii. For arguments in favor of the secular clerk, see Gerrard, 195, Gransden, 188–9. Cf. John of Worcester, 3, 213.

alternately extolled and excoriated for his mix of violence, secularity, wisdom, and forthrightness. Henry's image was crafted by far more than his obedience to canon law, and his contemporaries judged him as they would have judged any other great man, with his ecclesiastical position and *ordo* representing only one element.

An infamous episode at the abbey of Cluny during Henry's youth gives us a foreshadowing of some of the complaints leveled at Henry himself. He began his education around the beginning of the reign of Abbot Pontius (r. 1109–22), a man who was among the most controversial of Cluny's leaders. Pontius was a powerful ecclesiastical figure, and one discussed as a candidate for pope during the papal election held at Cluny in 1119 (as a rival to the eventual winner, Guy of Vienne), though his perceived pride and arrogance made him too many enemies for him to prevail.[3] While most contemporaries found Pontius's pride overbearing, for Orderic Vitalis it was a measure of his 'noble spirit' (magnanimous).[4] Orderic saw Pontius as demonstrating strength and virility in meeting the charges of his foes, and this was to be celebrated. When Pontius's enemies appealed to the pope against him, the abbot resigned his office in a fury (a move that even Orderic condemned as 'foolish') and went on a pilgrimage to the Holy Land.[5] Upon his return (having been replaced by Peter the Venerable) he tried to regain his position through force, though Orderic once again sought to minimize Pontius's actions by claiming that the armed mob bore him into the abbey against his will.[6] He was excommunicated, and upon traveling to Rome to argue his case, he was arrested, imprisoned, and died in 1127. During this difficult circumstance, Henry was made abbot of Glastonbury by Henry I of England. Henry thus went to Glastonbury having already seen the value of loyalty, the utility and dangers of violence, and the importance of maintaining social order.

For many contemporary observers, especially those of the Cistercian order (though Cistercians were known to embrace militaristic imagery as well) and even some modern scholars, this episode was the natural outcome of the focus on military imagery that was popular in Cluniac monasteries.[7] Many Cluniac monks were sons of powerful noble families where military exploits and the cult

---

[3] Stanley A. Chodorow, 'Ecclesiastical Politics and the Ending of the Investiture Contest: The Papal Election of 1119', *Speculum* 46 (Oct. 1971), 625 and 627.
[4] Orderic Vitalis, *The Ecclesiastical History of Orderic Vitalis*, trans. Marjorie Chibnall, Vol. 6 (Oxford, 2002), 269.
[5] Ibid., 311.
[6] Ibid., 313.
[7] Katherine Allen Smith, 'Saints in Shining Armor: Martial Asceticism and Masculine Models of Sanctity, ca.1050–1250', *Speculum* 83 (2008), 573.

of chivalry were prevalent.[8] Furthermore, Cluniac monks were exhorted to consider themselves knights of Christ, engaged in a constant military battle against the forces of Satan, and this ideology and liturgy inherently promoted a valorization of warfare. This led to the blurring of the lines between the mentalities of knights and monks. This similarity could extend to the internal structure of the monastic community, which often became a surrogate for the noble *familia* and could be torn by the same seigniorial tensions.[9] In the case of Pontius, he was the leader of one noble 'clan' within the monastery, and they fought out, this time literally, the same factional disputes within the monastery walls as those that tore the seigniorial class outside of them.[10]

Only three years after being made abbot of Glastonbury, Henry was elevated to the powerful and wealthy bishopric of Winchester. He then obtained a papal dispensation to pluralistically hold both positions for his entire life. What is even more striking about his pluralism was that Henry was a devotee of the Gregorian reformed papacy and church, which frowned on simony, pluralism, and a variety of other clerical abuses.[11] Henry's position as bishop of Winchester, however, was a far more important base of power than that of abbot of Glastonbury. It was as bishop that Henry advanced his fortunes, and those of his preferred political faction, through all conceivable means, ecclesiastical, political, and military. Like his great-uncle Odo, there is no evidence that Henry saw tension between belonging to the clerical *ordo* and engaging in warfare. In fact, he probably saw active warfare as a necessary and righteous method of advancing peace in the realm.

Henry was instrumental in aiding Stephen's ascent to the throne (over the claim of his cousin Matilda), and was credited by contemporaries with smoothing over potential opposition from among the ecclesiastical elites. He was able to convince the archbishop of Canterbury, William de Corbeil, and Roger, bishop of Salisbury (who had served as Henry I's justiciar on many occasions) to support Stephen.[12] This was a two-fold success, since it not only secured the cooperation of many of the most powerful figures within the English church hierarchy, but also brought over many of the highest-ranking figures within the English

---

[8] Senette, 22. cf. Smith, *War and the Making of Medieval Monastic Culture*, 123.
[9] Dominique Iogna-Prat, *Order and Exclusion: Cluny and Christendom Face Heresy, Judaism, and Islam (1000–1150)*, tr. Graham R. Edwards (Ithaca, 2002), 92–3.
[10] Ibid. See also Edmund King, *King Stephen* (New Haven, 2010), 37.
[11] Ilicia Jo Sprey, 'Papal Legates in English Politics, 1100–1272' (Ph.D. dissertation, University of Virginia, 1998), 159.
[12] Malmesbury strenuously defended Bishop Roger, known for being an administrative wizard, as a pious cleric, and he applauded his direction of Henry I. See Björn Weiler, 'William of Malmesbury, King Henry I, and the *Gesta Regum Anglorum*', *Anglo-Norman Studies* 31, ed. C.P. Lewis (Woodbridge, 2008), 164–5.

royal administrative apparatus.[13] These leading churchmen, powerful in their own rights, also gave valuable cover to their secular peers, many of whom had sworn to uphold Matilda's claim to be the legitimate heir. The repudiation of this oath was made a little easier by the convenient tale told by Hugh Bigod, the king's steward, that Henry I on his deathbed had absolved his men of that oath, and that the original oath had been extracted from the nobles under duress.[14] While many contemporaries suspected Hugh's story to be false, it still was enough to legitimize the *fait accompli* of Stephen's accession and to spur the archbishop to consecrate the new king.[15]

Henry's actions in support of his brother were generally seen at the time, even by those predisposed against Stephen, as evidence of his loyalty. William of Malmesbury, an adherent of Matilda's party, and who dedicated his *Historia Novella* to Matilda's half-brother Earl Robert of Gloucester, saw Henry's actions as being dictated by an earnest desire to secure the well-being of the church. In fact, Henry was 'allured indeed by a very strong hope that Stephen would continue the ways of his grandfather William in the governance of the kingdom, especially as regards strict uprightness in Church affairs.'[16] Henry saw in his brother an opportunity to secure a much more beneficial balance of power in favor of ecclesiastical privilege, especially as it pertained to royal prerogatives. Stephen promised to forbid simony within the kingdom, a crucial plank in the Gregorian reforms, and to forgo redirecting the revenues from vacant sees into the royal coffers while the position remained vacant.[17] These concessions were solidified in the 1136 Oxford Charter of Liberties.[18] Henry's immediate importance in the counsels of his brother is manifest in the fact that he witnessed the charter third, immediately after Archbishop William and Archbishop Hugh of Rouen, and ahead of men such as Bishop Roger of Salisbury and Bishop Alexander of Lincoln, who had been preeminent under Henry I. Of further interest is that the clerics and nobles reserved the right to retract their oaths of loyalty to Stephen if he violated these liberties.

---

[13] Ibid., 161–2.

[14] King, *King Stephen*, 49.

[15] For discussions of the succession in general, see R.H.C. Davis, *King Stephen* (Berkeley, 1967), 15–17; John Appleby, *The Troubled Reign of King Stephen* (London, 1969), 19–25; H.A. Cronne, *The Reign of Stephen, 1135–1154* (London, 1970), 29–31; Donald Matthew, *King Stephen* (London, 2002), 59–67; King, *King Stephen*, 46–81.

[16] William of Malmesbury, *Historia Novella*, ed. and trans. K.R. Potter (London, 1955), 15. Cf. *Gesta Stephani*, ed. and trans. K.R. Potter, intro. R.H.C. Davis (Oxford, 1976), 9.

[17] Malmesbury, *Historia Novella*, 19; Senette, 141–3.

[18] *Select Charters and Other Illustrations of English Constitutional History from the Earliest Times to the Reign of Edward the First*, ed. William Stubbs, 9th Edition (Oxford, 1929), 142–4.

Henry (as Odo of Bayeux had been for William I) was instrumental in helping Stephen to solidify his position on the throne. Stephen, like William I, faced not only the usual noble attempts to carve out a greater share of power that often accompanied the accession of a new king, but also questions about his very legitimacy. Prior to 1135 there is no evidence of discussions to make him king, no discussion of his claims to the throne, and no groundswell of support for it. Indeed, even among the brothers of Blois, there was some expectation that his elder brother Theobald would make a bid for the throne, rather than Stephen himself.[19] Stephen also had one of the more damaging problems facing a new king: while he was renowned as a chivalrous knight and warrior, he quickly developed a reputation for being capricious and untrustworthy.[20] A perfidious nature and reputation for laxity would engender more political unrest and would undermine royal authority more effectively than would an open rebellion by a collection of nobles who could be met head on and defeated. Stephen's support was fragile and uncertain, which led the king to become untrusting and paranoid about his supporters, and thereby further undermined their loyalty to him.

Henry's role in all of this was to provide the firm guiding hand that his brother lacked. This was nowhere more evident than in the first major military test of Stephen's reign, the rebellion of Baldwin de Redvers. Baldwin's rebellion was based at the city of Exeter and threatened to undermine royal authority in the southwest. Exeter, a large and wealthy city, provided a firm basis for revolt, and Baldwin de Redvers himself was 'a man of eminent rank and birth.'[21] Baldwin was a suspected adherent of Empress Matilda's party, and he held a number of castles in addition to Exeter. When he raised the flag of revolt, King Stephen responded with speed and alacrity, assembling a large royal army and besieging the castle. The size of his army was a blessing and a curse, since by necessity it contained a large number of men whose loyalty to Stephen was dubious at best, and whose sympathies lay with the men besieged in Exeter, rather than the king.

While both contemporary chroniclers and modern historians differ as to the relative benefits of the outcome of the siege, all are in agreement regarding the importance of Bishop Henry's contribution. In this case it was not his direct use of military force that mattered but, rather, his strategic sense and military knowledge. After the castle had been under siege for three months the wells ran dry. The author of the *Gesta Stephani* saw this as a clear indication of God's wrath upon

---

[19] David Carpenter, *The Struggle for Mastery: Britain 1066–1284* (Oxford, 2003), 163.
[20] Orderic Vitalis, 6, 204–5 for a discussion of his knightly qualities, 197 for a foreshadowing of his capricious nature.
[21] *Gesta Stephani*, 31.

the disloyal men rebelling against their king.[22] The garrison sent out two men to negotiate with the king and to get word to their sympathizers within the king's army about how dire conditions truly were inside.[23] They sought generous terms from the king, and offered up the castle in return for safe conduct for the garrison. Knowing Stephen's reputation for affability and malleability, they intended to placate the king with sugared words, but the king 'under the persuasion of his brother the Bishop of Winchester's advice, showed them a front of iron, refused to listen to them, and drove them from his presence with threats …'[24] For the author of the *Gesta Stephani*, Henry was the iron in Stephen's spine, but he was possessed also of keen military insight.

The *Gesta Stephani* made a point of including Henry's reasoning for denying the requests of the besieged for mercy. As the men conversed with the king, the bishop had observed that they were suffering from a want of water. He saw

> their sagging and wasted skin, the look of torpor on their faces, drained of the normal supply of blood, and their lips drawn back from gaping mouths, perceived that they were suffering from agonies of thirst and that therefore it was anything but wise to give them permission to leave the castle, it being certain that they would very soon surrender on whatever terms the besieger desired.[25]

This observation combined an intimate knowledge of siege-craft and a pragmatic political outlook. Henry understood clearly that the castle would capitulate soon enough, so any mercy from the king was unneeded. Additionally, Henry saw that Stephen needed to show ruthlessness toward his enemies on a large scale. He had shown mettle in dealing with the small-scale rebellion at Bampton earlier in the year, but he needed to solidify that impression with a similarly strong performance at Exeter. While Henry understood this reality clearly, Stephen did not. Eventually barons within the king's army who sympathized with the besieged impressed upon the king the need to show mercy, and thereby win more hearts to his side. The author of the *Gesta* was clearly unimpressed with this decision, since it had the opposite effect, and even Henry of Huntingdon complained that

---

[22] *Gesta Stephani*, 39.
[23] Chief among probable sympathizers was Robert, earl of Gloucester. See *Gesta Stephani*, 40, n. 1.
[24] Ibid., 41.
[25] Ibid. 'quia episcopus, laxa et effeta eorum cute conspecta, uultibus remissis et a naturali succo uacuatis, labris dispanso hiatu retractis, anhela eos siti laborare deprehendit, ideoque nequaquam consultum esse progrediendi de castello permissum eis indulgere, cum ratum esset in proximo eos ad uotum suum, quocumque modo exoptabant, cessuros'.

Stephen should have listened to Bishop Henry's advice in order to avoid the bloodshed that ensued, because he had shown himself to be weak.[26] Stephen's clemency showed the king's weakness and changeable nature, and instead of rallying men to his side, it further empowered his enemies.

Orderic Vitalis recounted that upon Stephen's return to England in 1137 (he had been in Normandy unsuccessfully pressing his rights there) he laid siege to the castle of Bedford around Christmas. This took the garrison by surprise because it was such an unseasonable time to launch an attack, and Stephen had gone against 'the advice of his brother Henry, bishop of Winchester.'[27] While it is was true that the garrison was probably not expecting an attack during the winter, this was also a highly risky military maneuver for the king, since his army would be exposed to the elements and face difficulties in resupply. Nevertheless, despite Henry's opposition to the plan, he demonstrated his value (and perceived importance) by accepting the castle's surrender – in fact, the castle refused to surrender to Stephen, and would capitulate only when Henry himself arrived. Henry served as the chief negotiator between the king and garrison, and convinced them to lay down arms.

In these early campaigns to pacify England and support Stephen's reign (he was the consecrated king and Matilda had not yet raised the flag of revolt) Henry's military actions earned little, if any, criticism from observers. His clerical status was not seen as rendering his presence on the battlefield illegitimate, nor scandalous. No chronicler bemoaned Henry's place at the siege of Exeter, nor his active counsels against mercy or clemency. In fact, if anything, his actions and advice were shown to be correct. The author of the *Gesta Stephani*, who later did criticize Henry for his perceived knightliness, saw neither problem nor contradiction in Henry's role as both a prelate and military strategist. In fact, Henry's actions at Exeter served to underscore that it was not warfare that necessarily angered contemporary observers but, rather, the cause for which that warfare was used, or the manner and display with which it was indulged.

We can see a similar set of priorities at work in the descriptions of Archbishop Thurstan of York's actions in defense of the north of England against the Scots in 1138.[28] Thurstan was instrumental in rallying the forces of the northern barons against the Scots, and he was presented as a hero in every account by contemporary and later chroniclers. Even his desire to appear on the battlefield in person as

---

[26] Ibid., 43; Henry of Huntingdon, *Historia Anglorum*, ed. and trans. Diana Greenway (Oxford, 1996), 708–9; Senette, 158.

[27] Orderic Vitalis, 6, 511.

[28] For a good overview of this campaign, see Bachrach, *Religion and the Conduct of War c.300–1215*, 153–60. See also King, *King Stephen*, 84–94.

a general was met with pride at his bravery and resolve. His decision to send his priests leading their parishioners into battle (though we are not sure of their specific role in the fighting) similarly met with no complaint, and was proudly trumpeted by those reporting on the events. The image that emerges in the chroniclers' treatment of this event is that clerics who used military means to defend royal interests and the *patria* against invasion were to be lauded, not criticized.

Prior Richard of Hexham (along with his contemporary John) wrote a continuation of the chronicle of Symeon of Durham and set the stage for Thurstan's heroism when he wrote of the vicious atrocities committed by the Scots as they made their way south in English territory. Richard commented that while pillaging and plundering happened in every war, this invasion had surpassed all previous examples.[29] Richard credited Thurstan as being among the first to rouse the men of Yorkshire to mount a defense against the Scottish invasion. He wrote that the archbishop 'greatly exerted himself in this emergency', and he then explained Thurstan's vital role as a unifying figure, since many of the barons were mistrustful of one another.[30] King Stephen was abroad and the nobles suspected each other of colluding with the Scots. The dissension and mutual distrust between the northern nobles meant that they might have abandoned the defense of the country,

> had not their archbishop, Turstin [sic], a man of great firmness and worth, animated them by his counsel and exhortations. For, being the shepherd of their souls, he would not, like a hireling on the approach of the wolf, seek safety in flight, but rather, pierced with the deepest emotions of pity at the dispersion and ruin of his flock, he applied all his energy and labours to counteract these great evils.[31]

---

[29] Richard of Hexham, *The Acts of Stephen, and the Battle of the Standard, The Church Historians of England*, ed. and trans. Joseph Stevenson, Vol. 4, Pt. 1 (London, 1856), 42–5. For the original, see Richard of Hexham, *De Gestis Regis Stephani et de Bello Standardii*, ed. Richard Howlett, Vol. 3 (London, 1886), 151–3.

[30] Richard of Hexham, Stevenson, 47. For the original, see Richard of Hexham, Howlett, 159. 'scilicet Turstinus archiepiscopus, qui, ut consequentur apparebit, maxime se de hoc negotio intromisit.'

[31] Richard of Hexham, Stephenson, 47–8. 'nisi Turstinus eorum archiepiscopus, magnae constantiae atque probitatis vir, semone ac consilio suo illos animasset. Quippe cum esset pastor animarum illorum, non more mercennarii infestante lupo de fuga sibi praesidium sperabat, seb potius super gregis sui dispersione ac pernicie, atque patriae suae destructione, gravissimo compassionis dolore sauciatus, omni studio et conatu tantis malis remedium quaerebat.' See Richard of Hexham, Howlett, 160. Cf. Aelred of Rievaulx, *Relatio de Standardo*, trans. Jane Freeland, ed. Marsha Dutton (Kalamazoo, 2005), 265–6. For the original see Aelred of Rievaulx, *Relatio de Standardo*, ed. Richard Howlett, Vol. 3 (London, 1886), 181–3.

Thurstan's charge was two-fold: he was responsible for providing leadership in lieu of the king – a point that was reinforced a few sentences later when Richard claimed that Thurstan was leading the men through a royal warrant – there was the requirement for him to protect his flock from attack, as evidenced by the reference to John 10:12.[32] Thurstan's actions demonstrate not only his sense of loyalty to the king, but also a sense that churchmen had a major role to play in creating social and political stability.[33] Richard wrote that Thurstan promised the barons that 'the priests of his diocese, bearing crosses, should march with them to battle with their parishioners, and that he also, God willing, designed to be present with his men in the engagement.'[34] In the end he was unable to go because of poor health, but his intention, and the praiseworthy nature of it in Richard's eyes, was clear. The fact that the English were entirely victorious in the battle was a further demonstration of the righteousness of both their cause and Thurstan's actions, especially since the Scots reportedly far outnumbered them.[35] In the eyes of the Hexham chroniclers, his desire to be present on the field of battle with his own contingent of men, defending his region and his king, was evidence of his resolve and valor, rather than a cause for criticism.[36]

Abbot Aelred of Rievaulx's description of the battle of the Standard in his *Relatio de Standardo* (written in the early years of Henry II) casts the conflict in terms of holy war, with the Scots playing the role of the Saracens. Aelred was a

---

[32] Richard of Hexham, Stevenson, 47–8. John 10:12 references the importance of a shepherd not abandoning his flock – 'mercennarius et qui non est pastor cuius non sunt oves propriae videt lupum venientem et dimittit oves et fugit et lupus rapit et dispergit oves.'

[33] C.J. Holdsworth, 'Peacemaking in the Twelfth Century', *Anglo-Norman Studies* 19 (Woodbriedge, 1997), 7–11. Cf. Hollister, *Henry I*, 235. Jean Truax argues that his prior friendliness towards the house of Blois could have bolstered Thurstan's support for Stephen, in addition to his basic loyalty to the kingship. See Jean A. Truax, 'All Roads Lead to Chartres: The House of Blois, the Papacy, and the Anglo-Norman Succession of 1135', *Anglo-Norman Studies* 31, ed. C.P. Lewis (Woodbridge, 2008), 122–6. Truax also points out that Thurstan was close friend to a number of popes in the early twelfth century, and one wonders whether Thurstan's political position and personal affection might have aided Bishop Henry of Winchester as well as Stephen.

[34] Richard of Hexham, Stevenson, 48. 'Promisit etiam eis quod suae diocesis presbyteros singulos, cum crucibus et parochianus suis, pariter cum illis in bellum procedere faceret, et quod ipse cum suis bello interesse, Deo disponente, cogitabat.' Richard of Hexham, Howlett, 161.

[35] Richard of Hexham, 50.

[36] Gerrard casts Thurstan's role at the Standard as a fulfillment of his pastoral role. See Gerrard, 174–6. For a discussion of the political implications of Thurstan's role at the Standard, see Janet Burton, 'Citadels of God: Monasteries, Violence, and the Struggle for Power in Northern England, 1135–1154', *Anglo-Norman Studies* 31, ed. C.P. Lewis (Woodbridge, 2008), 21–2.

renowned historian and spiritual author in twelfth-century England, enjoying the support of both king and clerics. His canonization in 1191, only twenty-four years after his death, speaks to his contemporary reputation. For him, the invasion of England was akin to the assaults against the Holy Land by the Muslims, and thus the Anglo-Norman defenders were in a position to receive the same divine assistance and aid as did the crusaders.[37] Aelred's battle rhetoric was somewhat unique, especially considering the generally formulaic nature of pre-battle speeches. Walter Espec's (his friend and the founder of the monastery at Rievaulx) speech went far beyond the standard invocations of divine aid for the Anglo-Normans, and gave assurances that the 'whole heavenly court will fight with them [the Anglo-Norman army].'[38] He claimed that the nobility of Heaven, including St. Michael and St. Peter, would follow their Lord Christ into battle alongside the English army. Even further, 'Christ himself will take up arms and shield and rise up to aid us.'[39] For Walter (and Aelred) Christ would be present both physically in the form of the consecrated host present in the pyx atop the masthead (from which the battle derived its name), as well as metaphysically in the press of battle. If the Lord of Hosts himself was present in defense of this cause, how could Thurstan's own presence on the battlefield be anything other than praiseworthy?

Thurstan and Henry's steadfast defense of Stephen's interests put the new king on a relatively firm footing versus his enemies by 1139. However, that year would prove to be Stephen's high-water mark, due mainly to his souring relationship with the ecclesiastical hierarchy and the return to England of Earl Robert of Gloucester (Matilda's half-brother) to fight for his sister's cause. In 1139 Stephen decided to seize and imprison Roger, bishop of Salisbury, and his nephews Bishop Alexander of Lincoln and Roger le Poer, the royal chancellor. Traditionally, historians have seen the arrest of these two bishops as the turning point in the civil war against Stephen, at least until his release from prison at the end of 1141. Seizing the bishops, it has been argued, deprived Stephen of the support of many ecclesiasti-

---

[37] John Bliese, 'The Battle Rhetoric of Aelred of Rievaulx', *HSJ* 1(1989), 100–7.
[38] John Bliese, 'Aelred of Rievaulx's Rhetoric and Morale at the Battle of the Standard, 1138', *Albion* 20 (Winter, 1988), 554. See also Bachrach, *Religion and the Conduct of War*, 156–7.
[39] Bliese, 'Battle of the Standard', 554. The entire section reads, 'Aderit Michael cum angelis suam ulturus injuriam, cuius ecclesiam humano sanguine foedaverarunt, cuius altare superposito capite humano polluerunt. Petrus cum Apostolis pugnabit pro nobis, quorum basilicas nunc in stabulum, nunc in prostibulum converterunt. Sancti martyres nostra praecedent agmina, quorum incederunt memorias, quorum atria caedibus impleverunt. Virgines sanctae licet pugnae dubitent interesse, pro nobis tamen oration pugnabunt. **Amplius, dico, ipse Christus apprehendet arma et scutum, et exurget in adjutorium nobis.**' (Emphasis mine) *Relatio de Standardo*, Aelred of Rievaulx, ed. Howlett, 188–9.

cal lords. His violent disregard for canonical prohibitions against laying hands on clerics turned many against him, and it also deprived him of his most able administrators. It further reinforced the image of the king as an untrustworthy and capricious ruler who played fast and loose with chivalric notions of loyalty.[40] It is not within our purpose, however, to revisit this event, nor to take a firm stance on its impact relative to Stephen's ability to effectively administer the country. While it did lead to a famous estrangement between Stephen and Henry (when Henry, as legate, summoned the king to an ecclesiastical council to answer for his actions), it did not permanently destroy the comity between the two men, nor did it fundamentally alter Henry's use and embrace of warfare. What did affect Henry's role as a general were the landing in England of Matilda, and Henry's torn loyalties between his king and his legatine role as peacemaker.

When Matilda landed in England in 1139, Henry was still among his brother's chief military advisors and commanders. Earl Robert was in Gloucester, while the Empress landed at the castle of Arundel. Stephen immediately hastened to the area to besiege her and to take her into custody. Henry arrived at the siege at the head of 'a large bodyguard of cavalry' (*cum multa equestrium*), and advised Stephen to allow Matilda to depart and travel to her brother.[41] Henry argued that this would place all of the king's enemies in one place, where they could be more easily dealt with, and also that if the king was entirely focused on the siege of Arundel, Robert and his adherents would be able to make bloody mayhem throughout the rest of the country. Henry believed that 'when both with their forces had been brought into one place he [Stephen] might more easily devote himself to shattering their enterprise and might more quickly arrive with all his forces for a heavier attack.'[42] Ultimately this decision backfired for the king, since it allowed them to

---

[40] See Marjorie Chibnall, *The Empress Matilda* (Oxford, 1991), 79–80; H.A. Cronne, *The Reign of King Stephen*, 37–9; Davis, *King Stephen*, 29–35; Appleby, *The Troubled Reign of King Stephen*, 64–78; Craig M. Nakashian, 'The Use and Impact of the English Levied Soldiers in Anglo-Norman England', *Comitatus: A Journal of Medieval and Renaissance Studies* 37 (2006), 27–9; Thomas Callahan Jr., 'The Arrest of the Bishops at Stephen's Court: A Reassessment', *HSJ* 4, ed. Robert B. Patterson (1993). For views that do not see the arrest of the bishops as a crushing blow to Stephen, see Matthew, *King Stephen*, 91–3 and Graeme White, *Restoration and Reform, 1153–1165: Recovery from Civil War in England* (Cambridge, 2000), 23–5; Stephen Marritt, 'King Stephen and the Bishops', *Anglo-Norman Studies* 24, ed. John Gillingham (Woodbridge, 2002), 129–144. For a discussion of the political entanglements of Nigel, bishop of Ely, see Jennifer Paxton, 'Monks and Bishops: The Purpose of the *Liber Eliensis*', *HSJ* 11 (2003), 17–30; *Liber Eliensis: A History of the Isle of Ely from the Seventh to the Twelfth Centuries*, trans. Janet Fairweather (Woodbridge, 2005), 346–468.
[41] *Gesta Stephani*, 89.
[42] Ibid.

concentrate their power in the southwest and forge a separatist regime based in Bristol. Contemporaries and modern historians have used Henry's advice to call his loyalty to Stephen into question, and even the author of the *Gesta Stephani* reported rumors that Henry had met secretly with Robert of Gloucester, though he wrote that these were probably untrue.[43] Henry's advice was actually not as bad as it would seem on the face of it. His reasoning was not necessarily faulty, if one recalls the successful precedent of 1088, when William II trapped all of his major enemies in the castle of Rochester and was able to eliminate them all together. Henry also was anticipating a larger groundswell of support for the Empress than actually happened. Had large segments of the country simultaneously erupted into rebellion, the king would have been caught between numerous enemy forces and separated from his base of support in the southeast.

Between 1139 and 1141, we do not have much evidence of Bishop Henry serving as a primary military commander for Stephen. This could be fallout from the church council in which he summoned the king to answer for arresting Roger of Salisbury and Roger le Poer, or it could be a reflection of his new role as papal legate. As the papal legate, Henry might have initially seen his role as a mediator between Stephen and Matilda, rather than as an adherent of the royal party. While it is not likely that he desired the deposing of his brother in favor of his cousin Matilda, if he partially disassociated himself from Stephen, he could plausibly seek to negotiate between the two sides. Even if that reasoning is sound, the situation changed drastically after Stephen was captured at the battle of Lincoln in 1141. In Stephen's capture (as God's judgment for his assaults on the church, according to the *Gesta Stephani*) Henry was faced with a very difficult choice.[44] With the king in prison, royal resistance to the Empress's party collapsed and only a handful of nobles remained loyal to the king. The Empress and Robert of Gloucester immediately sent letters to Henry to woo him to their side, and to entice him to use his office of legate to offer them legitimacy. Matilda wrote to Henry 'because he was reckoned to surpass all the great men of England in judgement and wisdom and to be their superior in virtue and wealth.'[45] The author of the *Gesta Stephani* assumed that Henry's inclination was to continue supporting the king, since he was his brother and because Stephen was still the anointed ruler of England. On the other hand, William of Malmesbury claimed that Henry had turned from Stephen's cause because of his arrest of the bishops and Henry's desire to see peace in the realm.[46] Ultimately, Henry chose to acquiesce to the Empress, though he

---

[43] Ibid.
[44] Ibid., 113.
[45] Ibid., 119.
[46] Malmesbury, *Historia Novella*, 53.

would continue to watch for a time to aid in Stephen's restoration. The author of the *Gesta* had a vested interest in putting as good a face as possible on Henry's flip-flopping, and he was writing during a time (1148) when he had the benefits of hindsight as well as a belief that Stephen would emerge from the civil war as the victor. A demonstration of the importance of military reasoning to Henry's decision-making process can be seen in that one of the factors in his decision to support the Empress was that he had not had time to provision nor to garrison his castles well enough to withstand a concerted siege.[47]

The alliance between Henry and the Empress was not destined to last very long. Matilda showed herself to be a vindictive, prideful, and arrogant ruler. When she decided to disinherit Stephen's son (and Henry's nephew) Eustace of the county of Boulogne, the bishop took a leading role in rallying support against her.[48] It was believed at the time, and recorded in the *Gesta Stephani*, that Henry was instrumental in stirring up the Londoners to expel Matilda and in forcing her to flee the city.[49] Matilda and Robert fled to Oxford, then gathered an army to attack Henry's seat of power at Winchester.[50] Henry escaped from the city, called together the royalist barons, hired mercenaries at his own expense, and began harassing the Angevin army. He was joined by Queen Matilda, an army of Londoners, and royalist nobles. Henry then directed a vicious attack on the Angevin soldiers besieging his castles, and precipitated the burning of most of the town of Winchester, including over forty churches. According to William of Malmesbury, Henry himself ordered the burning of the city, and it was firebrands flung from Henry's own castles that ignited the conflagration.[51] If we believe Malmesbury, not only did Henry not hesitate to burn his own city in order to achieve his military goals, he also sought to benefit directly from the fire. One of the places burnt was the monastery of Hyde, which had an enormous crucifix wrought in gold and silver. William of Malmesbury wrote that 'it was then caught by the fire and fell to the ground and was afterwards stripped by the legate's order.'[52] Henry then used the money to reward his knights generously. While one might discount Malmesbury's account because of his adherence to Robert of Gloucester, his was not the only chronicle to record Henry's decision to destroy Winchester. Indeed, John of Worcester also mentioned it, and he did so in much more negative terms for Henry. He wrote that Henry ordered Earl Simon of Northampton, "'Behold, earl, you have my orders, concentrate on razing the city

---

[47] *Gesta Stephani*, 119; cf. Malmesbury, *Historia Novella*, 50–1; cf. John of Worcester, 3, 299.
[48] Malmesbury, *Historia Novella*, 57–8.
[49] *Gesta Stephani*, 125.
[50] Ibid., 127.
[51] Malmesbury, *Historia Novella*, 59–60.
[52] Ibid., 60.

to the ground." These words show the speaker's innermost feelings.'[53] John then went further in condemning Henry for attacking the monastery of Wherwell in pursuit of one of Matilda's partisans (though he is silent on the story that the church was fortified by men of the Empress to serve as a castle), and he repeated the story that Henry had sought to pillage the churches in his own city. He wrote,

> After these events, Bishop Henry's anger was slightly appeased, though his greed knew no limits, and at the suggestion of the prior of the recently-burned down New Minster, recovered from the ashes of the burnt cross fifty pounds of silver, thirty marks of gold, three crowns with the same number of footstools of the purest Arabian gold, adorned all over with precious stones, of beautiful and amazing workmanship.[54]

The outcome of the battle at Winchester led directly to an attack on the Empress's stronghold at Oxford, in which Robert of Gloucester was captured and later exchanged for Stephen. What is most important for our purposes in this brief look at Henry's actions at Winchester is that he is never condemned outright for his use of warfare, but rather he was condemned for the destruction his decisions caused and his potentially greedy motivations. This might sound like splitting hairs, but the distinction is crucial. He was criticized by hostile chroniclers for opposing Matilda, for breaking his oath to her, for ordering the burning of Winchester, and for seeking to benefit from its destruction. The fact that he was a churchman was not seen as antithetical to these actions, and had he done them on behalf of Matilda, these same chroniclers would probably have praised him. Had Henry manfully defended the Empress against one of the king's partisans, William of Ypres perhaps, the odds are that William, John, and other hostile chroniclers would have extolled his brave defense of her interests. The language used by Henry's detractors is not markedly different from that used to criticize other opponents of the chroniclers.

After Stephen's release Henry continued in his role as a royal commander, though he first had to make amends with Stephen for abandoning his cause, and

---

[53] John of Worcester, 3, 300–1. '"En comes, ego iussi, tu ista radere stude." Quibus dictis, patuerunt intima cordis dicentis.'

[54] John of Worcester, 3, 302–3. 'His ita gestis, presul Henricus, ira quantulumcumque sedata sed cupiditate admodum dilatata, suggerente priore Noui Monasterii nuperrime conflagrati, tulit ex combusta cruces quingentas argenti libras, auri quoque marcas triginta, diademata tria cum totidem scabellis ex auro Arabico purissimo, et lapidibus pretiosissimis undique operta, opere pulcherrimo et mirifico facta, eaque in suis recondidit thesauris.' Cf. *Gesta Stephani*, 133 for a more sympathetic take on the Wherwell episode.

this he did at an ecclesiastical council in which he formally restored Stephen as the legitimate king in the eyes of the papal delegation (i.e. himself) and explained his pivot to the Empress's cause. At this same council a letter from Pope Innocent II was read in which he chastised Henry for not trying harder to gain the release of his brother from prison. Innocent urged him to work to get the king released 'by any means, ecclesiastical or secular.'[55] It is noteworthy that the pope was calling on Henry to take a leading role, in his capacity as papal legate, in freeing the king, and he was asked to do so using whatever means were necessary, ecclesiastical as well as secular. Secular, in this context, almost certainly would have included military means. Henry then swore that he had served Matilda only under compulsion, and excommunicated all of her adherents, save her.[56]

The year 1142 saw Henry back alongside Stephen in his attempts to bring an end to the civil war. Stephen targeted Robert of Gloucester as his chief opponent and decided to launch an offensive to destroy him, gambling that if he could force Robert to give battle, and decisively defeat him, he could build on the momentum of getting out of prison and crush the Angevin party once and for all. Despite the known dangers of a pitched battle, Bishop Henry 'also came with a strong body of troops to aid his enterprise.'[57] The king's army was composed of the royal household, the troops under Bishop Henry's command, and a contingent of loyal barons and other nobles. Earl Robert decided to offer battle at Wilton, and engaged the royal army. Details of the battle are sketchy, as we rely almost entirely on the *Gesta Stephani* for accounts of it, but ultimately the king's army broke and fled, with the king and Henry barely avoiding capture.

The following year, Henry again engaged in battle, this time against William de Pont de l'Arche 'a man utterly loyal ... to King Henry and his descendents.'[58] The *Gesta Stephani* blamed William for various deprivations, and then recorded, with more than a little pride, that Henry defeated all of his attacks. Bishop Henry, 'with a very strong body of troops, always offered a firm and most resolute resistance to him and baffled all his attempts not only by force but by wise judgement.'[59] Henry's abilities as a commander are here explained in more detail, with equal parts bravery and wisdom. The author lauded Henry for his military wisdom and prowess. William wrote to the Empress asking her to send him reinforcements and a good commander to take on the bishop, further indicating Henry's military skill.

---

[55] Malmesbury, *Historia Novella*, 62.
[56] Ibid., 63.
[57] *Gesta Stephani*, 145.
[58] Ibid., 151.
[59] Ibid. 'Verum quia episcopus cum fortissima militantium manu fortiter semper et constantissime restitit, omnesque illus conatus non solum viribut sed et prudentiae suae discretione delusit.'

The Angevins sent Robert Fitz Hildebrand, 'a man of low birth indeed but also of tried military qualities.'[60] He was also 'a lustful man, drunken and unchaste', and he soon seduced William's wife and took over his castle. He then joined his forces to those of the king and bishop. Henry was more than happy to welcome him to the royal side, despite his reputation for disloyalty. God was not, apparently, as forgiving, and Fitz Hildebrand died of a wasting illness through His vengeance (according to chroniclers).

In a section probably written by 1148, the *Gesta Stephani* then bemoaned the effect that the civil war had on the state of the English church, and the English bishops in particular. Most, the author complained, were cowardly and incapable of standing against the nobles who were, in his view, ravaging the countryside at will. He wrote,

> But they, cowering in most dastardly fear, bent like a reed shaken by the wind, and since their salt had no savour they did not rise up to resist or set themselves as a wall before the house of Israel. For they should have met men wise in the flesh with the sword of God's word, which devours flesh, and to the sons of Belial [who were ravaging the country] they should bravely have presented the countenance of Jeremiah and the horned forehead of Moses.[61]

The bishops ought to have done more to protect the country, and specifically they ought to have wielded the sword of excommunication more effectively. The author of the *Gesta Stephani* specifically complained of bishops who offered excommunications on which they failed to follow through, or which were 'soon revoked.'[62] He also complained of those bishops who, rather than offering too weak a defense against their enemies, took matters into their own hands and fought violence with violence. Furthermore, these bishops began to behave just as, if not worse than, the men they were fighting against. The author wrote

> others (but it was no task for bishops) filled their castles full of provisions and stocks of arms, knights, and archers, and though they were supposed to be warding off the evil-doers who were plundering the goods of the Church showed themselves always more cruel and more merciless than those very evil-doers in oppressing their neighbours and plundering their goods. Likewise the bishops, the bishops themselves, though I am ashamed to say it, not indeed all but a great many out of the whole number, girt with swords and

---

[60] Ibid.
[61] Ibid., 157.
[62] Ibid.

wearing magnificent suits of armour, rode on horseback with the haughtiest destroyers of the country and took their share of the spoil;.[63]

The author was condemning churchmen who embraced the same tactics as the pillagers and warriors, and this arrow could not have missed Bishop Henry, as he was the highest-profile clerical general in the country. However, a closer examination shows us that, while the author did not relish the idea of clerics fighting, his condemnation was not quite as cut and dried as it seems, especially concerning his earlier praise of Henry's manful defense against William de Pont de l'Arche. His first complaint was that the bishops who 'were supposed to be warding off the evil-doers who were plundering the goods of the Church' instead showed 'themselves always more cruel and more merciless than those very evil-doers in oppressing their neighbours and plundering their goods.'[64] So, in fact, the complaint here was that the clerics were not doing enough to fight against the marauders, and instead had taken up arms for the detrimental purpose of further pillaging the countryside. The author wrote that he was ashamed to say that the bishops were 'girt with swords and wearing magnificent suits of armour' and they 'rode on horseback with the haughtiest destroyers of the country and took their share of the spoil.'[65] He was condemning the clerics for their pillaging and desire for spoils. The implicit counterpoint to this is that they ought to have spent their energies defending their flocks and the country from the pillagers. The language used here focuses on the pride, pomp, wealth, and worldliness of the bishops. They were going about acting and dressing as great secular lords. His condemnation of their riding in armor and armed does, however, indicate that he was offended by the behavior of churchmen who behaved as warriors, but he was more concerned that they were behaving as knights.

The *Gesta Stephani*'s condemnation of this 'knightly' behavior by clerics – and the author named Henry of Winchester, Alexander of Lincoln, and Roger de Clinton, bishop of Chester specifically as the worst offenders – calls to mind a similar description from Henry of Huntingdon. Henry of Huntingdon, in his *De Contemptu Mundi*, specifically condemned Henry of Blois as being a 'monstrous'

---

[63] Ibid. 'alii, quod tamen non erat opus episcoporum, castella sua escis et armorum copiis, militibus et sagitariis refertissime supplebant, dumque maleficos rerumque ecclesiasticarum direptores arcere putarentur, ipsis maleficis in vicinis suis opprimendis, in rebus eorum diripiendis crudeliores semper et magis immisericordes extiterant. Ipsi nihilominus, ipsi episcopi, quod pudet quidem dicere, non tamen omnes, sed plurimi ex omnibus, ferro accincti, armis decentissime instructi, cum patriae perversoribus superbissimis invebi equis, praedae participari.'

[64] Ibid.

[65] Ibid.

mixture of knight and monk. He wrote (after Henry's elevation to Winchester but before 1135), 'Now there sits in their place Henry, nephew of King Henry, who will be a new kind of monster, composed part pure and part corrupt, I mean part monk and part knight.'[66] This quotation, which has become rightly famous, is also very complex. On the surface it clearly condemned clerics who embraced knightliness; however, it was not necessarily churchmen who fought in wars that Henry was condemning but, rather, worldliness and excessive pride. Henry ignores or suppresses the military roles played by Anglo-Saxon bishops and abbots in the campaigns of 1016, but Henry's condemnation of the bishop of Winchester was written prior to 1135, and there is no evidence of Henry of Blois having a military role prior to the war.[67] Therefore, it was probably his worldliness and overall demeanor that Henry was complaining about, rather than some specific event of warfare.[68] He also showed an impressive amount of prescience in foreseeing that once hostilities did break out, Bishop Henry would happily throw himself into the fray.[69]

Henry of Huntingdon's displeasure with Bishop Henry's unification of the clerical and knightly lives did not stop him from offering copious praise for Alexander of Lincoln, to whom he dedicated his work, and who was at least as much a 'knightly' warrior as Henry.[70] Huntingdon called Alexander the 'flower of men' and wrote that he 'collects honour's treasures' through his generosity. Furthermore, Henry lauded men like Archbishop Lanfranc, Archbishop Anselm, Bishop Adhémar of le Puy, and Archbishop Thurstan as being holy and pious. He called Lanfranc 'a philosopher and outstanding man' and he referred to Anselm as 'a philosopher and saintly man'.[71] He wrote that Thurstan was 'praiseworthy in every way'.[72] Anselm, Lanfranc, and Thurstan all played vital military roles at one time or another, but they did so in causes that Henry supported, and they did so

---

[66] Henry of Huntingdon, 608–11.

[67] Ibid., 359 n. 65. It is, however, difficult to know whether Henry was purposefully suppressing their roles, or if his sources did not contain reference to their actions; Cf. ASC, 152; cf. John of Worcester, 492–3. John sought to also minimize the role played by the bishop and abbot by making it clear that they were on the battlefield only to 'pray to God for the soldiers fighting the battle.' This was despite a long tradition of Anglo-Saxon bishops and abbots taking active roles in combat.

[68] Ibid., 610 n. 68. It is also possible that Huntingdon was referring to Henry's Cluniac heritage.

[69] This also indicates, though it is purely speculative, that Bishop Henry did travel with a knightly retinue and was probably clad in armor and girt with a sword, even before the civil war.

[70] Henry of Huntingdon, 475.

[71] Ibid., 609.

[72] Ibid., 613.

without embracing the prideful and ostentatious 'knightliness' of men like Henry of Winchester. They used warfare sparingly and 'correctly', and never fell victim to the allure of worldliness. Even in the course of the description of events during the 'present time', Henry never condemned Bishop Henry for his activities in war during the civil war, and in fact he often downplayed any hint of scandal surrounding Henry. Thus, a cleric engaging in war was not condemned per se, only if he wedded it to 'worldliness' and made it his life's goal. So long as he remained principally a churchman rather than a knight, continued to behave with humility, and fought in causes that were embraced by the author, he could utilize righteous warfare without criticism.[73]

Both Henry of Huntingdon and the author of the *Gesta Stephani* bemoaned the 'knightly' pride of the bishops, who they thought ought to have shown more humility. Clerics could be active in warfare if necessary, but they ought to be so in the right causes and the right manner. This is confirmed by the *Gesta Stephani*'s account of an 'ideal' bishop – Robert de Béthune, bishop of Hereford. He was

> a man of religious devotion and most resolute character, [and he] did not stray from principles of religion or the path of justice but, taking up the weapons with which the Apostle heedfully arms and carefully equips the man of the Gospel, he manfully set himself like a shield of defence against the enemies of catholic peace.[74]

The *Gesta Stephani* was especially fond of Bishop Robert for his excommunication of Miles of Gloucester, one of the villains of the tale, and his former patron and earl. When Miles sent men to ravage Hereford's holdings, Bishop Robert gathered the clergy together and excommunicated the earl. Miles died a miserable death later that year, slain while hunting, due to God's vengeance.[75]

We can contrast this tale with that of Robert of Lewes, bishop of Bath (who may have been the author of the *Gesta*). Early in Stephen's reign, Bath was one of the few royal strongholds in the southwest, and was constantly harassed by the Angevin garrison in Bristol. The author retold of an attack on Bath by the citizens of Bristol. The bishop of Bath's soldiers surprised them and captured Geoffrey Talbot, a supporter of the Empress.[76] The rebels then offered the bishop of Bath safe conduct to come to discuss his release. The bishop, 'like a simple-minded

---

[73] This is further reinforced by his treatment of the near-legendary Bishop Ealhstan, who manfully fought against the pagan Danes.
[74] *Gesta Stephani*, 159.
[75] Ibid., 161.
[76] Ibid., 59.

man who believes every word, like another Jacob who lived guilelessly at home' was seized by them when he arrived and the author then eviscerated them in prose, saying that the attackers had laid 'sacrilegious hands on the preacher of the Gospel, the ministrant at God's holy table, and the venerable sower of all men's faith and religion, the steward of the grain in the Lord's granary, who carries in his breast the ark of God and the divine manna.'[77] The bishop acquiesced to their demands and released Geoffrey. When Stephen heard of this, he accused the bishop of colluding with his enemies and threatened to march on Bath to take him into custody. Cooler heads prevailed, probably Henry of Winchester, who was Robert of Lewes's patron, and the king eventually forgave the bishop.

In defending his decision to release Geoffrey to save his own skin, Robert fell back on the argument about the impropriety of a bishop's returning 'evil for evil' or being 'harmful himself to harm the harmful.'[78] Now, he was either taking the perfectly canonical position of the proper role and disposition of bishops, or he was using it as a useful defense against the king's anger at his release of Geoffrey. It seems very probable that it was a little of both. The author needed a reason why Robert had failed so completely, both to assuage the king and also to assuage his own honor. This early failure in the realm of warfare by Robert, a conventional bishop, probably colored the rest of the author's interpretation of warrior-clerics. He often praised Henry of Winchester, for example, for being manful in the face of danger and in resisting his enemies, but also condemned him for being overtly worldly and knightly. Henry's failure was that he behaved more like a knight in his dress, his demeanor, and his display, not that he used violence to achieve his ends, provided that they were laudatory. A final example will demonstrate this interpretation. When a companion of Brian fitz Count captured the Bishop of Winchester's castle at Lidelea

> the bishop, who was always wise in judgement and most vigorous in action, acted on his own behalf, gathered a mighty host, and with great energy built two castles in front of this one, and by garrisoning them adequately with knights and footmen reduced the besieged to the extremity of hunger.[79]

The castle eventually surrendered after Stephen defeated an attempt by Robert of Gloucester to relieve it. In this small vignette, we can see again the author's acceptance of righteous violence and military action by clerics. How can Henry have been 'wise in judgement and most vigorous in action', but also have been

---

[77] Ibid., 61.
[78] Ibid.
[79] Ibid., 211.

shameful for riding about in armor with a sword and leading armies? The answer is that both were true, and both were accurate. It could be acceptable for a cleric to lead armies, to prosecute sieges, and even if necessary to charge into battle, but he had to do so at all times as a cleric, and not a knight. While this might strike us as a semantic difference, since a man killed on a battlefield rarely asked the disposition of his assailant, yet it was hugely important to medieval observers. While the prescriptive notions of *ordines* did not influence actual behavior as much as theoreticians would have hoped, they did have an impact on what people considered acceptable behavior for clerics and others. So long as a cleric recalled his clerical status, and fought in a cause considered just by the observer, he could wield both swords entrusted to St. Peter by Christ.

Henry bolstered his image in his later years by spending two decades as an elder statesman within the church. After the civil war and Stephen's death in 1154, Henry had a long period of post-warfare activity, during which he wholly embraced his clerical role and seemingly put aside violence as a tool. His earlier life as a 'knightly' bishop was not held against him, and while he never again exercised the same amount of authority as he had as papal legate, Henry remained an important and impressive cleric in England. He was omnipresent during the Becket controversy, though he took a back seat to others in the conflict. In 1166 he was given a papal commission, along with Bishop William Turbe of Norwich, to investigate the Gilbertine houses of southern England.[80] This demonstrated that he was treated the same as his fellows, and given the deference due to him from his years of service and his ecclesiastical rank. Clearly, his earlier exploits in war were not sufficient to adversely affect his career.

Modern historians have used Henry's post-1154 career to argue either that he had 'reformed' (since they argue that warrior-clerics were guilty of malfeasance) or that the broader culture of the world of Henry II was no longer willing to accept clerics who mixed their ecclesiastical position with activity in warfare.[81] Michael Davis argues that Henry's later years worked to 'add polish to the past tarnishes to his reputation.'[82] To David Knowles, Henry's decision was because of a conscious recognition that his style of ecclesiastic was 'an anachronism in the new world of 1154.'[83] Knowles saw Henry as having embraced a wholly different persona after the death of Stephen in 1154, shedding his 'worldliness' in favor of a rededication

---

[80] Christopher Harper-Bill, 'Bishop William Turbe and the Diocese of Norwich, 1146–1174', *Anglo-Norman Studies* 7, ed. R. Allen Brown (1984), 148.

[81] Such a cultural change would have come as a surprise to Geoffrey Plantagenet, Thomas Becket, Hubert Walter, Peter des Roches, Philip of Dreux, and the rest of the high-ranking ecclesiastics who continued to take active military roles.

[82] Davis, *Henry of Blois*, 136.

[83] Knowles, *Saints and Scholars*, 52.

to his 'proper' role as a spiritual leader. Knowles writes that Henry's contemporaries 'agree that in this last period of his life his character had greatly changed; perhaps it would be more true to say that the deepest potentialities of his personality, long undeveloped beneath the turmoil of ambitious and worldly activities, now had freedom to spring into life and view.'[84] Davis echoes this interpretation of Henry's post-civil-war behavior, quoting Knowles to the effect that there was no room for a warlike bishop in the post-Stephen England. He writes,

> The time spent at Cluny allowed the old bishop to work for God and reflect. Time had acted like a soothing balm healing the festering sores of his political ambition. A different Henry remerged from his exile and henceforth he would take on a different role; that of elder statesman.[85]

Henry's transformation to 'a venerable and beloved elder statesman' was well underway.[86] What caused this apparently complete change of heart is not clear. One calls to mind the wonderful exchange between Peter O'Toole (playing Henry II) and Felix Aylmer (playing the archbishop of Canterbury) in the 1964 film *Becket*. When Henry asks for taxes from the church, and he is told that the church can support wars with only their prayers, he angrily replies that clerics fought happily enough at Hastings when there was booty to be won. The archbishop calmly responds, 'Those times are over. The priest is back in his sanctuary. It is peace time.'[87] Both Davis and Knowles approach Henry's life and career from the similar position that a warrior-cleric was somehow less 'legitimate' than one who abhorred military actions. However, Henry was not 'reborn' after 1154, after recognizing the error of his ways. In fact, what changed after 1154 was not Henry but, rather, the circumstances in which he operated. He had embraced warfare between 1135 and 1154 because it served his purposes as the brother to the king, as the papal legate seeking to bring peace to the realm, and as a major landholder during a time of civil war. There was no civil war in England after 1154, and the only major rebellion within the kingdom during Henry II's reign occurred two years after Bishop Henry's death.[88] Changing circumstances do not demonstrate a changing ideology.

---

[84] Ibid., 53.
[85] Davis, *Henry of Blois*, 124.
[86] Knowles, *Saints and Scholars*, 53.
[87] *Becket*, DVD, directed by Peter Glenville (1964; Shepperton, England: Paramount Pictures/MPI Media Group, 2007).
[88] It is certainly interesting to consider how Henry, had he been alive and in his prime, would have behaved during the Great Rebellion of 1173–74.

CHAPTER 7

The Angevins, Part I
(Henry II and Richard I) Royal Servants*

STEPHEN's adoption of Henry Plantagenet, son of Matilda and Count Geoffrey of Anjou, in 1153 brought an end to the civil war in England. Henry II became king in 1154 on Stephen's death, and his power and titles grew to make him one of the strongest and most influential rulers of the Middle Ages. His reign, and the reigns of his sons Richard and John, also featured continued military service from important churchmen. This chapter focuses on two men who primarily fought for Henry II himself – Thomas Becket and Henry's own illegitimate son, Geoffrey Plantagenet. Becket's military role as chancellor in Henry's campaigns in France, and its portrayal by contemporaries, is instructive of how warrior-clerics in the second half of the twelfth century could be presented, especially when their actions were on behalf of a legitimate ruler. Geoffrey, archdeacon and bishop-elect of Lincoln (1173–82), archbishop of York (1191–1212), was a hybrid between directors of military affairs, such as Lanfranc and Anselm, and career generals, such as Geoffrey de Montbray, bishop of Coutances. Geoffrey owed his elevation and social position to Henry II's favor, and his loyalty to the king was never in question. His dedication to the elder king was so marked (especially compared to Henry's legitimate sons) that the king was known to remark, in jest and frustration, that Geoffrey was, in fact, his only 'true' son. Despite resigning his election to Lincoln, so that he would be freer to serve as royal chancellor, he was still elected and consecrated as archbishop of York upon the death of his father and elevation of his brother Richard. Both Geoffrey and Becket parlayed their royal service into exalted ecclesiastical positions and, despite their very different and controversial actions as archbishop, both enjoyed relatively positive images with their contemporaries in regards to their previous royal service.

I do not propose here to recount Becket's career, conflict with Henry II, murder, or subsequent canonization.[1] However, I do want to discuss his military

---

* I have written about Geoffrey Plantagenet's career elsewhere, and this chapter draws upon some of my earlier research and conclusions. See Craig M. Nakashian, "'All my sons are bastards': Geoffrey Plantagenet's Military Service to Henry II," in *Ecclesia et Violentia: Violence against the Church and Violence within the Church in the Middle Ages*, ed. Radosław Kotecki and Jacek Maciejewski (Newcastle-upon-Tyne, 2014), 122–40.

[1] The standard general treatments of Becket's life and career are still David Knowles, *Thomas Becket* (Stanford, 1971) and Frank Barlow, *Thomas Becket* (Berkeley, 1986).

actions as chancellor, and the treatment of these actions by his biographers, primarily William FitzStephen and Herbert de Boseham.² As Hanna Vollrath has pointed out, there was no unified discourse about Thomas Becket; each author found a different avenue for discussion in understanding his life.³ While this is certainly true, and we shall see evidence of that discourse below, for the most part Becket provided one of the best examples of a churchman who embodied the 'turn from worldliness' narrative of reform ideology, and he fit into that narrative construct for both reformist contemporaries eager to present it as ideal, and modern historians hoping to find decreasing support for 'outdated' warrior-clerics.⁴ Since many of his biographers/hagiographers chose to ignore Becket's military actions while chancellor, it is even more interesting that William FitzStephen did not, and instead valorized them. Becket's embrace of warfare as chancellor demonstrates the easy relationship royal clerical servants had with war, and the difficulty some contemporaries had with categorizing it. His nomination by Henry II, probably a partial result of his fervent and effective military service to the king, and his near unanimous election as archbishop, albeit a result of this royal pressure, also shows that his personal conduct in war

---

For a more popular history of Becket based on the posthumous publication of William Urry's manuscript on Becket, see William Urry, Thomas Becket: His Last Days, ed. and intro. Peter A. Rowe (Stroud, 1999). Jean Truax gives a good account of the state of the archbishopric upon Becket's elevation. See Truax, Heirs of Anselm and Ancestors of Becket, 181–8. Finally, for a more focused treatment of Becket's portrayal by his biographers, see Michael Staunton, Thomas Becket and His Biographers (Woodbridge, 2006). For an excellent narrative description of Becket's military career see John D. Hosler, 'The Brief Military Career of Thomas Becket', HSJ 15 (2004), 000–00.

[2] I have chosen these two biographers in particular because both served Becket as chancellor and archbishop, and thus their accounts come largely from first-hand experiences with Thomas. I primarily use William FitzStephen because he wrote extensively about Thomas's time as chancellor. See Knowles, Thomas Becket, 33. See also Hanna Vollrath, 'Was Thomas Becket Chaste? Understanding Episodes in the Becket Lives', Anglo-Norman Studies 27, ed. John Gillingham (Woodbridge, 2005), 201.

[3] Vollrath, 198. Staunton, Thomas Becket and His Biographers. For a discussion on the use of hagiography, see Felice Lifshitz, 'Beyond Positivism and Genre: "Hagiographical" Texts as Historical Narrative', Viator 25 (1994), 95–113.

[4] In discussing St. Hugh of Lincoln (d. 1200), Karl Leyser posited that Hugh's dedication to an ascetic lifestyle 'enabled him to dissociate himself and to inspire awe and hit the consciences of men in high places who were bound to live in a perpetual state of conflict between their new professional secular tasks and the inner dictates of their clerical ordo.' See Karl Leyser, 'The Angevin Kings and the Holy Man', Communications and Power in Medieval Europe: The Gregorian Revolution and Beyond, ed. Timothy Reuter (London, 1994), 159. Leyser's insight is well taken, even if it assumes an inherent conflict between secular tasks and clerical identity. For many clerics it certainly did, but as this study has shown, it was not an all-encompassing outlook.

did not disqualify him from the archbishopric in the eyes of his contemporaries, nor did it prove to be an insurmountable obstacle for Henry to overcome.[5] While Becket's previous service to Henry II alarmed reformist clerics devoted to ecclesiastical independence (at least until royal power was needed to protect their interests), he was perfectly in keeping with Henry's desire to return to a tradition of cooperation between the archbishop of Canterbury and the king.[6] Thomas would probably not have been as acceptable a candidate to modern historians, however. Modern commentators have often adopted the ideology of twelfth-century reformers as normative, and have usually judged Becket (and other contemporary churchmen) in those terms. David Knowles, in his 1971 biography of Becket, criticizes his opulent lifestyle in language that could have been borrowed from Bernard de Clairvaux

> we seem to note in Thomas a love of the display of wealth and expensive things which is open to criticism, not only as unbecoming a cleric and even in a devout Christian, but because there is in it a note of rhetoric, if not of vulgarity, that is inconsistent with a character of true dignity.[7]

Knowles commented on, and condemned, Becket's perceived worldliness, and he saw Becket's activity in warfare as an implied part of that fault. Knowles's complaint is also highlighted by Frank Barlow in his 1986 biography of Becket. Barlow writes that 'Thomas gloried in all the pomps of the world' and that William FitzStephen depicted Becket and Henry II 'as boon companions, in and out of each other's apartments, gaming, fowling and hunting together, as close off duty as on.'[8] Barlow goes further, explaining that when Becket became a deacon he 'was now precluded from marrying, bearing arms and pursuing other unsuitable activities.'[9] The prohibitions on behavior mentioned in these canons do not seem to have concerned his contemporaries, and Barlow theorizes that this was due to Becket's background as a secular, rather than regular, cleric.[10] Barlow makes

---

[5] The only bishop to speak against his election, Gilbert Foliot, probably did so as much out of a desire for the office himself as he did out of concerns for Thomas's closeness to the king. See Adrian Morey and C.N.L. Brooke, *Gilbert Foliot and His Letters* (Cambridge, 1965), 170. Indeed, David Knowles admitted that there was no public protest at his election. Furthermore, he characterized the election as unanimous, as was the application to the pope for a *pallium*. See Knowles, *Thomas Becket*, 52.

[6] Archbishops Dunstan and Lanfranc were two exemplars that Henry could look to for emulation.

[7] Knowles, *Thomas Becket*, 39.

[8] Barlow, *Thomas Becket*, 44.

[9] Ibid., 38.

[10] Ibid., 58–9.

the case that the cultural acceptance of warrior-clerics was based on legalistic definitions of status as distinguishing between a monk and a secular cleric. This is an intriguing argument, though it would call into question why a number of Becket's biographers found it necessary to explain away his secular (if not his military) actions as chancellor, or to use them as a precursor to his turning from secular to spiritual concerns. Barlow is essentially arguing that secular clerics had greater leeway to engage in "worldly" activities than did monks. Douglas Senette makes a similar argument vis-à-vis Bishop Henry of Winchester, and we can see, perhaps, such a conception reflected in Henry of Huntingdon's complaints regarding Henry. There is some truth to their distinction, and while we cannot know exactly how many contemporaries held such views, overall it represents a further demonstration of the full spectrum of beliefs and ideologies that existed in regards to warrior-clerics. It could also help to explain the differences in behavior of men such as Anselm and Lanfranc, versus those such as Odo of Bayeux and Geoffrey Plantagenet.

Among the numerous contemporaries who wrote *Lives* of Thomas Becket after his murder, William FitzStephen and Herbert de Boseham offered two of the most intimate portrayals of him.[11] William served Becket as chancellor and archbishop, and was a witness to his murder.[12] He created a stark duality of interests in the figure of Thomas Becket, but a commonality of personality. He described Becket as a fanatically devoted servant, first to Henry II as chancellor, then to God as archbishop. However, in spite of the shift in loyalty, FitzStephen offered an image of Becket that was praiseworthy in both professions.[13] This was in contrast to how John of Salisbury (also a former clerk of Becket's) and William of Canterbury approached Becket's time as chancellor. John, in his brief account of Becket's chancellorship, reinforced FitzStephen's argument that Becket did

---

[11] Michael Staunton referred to William FitzStephen's account as the 'most appealing' of the *Lives* and one that filled in many sections of Thomas's life and career left out by other biographers. See Staunton, *Lives of Thomas Becket*, 56. For the entire section on William FitzStephen, see 56–62. William maintained close ties to the royal court after Becket's exile, which could certainly explain his approach to Becket's achievements as chancellor, as well as why the other Becket biographers do not refer to him. See Staunton, *Lives of Thomas Becket*, 8–9.

[12] Hosler points out that William 'was perhaps the best-informed of all of Becket's biographers because he personally knew his subject both during and after his chancellorship and composed his *Life* soon after the martyrdom.' Hosler, 89.

[13] Also of note is that FitzStephen credited Becket's elevation to chancellor to 'the noble Henry, bishop of Winchester'. Not only was William praising Henry, bishop of Winchester, but he also created an important link between the young Becket and a man who had successfully unified his clerical career with active warfare. See *English Historical Documents*, 2, 705.

not relish some of the worldly activities of being chancellor, and William of Canterbury contended that the 'more Thomas climbed in the secular world, the more humble he was at heart, whatever he appeared to be.'[14] John and William of Canterbury were interested in showing that Becket was always 'saintly' – an ascetic holy man who spurned inwardly those worldly things required of his office. FitzStephen's account contains some of these elements as well, especially in terms of the 'worldly' activities, but he lauds Becket for his service to Henry II and for his military achievements.

In FitzStephen's account, Becket did good and laudable things as chancellor. He helped Henry II bring peace and stability to a country wracked by fifteen years of civil war, as well as making sure that vacant ecclesiastical offices were filled without hint of simony.[15] Furthermore, he resisted the temptation to take incomes from these churches himself, though he could have, but instead found them worthy holders.[16] When Becket entertained the nobility and other wealthy figures, he did so in order to collect rich alms from them, thereby turning something worldly into something holy. When he played at the activities of the nobility – hunting, sports, and chess – he did so 'in a perfunctory manner, not with commitment.'[17] Finally, despite the promptings of his king, Becket did not indulge in lechery. William did not decry Becket's secular actions as chancellor (despite his being a churchman), but he considered it more laudable that Becket put aside the worldly interests of the secular court, specifically his clothing, dining habits, and lifestyle, in favor of living a more simple and ascetic life. While Staunton argues that FitzStephen included Becket's ostentatious embassy to the French king and his military exploits in order to build 'up the image of Thomas in the secular world so as to heighten the dramatic charge of his change of life upon becoming archbishop', I believe that William, alone among the contemporary biographers of Becket, tried to craft an image of the slain archbishop that sanctified him, but did so within the context and confines of being acceptable and prescriptive within the royal court – a difficulty obviously exacerbated by the realities of Becket's murder.[18]

Staunton also makes an intriguing argument, following on that of Scattergood, that FitzStephen was using his description of London at the start of his *Life* to construct a complex dichotomy between the classical and Christian, secular and spiritual, within Becket's life. Classical authors often began their works by

---

[14] Staunton, *Lives of Thomas Becket*, 53–5. See also Vollrath, 203.
[15] Staunton, *Lives of Thomas Becket*, 49.
[16] Ibid., 50.
[17] Ibid.
[18] Staunton, *Thomas Becket and His Biographers*, 59.

extolling Rome, so FitzStephen was showing the glory of Becket's secular achievements before showing his greater glory in spiritual ones. Staunton also points out that FitzStephen's account of Becket's pre-archiepiscopal life and career bristles with classical references, but no Christian ones, whereas his archiepiscopal career is flooded with Christian references.[19] Staunton's interpretation is an appealing one, since it casts the secular side of Becket's life not as inherently horrid and sinful, needing to be washed away by his complete transformation as archbishop but, rather, as valuable and meritorious, just not as valuable and meritorious as his later actions as archbishop. His service to his king was a firm and praiseworthy foundation for his later service to Christ.

Becket's role in the 1159 campaign in Aquitaine has received more assessment and analysis by modern historians than it did by his contemporaries.[20] Only William FitzStephen discussed it at length, while other biographers such as Edward Grim merely referred to it (negatively), and used it as evidence to contrast with his time as archbishop.[21] FitzStephen lauds Becket's military acumen, especially regarding his arguments in favor of attacking the city of Toulouse. Henry's other generals counseled him not to attack the city, because his liegelord Louis VII, king of France, had entered the city with a small force. William bemoaned that Becket's advice was ignored, and instead that Henry had listened to his 'untrustworthy' (*vana*) other advisors, and the opportunity to take the city was lost.[22] According to FitzStephen, Becket showed more military wisdom and

---

[19] Ibid., 82–3.
[20] See Jane P. Martindale, '"An unfinished business": Angevin Politics and the Siege of Toulouse (1159)', *Anglo-Norman Studies* 23, ed. John Gillingham (2001), 115-154; John Hosler, 'The Brief Military Career of Thomas Becket'. See also Richard Benjamin, 'A Forty Years War: Toulouse and the Plantagenets, 1156-96', *Historical Research* 61 (1988), 272-4.
[21] Grim wrote, '"Who can tell", he asks, "how much death, how much persecution he inflicted", and he goes on to say that Thomas attacked and destroyed villages and towns, that he burnt houses and other possessions without compunction and that he was relentless in fighting his king's enemies. 'But in all this (although others may think differently about it), his body was chaste and his heart was humble, but among the humble only, for among the mighty ones he appeared mightier and more sublime than they did.' Quoted in Vollrath, 206. The original passage in Grim reads, 'Sed inter his omnibus (licet aliter aliqui aestimaverint) corpore castus, corde humilis, sed inter humiles, nam inter potentes potentior ipse ac sublimior apparebat'. See *MTB*, 2, 365.
[22] The passage reads, 'de propria familia lectam manum, septingentos milites habebat. Et quidem, si eius paritum esset consilio, urbem Tolosam, et regem Franciae, qui favore sororis comitissae Constantiae se immiserat, sed et improvide sine exercitu et manu forti, invasissent et cepissent; tantus erat regis Anglorum exercitus. Sed vana superstitione et reverentia rex tentus consilio aliorum, super urbem, in qua esset dominus suus rex Franciae, irruere noluit'. William FitzStephen, *Vita S. Thomae, MTB*, 3, 33-4. Henry also

bravery than did his secular peers.²³ FitzStephen saw value in what Becket did as chancellor, much as Eadmer saw value in Anselm's aid to Henry I (discussed in chapter 5). Such an interpretation is strengthened by the fact that both John of Salisbury (who dedicated his *Policraticus* to Becket while the chancellor was besieging Toulouse) and Stephen of Rouen (author of the *Draco Normannicus*) do not fault Becket for his military leadership in the campaign because they accept the overall justice of Henry's cause in France.²⁴

FitzStephen then related more about the campaign, including the seizure of Cahores and the crossing of the Garonne. He was creating and using Becket's reputation as a canny general to increase his honor, especially as opposed to the 'untrustworthy' (and perhaps even cowardly) secular lords who had argued for retreat. For Martindale, this was further evidence of FitzStephen seeking to build a strong contrast between Becket the secular man, and Becket the spiritual one. For William Urry, on the other hand, Becket's campaign was violent, destructive, and worthy of condemnation. After detailing his actions at Toulouse, he writes, 'Becket fell back on Quercy and conducted a savage and cruel dragonnade, slaughtering and burning, as recorded by shocked biographers.'²⁵ Urry went further and explained that 'Becket's military activities are not attractive to the modern mind.'²⁶ Far from being the scandalized biographer Urry refers to, William FitzStephen seemingly purposely created a Becket who was braver and more of a ruthless general than men for whom it was expected to be the purpose of their *ordo*. Furthermore, FitzStephen did so in a way that intimated that Becket's behavior and defense of the king's interests was praiseworthy. In this case, we are put in mind of how the *Gesta Stephani* treated Henry of Winchester's advice

---

might have quite seriously believed that assaulting a city in which his liege-lord (Louis VII) was present was an assault on the prestige of kingship. See Matthew Strickland, 'Against the Lord's Anointed: Aspects of Warfare and Baronial Rebellion in England and Normandy 1075-1265', *Law and Government in Medieval England and Normandy: Essays in Honour of Sir James Holt*, ed. G. Garnett and J. Hudson (Cambridge, 1994), 63-4.

²³ Martindale, 136. Martindale cautions us that William might have been inflating Becket's role in the siege in order to 'emphasize the contrast between the conduct and attitudes of Thomas as chancellor and Thomas as archbishop.' Such an interpretation would be perfectly in keeping with seeing Becket's life in the Saul/Paul conversion trope.

²⁴ Martindale, 121-4.

²⁵ Urry, *Thomas Becket*, 5. Martindale writes that Becket was 'entrusted with the work of organizing this, although possibly the role which he played in the direction of these secular affairs is emphasized in works written after his murder, either in order to emphasize how much the king had owed to his chancellor, or to make an even more dramatic contrast with Becket's conversion to a severe religious life at a later date.' See Martindale, 142.

²⁶ Ibid., 3.

to King Stephen at the siege of Exeter (discussed in chapter 6), whereby Henry's advice to be firm and unsympathetic was contrasted with the (ultimately incorrect) advice of the secular nobles to offer the garrison generous terms to surrender.

FitzStephen then discussed Becket's military achievements on the 1161-62 Gisors campaign. In a section regarding the war in France, William highlighted the size of Becket's command (seven hundred *equites*, another twelve hundred *stipendarios milites*, and four thousand *servientium*) and his important function as a military paymaster and administrator.[27] Becket's role as general was merely a precursor to his actively performing deeds of chivalric prowess. Hosler notes that 'the chancellor found opportunity to distinguish himself on the battlefield. Despite his riding with a more seasoned company than he, Becket is said to have been the most daring warrior of all.'[28] FitzStephen wrote, without condemnation and with a hint of pride, about Becket's victorious joust with the 'strong' (*valente*) French knight Engelram de Trie. Becket, 'despite being a cleric', struck and unhorsed Engelram, and gained his charger.[29] FitzStephen demonstrates Becket's courage and achievement by specifically mentioning Engelram's strength and bravery, and then contrasting it with Becket's clerical status. It does not seem that he mentioned Becket's status in order to condemn him for jousting but, rather, as in the above example of his advice at Toulouse, to show that he excelled in activities that were outside his normal occupation and to create an even stronger contrast with Engelram. Just as he was a better military advisor than Henry II's other generals outside of Toulouse, here too he was a better warrior than the professional knight Engelram.

Herbert de Boseham also briefly discussed Becket's career as chancellor. While he complained about the poor effect the elevation to chancellor had on Becket's morals, and he decried the future archbishop's turn towards worldly opulence and secular comforts, he did not specifically condemn Becket's military actions.[30]

---

[27] William FitzStephen, 34-5.
[28] Hosler, 94. Becket's jousting with the enemy also shows the difficulty in separating being a 'general' and a 'warrior' in medieval combat.
[29] The entire passage reads, 'Ipsemet, clericus cum esset, cum valente milite Franco, Engelramno de Tria, e regione subsiditis equo calcaribus veniente armato, lancea demissa et equo admisso congressus, ipsum equo dejecit, et dextrarium lucrifecit.' William FitzStephen, 35. Hosler claims that Becket 'won high praise from the French nobles and Louis VII' for his defeat of Engelram. See Hosler, 94.
[30] Herbert de Boseham, *MTB*, 3, 172-5. Herbert did comment on Thomas's achievements on the Toulouse campaign, writing, 'qualiter videlicet et quam industrie munitiones quinque munitissimas, in Franciae et Normanniae sitas confinio, domino suo regi, ad cuius tamen ius ab antiquo spectare dignoscebantur a rege Francorum per matrimonium, sine ferro, sine gladio, absque lancea, absque pugna, in omni regum dilectione et pace revocaverit, Gizortium scilicet, castrum munitissimum, et alia quatuor.'

William and Herbert both comment that once Becket was elevated to the archbishopric, he put aside the secular duties of chancellor and turned fully to concerns of the spirit. His putting aside of worldly concerns and interests, including fine food, comfortable clothing, and hunting, is one of the most celebrated aspects of his biography, and was used by authors to speak of his inherent holiness, and also to fit Thomas into the Saul/Paul conversion mechanism important to Christian exegesis.[31] While there was some question as to how 'authentic' Becket's secularity had been, there was no debate that once he became archbishop he dedicated himself with monastic fervor to spiritual, rather than worldly, concerns.[32] John Hosler has interpreted the course of Becket's career by arguing that the 'saintly Becket could be no warrior, so it was his conversion in 1162 from a man of the world to a man of God that first captured the attention of his biographers.'[33] Hosler is certainly correct that most of Becket's biographers wanted to focus on the martyred archbishop's spirituality, rather than his military achievements, but we are still left with William FitzStephen's depiction of Becket. He saw his previous achievements in war on behalf of Henry II as still sufficiently glorious to include them in his biography without using them as a foil for Becket's later rejection of 'worldliness'. For FitzStephen, Becket's devotion to Henry II and to God demonstrated his good sense and character, and thus his saintliness was seen in all his endeavors.[34]

Geoffrey Plantagenet was, like Becket, a controversial figure for contemporaries, though he received generally positive treatment from the chroniclers of the reigns of his father and brothers.[35] Walter Map was his primary critic, but, as

---

[31] Staunton argues that Becket's biographers 'strike a balance between Becket's virtues and the limits of his achievements ... [but] they consistently claim that the roots of his later greatness lay in his earlier life.' Staunton, *Thomas Becket and His Biographers*, 78. For how this fits into the broader Christian ideology, see pages 88–90, 96. See also Michael Staunton, 'Thomas Becket's Conversion', *Anglo-Norman Studies* 21 (1999), 193–4. It is interesting that his biographers focused so much on Becket's elevation as archbishop for the moment of his 'transformation', rather than his ordination as deacon, which subjected him to canon law. See Vollrath, 205–7.

[32] For a description of Becket's austerity measures, see William FitzStephen, 37–41.

[33] Hosler, 99.

[34] Hosler argues that FitzStephen was perhaps overly sympathetic towards Becket, and that he only 'deigns' to discuss Becket's activities in warfare. He 'frequently advances the proposition that Becket possessed irreproachable good faith and splendid character.' See Hosler, 89. Daniel Gerrard convincingly argues that it is 'inappropriate' to say that FitzStephen was uncomfortable with Becket's warfare, because 'Becket's military activities are not held in tension with his sacred status, they are part of it.' Gerrard, 202. Vollrath also sees FitzStephen as celebrating both Becket's religious fervor and his worldly splendor. See Vollrath, 206.

[35] Thomas Jones argues that Geoffrey was generally disliked by the chroniclers of the period, but his only citation was when Walter Map called his mother a whore.

we will see below, this was not based on Geoffrey's conduct in war but, rather, on a clash of personalities. Most chroniclers generally either praised Geoffrey's steadfast support of the king or treated him much the same as they did other secular and ecclesiastical lords and nobles. Geoffrey's loyalty to Henry II, among the most important chivalric attributes a man could show to his king, was in marked contrast to that of his half-brothers, and many other Anglo-Norman and Angevin prelates, which worked in his reputation's favor.[36] Geoffrey gained great sympathy when he was assaulted and imprisoned by William Longchamp in 1191, and he became a paragon of ecclesiastical fortitude when he willingly went into exile during the reign of King John. At no point was Geoffrey overtly condemned for being involved in military affairs, unlike his contemporary Philip of Dreux, bishop of Beauvais (whose career is discussed in chapter 8). Geoffrey was a firm supporter of Henry II, and he readily embraced the role of general for his father. His military activities, however, declined during the reigns of his brothers Richard and John, when he was archbishop of York. There is no overt evidence to explain why this change happened, but it is reasonable to assume that it derived in part from his devotion to Henry; he was probably not as interested in personally aiding his brothers as was his father (though he did participate in the wars of the 1190s, during Richard's captivity). Furthermore, as archbishop of York, he had more ecclesiastical responsibilities than he did as archdeacon or bishop-elect of Lincoln. He apparently emphasized his ecclesiastical responsibilities – including a long-running conflict with Canterbury over primacy – over those of being a general. Lastly, during the period of Geoffrey's active career after Henry II's death there were not many opportunities for him to lead armies; there were no Scottish invasions, for instance, that would have enabled him as archbishop of York to raise armies in opposition, and he died before the period of the baronial rebellions and French invasion.[37]

Geoffrey's primary opportunity for generalship was during the Great Rebellion

---

See Thomas Jones, *War of the Generations: The Revolt of 1173–1174* (Ann Arbor, 1980), 37.

[36] Richard, abbot of Tournai, and William, archbishop of Sens, were two early supporters of Henry the Young King. See *Gesta Regis Henrici Secundi Benedicti Abbatis: Chronicle of the Reigns of Henry II and Richard I, 1169–1192, Known Commonly Under the Name of Benedict of Peterborough*, ed. William Stubbs, Vol. 1 (London, 1867), 46–7.

[37] Opportunity is one of the least acknowledged variables in assessing the cultural ideals of warrior-clerics. Many clergymen held office during periods of relative peace, and since they were not free to devote themselves fully to chivalric culture, unlike knights or nobles, they often had to wait for the war to come to them. This can artificially deflate the popularity of chivalric culture among clerics as it survives in contemporary materials and can reduce the numbers of clerics that we see as 'warriors'.

against Henry II in 1173 and 1174.[38] The rebellion was the greatest threat that the elder Henry had faced since becoming king and it centered on his eldest surviving son, Henry the Young King. Young Henry, having already been crowned, was able to count on the support of a variety of secular and ecclesiastical nobles in England and Normandy, as well as his father-in-law, King Louis VII of France. Henry II defended his continental holdings personally, while his surrogates in the royal administration engaged the rebels in England, with Geoffrey himself as one of the most important and successful of the royal commanders. During the campaigns against the rebels, Geoffrey led royal armies against the castles of Kinnard Ferry on May 5, 1174 and Kirkby Malzeard in July of 1174, which were held by Roger de Montbray, as well as helping to secure the north of England against the Scots.[39]

Geoffrey's life was a subject of interest for numerous chroniclers and authors during the late twelfth and early thirteenth centuries, but no one dedicated more time and effort to his career than did Gerald of Wales, who wrote a *Vita* of Geoffrey as part of his *Speculum ecclesiae* (Mirror of the Church). The other lives contained in the *Speculum* were all of saints, or men (such as Remigius of Fécamp) that Gerald was trying to get canonized. Geoffrey's inclusion in this list speaks volumes about Gerald's conception of his relative importance and general worthiness. Despite the work's probably limited contemporary circulation, it is valuable for gaining an insight into how Gerald viewed warrior-clerics.[40] As will be seen below, Gerald did not have any overt problems with clerics in military roles, provided that they behaved honorably and fought in causes that Gerald himself deemed worthy.[41] To that end, he portrayed Geoffrey as a solid protector of his father's rights and rule in England. In discussing Geoffrey's successful

---

[38] See especially *English Episcopal Acta I: Lincoln 1067–1185*, ed. David M. Smith (Oxford, 1980), xxxviii. See Decima Douie, *Archbishop Geoffrey Plantagenet and the Chapter of York* (York, 1960), esp. 3. She considered him better suited for a military career, rather than an ecclesiastical one, due to his interests and aptitudes in warfare.

[39] *English Episcopal Acta I*, xxxviii. For an overview of his campaigning, see *Gesta Regis Henrici Secundi*, 68–9.

[40] Gerald of Wales, *Speculum Ecclesiae: De Vita Galfridi Archiepiscopi Eboracensis: Sive Certamina Galfridi Eboracensis Archiepiscopi*, ed. J.S Brewer, Vol. 4 (London, 1873), vii. Brewer attributed the poor circulation of the manuscript to Gerald's relative lack of favor in court circles by the end of his life, and his propensity to include embarrassing stories about monastic life in his works, which would not have endeared him to his monastic copiers.

[41] In Distinction IV of the *Speculum*, Gerald included a list of how bishops and others clerics ought to behave, and how they failed to do so, but there was not any overt mention of warfare one way or the other. Gerald did not have major problems with it, or he did not see it as a major problem among clerics. Considering the number of clerics who were active in warfare, and the vitriol directed at them by canonists and reformers, we can reasonably assume the former.

assault on a castle of Roger de Montbray's, Gerald spoke of him as fighting for his father and his country (*pro patre simul et patria dimicare*).[42] He was fighting for two licit causes: as a son defending his father and as a lord defending his king and country. His defense of England and the rightful rule of Henry II were contrasted with the treasonous behavior of Henry the Young King, Richard, and nobles like the aforementioned Roger. Geoffrey's defense of the king in the face of noble rebellion was in keeping with the general tradition of ecclesiastical lords serving as royal defenders. His defense of England in the face of rapine and pillage was in keeping with the growing popularity of the idea of the right and duty to defend the *patria*, a result of increased attention and adherence to notions of Roman law.[43] Finally, his support of his father, especially as contrasted with the rebellion of his brothers, allowed Geoffrey to tap into the basic Christian antipathy towards sons who rebelled against fathers.[44]

Geoffrey's loyalty, when compared with the disloyalty of Henry and Richard, was instrumental in securing him a positive reputation among most chroniclers. A few pages later, Gerald depicted the famous scene in which Henry II directly contrasted Geoffrey's loyalty with the perfidy of his brothers. Gerald quotes Henry as claiming that Geoffrey was his only truly legitimate son, while his other sons were the real bastards.[45] Clearly, Geoffrey had done right in standing by Henry II, but

---

[42] Gerald of Wales, *Speculum Ecclesiae*, 364-5. The entire Capitula read, 'Sed quoniam facilius est ardentes favillas ore comprimere, quam innatae strenuitatis audaciam imminente necessitates articulo dissimulare; vacillantibus jam fere cunctis, et a fidelitate vel clam vel palam recedentibus; contra suorum omnium monita ad armatam militiam se proripiens, pro patre simul et patria dimicare, seque pro populo clipeum opponere, laudabili animositate, decrevit. Convocatis itaque militibus multis, et stipendiariis undique confluentibus, ad castellum Rogeri de Mumbrai, qui inter boreales regni barones non modicus extiterat, et inter primos filiis contra patrem adhaeserat, circa viginti millia ab urbe Lincolniensi distans, totamque provinciam caedibus, incendiis et depraedationibus vastans, primo vexilla convertit. Erat autem oppido nomen *Insula*, eo quo aquis ex omni latere complecteretur et valde inexpugnabile hactenus haberetur. Veruntamen quia subito nimis et inopinatus advenerat; castenses, qui prae nimia securitate et negligentia nil tale timentes sibi in alimonies non providerant, statim ad deditionem sunt compulsi. Unde patet, quia incauta est simper nimia praesumptio et sui negligens. Timor autem prospicere futuris admonet, et diligentiam docet in prosperis et providentiam. Destructa igitur et deleta penitus praedonum spelunca, provincial egregie pacificata, victor ad propria remeavit.'

[43] This reliance on the idea of defending the *patria* was also used by Philip of Dreux in his letters to Celestine III as a defense for his actions on the battlefield.

[44] See Geoffrey of Coldingham, *Historiae Dunelmensis Scriptores Tres, Gaufridus de Coldingham, Robertus de Graystanes et Willielmus de Chambre*, ed. James Raine (Surtees Society, 1839), 10. For the story of Absalom's rebellion against King David, see 2 Samuel 14-19.

[45] Gerald of Wales, *Speculum ecclesiae*, 367-8. The whole passage read, 'Quinimmo ut

what is most interesting is that his actions were judged purely on those grounds. His status as an archdeacon, even a bishop-elect (though not yet a priest), did not matter in terms of his embrace of a military leadership role. According to Gerald, the defense of Henry II and England was a noble and correct course of action, and thus Geoffrey was noble and correct for pursuing it. Gerald certainly did not believe that Geoffrey's status as a churchman ought to have compelled him to stand apart from the Great Rebellion and let it run its course. On the contrary, he was right and laudable for taking an active role in aiding the king.

This *pater et patria*-first conception of loyalty and laudability was also found in the chronicle of Jordan Fantosme. Fantosme, a troubadour and cleric from Winchester, wrote a verse account of the Great Rebellion. In discussing the state of the royal response to the rebellion, Jordan recorded, or created, a conversation between Bishop Richard of Winchester and Henry II. Henry asked about the loyalty of various nobles in opposing the Scots, and then he asked whether Geoffrey remained loyal, to which Winchester responded "'He is, sire, truly your cordial friend; He has enough of chevaliers and good border-serjeants.'"[46] Geoffrey was standing against the king's enemies and the invaders of England. He was listed along with other nobles, and there is no indication that he was treated or considered differently by Richard of Winchester, Henry II, or even Jordan Fantosme due to his ecclesiastical status. Indeed, his actions, not his *ordo*, were what determined the treatment he received in contemporary writings.

Following the Great Rebellion, Geoffrey continued his military service to his father, though he resigned his election to Lincoln in order to do so more fully. Pope Lucius III had ordered that Geoffrey either undergo ordination and consecration, or forgo the see of Lincoln. Geoffrey acquiesced and abandoned the see, citing his desire to serve the king and to continue his military exploits as the reason. Clearly there was a tension here between serving as a bishop and as a general, as we have seen before, but it is interesting that neither the pope nor Geoffrey saw such services as mutually exclusive, considering Geoffrey's military roles prior to his election to the diocese. In fact, Geoffrey's election to Lincoln had

brevi eloquio laudis ad cumulum multa concludam, nullum in regno grave periculum, nullum urgens instabat incommodum, in quo viri virtus innata strenuitate non eniteret. Ubique nimirum, sicut in regis Scotoum apud Anwicense castrum non longe post interceptione, et in aliis multis, per se et per suos, fideliter ut decebat et naturaliter patri filius assistebat; adeo quidem ut apud Huntendunnense munipium, quod paulo post deletum fuit, cum patri septies xx militum agmine septus praeter alios armatos quamplurimos occurrisset, rex gavisus in multorum audientia dixisse memoratur: "Alii filii mei se revera bastardos, iste vero solus se legitimum et verus esse probavit.'"

[46] Jordan Fantosme, *Chronicle*, ed. and trans. Francisque Michel (London, 1840), Lines 1556–59. 'Il est, sire, veirement vostre charneus amis; Asez ad chevaliers e bons serjanz marchis.'

been confirmed already by the pope in the same year that he was helping to suppress the Great Rebellion.[47] Clearly, his very active military role did not undermine his abilities to hold higher office, as the pope actually was attempting to engineer his consecration to that office, rather than trying to find ways to nullify it.

However, Geoffrey and Lucius were both concerned about the ability of a man to hold a full-time military command while also serving as a full-time bishop. Indeed, we can and should read Geoffrey's decision to forgo the office of bishop of Lincoln as an attempt to give himself more time and flexibility to serve the king. Service to Henry II was always his primary goal, and even absentee bishops had responsibilities and duties that could interfere with their ability to be wholehearted royal servants. Geoffrey's reticence to undergo ordination and consecration as a bishop during the life of Henry II, but his ready acceptance of the office of York after the king's death, can be explained by his desire not to place any additional official commitments between himself and serving his father. Geoffrey himself claimed in his letter to Lucius III that this was the primary motivation. According to Roger of Howden, a royal cleric and partisan of Henry II, Geoffrey wrote that he was 'sensible of his own insufficiency, and considering that he was not competent to perform the duties of so arduous an office, preferred to renounce the episcopal office, rather than undertake to bear a burden which he could not support.'[48] After consultation with his father and other clerics he responded, 'I have come to a different determination as to my mode of life and profession, wishing for a time to serve in a military capacity under the orders of the king, my father, and to refrain from interfering in episcopal matters.'[49] Taking into account the typically modest nature of Geoffrey's self-reflection, we can still see some remarkable aspects of his understanding of the interplay between warfare and being a cleric. On the surface there does exist a basic acceptance of the idea that there was a different *'vita et statu meo disposui'* associated with being a soldier rather than a cleric. However, rather than seeing this in a general sense, Geoffrey linked this profession directly with service to his father. What he was saying was that being a bishop necessarily complicated the professional soldier's life, and that he would much prefer to serve his father as a soldier, rather than to have to interfere 'in episcopal matters'. Thus, he was not arguing that a cleric could not be active in warfare, as he himself had done but, rather, that taking on the office and responsibility of a bishop would detract from his ability to serve Henry II, and that

---

[47] Roger of Howden, *Chronica Magistri*, ed. William Stubbs, Vol. 2 (London, 1869), 58.
[48] Roger of Howden, *Annals*, trand. Henry T. Riley, Vol. 2 (London, 1853), 2.
[49] Ibid., 3. 'qui praesentes aderant, aliter de vita et statu meo disposui, volens patris mei obsequiis militare ad tempus, et ab episcopalibus abstinere.' See *Chronica Magistri*, Vol. 2, 254–5.

he was not willing to make that sacrifice. Furthermore, Geoffrey did not shy away from involvement in military affairs as archbishop of York, which would further underscore the fact that he did not see these two professions as mutually exclusive.

During his career as chancellor, Geoffrey served his father as an important military commander in Normandy, and was thus the beneficiary of positive treatment in the writings of Howden. He was entrusted with various royal castles, and was in charge of coordinating large sections of the royal military. During a rebellion by his half-brother Richard, Geoffrey was in charge of relieving royal castles that were under siege. Gerald of Wales wrote that Geoffrey had been entrusted with almost all of the royal army.[50] Richard and his Norman allies were besieging various Norman fortifications, and Geoffrey's role was to bring up the royal army in relief. As is noted, he brought 'almost the whole army', indicating the importance of his military position. He also supported Henry II and came to his aid, again in contrast to Prince Richard.[51] Geoffrey was depicted as both a dutiful son and a loyal royal commander and servant. His contemporaries judged him according to his actions and personality, not his ecclesiastical status.[52]

The lack of comment about Geoffrey's mixing of military business with ecclesiastical position is especially interesting in light of the legislation of the Council of Westminster of July 1175. Archbishop Richard of Canterbury held a provincial synod that promulgated decrees forbidding clerics from presiding over 'blood' judgments or from taking up arms or wearing armor.[53] The idea proposed by this canon, that a man could not serve both God and the secular world, in theory applied to matters beyond being armed and military service, but in its very generality it demonstrated its distance from reality. The same year that this council

---

[50] Gerald of Wales, *Speculum ecclesiae*, 369. 'cancellarius cum exercitu fere toto versus Aleconam divertit.'

[51] Ibid. 'Unde statim cum centum militibus bene paratis et electis patrem non absque periculo sequens, cunctis nimirum interjacentibus viis jam propemodum ab hoste occupatis, rebus in afflictis cum gaudio mango a patre susceptus, se ei apud Savingni fideliter adjunxit.'

[52] The legal question of whether a bishop-elect was technically considered a 'cleric' is an interesting one. As a study of cultural reception, we can be reasonably sure that archdeacons elected as bishops, even if not ordained priests, were considered churchmen by contemporaries, even if not by strict canonists. Innocent III's intervention on behalf of the captured bishop-elect of Cambrai, and the interdict threatened by Peter of Capua were he not released, would seem to support this interpretation. See Roger of Howden, *Annals*, 2, 94.

[53] Roger of Howden, *Annals*, 1, 392. Councils and Synods, 1, 2, 988. 'Quicunque ex clero videntur esse arma non sumant nec armati incedant, sed professionis sue vocabulum religiosis moribus et religioso habitu prebeant. Quod si contempserint tanquam sacrorum canonum contemptores et ecclesiastice auctoritatis prophanatores proprii gradus amissione multentur, quia non possunt simul Deo et seculo militare.'

was convened also saw Geoffrey's election to the see of Lincoln confirmed by Pope Alexander III. It was certainly ironic that Geoffrey's election was confirmed the same year as the Council of Westminster, and so soon after his active part in suppressing the Great Rebellion.

Nothing in Geoffrey's past prevented him from gaining election, confirmation, and consecration to the see of York.[54] It did, however, provide useful fodder for his political opponents to contest his election, including Hubert Walter, the dean of York (himself a warrior-cleric, discussed in the next chapter), and Hugh de Puiset, bishop of Durham.[55] They were angered that Geoffrey had been elected by the canons of York without them being present, and thus being unable to cast the first votes, as they claimed was their right.[56] King Richard ordered that the circumstances revert to how they were before Henry II's death until the case could be settled. Furthermore, Archbishop Baldwin of Canterbury insisted that Geoffrey could receive neither consecration nor priestly orders from anyone but himself.[57] Hubert Walter and Hugh de Puiset claimed that Geoffrey's election was not canonical, that he was a murderer, and that he was born out of adultery. Despite these charges his election was confirmed by cardinal John of Anagni, the papal legate. In return for a promise of three thousand pounds Richard confirmed the election and invested his brother with the archbishopric, after which de Puiset and Walter were reconciled with Geoffrey.[58]

Regardless of the charges initially leveled against him, Geoffrey was consecrated in 1191 by William, archbishop of Tours. He then returned to England, despite his oath to Richard not to enter the country during the three years after Richard had left for the Holy Land. He was forbidden to land by his successor as royal chancellor, William Longchamp, bishop of Ely. Upon landing, Geoffrey was arrested by the chancellor and imprisoned, before being released on the order of Prince John.[59] This crisis precipitated the deposition of William Longchamp and his flight from England. Hugh, bishop of Coventry, wrote a letter regarding the deposition in which he excoriated Longchamp for imprisoning Geoffrey, and more generally for his overall lifestyle. He accused him of besieging Geoffrey in a church, and then violently tearing him away from its sanctuary.[60] Geoffrey was

---

[54] Roger of Howden, *Chronica Magistri*, 3, 7.
[55] Hubert Walter's opposition stemmed largely from Geoffrey's seizure of the estates of York, some of which were held by men of Hubert's. See *Gesta Regis Henrici Secundi*, 2, 73.
[56] Roger of Howden, *Chronica Magistri*, 3, 7–17.
[57] Ibid., 17.
[58] Ibid., 27.
[59] Ibid., 138.
[60] Ibid., 141–7.

described in perfectly innocent terms – he was the wronged, humble, peaceful figure, rather than a violent, secular, warrior pseudo-archbishop. He was the blameless victim of Longchamp's aggression, which is in marked contrast to other contemporary imprisoned bishops such as Philip of Dreux, bishop of Beauvais, or Philip, the bishop-elect of Cambrai (as discussed in the next chapter). In a further contrast to Geoffrey, Hugh of Coventry portrayed William Longchamp as the warlike and knightly offender. After falling from favor, William retreated to the Tower of London, clothed in a coat of mail, then fled to the seashore disguised as a woman.[61] Hugh mentions how funny it was that he was dressed as a woman, since he was 'accustomed much more frequently to wear the knight's coat of mail.'[62] William's portrayal as a knightly figure was designed to exacerbate the image of him as bound up in secularity and insufficiently concerned with spiritual affairs. Longchamp's position was publically defended by Peter of Blois, archdeacon of Bath. In addition to defending his character and actions in general terms, Peter also specifically answered the charges of Longchamp's secularity. He described William as 'one beloved by God, and men, a man amiable, wise, generous, kind, and meek, bounteous and liberal to the highest degree'.[63]

In each case the general assumption was that secularity and knightly behavior were to be criticized in clerics, even among defenders of specific clerics such as William. However, as we saw in chapter 6 regarding Henry of Winchester, this condemnation did not include avoiding royal service, or even leading royal armies. William, Geoffrey, and Hubert Walter (as we will see in chapter 8) were often not condemned for acting as royal partisans. Rather, it was their demeanor and overall level of worldliness that was frowned upon, and even then usually only when it served the larger political purposes of those issuing the complaints. This was seen in the treatment of the military campaigns of 1193 on behalf of Richard. While Richard was gaining his release from prison his partisans in England launched a series of campaigns designed to secure the country for the soon-to-be-released king, and to drive his opponents, including Prince John, from power. The royal forces laid siege to a variety of castles held by John, and Geoffrey was a

---

[61] Ibid.
[62] Ibid.
[63] Ibid., 148–50. For letters from William in his own defense, see 152–5. Richard of Devizes and William of Newburgh also discussed William Longchamp at great length. As Nancy Partner explains, 'Richard always refers to Longchamp as "the chancellor," to remind his readers of what Longchamp was; William of Newburgh always refers to him as "the bishop," to remind us what he was not.' See Partner, *Serious Entertainments*, 169. She argues that in the eyes of Richard of Devizes, 'Longchamp's worst offenses were his interference in monastic affairs … his actions against the interests of the bishop of Winchester, and his excessive aggrandizement of himself and his relations.' Partner, *Serious Entertainments*, 170.

central figure in this effort. Howden wrote, 'Geoffrey, archbishop of York, Hugh Bardolph, the king's justiciary, the sheriff of York, and William de Stuteville, assembling their forces, came to Doncaster, and fortified it.'[64] Geoffrey was one of the fiercest partisans on behalf of Richard, and his enthusiasm caused a rift with his fellow generals. Geoffrey wanted to proceed further and besiege the castle of Tickhill, but Hugh and William balked, as they were liegemen of John. Upon this 'the archbishop of York left them, with his people, calling them traitors to the king and his realm.'[65] Geoffrey was in favor of bringing the royal army to Tickhill to reinforce his old foe, and now ally, Hugh de Puiset, bishop of Durham, who was in charge of prosecuting that siege.[66] Hubert Walter, bishop of Salisbury and Richard's justiciar, led the siege of Marlborough.[67]

Geoffrey's ecclesiastical conflicts with the chapter of York also give us an opportunity to examine how he was viewed and how his military activities were treated. The main conflict was over who had the right to appoint the Dean of York.[68] Soon after this matter was resolved in the presence of the pope, Geoffrey's enemies began to slander him, 'declaring that he was a violent spoliator of themselves and the other clergy, a dishonest extortioner, that he had with an armed band broken open the doors of churches.'[69] Furthermore he 'quite despised his duties as archbishop, and was devoted to hawking, hunting, and other military pursuits. For these, and for other reasons, they sought to depose him.'[70] Howden certainly seems to have had more sympathy for Geoffrey than for his attackers. This is evident from his use of terms like 'slander' to describe their attacks, and by pointing out that they were ungrateful for the largesse Geoffrey had showed them, going so far as to quote Isaiah 1:2 – 'I have nourished and brought up children, and they have rebelled against me.'[71] By comparing this dissension to the illegitimate rebelliousness of a son against a father, Howden was undermining the position

---

[64] Roger of Howden, *Chronica Magistri*, 3, 206.
[65] Ibid.
[66] Ibid., 237. Hugh was a cleric who also had an easy relationship with warfare. He had purchased the earldom of Northumbria, and was readily girded with the sword of office. As a nephew to King Stephen and Henry of Winchester, he was very much in keeping with the other clerics profiled in this study. For coverage of how Hugh managed his military affairs in the North in 1173-74, see G.V. Scammell, *Hugh du Puiset, Bishop of Durham* (Cambridge, 1956), esp. 36-9.
[67] Roger of Howden, *Annals*, 2, 314. Walter also received a legateship in 1195 from Pope Celestine III, demonstrating further that military commands did not compromise ecclesiastical elevation.
[68] Roger of Howden, *Chronica Magistri*, 3, 229.
[69] Roger of Howden, *Annals*, 2, 308-9.
[70] Ibid.
[71] Ibid.

of Geoffrey's enemies, and lending credibility to Geoffrey himself, though he acknowledged that Geoffrey did not help himself, due to his arrogant manner.[72]

Eventually Pope Celestine III was compelled to direct an inquiry into Geoffrey's behavior and the complaints of the Dean of York. In 1194 he wrote a letter directing an inquisition into Geoffrey's alleged excesses.[73] He reiterated the charges from the clergy and chapter at York, namely that Geoffrey was ignoring his episcopal duties, and instead was engaging in a life of hunting, hawking, and military pursuits. The condemnation is equal, it seems, for the lack of attention to episcopal duties as it is for the worldly replacement activities, namely, violent, military pursuits. In 1195 the pope again answered the complaints of Simon, dean of York, which were again based on Geoffrey's perceived lack of attention to his episcopal duties and his interest in secular activities. Instead of engaging in episcopal activities, his opponents claimed, he was 'giving the whole of his attention to hunting and hawking, and was engaged in other things which were derogatory in no slight degree to the pontifical office entrusted to him and to his honor.'[74] This description of Geoffrey's behavior was ultimately accepted by the pope, who condemned his life as disgraceful and who complained that since assuming the archbishopric Geoffrey had occupied himself 'with hunting and hawking, and other military pursuits' and that he refused to engage in his episcopal duties.[75] He had also led an armed band to attack the 'greater church' and carried off materials belonging to the canons.[76] Geoffrey traveled to Rome and persuaded the pope to forgive him. Howden tells us that the pope followed the advice of his whole court in absolving Geoffrey.[77]

Celestine's primary complaint against Geoffrey was more than that he was interested in military or secular activities. While these interests were not ideal in Celestine's eyes, Geoffrey's primary faults were that he had ignored his ecclesiastical and spiritual duties, and that he had fallen into worldly pursuits. His political opponents in York, the Dean and Chapter, were able to use his actions in warfare against him with Pope Celestine III, a noted opponent of warrior-clerics (i.e. Philip of Dreux), though a supporter of King Richard. However, even the pope had to couch his disapproval in the context of Geoffrey's failure to live up to the ecclesiastical duties of his office. The pope's opposition was tempered by his political affection for Richard, and thus Geoffrey was able to re-secure the pope's support, and it is notable that Howden claimed that Celestine was following the

---

[72] Ibid., 356.
[73] Roger of Howden, *Chronica Magistri*, 3, 279–81.
[74] Ibid., 312–16.
[75] Roger of Howden, *Annals*, 2, 379.
[76] Ibid., 380.
[77] Ibid., 389–90.

advice of his 'whole' court in welcoming Geoffrey back into his good graces. The pope's hardline stance against clerical warriors was not, apparently, shared by many of his courtiers.

The only contemporary author who was overtly and consistently hostile to Geoffrey Plantagenet was Walter Map.[78] Map was among the more personally interesting twelfth-century writers, and his *De Nugis Curialium* presented a series of anecdotal stories designed to illuminate, often sarcastically and humorously, the life he saw around him at court. Map was born around 1140 in the area of Hereford, and his family served Henry II.[79] Walter had a complex view of proper clerical behavior in terms of warfare, though in general his opinion was that warfare had no role to play in religion. For instance, Map hated Bernard de Clairvaux and excoriated the Templars for their use of the sword in defense of Christ, because of Christ's invocation against Peter's using the sword to defend him in the garden of Gethsemane.[80] Two of his stories in the *De Nugis Curialium* also serve to show his opinions. Each involved monks who left the monastery to rejoin earthly combat, and in their deaths we can detect Map's displeasure, but also his partial ambiguity regarding the ideal clerical role in warfare.

In the first story the Cluniac monk Guichard de Beaujeu joined the monastery in his 'extreme old age', but then petitioned his abbot for leave to restore 'with armed hand to the aforesaid Humbert, his son, all his land which this son had lost through the power of his enemies and through his own weakness. Returning to the convent, he was ever devoutly constant to his vows and closed his life with a fair ending.'[81] At a later place in the text (though it may have been written first), Map returned to the story of Guichard. In this account, Guichard was allowed to leave the monastery, though the abbot enjoined him against using arms, and forced him to promise to return at the end of hostilities and undergo penance.[82] The monk led his men against the enemy in 'fierce and furious onslaughts' and with 'persistent courage'.[83] He secured a truce and received pledges of peace. He was, however, betrayed and forced to join battle once again. He rallied his men and stood in the center of them unarmed. He finally donned armor and charged

---

[78] Identifying Map as the only author hostile to Geoffrey is dangerously close to an argument *ex silencio*, but we can be reasonably sure that, had Geoffrey's military behavior been truly beyond the pale, more of our surviving authors would have reflected that view.

[79] Walter Map, *De Nugis Curialium*, trans. Frederick Tupper and Marbury Bladen (New York, 1924), xi. For a basic overview of his social beliefs, see xiii–xiv.

[80] Ibid., 37.

[81] Ibid., 23.

[82] Ibid., 215–16.

[83] Ibid.

into the fray, wreaking havoc on his enemies. After winning the victory, he 'sorted the spoils as he wished.'[84] After this bit of military excitement, he headed back to the monastery, but was ambushed and mortally wounded. He confessed himself to a nearby youth, despite the boy's 'unfitness' for the confession. He died 'in the faith of Christ, and with the good hope and glowing zest of repentance.'[85] The monk had done wrong in leaving the monastery, despite his abbot's allowance, but had died rightly in repentance to Christ for his transgression.

A second story advanced similar themes. Another monk of Cluny, a 'noble and mighty man', sought the leave of his abbot to rejoin the world of earthly combat.[86] After suffering defeats in warfare 'he seemed … ever born anew to battle; and, as though kindled with reviving rage, he rushed the more keenly upon his foes and, whether they ran or whether they resisted, he unwearied stuck to them like glue.'[87] After cornering him, his enemies cautiously approached, 'But the monk, in the midst of his foes, like a whirlwind in the midst of dust, or rather like a tempest venting its wrath, scattered his opponents and so stupefied them by his great valour that they saw no safety save in flight.'[88] He did not allow them to escape, but pursued them despite being heavily outnumbered, 'and the opposing soldiers, in the effort to save their masters from him, all became the prey of a single monk.'[89] One enemy soldier got away, doubled back, and mingled in with the monk's men. The monk had stripped off his armor and was reclining in the shade. The enemy soldier pierced him with a dart. 'The monk, knowing that he was near to death, confessed to his page, who alone was by, and asked that penance be imposed upon him.'[90] The penance he asked for was that his soul would be in Hell until Doomsday to save him from seeing God's 'countenance full of rage and wrath' at the end of time.[91]

What do these two similar stories tell us about Map's conception of warrior-clerics in the abstract? Map presented the monks as noble and courageous, but too eager to return to the travails and sins of the world. They fought in generally acceptable causes, or at least, not in infamous ones, and, given Map's propensity to skewer rhetorically those whom he disagreed with, we can interpret his relative restraint as demonstrative of some ambivalence. There is a definite tone of

---

[84] Ibid., 217.
[85] Ibid., 218.
[86] Ibid., 23.
[87] Ibid.
[88] Ibid., 23–4.
[89] Ibid.
[90] Ibid.
[91] Ibid. Regretting his violence, or his pride, the monk chose an exceedingly heavy penance for himself.

approval in Map with regards to the harsh penance the monk chose for himself. While the monk ought to have restrained himself from earthly warfare, he recognized his failings and faced his fate bravely. Recalling the mercy of Jesus, Map wrote, 'Here may be recalled to memory the words of mercy which He spoke: "In whatever hour the sinner mourneth, he shall be saved." In what wise was this monk able to mourn and yet did not do so?'[92] In an ideal world these monks would not have had cause to return to the world of earthly combat, but, having done so, they met their end as the Lord had foretold in the Garden of Gethsemane.[93] They were brave in facing enemies and in facing the wrath of God, which was laudable, but they had violated the prescriptions of their *ordo* by rejoining earthly combat and thus were condemned for this transgression.

These insights help us to understand Map's reaction to Geoffrey Plantagenet. Walter Map hated Geoffrey Plantagenet. He hated his base-born mother (whom he described as a 'harlot' who had tricked Henry II into accepting a son that was not actually his), he hated that Geoffrey was elected to the see of Lincoln, he hated that Geoffrey had exacted money from Map's own church, and he hated that Geoffrey's loyalty was to Henry II first, and God second.[94] In all of this vitriol, Map never condemned or criticized Geoffrey for his being a warrior. He never complained that Geoffrey was more a knight than a cleric. Map probably saw Geoffrey's military actions as simply a fact of his position in the world, and not as something particularly condemnable. Being active in war was a morally neutral facet of Geoffrey's life; if it had been otherwise, we can be sure that Map would have used it as a cudgel against him. As we saw with Walter Map's complaints regarding Geoffrey Plantagenet's secularity, it was not his role as general that annoyed Map (and others) but, rather, the perception that Geoffrey counted Henry II as his primary lord, rather than God. Being a general was no different from being a justiciar or chancellor. It was the prioritizing of secular service that was the primary problem, not the actual conduct in war. Men such as Geoffrey and Thomas Becket were balancing loyalties to their king and to God, and were straddling the line between acceptable devotion to both lords.

---

[92] Ibid.

[93] Map was not uniformly hostile to the world of warfare and combat. He told the story of a knight, Hamericus, who was wealthy but had a limited reputation. He thus attended a tournament. On his way he stopped to hear Mass and thus missed the tournament. Upon reaching his friends, they congratulated him on his victories there. He realized that 'the Lord had given him a deputy, so that his comrades might have no joy from their irreverence of the mass or he have grief from his reverence.' See page 37.

[94] Ibid., 299–311.

CHAPTER 8

The Angevins, Part II (Richard, John, and Henry III) Crusaders for King and Christ

THE later twelfth and early thirteenth centuries saw the culmination of a number of the phenomena we have been discussing. These include, but are not limited to, the zenith of crusader activity, especially among the English (mainly as a result of the fall of Jerusalem in 1187 to the Islamic forces under Saladin), attempts by kings to centralize control over their kingdoms, especially John in England and Philip II in France, and attempts by the papacy to centralize control over Christianity, namely in the figures of Innocent III and Gregory IX. Large-scale expeditions to the Holy Land were launched by leading figures in Europe, including Frederick Barbarossa, King Richard I of England, King Philip II of France, and Frederick II of Germany. Richard I brought a sizeable number of the higher-ranking clergy with him, as they were powerful churchmen and also important members of his government. We begin our examination with Hubert Walter, bishop of Salisbury (r. 1189–93), archbishop of Canterbury (1193–1205), chancellor to Richard I, and legate of Celestine III (1195–98), and with his predecessor, Archbishop Baldwin of Canterbury. The reputations of Hubert and Baldwin will be contrasted with that of Philip of Dreux (a servant of Philip II of France, who was active in warfare against the Angevin kings), and his experiences will demonstrate the cardinal importance of political ideology, pragmatism, and perceived worldliness in determining how a churchmen's military violence would be portrayed by contemporaries. Our final figure, Peter des Roches, parlayed his military activities into reaching the height of political and ecclesiastical power, serving both as a bishop and as regent for the young Henry III. He achieved these powers, and the respect of contemporaries, despite (or because of) his embrace of active fighting in battle. These men were comfortable in warfare, wore armor, bore weapons, and used them personally in battle, and yet they rose to great heights of power in the secular and ecclesiastical hierarchies, and were often praised for their devotion to God and king.

Hubert Walter (c.1160–1205) was one of the most important ecclesiastical figures during the reigns of Richard I and John, and his family had a long history of royal service. His uncle, Ranulf Glanvill, was the chief justiciar of Henry II, beginning in 1178, and Walter himself was elevated to his uncle's household by the time he was twenty.[1] He entered royal service in the early 1180s, and served his uncle in a variety of roles as a diplomat, treasurer, and judge.[2] He was a consummate royal official and ecclesiastical noble, serving as bishop of Salisbury, archbishop of Canterbury, chief justiciar, chancellor, and a royal judge over a period of twenty years. He was also a controversial figure for contemporaries; some reviled him for his perceived preference for royal service rather than ecclesiastical priorities (though Hubert himself was rather studious about keeping the two roles separate, at least in regards to his two households), while others saw him as standing up virtuously for his rightful king (Richard I) and defending his spiritual Lord on crusade.[3]

Gerald of Wales (the great promoter of Geoffrey Plantagenet) complained that Hubert had been schooled in the Exchequer, rather than in canon law. He wrote that the bishop (like many of his colleagues) had come, 'From the Exchequer ... This was the academy, this was the school, in which he had already grown old, from which he was called to all the grades of his [ecclesiastical] dignities, like nearly all the English bishops.'[4] Gervase of Canterbury criticized Hubert for being more concerned with the things of this world, instead of those of the next.[5] In keeping with the evidence presented for other clerics in this book, most contemporaries complained about Walter's worldly fascination with finance and royal power, rather than about his active use of military force. In fact, William of Newburgh, who was himself rather condemnatory of clerics' taking on secular responsibilities, praised Hubert throughout his work, even for his military activities.[6] Indeed, one of the first things that Bishop Hubert did after his elevation

---

[1] For Glanvill's appointment and early changes to royal government, see W.L. Warren, *Henry II* (New Haven, 2000), 294–5.

[2] For Hubert's early career, see C.R. Cheney, *Hubert Walter* (Stanford, 1967), 16–30.

[3] Richard Heiser, 'The Households of the Justiciars of Richard I: An Inquiry into the Second Level of Medieval English Government', *HSJ* 2, ed. Robert. B. Patterson (1990), 223–31, esp. 229.

[4] M.T. Clanchy, *From Memory to Written Record, England, 1066–1307* (Cambridge, 1979), 52. Original found in Gerald of Wales, *Opera*, ed. J.S. Brewer, Vol. 3 (London, 1891), 28. The whole section reads, 'et archiepiscopus unde? a scaccario, et quid scaccarium? Locus in Anglia publici ærarii, Londoniis scilicet tabula quasi quadrata, ubi fiscales census colliguntur et computantur; ab hoc studio, ab hoc gymnasio, in qua jam senuit, ad omnes dignitatum suarum gradus, sicut omnes fere Anglicani episcopi, vocatus fuit.'

[5] Cheney, *Hubert Walter*, 36.

[6] John Gillingham, 'Historian as Judge', 1276–78. Gillingham theorizes that Newburgh's general approval of the crusading movement led him to accept Hubert's actions, though the fact that this approval apparently extended to Hubert's military actions back in England demonstrates perhaps that a broader approach is necessary than relying on Newburgh's crusading fervor. See below, note 44.

to the episcopate was to join his king, Richard I, on the Third Crusade. During the crusade Hubert engaged personally in a number of chivalric acts of violence, and he was almost universally lauded for this behavior by contemporaries. As we have seen before, since the military force was directed towards a perceived salutary purpose – the defeat of the infidel – it was generally praiseworthy, whereas his service as a royal justice could detract from his devotion to his ecclesiastical duties, and thus was more circumspect.

The Third Crusade was the result of the Christian defeat at the battle of Hattin in 1187, and the subsequent capture of Jerusalem by Saladin. The complete failure of the Second Crusade in 1147 had undermined enthusiasm for large-scale crusading campaigns and there was concern that support for crusading in western Europe was flagging. Prior to the defeat at Hattin, 'crusading appeared to have run its course, a model of holy war that, in the shape taken since 1095, had served its turn and lost its fierce popular resonances.'[7] The defeat at Hattin and loss of Jerusalem, in the hands of Latin Christians since its capture on the First Crusade in 1099, came as a shock to observers. Pope Urban III reportedly died of grief upon hearing of the disaster, and his successor Gregory VIII issued a papal bull, *Audita Tremendi*, which called for an expedition to retake the holy city. When news reached western Europe, the first ruler north of the Alps to take the cross was Henry II's son Richard, count of Poitou.[8] Upon becoming king in 1189, Richard made preparations to make an expedition to the Holy Land, accompanied by King Phillip II of France. Separate expeditions were planned and launched by Frederick Barbarossa, emperor of the Holy Roman Empire, Henry, count of Champagne, and a fleet launched from Sicily that succeeded in disrupting Muslim naval operations along the Levantine coast.[9] A number of English chroniclers wrote extensively about the Third Crusade, notably Roger of Howden (himself a crusader), Ralph of Coggeshall, and Ralph of Diceto.[10]

Hubert Walter's military activities began when he accompanied Richard I on crusade. He had been elevated by Richard to the bishopric of Salisbury in 1189, and with the forcing out of his uncle Ranulf Glanvill as justiciar he began to take on a larger role in royal governance. Hubert was joined on the crusade by Baldwin, the aged archbishop of Canterbury.[11] While the majority of the recruits were

---

[7] Christopher Tyerman, *God's War: A New History of the Crusades* (Cambridge, MA, 2008), 342. For the political and military developments in Outremer leading up to the battle of Hattin in 1187, see pages 341–66.
[8] For the battle of Hattin and the fall of Jerusalem, see ibid., 366–74.
[9] See Andrew Jotischky, *Crusading and the Crusading States* (Harlow, 2004), 155–63.
[10] Tyerman, *England and the Crusades*, 83–4. Tyerman also points out that Gervase of Canterbury never showed much interest in nor approval of the crusades.
[11] Tyerman, *God's War*, 395.

soldiers, clerics were sought out as well, though primarily as preachers, morale-builders, scribes, accountants, secretaries, and quartermasters.[12] At the upper echelons of the army, however, these distinctions were not nearly as important, as both Baldwin and Hubert Walter took on active roles as generals and warriors (in Hubert's case).

When the English army reached Marseilles in August of 1190, Richard split it into two sections. One detachment under the king continued south by land to Sicily, while a second detachment under the command of Baldwin and Hubert went directly by sea to the Holy Land. They arrived outside of Acre two months later, at about the same time as the remnants of the German army (who had straggled in after Barbarossa died in 1190). The city had been under siege since August of 1189, and the Christians had successfully kept it besieged despite attempts by Saladin to raise the siege and resupply the city. The arrival by the English bolstered the strength of the Christian forces, but also helped to exacerbate the ethnic and national divisions within the crusader camp between the English, French, Frisians, Danes, and Germans, among others.[13] During the siege, both Baldwin and Hubert were singled out by the compiler of the *Itinerarium Peregrinorum et Gesta Regis Ricardi* (probably Prior Richard of Holy Trinity in London) for their meritorious military actions on behalf of the Christian war effort.[14] Richard had compiled the *Itinerarium* from a number of sources, including a continuation of William of Tyre's *History of Deeds Done Beyond the Sea*, a shorter version of the *Itinerarium* that dated from the time of the Third Crusade itself, and the *L'Estoire de la Guerre Sainte* by the Anglo-Norman poet Ambroise. There is also some evidence that Richard himself was a participant and observer on the crusade.[15] The *Itinerarium* is unflinching in its praise for the military prowess of the clerics on crusade, and specifically Hubert and Baldwin's achievements in battle.

In discussing the general actions of clerics during the siege of Acre, Richard unified the spiritual and the military power of the clergy, writing 'The clergy, however, claimed no small part of the military glory; for the abbots and prelates led their cohorts, and they boldly fought for the faith, joyfully striving for the law of God.'[16] These clerics were no mere preachers or scribes; they were taking active

---

[12] Ibid., 396. See also Bachrach, *Religion and the Conduct of War*, 127–8.
[13] Tyerman, *God's War*, 428–9.
[14] Helen J. Nicholson, *Chronicle of the Third Crusade: A Translation of the Itinerarium Peregrinorum et Gesta Regis Ricardi* (Aldershot, 1997), 7.
[15] Ibid., 12–13. For a general explanation of the provenance of this complex text, ibid., 5–15.
[16] *Itinerarium Peregrinorum et Gesta Regis Ricardi*, ed. William Stubbs, Vol. 1 (London, 1864), 116. 'Clerus autem non modicum militaris gloiae partem vendicat; nam et abbates, et praesules suas educunt cohortes, et pro fide fidenter dimicant, pro lege Dei laeti contendunt.'

parts in the battle and led their retinues personally into the fray. This behavior, far from garnering criticism, was salutary and laudable. They were fighting for the faith, a worthy cause that rendered their actions worthy as well. Richard, following the sources he was using, saw nothing to be criticized in this behavior. The *Itinerarium* focused on the value of the clerical military activity by then singling out the actions of Baldwin and Hubert for special praise, writing, 'Truly the venerable Baldwin, archbishop of Canterbury, distinguished himself as a soldier, above and beyond the others; although his aged weakness might have invited feebleness, he nevertheless overcame this natural defect by his perfect bravery.'[17] Baldwin, probably aged 75 and only weeks away from his death (on November 19, 1190,) had summoned up the energy and courage to lead his men personally at the siege of Acre. He presented himself to the troops, and he rallied them around his standard, which bore the name of Thomas Becket, the recently martyred archbishop of Canterbury. Baldwin 'procured a handsome and worthy troop' for the banner of St. Thomas, which consisted of two hundred knights and three hundred other soldiers who were in his pay.[18] Once Baldwin had the troops gathered, he took it upon himself to grant absolution to them for the forthcoming battle. He and Duke Frederick of Swabia and Count Theobald of Blois, were the primary commanders of the Christian camp.[19] Richard used this opportunity to elevate the military role of Baldwin, and the clergy in general, alongside (and in some cases above) that of the lay rulers.

The *Itinerarium* then magnified the military actions of Hubert Walter. He wrote, 'the stout-hearted (*magnanimus*) bishop of Salisbury could not bear to absent himself from the expedition, but distinguished himself in the battle. He did what a soldier should in the field, a leader in the camp, a pastor in the church.'[20] His military service encapsulated not just the acceptable nature of clerical involvement in battle, but its laudable character as well. He was *magnanimus*, and a 'great man', who took virile actions on behalf of Christianity and his king. Richard then gave the wonderful formulation that Hubert was someone who had the virtues of an armed soldier, a military leader, and a spiritual pastor, and who knew when

---

[17] Ibid. 'Sane venerbilis archipraesul Cantuariorum Baldewinus inter caeteros et prae caeteris insignias militat: quem licet ad segnitiem senilis invitet infirmitas, naturae tamen defectum virtutum perfectione transcendit.'

[18] Ibid. 'Hic vexillum cui gloriosus martyr Thomas inscriptus fuerat, praeminentius prodire faciens, eidem comitatus decoros et dignors procurat; nam et milites ducenti et trecenti satellites, viri sancti stipendiis pugnaturi sequuntur.'

[19] Ibid.

[20] Translation from Cheney, *Hubert Walter*, 35. Original in *Itinerarium Peregrinorum et Gesta Regis Ricardi*, 116. 'Verum magnanimus Saresbyriensis antistes, ab expeditione abesse non sustinet, sed partem belli moderatur insignem, cuius virtus in armis militem, in castris ducem, in ecclesiasticis implet pastorem.'

to take on each role. C.R. Cheney, one of Hubert's modern biographers, argues that '[e]ven if Archbishop Hubert was scrupulous not to bear arms in defiance of the canons, his generalship was a reproach against him.'[21] While canonists would have certainly agreed with this sentiment, the evidence demonstrates that other contemporaries saw active military prowess as a laudatory trait in a prelate, provided it was done for the right purposes.

Hubert himself was curious about the proper role clerics ought to play on crusade. He wrote a letter to Pope Innocent III asking for clarification on the status and obligations of clerical crusaders. Innocent's reply is interesting,

> Concerning clerics we reply that, since clerical duties render them inapt for fighting, unless they are energetic in counsel or trained in the art of preaching or engaged in the service of great men, or else are so rich and powerful that they can bring others as soldiers with them at their expense, it is more expedient to allow them to compound than to oblige them to fulfill their vow, if need arises or if it seems useful.[22]

Innocent saw the function of most clerics on crusade as one of support; they were there to preach and absolve. However, he believed that the primary purpose of the crusade was military, and thus if a cleric was 'so rich and powerful' that he could bring his own retinue of warriors, that would be fine. He did not necessarily condemn clerics who were actively engaged in the fighting; rather, he assumed that most of them could not afford to support soldiers, nor would they be particularly adept at fighting themselves. While clerics such as Hubert Walter might have been effective soldiers, most others were better suited to the scriptorium, rather than the battlefield. John Gillingham, in his work on the reign of Richard I, argues that Hubert's worldly interests, including his military ones, caused contemporaries to feel 'uncomfortable'. He writes, 'the sight of a clerk as deeply immersed in secular business, financial, judicial, even military, as Hubert Walter was, often made ecclesiastics uncomfortable, whether they attacked him for it or whether they went out of their way to justify him, as Ralph of Diceto did.'[23] Rather than trying to argue that Ralph of Diceto was so uncomfortable with Hubert Walter that he sought to over-compensate by effusive praise, I believe that the evidence shows willingness by contemporaries to engage with and consider the military achievements and activities of prelates at a more subtle level, one beyond pure canonical obedience.

---

[21] Cheney, *Hubert Walter*, 99.
[22] Ibid., 130.
[23] John Gillingham, *Richard I* (New Haven, 2002), 274.

Hubert was again at the forefront of the fighting in a later tale in the *Itinerarium* in which the Muslims attacked the Christian army outside of Betenoble, a tale found in Ambroise's poem, but with an added section praising Hubert's military prowess. While staying outside of Betenoble in June 1192, the Christian army was ambushed by two hundred Muslims, and Hubert acted quickly to rescue the count of Perche and save the Christian camp. As the Christians grew weary during the long combat, Richard recorded that the count of Perche heard the conflict and came to their aid. However, he proved to be *timide*, and his men began to waver, at which point the Christian army was rescued by the timely and courageous assistance of the bishop of Salisbury.[24] Not only did Hubert Walter intervene and help drive back the Muslim assault, but Richard contrasted his bravery and alacrity with the timidity of the count of Perche. It is especially interesting that Hubert's deeds were specifically added to the basic story as told by Ambroise. Richard, or whoever wrote the original account, wanted to draw extra attention to the bishop of Salisbury's exploits. We know that Ambroise himself did not have a problem giving Hubert praise for his prowess, as he claimed that in 'July 1191, at a bold assault on the walls of Acre, the bishop's banner was seen in the breach with those of the earl of Leicester and the count of La Marche.'[25] In each case, Hubert was taking an active role in combat alongside powerful lay figures, and was being favorably compared to them for his prowess, bravery, and military effectiveness. His high clerical status did not prevent his doing of manly military deeds, nor did it reflect poorly on his character.

Ralph of Diceto, the dean of St. Paul's cathedral, also commented on Hubert's activities on crusade, especially in the wake of the death of Archbishop Baldwin in November of 1190. Ralph, who had a generally positive opinion of Hubert, wrote that the bishop of Salisbury was a faithful executor of the dead archbishop's will. He used the money for pious uses, as well as military ones, and one suspects that for Ralph these two elements were mutually supporting. He wrote, 'Concerned about the lack of sentries in the camp, the bishop spent Baldwin's money on wages for twenty knights and fifty serjeants to meet this need.'[26] Hubert also gave alms

---

[24] *Itinerarium Peregrinorum et Gesta Regis Ricardi*, 372. 'Jam nimium nostri fatigati pondere belli, fluctuare coeperunt, et ecce! Deo providente, audito congredientium tumultu, eo venit comes de Perche, qui tamen se timide habuit; Episcopus vero Saresberiensis cum turma sua nisi citius occurrisset, Franci confunderentur in illa die.' See also Cheney, *Hubert Walter*, 36.

[25] Cheney, *Hubert Walter*, 36. The original passage reads, 'E la fud la baniere al conte/ De Leicestre en icel conte;/ Si fud la mon seignor Andriu/ De Chavingni en icel liu;/ La seignor Hugon ensement/ Le Brun i vint mult richement,/ E l'evesque de Salesbires,/ E autres de plusors matires.' See Ambroise, *L'Estoire de la Guerre Sainte*, ed. Gaston Paris (Paris, 1897), 133–4, lines 4995–5002.

[26] Cheney, *Hubert Walter*, 35.

to the poor out of the money, which Diceto characterized as being like 'a good prelate'.[27] Later, Diceto detailed how Hubert oversaw the pious correction of pilgrims who had broken the prohibition against the eating of meat during Lent. What is especially telling about these anecdotes is that they come before and after the accounts of his valorous exploits in combat. The chroniclers all spoke to his piety in all of these stories. Whether Hubert was dispensing alms, correcting pilgrims, fighting in battle, or posting sentries, he was actively engaged in pious work for God, and thus was behaving in a manner consistent with being a good pastor. This description of Hubert meshes with that given of Ralph of Hauterive, archdeacon of Colchester. He 'who rallied a rout in the dark days of July 1190, was a man, so it was said, "of renown in learning and fame in arms."'[28] He was the nephew of Gilbert Foliot, colleague of Ralph of Diceto, 'who praised his martial prowess', a royal justice, and master of the school of St. Paul's. Tyerman concludes that he was 'no termagant hedge-priest but an aristocrat of the church who shared the aptitude of his class for war, if not the instincts.'[29] Tyerman's point is well taken. Men such as Ralph and Hubert were invested in the traditional chivalric cultural structure which rewarded displays of prowess, bravery, and loyalty.

After Richard's arrival in the Holy Land in 1191, Hubert worked with the king to prosecute the military campaign and to oversee the spiritual well-being of the English army. His acclaim and renown in the army actually grew with the coming of the king and the many other secular military leaders; Cheney argues that the evidence demonstrates that Hubert's 'prestige grew with the scale of operations.'[30] His success during the siege of Acre, and his active embrace of a leadership role on the death of Archbishop Baldwin, impressed King Richard and enhanced the bishop's stock with the tough-minded and action-focused king. Gervase, wrote that 'Hubert, bishop of Salisbury, at Acre enjoyed favor in all eyes, and in military things he was truly magnificent, so that likewise he was admired by king Richard.'[31] Gervase further explained that Hubert was a skilled administrator, though a poor speaker, and that he was also more concerned with the things of the mortal world, rather than the spiritual.[32] As Gervase was writing after the events of Hubert's entire reign as archbishop of Canterbury, it is difficult to

---

[27] Ibid.
[28] Tyerman, *England and the Crusades*, 74.
[29] Ibid.
[30] Cheney, *Hubert Walter*, 36.
[31] Gervase of Canterbury, *Actus Pontificum Cantuariensis Ecclesia*, ed. William Stubbs, II (London, 1880), 406. 'Hubertus Sarisberiensis episcopus, apud Accon in omnium oculis gratiosus, et in re militari adeo magnificus, ut etiam regi Ricardo esset admirandus.'
[32] Ibid. 'Regni itaque negotiis intentus, humana magis quam divina curabat, et omnia regni novit iurs.'

say that he was specifically complaining about his military activities on crusade, rather than offering a retrospective on his entire career. His complaint seems to be based more on Hubert's general political activity and perceived worldliness once he returned to England.

Over the course of the rest of the crusade, Hubert 'continued to distinguish himself in military affairs, conducted diplomatic negotiations, and remained the good pastor of the English pilgrims.'[33] When Richard fell ill in August of 1192, it was Hubert 'who restored morale in the camp, took the initiative in summoning a council of war, and argued compellingly for an immediate truce with Saladin.'[34] Once the truce was agreed to, Hubert led one of the convoys of pilgrims into Jerusalem. According to Ambroise, Saladin 'respected him for his valour and renown and rank.'[35] He dined with Saladin, and he 'extracted from Saladin a promise to allow a skeleton staff of Latin clergy to officiate at the Holy Sepulchre, at the church of the Nativity in Bethlehem and the church of the Annunciation in Nazareth.'[36] Ambroise claimed that Hubert sought this concession, 'So he could boast that he had put God again in possession of services which He was no longer enjoying.'[37] Ambroise's comment illuminates the double-edged sword for churchmen who were politically active. They had always to walk a fine line between being perceived as ineffective (for not manfully defending Christ and King) and having their pride in success seen as worldly. In either case, it was only this political behavior that raised a whiff of ire from the Anglo-Norman poet, rather than Hubert's military actions.

The admiration that Hubert earned from King Richard also led to his preferment for the archbishopric of Canterbury.[38] Baldwin's death, and the death one month later of Reginald de Bohun, bishop of Bath, who had been elected to replace him, created an opening for Richard to fill. After a two-year hiatus, Richard recommended Hubert for the post, and in letters to his mother, Eleanor, and the justiciars in England, dated March 30, 1193, Richard spoke glowingly of the 'venerable' bishop of Salisbury. He discussed Hubert's contributions to the crusade, and referenced the 'pains and perils' that Hubert had 'exposed himself and his men' to 'for the sake of God's name and the relief of the East.'[39] Hubert

---

[33] Cheney, *Hubert Walter*, 36.
[34] Ibid.
[35] Ibid.
[36] Tyerman, *God's War*, 471.
[37] Cheney, *Hubert Walter*, 36.
[38] Tyerman, *England and the Crusades*, 68–9. Philip of Poitou also probably gained advancement to the see of Durham for the service he rendered on crusade.
[39] Cheney, *Hubert Walter*, 39. The original is found in *Epistolae Cantuarienses*, ed. William Stubbs, Vol. 2 (London, 1865), 362–3. 'Quantis laboribus et periculis venerabilis

was subsequently elected archbishop of Canterbury, a post he held until his death in 1205. Richard portrayed Hubert's elevation as a clear result of the bishop's actions on crusade, explicitly including those in battle.

Hubert's active military life generally won praise from chroniclers, with the most famous exception of Gerald of Wales. C.R. Cheney quotes Gerald's satirical praise of the archbishop:

> Blessed be God [wrote Gerald] who has taught your hands to war and your fingers to fight. Blessed be God who by the hand of his anointed has given such a glorious victory over the enemy. And blessed be his holy name who has ordained that this great realm should be ruled by law and pacified by arms through the unwearied labour of his pontiff and primate, strong both in spiritual and worldly warfare, fighting with either sword, and by his marvelous skill moulding himself to meet the vicissitudes of these times.[40]

Given Gerald's support for Geoffrey Plantagenet (also a renowned warrior-cleric), we must contextualize his hatred of Hubert – he probably wrote these particular lines in reference to a July 1198 campaign that Hubert had led against the Welsh. Furthermore, Gerald had sued Hubert over an unrelated political matter, and he used 'every scandalous story and rhetorical trick he could muster to discredit the archbishop and all his agents.'[41] Later in life Gerald regretted his intemperate hatred of the archbishop, and partially retracted some of his strongest invectives.[42] He admitted that he had relied on 'gossip' to blacken Hubert's character, but this does not account for his use of Hubert's military actions as a mechanism for discrediting him. Hubert's military achievements were hardly the result of 'gossip', but were, rather, large parts of his public persona and cause for celebration among his supporters. That Gerald saw them as a useful tool to denigrate him demonstrates the cultural grey area of clerical military exploits, and the importance that political partisanship and pragmatism could play in these descriptions. Hubert's

Hubertus Saresberiensis episcopus, in ultramarinis partibus propter nomen Domini et succursum terrae Orientalis.' Cf. Gillingham, *Richard I*, 238.

[40] Cheney, *Hubert Walter*, 99. The original is found in Gerald of Wales, *Opera*, ed. J.S Brewer, Vol. 1 (London, 1861), 96. 'Benedictus Deus, qui docuit manus vestras et digitos vestros ad bellum. Benedictus Deus, qui tam gloriosam in manu Christi sui victoriam de hostile populo fecit. Et benedictum nomen eius santum, qui tam strenua pontificis sui et primatis industria, utraque militia vigente et utroque gladio dimicante, miro moderamine temporum vicissitudini se cooptante, regni amplitudinem et legibus regi statuit et armis pacificari.' This was, of course, the same Gerald who extolled the virtues of Geoffrey of Plantagenet.

[41] Cheney, *Hubert Walter*, 106.

[42] Ibid., 178.

military achievements could at once be laudable and praiseworthy to Ambroise and the author of the *Itinerarium*, but horrible and deserving of condemnation to Gerald of Wales (despite his support of a different warrior-cleric in Geoffrey Plantagenet). Gerald himself illuminates this debate in his final summation of the archbishop's life and career. He wrote that while he was 'a courageous and energetic man', he also should have been more focused on divine matters, rather than earthly ones (mirroring the criticisms found in Gervase). Furthermore, Hubert had been a vital check on the exactions of the crown, and with him dead, tyranny grew worse. Gerald wrote

> Nevertheless, he was a restraint upon the king and an obstacle to tyranny. He was the peace and solace of people and, in his day, the refuge in need of rich and poor alike against the oppressions of the government, as is evident from what has happened since. For no sooner was he dead than tyranny grew stronger in the realm, and as though a barrier had been broken down a more shameless and unwise arrogance has raged in both secular and religious affairs.[43]

A powerful and military-minded prelate could make a number of contemporaries uncomfortable, as it undermined the division of society into *ordines*. Conversely, such a prelate could also defend his flock from far worse problems such as violence and financial ruin. For William of Newburgh, Hubert's actions on the crusade were self-evidently justifiable – he was fighting the enemies of Christ. For his warfare back in England, however, William had to point to the fact that Hubert fought in '"just and necessary"' wars on behalf of the king.[44] His actions, such as his personal command at the siege of Marlborough in February of 1194, made his military exploits laudable. As we saw with Newburgh's recounting of the two bishops fighting (discussed in the Introduction), the motivation and intention of the clerics was the primary determinant of the licitness of his behavior. Hubert was fighting to stamp out rebellion, rather than to expand his worldly glory, and thus he was laudable, but this was a more culturally contested justification than that of the crusader.

---

[43] Ibid., 178. Erat hic autem principis fraenum et tyrannidis obstaculum, populi pax et solatium, maiorum partier et minorum suis diebus contra publicae potestatis oppressions in necessitate refugium; sicut ex post factis palam fuit. Ipso namque defunct statim in regno tyrannis invaluit, et tanquam rupto repagulo non solum in humanas verum etiam res divinas impudens et impudens contumacia crevit. Gerald, *Opera*, Vol. 1, 427.

[44] Gillingham, 'Historian as Judge', 1278. Gillingham theorizes that Newburgh's overall approval of the crusades colored his view of Hubert throughout his work. See page 1283.

Hubert Walter's achievements as a crusader in battle earned him almost unreserved praised from his contemporaries; but what of clerics in the later twelfth century who fought as partisans of their kings – a more morally-contested role (though often still admired)? We will consider here in some detail the exploits and actions of Philip of Dreux and Peter des Roches. Philip of Dreux, bishop of Beauvais (r. 1175–1217), was the uterine cousin of Philip II of France, and he served as one of that king's most important commanders, soldiers, and diplomats.[45] Peter des Roches was the bishop of Winchester (r. 1205–38) under the English kings John and Henry III, and he took a leading role in administering the kingdom for John, as well as serving as one of the regents and protectors of the infant Henry. Contemporaries wrote of Philip and Peter as leading armies on campaign, leading men in battle, and actively fighting in battle themselves.

We will focus on Philip's most celebrated military activities, his actions at the battle of Bouvines in 1214, and the treatment he received after his capture by partisans of Richard I in 1197. The response to his military actions at Bouvines reinforces the basic desire seen elsewhere to laud a bishop who did manly deeds and fought in a just cause for his king, while also being sensitive to both the canonical proscriptions against clerics fighting in war and the delicate ideological boundaries between clergy and laity. These same concerns were evident in how Philip's imprisonment was portrayed in English sources and the supposed papal responses to his imprisonment. Pope Celestine, eager to strengthen his alliance with Richard I, probably used Philip's use of arms as a pretext to consign him to an English prison, whereas Innocent, with his desire to strengthen papal prerogatives and to garner widespread support for the crusade that he was calling for, immediately sought his release.

Philip's military activities appeared most strikingly in his leadership and individual combat role at Bouvines. The best contemporary chronicle that recorded these events is that of William the Breton, a royal cleric of Philip II, and someone

---

[45] For treatment of his contemporary importance, see Roger of Howden, *Annals*, Vol. 1, 372. See also Marcel Pacaut, *Louis VII et son Royaume* (Paris, 1964), 109 and 115–17. I justify including him in our examination for the same reasons that Daniel Gerrard does in his dissertation on the military activities of English clerics. Philip of Dreux was imprisoned by the English, and his exploits were treated at length by English sources. Gerrard, 55. I have expanded that justification to include Philip's actions at Bouvines. I shall not analyze the actions of Guerin of Senlis, however, despite his leadership at the battle. As chancellor of France, as well as a Hospitaller, he would be a fascinating study, but it would unnecessarily broaden the scope of this project. It should be noted, however, that he did not receive the same level of criticism as his compatriot Philip of Dreux. See Elizabeth M. Hallam, 'Monasteries as "War Memorials": Battle Abbey and La Victoire', *The Church and War*, ed. W.J. Sheils, *Studies in Church History* 20 (London, 1983), 54–6.

who was probably present at the battle. Philip's role as bishop of Beauvais was related in the *Philippidos* of William, which was designed to glorify Philip's contribution to the king's great victory over the forces of Otto IV of Germany and John of England, but to do so in such a way as to minimize potential criticisms of that role from canonically minded observers.[46] Georges Duby interpreted Philip of Dreux's actions, and the phenomenon of men like him, as being reflective of the shared military culture of noble households in the late twelfth and early thirteenth centuries. This commonality of secular culture was also reflected in the changing nature of the backgrounds of clerics who were advanced to high office. He argued that monasticism began to lose ground in the mid-twelfth century and thereafter

> the major role in the Church is held by the clerks who have always remained intimately connected with military society. We see canons fight like braves against *routiers* to defend the possessions of their cathedrals. Bishops fight as well, like the Bishop of Beauvais, Philip of Dreux, who was wielding a mace at Bouvines, and who, fifteen years earlier, had been captured by a *cottereaux* chief, not as a prelate, says the *Chanson de Guillaume le Maréchal*, 'but as a knight, all armed and the helmet laced tight.'[47]

While Duby saw this as a largely northern French phenomenon, whereby young clerics rubbed shoulders with young knights in households and thus came to share some of their chivalric cultural leanings, this shared culture of the nobility was common to a number of the clerics examined in this book. What is especially interesting is that this behavior existed among clerics from non-noble backgrounds as well, so it appears that there was a broader cultural acceptance of such military behavior by clerics than can be explained by direct transference of socially determined ideology.[48]

---

[46] This attempt at minimizing was especially important in light of the tense relations between Innocent III, who had backed John, and Philip II.

[47] Georges Duby, *The Legend of Bouvines: War, Religion and Culture in the Middle Ages*, trans. Catherine Tihanyi (Berkeley, 1990), 100. Duby saw Bouvines as the perfect example of the three orders of medieval society interacting, with each playing its proper role. He wrote, 'This was the case on the battlefield as well as in life: at his feet, the workers of the communal militias; at his head, the chaplains, dispensers of liturgy – it was only right that the latter devote themselves completely to their profession and that, in order to sing psalms well, they should live very comfortably from the profits of a seignory. Finally, there were the men of war who gave support to the King's avenging arm.' See page 133.

[48] It is also important to realize that many clerics from humbler backgrounds were criticized by contemporaries precisely because of their lesser status. See Bouchard, *Strong of Body*, 157.

Philip of Dreux's career demonstrated the importance of shared cultural values and royal service. His devotion to royal service led him to the battlefield, and his experience growing up in a noble household very probably contributed to his ability to be effective in hand-to-hand combat once he got the opportunity. William the Breton provided the best account of Philip's actions in battle, and he claimed that during the fighting, Philip grew increasingly distressed at the course of the battle, and the losses suffered by the division under his command. He saw the English commander, King John's half-brother William 'Longsword', wreaking havoc on the French troops, and he decided to take matters into his own hands. William wrote, 'since by chance he happened to have a mace in his hand, hiding his identity of bishop, he hits the Englishman on the top of the head, shatters his helmet, and throws him to the ground forcing him to leave on it the imprint of his whole body.'[49] We immediately notice William's attempt to minimize the fact that Philip engaged personally in combat, by claiming that he had only accidentally found a mace in his hands. A reader would probably note the improbable nature of this happenstance, and would also note that the mace is not known to be a ranged weapon, and therefore Bishop Philip must have been in very close proximity to his intended target. Philip's proximity to the fighting also demonstrates the difficulty of leading men into a medieval battle without becoming embroiled in the mêlée itself. William was making a valiant attempt to give credit to Bishop Philip for changing the course of the battle in the French favor, but at the same time minimizing the controversial nature of his actions.[50] William continued in this attempt in the subsequent lines

> And, since the author of such a noble deed could not remain unnoticed, and since a bishop should not be known to have carried arms, he tries to hide as much as possible and gives orders to John, whom Nesle obeys by the right of his ancestors, to put the warrior in chains and to receive the prize for the deed. Then the bishop, throwing down several more men with his mace, again renounces his titles of honor and his victories in favor of other knights so as

---

[49] Translation from *The Legend of Bouvines*, Book 11, verses 538–58; original in William the Breton, *Philippidos*, Liber 11, verses 538–58. Utque tenebat/ Clavam forte manu, sic illum, dissimulato/ Presule, percussit in summon vertice, fracta/ Casside, quod sterni tellure coegit eumdem,/ Corporis et longi signare charactere terram./ Et quasi celari facti tam nobilis auctor/ Possit, neve queat presul gerere arma notary,/ Dissimulare studet quantum licet, atque Johanni,/ Servit adhuc partum cui jure Nigella suorum,/ Hunc vincere jubet, et sumere premia facti./ Six plerosque alios clava sternebat eadem,/ Militibus super hoc titulum palmamque resignans,/ Accusaretur operam ne forte sacerdos/ Gessisse illicitam, cui nunquam talibus inter/ Esse licet, ne cede manus oculosve profanet;/ Non tame nest vetitum defendere seque suosque.

[50] See Duby, *Legend of Bouvines*, 123.

not to be accused of having done work unlawful for a priest, as a priest is never allowed to be present at such encounters since he must not desecrate either his hands or his eyes with blood.[51]

Philip was forgoing the typical chivalric honor of claiming credit for his victories, ostensibly to avoid canonical censure, but he also was demonstrating the laudable trait of humility and selflessness. Philip was not seeking glory in his victories but, rather, seeking victory for his king. As seen by literary examples such as Chretien de Troyes' Yvain (who fights anonymously to regain his wife after privileging his knightly honor over courtly love), humility could be a chivalric trait. William ensures that Philip received both the honor associated with humility, and also the honor associated with chivalric prowess and loyalty, by publicizing the event. Fighting for glory would have meant that Philip was becoming more 'worldly', with the full implications for the transcendence of identity that entails. As we have seen previously, churchmen were more often condemned for their worldly mannerisms, dress, and affectation, than for merely taking part in battle.

Philip's royalist focus was evident in William's last attempt to defend his actions: 'It is not forbidden, however, to defend oneself and one's people provided that this defense does not exceed legitimate limits.'[52] This final line demonstrates the importance of royal service as a motivator and defense of warrior-clerics, and it echoes the argument Philip made in 1197 upon his capture and imprisonment by Richard I. William the Breton straddled the canonical line that clerics ought not to be armed, nor should they fight, but he seems to have endorsed the idea, promulgated by some Decretalists, that defense of one's person and people was a legitimate reason to fight, provided that it was within certain limits.[53] The king was fighting a legitimate war in defense of the *patria*, and Philip was helping him to achieve this very laudable end. His attempts to 'sanitize' (in his own conception) Philip's actions, but also to defend them and give him credit and honor for helping the French cause in battle, show the debate over licit clerical military behavior.

---

[51] Ibid. William's understanding of canon law was that it forbade clerics from even being at a battle. Philip's active embrace of violence must have been an even greater problem for William to circumvent. He wrote that even seeing a battle was polluting for a cleric, but we are left to wonder whether this was his own view, or his understanding of canonical views.

[52] Ibid.

[53] Duggan makes the argument that Philip of Dreux's actions are indicative of the acceptance within canon law of clerics' taking part in battle. See Duggan, *Armsbearing and the Clergy*, 222-3. Jim Bradbury argues, however, that Philip behaved in a 'most unbishoply manner' and that his actions at Bouvines were readily condemned by his contemporaries. See Jim Bradbury, *Philip Augustus: King of France 1180-1223* (New York, 1998), 307. Cf. Gerrard, 238-9.

Philip had already participated in the debate over warrior-clerics after his capture by the English in 1197.[54] After being captured in battle, he was taken into custody and imprisoned at the Angevin stronghold of Chinon.[55] His city had been attacked by mercenary Brabanters, and the bishop, along with William de Merle, led a large force against them. Roger of Howden mentioned specifically that Philip was bearing arms as he led his men.[56] Roger himself did not criticize Philip for bearing arms, though he included in his chronicle an exchange of letters in which Celestine III condemned Philip to his fate in prison because he had embraced earthly weapons, though it is an open question whether the letters were real (as argued by Bradbury), spurious (as argued by Brundage), or invented as part of English propaganda (as argued by Gillingham).[57] Whether they were real or forgeries matters a great deal if we want to understand the views of Celestine III on warrior-clerics, but much less so if we are interested in how the debate was carried on in a broader cultural context.

Philip had played a major role in prosecuting the king's wars against Richard I prior to 1197, and had thus earned the enmity of the English king. In 1188 Philip II of France invaded Berry, with Philip sending his army to ravage the lands of the king of England, and 'On this, Philip, bishop of Beauvais, entered Normandy with an army, and ravaged with fire Blangeville, a town belonging to the earl [sic] of Auch, and Aumarle, a castle of William, earl of Mandeville, together with the adjoining provinces.'[58] After his capture, Philip supposedly sent a letter to the pope with his brother, the bishop of Orleans. He sought to ameliorate his position with the pope by stressing that his actions had been in defense of his city, that Richard had been attacking the lands of his liege-lord, the king of France, and that he had employed mercenary troops, whom he referred to as 'apostates'.[59] Philip then argued that his defense of the region was justified in Roman law. Recalling 'the legal maxim, "It is lawful to repel force by force," and by that other one, "Fight for your country," mingling in the throng of warriors and citizens,

---

[54] William the Breton, *Chronicle*, 94. Cf. William the Breton, *Philippide*, V, 331. Cf. Ralph of Diceto, *Ymagines Historiarum*, ed. William Stubbs, II (London, 1876), 152–8. Diceto also recounted numerous military actions by clerics on the Third Crusade. See 79–84.

[55] William the Breton, *Philippide*, Vol. 8, 397.

[56] Roger of Howden, *Chronica Magistri*, ed. William Stubbs, Vol. 4, 16. 'una cum filio suo, et militibus multis et plebe armata, exierunt et ipsi armati.'

[57] Bradbury, *Philip Augustus*, 122–3; James Brundage, 'The Crusade of Richard I: Two Canonical Quaestiones', *Speculum* 38 (1963), 446, n. 12; John Gillingham, 'Royal Newsletters, Forgeries and English Historians: Some Links between Court and History in the Reign of Richard I', *La Cour Plantagenêt (1154–1204)*, ed. M. Aurell (Poitiers, 2000), 171–85. See also Gerrard, 180.

[58] Roger of Howden, *Chronica Magistri*, Vol. 2, 344.

[59] Roger of Howden, *Annals*, Vol. 1, 401.

and in the ranks of the nobles, I went forth to meet the enemy in their onward career.'[60] His use of Roman law is interesting for several reasons. The first is that it demonstrates the growing importance that Roman law played in conceptions of licit behavior, and the second is that Philip was appealing to it for actions that were in direct contravention of canon law. While the evolving canon law of the church included a fair amount of Roman precedent, this direct appeal to Roman law as taking precedence over canon law demonstrates Philip's conception of a justifiable legal basis for clerical behavior that transcended relying only on canon law. Philip could have also pointed to a long tradition of clerics taking active roles in defending their cities and regions, and not being criticized for it – we have examined some already, such as Archbishop Anselm of Canterbury in 1095 and Archbishop Thurstan of York in 1138.

Celestine's response, according to Howden, was even more remarkable for our purposes. After wishing Philip a full and speedy recovery 'from his course of error', the pope went on to excoriate him for his decision to go about armed.[61] In a wonderfully poetic and memorably eviscerating passage, Howden recorded Celestine as saying that Philip had thrown aside his status as a peaceful bishop, and had instead embraced the warlike nature of the knight.

> In your rashness perverting the order and course of things, you have borne the shield in place of the chasuble, the sword in place of the stole, the hauberk for the alb, the helmet for the mitre, and the banner for the pastoral staff; not wishing, as you allege, to repel violence but valour, by violence; not fighting for your country, but against your country.[62]

Perhaps lost in the dualistic imagery of a cleric casting off his spiritual armor and donning the armor of this world is the final line in which Celestine drew attention to his own political leanings (and thus perhaps demonstrating the letter's English origins). Celestine rejected the French contention that they were merely defending their territory against English attack, and instead sided with Richard in arguing that the French had begun the hostilities and therefore the English king was muscularly defending himself against them. While Celestine agreed with Philip that defending one's *patria* was a licit opportunity to use arms

---

[60] Ibid.
[61] Ibid., 402.
[62] Ibid. Praesulum namque pacificum exuens, militem bellicosum induisti: clypeum pro infula, gladium pro stola, loricam pro alba, galeam pro mitra, lanceam pro baculo pastorali, ordinem rerum et seriem pervertens, temerarious baiulasti; non vim, sicut allegas, sed virtutem vi repellere volens, non pro patria, sed contra patriam pugnans. See Roger of Howden *Chronica Magistri*, Vol. 4, 23–4.

(though presumably still not personally by a cleric), he explained that this did not apply to Philip, since he was the aggressor. Celestine concluded by claiming to have written letters to Richard to release Philip, but this very weak and perfunctory effort met with no success, and Celestine chose not to pursue the matter further. Roger of Wendover, a continuator of the St. Albans chronicle, explained the pope's reticence by writing that Richard had sent Philip's armor to Celestine and asked if it was 'his son's coat or not.'[63] Celestine replied, 'He is no son of mine nor of the church, let him be ransomed at the king's pleasure, for he is a soldier of Man rather than of Christ!'[64] In the ideological construction of Celestine (or the English forger), simply wearing armor made one a soldier, and thus presumably was enough to deny one the protections of being a member of the clergy.[65] A cleric's using weapons and armor to protect himself was egregious enough to deny him the protection of clergy; he need not necessarily have shed blood. Celestine's opposition to Philip's actions was not maintained by his successor as pope, Innocent III.[66] Very soon after assuming the papacy he sent Peter of Capua to Richard, demanding Philip's release, but Richard angrily refused, 'offering to castrate the legate for his troubles!'[67] As Peter was trying to enlist Richard's support for the budding crusade, he did not pursue the matter further. After Richard died unexpectedly in 1199, however, a prisoner exchange was arranged whereby Philip was released, and Philip Augustus agreed to release the bishop-elect of Cambrai, whom he had captured in battle.[68] Neither of the two warrior bishops faced further ecclesiastical censure or deprivation of office for his activities in warfare.

The final figure in our study, Bishop Peter des Roches of Winchester, elicited less hand-wringing among contemporaries than did Philip of Dreux. He played active roles in the campaigns against the French army of Prince Louis that invaded England in 1217, on crusade with Frederick II, and in command of a papal army towards the end of his life. Roger of Wendover wrote of Peter's elevation in 1205 that he was 'a man of the knightly order and skilled in the ways of war.'[69] He was

---

[63] Roger of Wendover, *Flowers of History*, trans. J.A. Giles, Vol. 2 (London, 1849), 148.
[64] Ibid.
[65] This recalls the language of the peace council of Charroux in 989 in which clerics forfeited the protections of the Peace of God if they were armed or armored.
[66] Innocent III was also interested in solving the political discord between Philip II and Richard I in preparation for a crusade. See Vincent Ryan, 'Richard I and the Early Evolution of the Fourth Crusade', *The Fourth Crusade: Event, Aftermath, and Perceptions*, ed. Thomas F. Madden (Aldershot, 2008), 7–8.
[67] Bradbury, *Philip Augustus*, 123.
[68] Ibid., 133.
[69] Roger of Wendover, *Flores Historiarum*, ed. H.G. Hewlett, II (London, 1887). 9. 'vir equestris ordinis et in rebus bellicis eruditus'.

chosen specifically for his knightly qualities and because of his loyalty to King John and his willingness to advance the king's interests.[70] His election was eventually confirmed by Innocent III, with the pope consecrating him in person, and he was soon given legatine authority in England. Peter served John in a variety of roles, including as justiciar when the king was out of the country. One such event in 1214 has elicited the pejorative comment from W.L. Warren that John left the country 'and its government to the strong, if not too clean, hands of his ablest henchmen. Peter des Roches, foreign adventurer and bishop of Winchester …'[71] In addition to showing Bishop Peter's importance, Warren's comment also demonstrates the normative bias inherent in most treatments of warrior-clerics. This attitude is also in keeping with the broader approach to Peter des Roches by modern historians. They have often seen him as 'a warrior and financier first and foremost, a bishop in little more than name.'[72] Contemporaries, however, were much more pragmatic about the value of Peter's actions, and the licit nature of his military activities.

Peter was a trusted advisor and military commander during Richard and John's reigns. He spent a large amount of time in the royal chamber, and was intimately involved in Richard's wars in France, paying ransoms, overseeing the payment of crossbowmen, and in negotiations over truces, among other duties.[73] In 1205 he was elected to the bishopric of Winchester with the support of King John, and with letters of support from Barthelemey de Vendôme, archbishop of Tours. Whereas Nicholas Vincent uses this fact to reinforce his contention (probably accurate) that des Roches was not, in fact, a 'Poitevin', as his English detractors claimed, but, rather, from Touraine, it is also important in that the archbishop was willing to support his election, despite (or perhaps because of) Peter's previous military actions.[74] Peter had served as both the treasurer and archdeacon of Poitiers during Barthelemey's episcopate, and the archbishop's decision to support and endorse his candidacy speaks to the multiplicity of perceptions regarding warrior-clerics. Peter's election was met with some scorn from observers, however, who derided him as a courtier-bishop and someone more concerned with secular, rather than spiritual affairs. Vincent argues that while 'commentators have regarded him as a churchman in little more than name … the pope clearly believed that he possessed some redeeming features. Perhaps

---

[70] As Fred Cazel has pointed out, Peter had no qualms about elevating the interests of the king above those of the 'law'. See Fred A. Cazel Jr., 'Intertwined Careers: Hubert de Burgh and Peter des Roches', *HSJ* 1 (1989), 173.
[71] W.L. Warren, *King John* (Berkeley, 1978), 217.
[72] Vincent, 4.
[73] Ibid., 19–20.
[74] Ibid.

above all, Innocent [III] hoped that would serve as a channel of communication with King John.'[75] Such an interpretation is supported by other examples of Innocent's political outlook, including his intercession for Philip of Dreux, discussed above. It is also possible, of course, that Innocent saw in Peter the sort of prelate who could be useful leading papal armies, or functioning effectively on crusade, two things that des Roches did successfully later in his career.

Upon becoming bishop, Peter continued his active military role. He served as a commander both in a continental campaign and on a royal expedition into Wales. On the Welsh campaign he was one of the three named commanders of the army, and the annalist recorded that they established three castles against the Welsh.[76] During his episcopate, his household earned the reputation, no doubt spurred on by his successes in war, for being more notable in its martial exploits rather than in its piety.[77] He was the chief English prelate to stand by the king during the Interdict imposed by Innocent III over the king's refusal to allow Stephen Langton, the pope's choice for archbishop of Canterbury, into the country, and Peter's decision to stay and serve the king probably did not endear him to contemporary authors (or modern historians). This loyalty to John earned him the ire of his episcopal colleagues. Vincent reckons, with some amusement, that 'While exiled churchmen bewailed the liberties of the church, the bishop of Winchester was busy at the Exchequer or in leading a royal army into Wales.'[78] Peter's loyalty to John also probably galled Innocent III, who had supported his elevation. However, with the ending of the Interdict in 1213, and John's surrendering England to papal protection, des Roches was once again on the winning side of the political argument. He was not forced to do penance for his decision to stay at court, nor had he been suspended from office during the five-year Interdict.[79] In fact, he enjoyed papal support in his election in 1214 to the archbishopric of York, over the strenuous objections of Langton.[80] Langton, however, successfully organized opposition to des Roches, and managed to delay confirmation until support for his elevation collapsed.

[75] Ibid., 52.
[76] Ibid., 62. *Annales Prioratus de Dunstaplia*, ed. H.R. Luard, Vol. 3 (London, 1866), 32. 'Iterim Galfridus filius Petri justiciarius, et comes Cestriae, et episcopus Wintoniensis grandes exercitus duxerunt in Walliam; et contra Wallenses tria castella firmaverunt Ibidem.'
[77] Vincent, 63.
[78] Ibid., 69.
[79] Vincent theorizes that Peter had been tasked with administering John's excommunication, which, if true, would account for the lack of ecclesiastical penalties against him. See Vincent, 80.
[80] Innocent also sided with des Roches over protecting Richard Marsh, another courtier and adherent of John, against attempts at censure headed up by Langton. See Vincent, 96–7.

Despite his failure to become an archbishop, Peter continued to faithfully serve John for the remainder of his reign. During the period of mounting baronial opposition to the king, Innocent III instructed Peter des Roches and his royal colleagues to support King John against the rebels, whom he termed "'worse than Saracens, for they are trying to depose a king who, would succour the Holy Land.'"[81] Upon John's death Peter oversaw the accession of Henry III in 1216 at the age of nine, and he personally crowned the young king. In fact, his most famous military achievements came on behalf of Henry III during the French invasion led by Prince Louis. The *History of William Marshal* provides some of the best evidence for Peter des Roches's military actions on behalf of John and Henry III. At the siege of Torksey Peter led the fourth division of the royal army, earning praise from the author and earning the sobriquet 'worthy' (*buens*) from the poet.[82] William Marshal then gave a rousing address, and in his wisdom he 'entrusted his crossbowmen to Peter, the worthy bishop of Winchester, who was in charge of leading them, who had sound knowledge in that sphere, and who strove hard to perform well.'[83] There was no indication in the text of anything untoward about Peter's role as a military leader, nor the fact that he was especially adept at commanding crossbowmen. This last aspect is especially interesting, since crossbowmen had been condemned by the Second Lateran Council in 1139 and clerics were specifically prohibited from commanding them, according to the Fourth Lateran Council of 1215. This was a prohibition that des Roches ignored without consequence or criticism. Peter's role was presented only as laudable by the author of the *Histoire*. During the battle, Peter followed William Marshal 'shouting loudly and many times, in all directions: "This way! God is with the Marshal!"'[84] He actively led the royal troops in battle, and the author consciously linked him with the royalist hero William Marshal.

In a later battle, probably the great royalist victory at Lincoln, Peter was described as playing an even greater and more personal role. The author praised his knightly feats, writing,

> The worthy bishop of Winchester, Peter des Roches, who was in charge that day of advising our side, was not slow or slothful, and he knew how to make

---

[81] Tyerman, *England and the Crusades*, 136.
[82] *History of William Marshal*, ed. A.J. Holden, trans. S. Gregory, notes D. Crouch, Vol. 2 (London, 2004), 315, line 16259.
[83] *History of William Marshal*, 316–19, lines 16314–18. Nicholas Vincent points out that des Roches maintained crossbowmen 'regularly' on his estates, and that his *familiars* came not from the nobility but, rather, from mercenary constables and captains. See Vincent, 138.
[84] *History of William Marshal*, 332–3, Lines 16626–8.

use of his arms. In the company of his fine troop of men he gave chase, and in the course of that pursuit he did very well indeed, capturing knights as he went.[85]

Far from being condemned, Peter's active embrace of violence and his essentially chivalric feats of arms were cause for praise and fame. The *Histoire* had a highly royalist perspective, and it assessed Peter's actions on that basis. His support of the royal cause (the same cause as that of the hero, William Marshal) was what mattered for his reputation. His support of William Marshal and the cause of Henry III made his behavior laudable. For the author of the *Histoire*, his clerical status played little or no role in assessing the acceptability of his military actions. Nicholas Vincent argues that his training in Richard I's army probably gave him good strategic insights, and 'It was largely to the credit of des Roches that the combat developed along far different, far more advantageous lines than those envisaged by the army's veteran commander [William Marshal].'[86] Furthermore, he 'was very much the hero of the day' and even the chroniclers who were 'generally most hostile to des Roches, Wendover and the author of the *Histoire de Guillaume le Maréchal*, bury their enmity to marvel at his martial prowess.'[87] The battle was described by some chroniclers in explicitly crusader terms, with John's forces taking on the role of the holy defenders. Peter absolved the Angevin army before the battle, and his soldiers donned white crosses to signify their favor in God's eyes. Their victory went a long way towards proving that claim.[88]

Other sources were a little more circumspect about Peter's enthusiasm for military combat. The bishop came in for criticism in contemporary chronicles and songs for being worldly, but it was often for his devotion to the king's finances and his role at the Exchequer. That being said, one source did call him 'the arms-bearer of Winchester' (*Wintoniensis armiger*), but went on to criticize his monetary policy, rather than his embrace of military action.[89] Vincent argues that Peter was a conundrum for contemporaries, 'Even at the height of his triumph, at the battle of Lincoln in 1217, the chroniclers mingle respect for his military prowess with a suggestion that he was involved in the seamier professional side of

---

[85] Ibid., lines 16697–7004.
[86] Vincent, 137.
[87] Ibid., 139–40.
[88] See Tyerman, *England and the Crusades*, 138–40.
[89] See Flacius Illyricus, *Song on the Bishops*, *The Political Songs of England from the Reign of John to that of Edward II*, ed. and trans. Thomas Wright (London, 1839), 161. 'Wintoniensis armiger/ Praesidet ad Scaccarium,/ Ad computandum impiger,/ Piger ad Evangelium,/ Regis revolvens rotulum;Sic lucrum Lucam superat,/ Marco marcam praeponderat,/ Et librae librum subjicit.'

army life: the command of the king's highly unrespectable crossbowmen.'[90] This example represents a crucial distinction in the treatment of warrior-clerics. His actual fighting on behalf of the king was not as much of a problem as his embrace of, as Vincent puts it, 'the seamier professional side of army life'. Fighting in a licit cause was often seen as permissible, but transgressing normative boundaries between clerics and knights was cause for greater concern.

During des Roches' years in power after John's death, he worked closely with the papal legates to bring the English church into line with several of the reforms adopted at the Lateran Council of 1215.[91] He promulgated moral reforms, including laws against clerical drunkenness, and was zealous in carrying them out on his own estates, though less so at the Exchequer. Politically, des Roches was an important member of the regency government for young Henry III, in which he oversaw royal affairs alongside his rival Hubert de Burgh and William Marshal (until his death in 1219), and subsequently Pandulf de Masca, bishop of Norwich (and papal legate). His political machinations made him many enemies, and he was alternately in and out of favor over the next several years. He took the cross in 1221 after being accused of treason, but returned in 1223 and joined the anti-de Burgh faction. He continued his military activities, including the leading of a 'significant contingent of the army' against the Welsh that year.[92] His return was reasonably short lived, as he was forced from power by his political opponents, and so he took up a military command and joined the crusade of Frederick II in 1227. He led, along with Bishop William Brewer of Exeter, the English contingent in Frederick's army, despite Frederick's being excommunicated.[93] Peter placed the success of the crusade over the 'political designs of the papacy' and refused to shun contact with Frederick.[94] Frederick succeeded in reoccupying Jerusalem, by treaty rather

[90] Vincent, 4. Vincent claims that there 'are few parallels to the enthusiasm of the skill with which he [des Roches] resorted to arms. Hubert Walter had fought on crusade although bishop of Salisbury. In theory bishops might bear arms, though canon law restricted their choice of weapons and forbade the spilling of blood.' See page 137. Cf. Cazel, 175.

[91] Vincent, 172.

[92] Ibid., 211.

[93] Lloyd, *English Society and the Crusade*, 75. Lloyd categorizes clerics as among the 'non-combatants' that most crusade organizers sought to avoid, since they used resources but did not fight. See 72–81. Cf. Tyerman, *England and the Crusades*, 99–100.

[94] Vincent, 251. Vincent also theorizes that des Roches saw parallels between his support of Frederick, and his previous support of John during the Interdict. Tyerman argues that 'On crusade, however, the English bishops ignored papal strictures, cooperating fully with the emperor's agent Henry of Limbourg in 1227–1228 and with Frederick himself after his arrival in Palestine in 1228.' Rather than being 'pro-Frederick' we should see des Roches and Brewer as pragmatic. 'In fact they identified themselves with whichever group pursued an active and constructive policy, which the pullani appeared reluctant to follow.' Tyerman, *England and the Crusades*, 100.

than combat, and in March of 1229 des Roches accompanied him into the city, where the emperor was crowned in the Church of the Holy Sepulchre. While the nature of the retaking of Jerusalem caused some controversy, it largely enhanced des Roches' reputation back in England. As Vincent notes, des Roches 'returned to England *fêted* as warrior and statesman' and as a hero, though it also served to reinforce his image as an outsider and cosmopolitan in an England rapidly becoming more xenophobic.[95] Des Roches became embroiled in a number of political squabbles upon his return, and by 1234 he was driven again from high political office. He was rescued from obscurity by his overseas interests, and he 'accepted an invitation from the papacy to assist in Gregory IX's campaign against the rebellious citizens of Rome.'[96] He was a confidant of the pope, who was a celebrated canonist. While the pope did not give des Roches unqualified support, his endorsement, especially of des Roches's military abilities, demonstrates the importance and relative acceptability of warrior-clerics. The noted chronicler Matthew Paris makes explicit that the pope summoned him because of his great wealth, and his noted military reputation.[97] Peter ended his career as he had begun it, serving two lords on the battlefield.

In this final period of our study, we can see a number of important distinctions being made clear. For clerics who fought in the crusades, such as Baldwin of Canterbury, or especially Hubert Walter, there was virtually no overt criticism of their military roles. Their actions, whether on campaign or in battle itself, were held up as praiseworthy examples of clerics who were willing to put themselves in peril on behalf of Christ. For men such as Philip of Dreux and Peter des Roches, fighting for their kings proved to be somewhat more open to criticism than fighting on crusade. Partisans of the king or his cause would probably defend one's actions, whereas his adversaries would assail one. However, as we have seen with each man, the growing power of the papacy and the subsequent support of the pope was an important factor in determining the results of engaging in warfare. Innocent III proved to be open to supporting warrior-clerics, provided they fitted his larger political scheme, and his successor Gregory IX proved to be very similar.

---

[95] Vincent, 255. See also M.A. Pollock, *Scotland, England and France After the Loss of Normandy, 1204–1296* (Woodbridge, 2015), 115.

[96] Vincent, 470–1. Cf. Cazel, 180. See also Matthew Paris, *Chronica Majora*, Vol. 3, 272–3, 290–6, 309.

[97] Paris, *Chronica Majora*, Vol. 3, 304. 'et episcopus Wintoniensis, quem dominus Papa callide vocavit ad exercitum suum regendum, tum propter thesauri abundantiam, tum propter militandi peritiam'. Peter's military abilities must have been great, since the papal armies of the thirteenth century were undergoing the same 'professionalization' as other western powers. See D.P. Waley, 'Papal Armies in the Thirteenth Century', *EHR* 72 (Jan., 1957), 15–21.

Each of these men was heavily involved in the process of codifying and promulgating canon law, including canons condemning clerics who fought, and yet each embraced such clerics when it suited them. The utility of prowess in warfare was a very difficult weapon to cast aside, even for the vicar of Christ.

CONCLUSION

The Thirteenth Century and Beyond

THE preceding pages have highlighted the military activities of churchmen in England throughout the period from the Conquest through to the death of Peter des Roches, and that arguments persisted over the legitimacy of their military actions despite the hardening of canon law and the strengthening of the papacy.[1] However, we do not want to interpret the choice of period of this study (Anglo-Norman and Angevin England) to indicate that warrior-clerics and the arguments they inspired were indicative of that period alone. In fact, given more space and time, one could certainly see these arguments continuing on until the fifteenth century at the least, and perhaps even further. With that in mind, I will briefly survey some avenues of future research for those later periods.

The mid to late thirteenth century saw clerics arrayed on both sides of the Barons' Wars against Henry III, and many of the same ideological constructs seen previously were used to defend the actions of these men as they contended for control over the throne of England. James King argues that thirteenth-century England saw a conflict between two idealized clerical exemplars – St. Francis of Assisi and Friar Tuck. For him, clerical military activity was antithetical to the clerical vocation. He writes that 'the essence of the vocation of the cleric was spiritual and therefore, non-violent in nature.'[2] According to King, England settled this debate by embracing the Friar Tuck model (which, ironically, he finds incongruous with the previous period). Regardless of whether King sees this as mostly a thirteenth-century phenomenon, his recognition of the broad acceptance of the warlike model reinforces the evidence seen from the eleventh and twelfth centuries. Lawrence Duggan has traced what he believes is a loosening of the canonical prohibition on clerical arms-bearing to this same period, highlighting that in 1240, Bishop Walter de Cantilupe of Worcester promulgated new statutes that allowed clerics to bear defensive weapons when necessary, and Bishop Nicholas

---

[1] Duggan has argued that significant changes to the canonical ban on arms-bearing by clergy did not happen until after 1238. Duggan, *Armsbearing and the Clergy*, 1–5, 182.

[2] James R. King, 'The Friar Tuck Syndrome: Clerical Violence and the Barons' War', *The Final Argument: The Imprint of Violence on Society in Medieval and Early Modern Europe*, ed. Donald J. Kagay and Andrew L.J. Villalon (Woodbridge, 1998), 27. See also Duggan, *Armsbearing and the Clergy*, 27–33.

de Farnham of Durham issued statutes forbidding arms, "'except perhaps for defensive weapons in time of war and for compelling reasonable cause.'"[3] On the other hand, Bishop Robert Grosseteste (1235–53) issued statutes completely forbidding clerics to bear arms somewhere between 1239–43, possibly in reaction to the example of Peter des Roches (whom he hated), and it was his position (in favor of maintaining the ban) that was more popular among other English dioceses.[4]

With the accession of Edward I, Antony Bek was elevated to the bishopric of Durham, and in 1298 he commanded a division of the royal army at the battle of Falkirk. One of his knights, Ralph Basset of Drayton, very famously told Bek, "'It's not your place, bishop, to teach us how to fight; you ought to be saying mass.'"[5] Bek's response, however, was unequivocal, "'Go, if you want to celebrate Mass, for today we are all soldiers.'"[6] Bek's rejoinder, that they were all soldiers, echoes the earlier arguments that royal service and the defense of the kingdom trumped canonical prohibitions and the monopoly on licit violence enjoyed by the knightly *ordo*. Walter of Guisborough, who recorded this conversation, had previously described Basset as a *miles strenuus*, and Basset was essentially proved wrong by the epic victory that Edward's army soon won.[7] Bek demonstrated a keener grasp of tactics than the professional soldier, and thus Basset's criticism rang hollow to an audience familiar with the outcome of the battle.

Bek's career as a royal commander continued after Falkirk, and included sending men on further royal campaigns against Scotland, as well as a proposed royal campaign against Flanders.[8] In 1300 Edward I led a large-scale royal

---

[3] Duggan, *Armsbearing and the Clergy*, 182; original in *Councils and Synods*, 2:431, c. 36: 'ne clerici arma portent, presertim aggressionis, nisi forsan arma defensionis tempore belli ingurente et causa rationabili compellante.'

[4] Duggan, *Armsbearing and the Clergy*, 183–6.

[5] Schwyzer, 'Arms and the Bishop', 116. 'Non est tuum, episcope, docere nos in presenti de milicia qui te intromittere debes de missa.' See Walter of Guisborough, *Chronicle*, ed. Harry Rothwell, Camden Series 89 (London, 1957), 327–8. Cf. G.W.S. Barrow, *Robert Bruce and the Community of the Realm of Scotland* (Edinburgh, 1988), 102. A much later imaginative text of the battle, *The Wallace* by Blind Harry, also discussed Bek's importance to the English army. Written in the mid-fifteenth century, the poem credited Bek with leading a major division of the English army, and providing a crucial breakthrough against the Scots. It also commented on his leadership and cunning. See Blind Harry, *The Wallace*, ed. Anne McKim (Edinburgh, 2003), 310, Lines 202–4, 315, Lines 358–9.

[6] Guisborough, 327–8. '"Vade quidem", inquit, "missam celebrare si uis quoniam die hac que ad miliciam pertinent nos omnes faciemus."'

[7] Guisborough, 327. Cf. C.M. Fraser, *A History of Antony Bek* (Oxford, 1957), 75–6.

[8] For the royal order for men for the 1299 campaign, see *Records of Antony Bek: Bishop and Patriarch 1283–1311*, ed. C.M. Fraser, Surtees Society, 162 (Durham, 1953), 56. Cf. *Calendar of the Close Rolls, 1296–1302*, 323. For the Flemish call-up, see *Calendar of the Close Rolls, 1296–1302*, 113.

campaign to besiege the castle of Caerlaverock in southwestern Scotland. Antony Bek did not attend, but he sent one hundred and sixty men-at-arms to aid the king's endeavor. While the campaign was relatively limited in strategic scope, it did lead to the creation of an illustrated roll of arms detailing the contributions and chivalric actions of the major nobles of the English army. Bek was included in this list:

> the noble Bishop of Durham, the most vigilant [*plus vaillant*] clerk in the kingdom, a true mirror of Christianity; so, that I may tell you the truth, I would be understood that he was wise, eloquent, temperate, just, and chaste. Never was there a great man, nor like person, who regulated his life better. He was entirely free from pride, covetousness, and envy; not, however, that he wanted spirit to defend his rights, if he could not work upon his enemies by gentle measures, for so strongly was he influenced by a just conscience, that it was the astonishment of every one. In all the king's wars he appeared in noble array, with a great and expensive retinue.[9]

Bek was imbued with the traditional values associated with a pious cleric, especially in the reference to his wisdom, eloquence, temperance, justice, and chastity. His piety was such that the poet reckoned him a 'true mirror of Christianity'. There were monastic overtones to his humility and simplicity, demonstrating a 'regulated' lifestyle, and one in keeping with the best traditions of the humble churchman. However, the poet was also very clear that Bek was a worthy warrior and royal servant – he fought in 'all the king's wars'. He was a '*plus vaillant clerke*' in defense of Edward's interests. The poet also, perhaps answering the complaints of men like Guisborough that Bek was not sufficiently warlike, argued that Bek did not allow his devotion to piety and humility to get in the way of manfully defending his rights and performing his military responsibilities. He preferred gentleness and diplomacy to violence, but was possessed of the strength of character not to shirk from using force when necessary. Regardless of his mildness, humility, and preference for finding a diplomatic solution to conflicts, in 'all the king's wars he appeared in noble array, with a great and expensive retinue.'[10] His embrace of warfare was seen as a net positive for his position as bishop and a royal servant. The priorities of the poet were that Antony Bek served Edward well and effectively, and that he did so honorably; his humble and pious demeanor as bishop was seen as a bonus. The poet concluded his discussion of Bek by comparing him

---

[9] *The Siege of Carlaverock*, ed. N.H. Nicholas (London, 1828), 52–3.
[10] Ibid.

to Merlin, with Edward as King Arthur.[11] It is unlikely that Bek could have earned higher praise.[12] Regardless, in 1311 and 1312 the council of Vienne outlawed all clerical arms-bearing (again). The argument continued.

A generation later, facing a resurgent Scotland in the aftermath of the great English defeat at Bannockburn in 1314, northern clerics took on leadership roles in defending the region once again. The best example of clerics taking an active part in the fighting came in 1319 when William Melton, archbishop of York, led an army comprised of clerics and laymen against a Scottish invasion. On October 12 he engaged the Scots at the battle of Myton-on-Swale, and the English army was utterly routed. Rosalind Hill argues that Melton had 'no pretensions whatsoever to military leadership', but nevertheless 'put up a brave but inexpert resistance to the Scottish invaders of his province at the battle of Myton-on-Swale in 1319.'[13] Melton's disastrous attempt to turn back the Scottish invasion was probably based on his belief that he was right to defend his region and the interests of his king against the depredations of the Scots. James Raine, editor of a number of documents concerning this event for the Rolls Series, commented that 'Military men, in contempt for the clerical combatants, called that assemblage on the battle-field the chapter of Myton.'[14] As with Basset's complaints (though proven incorrect) regarding Antony Bek, one can see a sense from among professional warriors that clerics ought not to be on the battlefield, not necessarily because it violated canonical principles, but because it was likely to end in disaster.

As the fourteenth century wore on, clerics continued to take active roles in the wars between the English and Scots, and the English and the French. It wasn't just English clerics fighting – 'Fighting' Bishop Sinclair defended the Scottish coast in 1318 from English depredations, and at the battles of Neville's Cross and Crecy in 1346, clerics fought and fell on both sides.[15] In fact, as the period progressed

---

[11] Ibid.

[12] Andrew Spencer argues that Bek was 'the most powerful lord in the north-east' and that his absence from the Scottish campaign of 1298 made Warenne's defeat at Stirling more likely. See Andrew M. Spencer, 'John de Warenne, Guardian of Scotland, and the Battle of Stirling Bridge', *England and Scotland at War, c. 1296–1513*, ed. Andy King and David Simpkin (Leiden, 2012), 45.

[13] Rosalind Hill, 'An English Archbishop and the Scottish War of Independence', *The Innes Review* 22 (1971), 59.

[14] *Historical Papers and Letters from the Northern Registers*, ed. James Raine (London, 1873), xxviii. Raine records a letter from Melton dated November 16, 1319 in which the archbishop asked the abbot and convent of Welbeck for financial assistance due to his heavy losses at the battle of Myton-on-Swale. He lost a whole host of goods, including his horse and carriage, his silver and gold plate, and especially his armor. See page 295.

[15] A.K. McHardy, 'The English Clergy and the Hundred Years War', *The Church and War*, ed. W.J. Sheils, Studies in Church History 20 (Oxford, 1983), 173–4. H.J. Hewitt, *The*

and the warfare became more desperate, churchmen went from being unwelcome on the battlefield to being required to be there through arrays of the clergy.[16] Alison McHardy sees these developments as demonstrative of a blurring of the traditional lines between the *ordines* of medieval society, with clerics increasingly being involved in warfare, and laymen increasingly being involved in previously 'clerical' activities, such as education.[17] Among the best high-profile examples of this blurring occurred in the crusade of Henry Despenser, bishop of Norwich, against the Flemings in 1383. In France, Froissart wrote of an abbot at Hennecourt who, while defending his town, entered into hand-to-hand combat with a Flemish lord and defeated him. The monks then carried the sword as a trophy back to their church and venerated it as a relic. In the ordinances promulgated by Richard II and Henry V of England it was stipulated that only unarmed clerics were to be protected from capture in warfare.[18] All of these examples taken together, along with the famous arrays of clergy in England in the later fourteenth and early fifteenth centuries, demonstrate that clerical involvement in warfare continued throughout the later Middle Ages and into the early modern era.[19]

Moving into the sixteenth century, we see the survival of similar concerns on

Organisation of War under Edward III, 1338–62 (Manchester, 1966), 11 and 13 discusses the defense against the French. See also Andy King, 'A Good Chance for the Scots? The Recruitment of English Armies for Scotland and the Marches, 1337–1347', *England and Scotland at War, c. 1296–c.1513*, ed. Andy King and David Simpkin (Leiden, 2012), 119–56. For Bishop Sinclair, see Michael A. Penman, 'Faith in War: The Religious Experience of Scottish Soldiery, c.1100–c.1500', *Journal of Medieval History* 37 (2011), 296. Penman sees the use of clergy in warfare in the later fourteenth century as 'a remarkable change of policy.' See page 298.

[16] For these arrays, see *Calendar of the Patent Rolls*, 1405–8, 303 and 306. See also Bruce McNab, 'Obligations of the Church in English Society: Military Arrays of the Clergy, 1369–1418', *Order and Innovation in the Middle Ages: Essays in Honor of Joseph R. Strayer*, ed. W.C. Jordan, B. Mcnab and T.R. Ruiz (Princeton, 1976), 293–314.

[17] McHardy, 176–7.

[18] Anne Curry, 'The Military Ordinances of Henry V: Texts and Contexts', *War, Government and Aristocracy in the British Isles c.1150–1500: Essays in Honour of Michael Prestwich*, ed. Chris Given-Wilson, Ann Kettle, and Len Scales (Woodbridge, 2008), 223, 240; Nicholas Wright, *Knights and Peasants: The Hundred Years War in the French Countryside* (Woodbridge, 1998), 31. For originals see *The Black Book of the Admiralty*, ed. T. Twiss, Vol. 1 (London, 1871) 453, 460, 467, 469.

[19] Peter Heath, 'War and Peace in the Works of Erasmus: A Medieval Perspective', *The Medieval Military Revolution: State, Society and Military Change in Medieval and Early Modern Europe*, ed. Andrew Ayton and J.L. Price (London, 1998), 130–1. Hispanic bishops of the later Middle Ages and early modern period routinely joined their men in the field and armed their clergy. See Henry Kamen, 'Clerical Violence in a Catholic Society: The Hispanic World 1450–1720', *The Church and War*, ed. W.J. Sheils, *Studies in Church History* 20 (London, 1983) 201–4.

the eve of the Reformation.[20] In one of the most famous and critical commentaries on warrior-clerics, *Julius Excluded from Heaven*, a humanist author (probably Erasmus) depicted Pope Julius II (r.1503–1513) assaulting the gates of Heaven with an army to gain admittance.[21] Julius II was one of the most personally warlike of the late medieval popes, and he had actively led papal armies against recalcitrant Italian city-states. His warfare against fellow Christians was generally designed to expand papal power and authority in response to the aggrandizing of Borgia power under Pope Alexander VI, but it struck contemporaries such as Erasmus as indicative of all that was wrong with the medieval church.

When Julius approached the gates of Heaven and found them locked, he immediately began pounding on them. St. Peter, in charge of defending them, at first took him for 'a general of the armies, a stormer of cities.'[22] Peter refused him entry, and when Julius grew agitated, Peter responded, 'when I look you over from head to foot, I see many a sign of impiety and none of holiness … What sort of unnatural arrangement is it, that while you wear the robes of a priest of God, under them you are dressed in the bloody armor of a warrior?'[23] Julius then began to list his accomplishments, including his military conquests, in an effort to convince Peter to open the gates. Eventually Peter asked him why he continued to wear armor as pope, to which Julius responded, 'As if you don't know the holy pope wields two swords; you wouldn't want me to go into battle unarmed, would you?'[24] Julius then questioned Peter about his use of the sword in the Garden of Gethsemane. How could Peter condemn Julius for wielding it when he himself had done so? Erasmus had Peter defend himself by claiming that he was fighting for Christ, not himself, for the Lord, not for booty, and he fought not as a pope, but as a Jew who had not yet received the Holy Spirit. Furthermore, Christ told him to put his sword away 'as a clear warning that warfare of that sort was unbecoming to priests and even to Christians in general.'[25]

Erasmus was directly answering those clerics and theologians who had rejected the reformers' attempts to disassociate clerics from warfare. Julius was a particularly egregious example of a warrior-cleric, but Erasmus' complaints could have

---

[20] Duggan sees the increase in Muslim invasions and the religious wars after 1517 as making warrior-clerics more likely. Duggan, *Armsbearing and the Clergy*, 34.

[21] The conventional wisdom is that the *Julius Exclusus* was the work of Dutch humanist Desiderius Erasmus (1466–1536), though Lawrence Duggan claims that the evidence points to the English cleric and humanist Richard Pace. See Duggan, *Armsbearing and the Clergy*, 18.

[22] Desiderius Erasmus, *The Praise of Folly and Other Writings*, trans. Robert M. Adams (New York, 1989), 143.

[23] Ibid., 144.

[24] Ibid., 148.

[25] Ibid.

been directed against any of the clerics examined in this study. All of them took up the sword in one form or another, and did so in violation of Christ's invocation against violence (according to Erasmus). Erasmus came back to the Garden of Gethsemane, the central piece of biblical evidence used by reformers to argue against clerics' being involved in warfare. He rejected all of the other arguments used by clerics to justify active roles in war, and he based his opposition on what some would call the 'plain meaning' of the biblical message, which he thought was one of peace and pacifism. In a direct rejection of the scholastic hair splitting of the various canons regarding clerical militarism, Erasmus presented violence itself as inherently unchristian, and clerical violence especially as being against the most basic tenets of the religion. Ælfric of Eynsham would probably have nodded in agreement.

Bibliography

Primary Sources
The Acts of the Christian Martyrs, intro. and trans. Herbert Musurillo (Oxford, 1972)
Adam Marsh, *Letters*, ed. and trans. C.H. Lawrence, Vol. 1 (Oxford, 2006)
Adémar de Chabannes, *Chronique*, ed. Jules Chavanon (Paris, 1897)
Aelred of Rievaulx, *The Historical Works*, ed. Marsha L. Dutton, trans. Jane Patricia Freeland (Kalamazoo, 2005)
_____. *The Lives of the Northern Saints*, ed. Marsha L. Dutton, trans. Jane Patricia Freeland (Kalamazoo, 2006)
_____. *Relatio de Standardo*, ed. Richard Howlett (London, 1886)
Alcuin, *The Bishops, Kings, and Saints of York*, ed. Peter Godman (Oxford, 1982)
The Anglo-Saxon Chronicle, ed. and trans. Michael Swanton (Phoenix, 2000)
Anna Comnena, *The Alexiad*, trans. Elizabeth A.S. Dawes (New York, 1978)
Annales Prioratus de Dunstaplia, ed. H.R. Luard (London, 1866)
Anselm of Canterbury, *Letters*, trans. and annot. Walter Fröhlich, 3 vols. (Kalamazoo, 1994)
Arnulf of Lisieux, *Letters*, ed. Frank Barlow, Camden Third Series, Vol. 61 (London, 1939)
Asser, *Life of King Alfred*, trans. Simon Keynes and Michael Lapidge (London, 2004)
Bede, *Ecclesiastical History of the English People*, ed. Bertram Colgrave and R.A.B. Mynors (Oxford, 1969)
Bernard of Clairvaux, *Treatises III*, trans. Conrad Greenia (Collegeville, MN, 1977)
The Black Book of the Admiralty, ed. T. Twiss, Vol. 1 (London, 1871)
Blind Harry, *The Wallace*, ed. Anne McKim (Edinburgh, 2003)
Bonizo of Sutri, *Liber ad amicum*, ed. E. Dümmler. *Monumenta Germaniae Historica Ldl* 1 (1891)
The Book of Sainte Foy, trans. Pamela Sheingorn (Philadelphia, 1995)
Die Briefe des Heiligen Bonifatius und Lullus, ed. Michael Tangl, *Monumenta Germaniae Historica Epistolae Selectae*, Vol. 1 (Berlin, 1916)
Burchardus Wortatiensis Episcopus- Decretorum Libri Viginti, ed. Migne, *Patrologia Latina* 140 (Paris, 1880)
Caesarius of Heisterbach, *Dialogus Miraculorum*, ed. Joseph Strange, Vol. 2 (Cologne, 1851; reprint Ridgewood, NJ, 1966)

_____. *The Dialogue on Miracles*, trans. H. von E. Scott and C.C. Swinton Bland (London, 1929)
Calendar of the Close Rolls, Edward I, Vol. 4: 1296–1302 (London, 1906)
Calendar of the Patent Rolls, Henry IV, Vol. 3: 1405–8 (London, 1907)
Catalogue des Actes de Philippe-Auguste, par Léopold Delisle (Paris, 1856)
The Chanson d'Antioche: An Old French Account of the First Crusade, trans. Susan B. Edgington and Carol Sweetenham (Farnham, 2011)
La Chanson d'Aspremont, ed. Louis Brandin, 2 vols. (Paris, 1923–24)
Le Chanson de Roland: The Song of Roland, The French Corpus, ed. Joseph J. Duggan et al., 3 vols. (Turnhout, 2005)
Christine de Pisan, *The Book of Fayttes of Armes and of Chyvalrye*, trans. William Caxton, ed. A.T.P. Byles (London, 1932)
The Chronicle of Battle Abbey, ed. and trans. Eleanor Searle (Oxford, 1980)
The Chronicle of the Election of Hugh, Abbot of Bury St. Edmunds and Later Bishop of Ely, ed. and trans. R.M. Thompson (Oxford, 1974)
Chronicle of Melrose, ed. and trans. Joseph Stevenson, *Church Historians of England*, Vol. 4, Pt. 1 (London, 1856)
Chronicle of the Third Crusade: A translation of the Itinerarium Peregrinorum et Gesta Regis Ricardi, Helen J. Nicholson (Aldershot, 1997)
Chronicon Abbatiæ de Evesham, ed. William D. Macray (London, 1863)
Chronicon Angliae Petriburgense, ed. J.A. Giles (New York, 1967)
Chronicon de Lanercost, 1201–1346, ed. Joseph Stevenson (Edinburgh, 1839)
Chronique Latine de Guillaume de Nangis de 1113–1300 avec les continuations de cette chronique de 1300 A 1368, H. Géraud, Vol. 1 (New York, 1965)
Chroniques de Saint-Martial de Limoges ed. Duples-Agiers (Paris, 1874)
The Collection in Seventy-Four Titles: A Canon Law Manual of the Gregorian Reform, trans. and annot. John Gilchrist (Toronto, 1980)
The Conquest of Lisbon, trans. Charles Wendell David, foreword by Jonathan Phillips (New York, 1936, reprint 2001)
The Correspondence of Thomas Becket, Archbishop of Canterbury 1162–1170, ed. and trans. Anne J. Duggan, 2 vols. (Oxford, 2000)
Councils and Ecclesiastical Documents relating to Great Britain and Ireland, ed. Haddan and Stubbs, Vol. 1 (Oxford, 1869)
Councils and Ecclesiastical Documents relating to Great Britain and Ireland, ed. Haddan and Stubbs, Vol. 2, Pt. 1 (Oxford, 1873)
Councils and Ecclesiastical Documents relating to Great Britain and Ireland, ed. Haddan and Stubbs, Vol. 3 (Oxford, 1871)
Councils and Synods with Other Documents Relating to the English Church, ed. D. Whitelock, M. Brett, and C.N.L. Brooke, Vol. 1, 2 pts. (Oxford, 1981)
Councils and Synods with other Documents relating to the English Church, ed. F.M. Powicke and C.R. Cheney, Vol. 2, Pt. 2 (Oxford, 1964)
Crusade Charters 1138–1270, ed. Corliss Konwiser Slack, trans. Hugh Bernard Feiss (Tempe, 2001)
Decrees of the Ecumenical Councils, ed. Norman P. Tanner, Vol. 1: Nicaea I to Lateran V (Washington, D.C., 1990)

Desiderius Erasmus, *The Praise of Folly and Other Writings*, trans. Robert M. Adams (New York, 1989)
Les Deux Redactions en Vers du Moniage Guillaume, ed. Wilhelm Cloetta, Vol. 1 (Paris, 1906)
Documents on the Later Crusades, 1274–1580, ed. and trans. Norman Housley (New York, 1996)
Eadmer of Canterbury, *Historia Novorum in Anglia*, ed. M. Rule (London, 1884)
_____. *History of Recent Events in England*, trans. Geoffrey Bosanquet (London, 1964)
_____. *The Life of Saint Anselm, Archbishop of Canterbury*, ed. and trans. R.W. Southern (Oxford, 1962)
_____. *Lives and Miracles of Saints Oda, Dunstan, and Oswald*, ed. and trans. Andrew J. Turner and Bernard J. Muir (Oxford, 2006)
Eddius Stephanus, *The Life of Bishop Wilfrid*, trans. Bertram Colgrave (Cambridge, UK, 1927)
English Episcopal Acta I: Lincoln 1067–1185, ed. David M. Smith (Oxford, 1980)
English Episcopal Acta III: Canterbury 1193–1205, ed. C.R. Cheney and Eric John (Oxford, 1986)
English Episcopal Acta IV: Lincoln 1189–1206, ed. David M. Smith (Oxford, 1986)
English Episcopal Acta V: York 1070–1154, ed. Janet E. Burton (Oxford, 1988)
English Historical Documents, 1042–1189, ed. David C. Douglas and George W. Greenaway, Vol. 2 (London, 1961)
English Historical Documents, 1189–1327, ed. Harry Rothwell, Vol. 3 (London, 1975)
English Historical Documents, 1327–1485, ed. A.R. Myers, Vol. 4 (New York, 1969)
Epistolae Cantuarienses, ed. William Stubbs (London, 1865)
Epistulae et Chartae ad Historiam Primi Belli Sacri Spectantes, ed. Heinrich Hagenmeyer (Innsbruck, 1901)
The Epistolae Vagantes of Pope Gregory VII, ed. and trans. H.E.J. Cowdrey (Oxford, 1972)
Gallia Christiana, ed. H. Welter, Vol. 9 (Paris, 1899)
Gallia Christiana, ed. Denis de Sainte-Marthe, Vol. 11 (Paris, 1759)
Geoffrey of Coldingham, *Historiae Dunelmensis Scriptores Tres, Gaufridus de Coldingham, Robertus de Graystanes et Willielmus de Chambre*, ed. James Raine (Surtees Society, 1839)
Geoffrey Gaimar, *The Anglo-Norman Metrical Chronicle*, ed. Thomas Wright (New York, 1967)
Geoffrey Malaterra, *De Rebus Gestis Rogerii Calabriae et Siciliae Comitis et Roberti Guiscardi Ducis fratris eius*, ed. Ernesto Pontieri, Vol. 5 (Bologna, 1924)
Gerald of Wales, *Opera*, ed. J.S Brewer, Vol. 1 (London, 1861)
_____. *Opera*, ed. George Warner, Vol. 8 (London, 1891)
_____. *Speculum Ecclesiae: De Vita Galfridi Archiepiscopi Eboracensis: Sive Certamina Galfridi Eboracensis Archiepiscopi*, ed. J.S. Brewer, Vol. 4 (London, 1873)
_____. *Vita Sancti Remigii*, ed. James F. Dimock, Vol. 7 (London, 1877)

Gervase of Canterbury, *Actus Pontificum Cantuariensis Ecclesia*, ed. William Stubbs (London, 1880)
_____. *Historia*, trans. Joseph Stevenson, *The Church Historians of England*, Vol. 5, Pt. 1 (London, 1858)
Gesta Regis Henrici Secundi Benedicti Abbatis: Chronicle of the Reigns of Henry II and Richard I, 1169–1192, Known Commonly Under the Name of Benedict of Peterborough, ed. William Stubbs, 2 vols. (London, 1867)
Gesta Stephani, ed. and trans. K.R. Potter, intro. R.H.C. Davis (Oxford, 1976)
Gilbert Foliot, *Letters and Charters*, ed. Z.N. Brooke, Dom Adrian Morey, and C.N.L. Brooke (Cambridge, UK, 1967)
Les Grandes Chroniques de France, ed. M. Paulin (Paris, 1837)
Gratian: The Treatise on Laws (Decretum DD.1–20) with Ordinary Gloss, trans. Augustine Thompson and James Gordley (Washington, D.C., 1993)
Gregory VII, *Correspondence*, trans. Ephraim Emerton (New York, 1932)
Gregory of Tours, *The History of the Franks*, trans. O.M. Dalton, Vol. 2: Text (Oxford, 1927)
Guibert de Nogent: Histoire de sa Vie (1053–1124), ed. Georges Bourgin (Paris, 1907)
_____. *Memoirs*, in *A Monk's Confession: The Memoirs of Guibert de Nogent*, trans. Paul J. Archambault (University Park, 1996)
_____. *Memoirs*, in *Self and Society in Medieval France*, trans. John F. Benton (Toronto, 1984)
Guillaume d'Orange: Four Twelfth-Century Epics, trans. Joan M. Ferrante (New York, 2001)
Guy of Amiens, *The Carmen de Hastingae Proelio*, ed. Frank Barlow (Oxford, 1999)
_____. *The Carmen de Hastingae Proelio*, ed. Catherine Morton and Hope Muntz (Oxford, 1972)
Henry of Huntingdon, *Historia Anglorum*, ed. and trans. Diana Greenway (Oxford, 1996)
Henry of Livonia, *Chronicle*, trans. James A. Brundage (Madison, 1961)
Heroes of the French Epic, trans. Michael A.H. Newth (Woodbridge, 2005)
Historia Ecclesie Abbendonensis: The History of the Church of Abingdon, ed. and trans. John Hudson, Vol. 2 (Oxford, 2002)
The Historia Vie Hierosolimitane of Gilo of Paris, ed. and trans. C.W. Grocock and J.E. Siberry (Oxford, 1997)
Historiae Dunelmensis Scriptores Tres, Gaufridus de Coldingham, Robertus de Graystanes, et Willielmus de Chambre, Publications of the Surtees Society, Vol. 9 (London, 1839)
Historical Papers and Letters from the Northern Registers, ed. James Raine (London, 1873)
History of William Marshal, ed. A.J. Holden, trans. S. Gregory, notes D. Crouch, 2 vols. (London, 2002–4)
Holy Bible: Today's English Version with Deuterocanonicals/Apocrypha, American Bible Society (New York, 1978)
Honore Bonet, *The Tree of Battles*, trans. G.W. Coopland (Liverpool, 1949)

Illyricus, Flacius, *Song on the Bishops, The Political Songs of England from the Reign of John to that of Edward II*, ed. and trans. Thomas Wright (London, 1839)
Innocent III, *Selected Letters concerning England (1198-1216)*, ed. C.R. Cheney and W.H. Semple (London, 1953)
Itinerarium Peregrinorum et Gesta Regis Ricardi, ed. William Stubbs, Pt. 1 (London, 1864)
John of Hexham, *Chronicle*, trans. Joseph Stevenson, *The Church Historians of England*, Vol. 4, Pt. 1 (London, 1856)
John of Salisbury, *Historia Pontificalis*, ed. and trans. Marjorie Chibnall (Oxford, 1986)
_____. *Letters*, ed. W.J. Millor, S.J., and H.E. Butler, revised C.N.L. Brooke, Vol. 1: The Early Letters (1153-1161) (Oxford, 1986)
_____. *Letters*, ed. W.J. Millor, S.J., and C.N.L. Brooke, Vol. 2: The Later Letters (1163-1180) (Oxford, 1979)
_____. *Policraticus IV-IV*, ed. K.S.B. Keats-Rohan (Turnhout, 1993)
John of Worcester, *Chronicle*, ed. R.R. Darlington and P. McGurk, trans. Jennifer Bray and P. McGurk, 2 vols (Oxford, 1995-98)
Jordan Fantosme, *Chronicle*, ed. and trans. Francisque Michel (London, 1840)
Lanfranc, *Letters*, ed. and trans. Helen Clover and Margaret Gibson (Oxford, 1979)
Le Patourel, Jean, 'Geoffrey of Montbray, Bishop of Coutances, 1049-1093', *English Historical Review* 59 (1944), 129-61
The Letters of Gerbert with his Papal Privileges as Sylvester II, trans. Harriet Pratt Lattin (New York, 1961)
The Letters of Lanfranc Archbishop of Canterbury, ed. and trans. Helen Clover and Margaret Gibson, Vol. 1 (Oxford, 1979)
Liber Eliensis, ed. E.O. Blake, Camden Third Series, Vol. 92 (London, 1962)
Liber Eliensis: A History of the Isle of Ely from the Seventh Century to the Twelfth, trans. Janet Fairweather (Woodbridge, 2005)
Liber Miraculorum Sancte Fidis, ed. A. Bouillet (Paris, 1897)
The Lives of Thomas Becket, trans. and annot. Michael Staunton (Manchester, 2001)
Materials for the History of Thomas Becket, ed. J.C. Robertson and J.B. Sheppard. 7 vols. (London, 1875-85)
Milo Crispin, *Vita Lanfranci*, ed. D'Achery, *Lanfranci Opera (ut supra)*, ed. Migne (1854)
Les Narbonnais, ed. Hermann Suchier (Paris, 1898)
Oeuvres de Rigord et de Guillaume le Breton, ed. H. Francois Delabord, 2 vols. (Paris, 1882)
Orderic Vitalis, *The Ecclesiastical History*, ed. and trans. Marjorie Chibnall, 6 vols. (Oxford, 1969-90)
Ovid, *Metamorphoses*, trans. Allen Mandelbaum (London, 1993)
The Papal Reform of the Eleventh Century: Lives of Pope Leo IX and Pope Gregory VII, trans. and annot. I.S. Robinson (Manchester, 2004)
Peter of Celle, *Letters*, ed. Julian Haseldine (Oxford, 2001)

Peter the Venerable, *Letters*, ed. Giles Constable, 2 vols. (Cambridge, MA, 1967)
Prefaces to Canon Law Books in Latin Christianity, trans. Robert Somerville and Bruce C. Brasington (New Haven, 1998)
Ralph of Diceto, *Ymagines Historiarum*, ed. William Stubbs, Vol. 2 (London, 1876)
Ramon Llull, *Selected Works*, ed. and trans. Anthony Bonner, 2 vols. (Princeton, 1985)
Raymond of Aguilers, *Historia Francorum qui ceperunt Iherusalem*, Recueil des Historiens des Croisades, Vol. 3 (Paris, 1866)
Records of Antony Bek: Bishop and Patriarch 1283–1311, ed. C.M. Fraser, Surtees Society, Vol. 162 (Durham, 1953)
Regesta Regum Anglo-Normannorum, ed. H.W.C. Davis, Vol. I (Oxford, 1913)
Regularis Concordia, ed. T. Symons (London, 1953)
Richard of Devizes, *Chronicon*, ed. John T. Appleby (London, 1963)
_____. *De rebus gestis Ricardi Primi*, in *Chronicles of the Reigns of Stephen, Henry II and Richard I*, Vol. 3, ed. Richard Howlett (London, 1886)
Richard of Hexham, *Acts of Stephen*, trans. Joseph Stevenson, *The Church Historians of England*, Vol. 4, Pt. 1 (London, 1856)
_____. *De Gestis Regis Stephani et de Bello Standardii*, ed. Richard Howlett (London, 1886)
Robert de Monte, *Chronicle*, trans. Joseph Stevenson, *The Church Historians of England*, Vol. 4, Pt. 2 (London, 1856)
Rodulfus Glaber, *Opera*, ed. and trans. John France (Oxford, 1989)
Roger of Howden, *Annals*, trans. Henry T. Riley, 2 vols. (Lampeter, 1994; originally published in London, 1853)
_____. *Chronica Magistri*, ed. William Stubbs, Vols. 2–3 (London, 1869)
Roger of Wendover, *Flores Historiarum*, ed. H.G. Hewlett, Vol. 2 (London, 1887)
_____. *Flowers of History*, trans. J.A. Giles, Vol. 2 (London, 1849)
Ruotger, *Vita Brunonis Archiepiscopi Coloniensis*, ed. Irene Ott, *Monumenta Germaniae Historica Scriptores Rerum Germanicarum Nova Series X* (Weimar, 1951)
The Saint of London: The Life and Miracles of St. Erkenwald, ed. E. Gordon Whatley (Binghamton, 1989)
The Seven Ecumenical Councils of the Undivided Church, ed. Henry R. Percival (New York, 1901)
The Siege of Carlaverock, ed. N.H. Nicholas (London, 1828)
Simeon of Durham, *Works*, ed. and trans. Joseph Stevenson, Vol. 3, Part 2 (London, 1855)
Simon de St. Bertin, 'Gesta abbatum Sancti Bertini Sithensium', ed. O. Holder-Egger, *MGH SS*, Vol. 13
Sir Thomas Grey, *Scalacronica*, ed. Andy King, Surtees Society, Vol. 209 (Woodbridge, 2005)
The Song of Aspremont, trans. Michael A. Newth (New York, 1989)
The Song of Dermot and the Earl, ed. and trans. Goddard Henry Orpen (Oxford, 1892)

The Song of Roland: An Analytical Edition, ed. and trans. Gerard J. Brault, 2 vols. (London, 1978)
Suger, *The Deeds of Louis the Fat*, trans. Richard. Cusimano and John Moorhead (Washington, D.C., 1992)
_____. *Oeuvres*, ed. A. Lecoy de la Marche (Paris, 1868)
Sylvester II, *Letters*, trans. Harriet Pratt Lattin (New York, 1961)
Symeon of Durham, *Historical Works*, ed. and trans. Joseph Stevenson, Vol. 3, Pt. 2 (London, 1855)
_____. *Libellus de Exordio atque Procursu Istius, Hoc Est Dunhelmensis, Ecclesie*, ed. and trans. David Rollason (Oxford, 2000)
Thomas of Marlborough, *A History of the Abbey of Evesham*, ed. and trans. Jane Sayers and Leslie Watkiss (Oxford, 2003)
Three Eleventh-Century Anglo-Latin Saints' Lives: Vita S. Birini, Vita et miracula S. Kenelmi and *Vita S. Rumwoldi*, ed. and trans. Rosalind C. Love (Oxford, 1996)
Three Old French Chronicles of the Crusades, ed. and trans. Edward Noble Stone (Seattle, 1939)
Turpine's Story: A Middle English Translation of the Pseudo-Turpin Chronicle, ed. Stephen H.A. Shepherd (Oxford, 2004)
Two of the Saxon Chronicles Parallel, ed. Charles Plummer and John Earle, 2 vols. (Oxford, 1899–1929)
Vita Burchardi Episcopi, ed. G. Waitz, *Monumenta Germaniae Historica Scriptores*, Vol. 4 (Hanover, 1841)
Wace, *Roman de Rou*, ed. R. Andresen, 2 vols. (Heilbronn, 1877)
Walter Daniels, *Vita Ailredi Abbatis Rievall*, trans. F.M. Powicke (New York, 1951)
Walter of Guisborough, *Chronicle*, ed. Harry Rothwell, Camden Series 89 (London, 1957)
Walter Map, *De Nugis Curialium*, ed. and trans. M.R. James, rev. C.N.L. Brooke and R.A.B. Mynors (Oxford, 1983)
_____. *De Nugis Curialium*, trans. Frederick Tupper and Marbury Bladen Ogle (New York, 1924)
William of Malmesbury, *Gesta Pontificum Anglorum*, ed. and trans. Michael Winterbottom and Rodney M. Thomson (Oxford, 2007)
_____. *Gesta Regum Anglorum*, ed. and trans. R.A.B. Mynors, Michael Winterbottom, and Rodney M. Thomson (Oxford, 1999)
_____. *Life of Saint Wulfstan*, trans. J.H.F. Peile (Felinfach, 1934)
_____. *Historia Novella*, ed. and trans. K.R. Potter (London, 1955)
_____. *Saints' Lives*, ed. and trans. Michael Winterbottom and Rodney M. Thomson (Oxford, 2002)
_____. *Vita Wulfstani*, ed. Reginald R. Darlington (London, 1928)
William of Newburgh, *The Historia Rerum Anglicarum*, ed. Charles Johnson (New York, 1920)
_____. *Historia*, trans. Joseph Stevenson, *Church Historians of England*, Stevenson, Vol. 4, Pt. 2 (London, 1856)
William of Poitiers, *Gesta Guillelmi*, ed. and trans. R.H.C. Davis and Marjorie Chibnall (Oxford, 1998)

William Rishanger, *Chronicle*, ed. James Orchard Halliwell (London, 1840)
_____. *Chronicle*, ed. Henry Thomas Riley, Pt. 2 (London, 1865)
William of Tyre, *A History of Deeds Done Beyond the Sea*, trans. Emily Babcock and August Krey (New York, 1943)
Wulfstan's Canon Law Collection, ed. J.E. Cross and Andrew Hamer (Cambridge, 1999)
Wulfstan of Winchester, *The Life of St. Aethelwold*, ed. Michael Lapidge and Michael Winterbottom (Oxford, 1991)

Secondary Sources

Alvarez de las Asturias, Nicolás, 'The Use of the *Collectio Lanfranci*: The Evidence of the Manuscripts', *Bishops, Texts and the Use of Canon Law Around 1000: Essays in Honour of Martin Brett*, ed. Bruce C. Brasington and Kathleen G. Cushing (Aldergate, 2008), 121–8
Anderson, M.D., *History and Imagery in British Churches* (Edinburgh, 1971)
Appleby, John T., *The Troubled Reign of King Stephen* (London, 1969)
Arnold, Benjamin, 'German Bishops and their Military Retinues in the Medieval Empire', *German History*, Vol. 7 (1989), 161–83
Arthurian Literature in the Middle Ages: A Collaborative History, ed. Roger Sherman Loomis (Oxford, 1959)
Asbridge, Thomas, *The First Crusade: A New History: The Roots of Conflict Between Christianity and Islam* (Oxford, 2004)
Bachrach, Bernard S., 'The Northern Origins of the Peace Movement at Le Puy in 975', *Essays on the Peace of God: The Church and the People in Eleventh-Century France*, ed. Thomas Head and Richard Landes, *Historical Reflections/Reflexions Historiques* 14 (1987), 405–22
Bachrach, David S., 'The Ecclesia Anglicana Goes to War: Prayers, Propaganda, and Conquest during the Reign of Edward I of England, 1272–1307', *Albion* 36 (2004), 396–406
_____. *Religion and the Conduct of War c.300–c.1215* (Woodbridge, 2003)
Baldwin, John W., *The Government of Philip Augustus: Foundations of French Royal Power in the Middle Ages* (Berkeley, 1991)
Barber, Richard, *Henry Plantagenet 1133–1189* (New York, 1993)
Barlow, Frank, *The English Church 1066–1154* (London, 1979)
_____. *Thomas Becket* (Berkeley, 1986)
_____. *William Rufus* (New Haven, 1983; reprint, 2000)
Barrau, Julie, 'Gilbert Foliot et L'Ecriture un Exégète en Politique', *Anglo-Norman Studies* 27, ed. John Gillingham (2005), 16–31
Barrow, G.W.S., *Robert Bruce and The Community of the Realm of Scotland* (Edinburgh, 1988)
Barrow, Julia, 'Grades of Ordination and Clerical Careers, c. 900–1200', *Anglo-Norman Studies* 30, ed. C.P. Lewis (2008), 41–61
Barstow, Anne Llewellyn, *Married Priests and the Reforming Papacy: The Eleventh Century Debates* (New York, 1982)

Barthélemy, Dominique, *The Serf, the Knight, and the Historian*, trans. Graham Robert Edwards (Ithaca, 2009)
Bates, David, *Bishop Remigius of Lincoln 1067–1092* (Lincoln, 1992)
_____. 'The Character and Career of Odo, Bishop of Bayeux (1049/50–1097)', *Speculum* 50 (Jan., 1975), 1–20
_____. *Normandy Before 1066* (London, 1982)
_____. 'Le Rôle des Évêques dans L'élaboration des Actes Ducaux et Royaux Entre 1066 et 1087', *Les eveques normands du XI siecle, Pierre Boulet et Francois Neveux, Colloque de Cerisy-la-Salle*, 30 Septempbre–3 Octobre 1993 (Caen, 1995), 103–15
_____. 'Le patronage clerical et intellectuel de l'eveque Odon de Bayeux (1049/50–1097)', *Annales de Normandie, Serie des Congres des Societes historiques et archeologique de Normandie*, vol. 2 (1997), 105–14
Becket. DVD. Directed by Peter Glenville. 1964. Shepperton, England: Paramount Pictures/MPI Media Group, 2007.
Benham, J.E.M., 'Anglo-French Peace Conferences in the Twelfth Century', *Anglo-Norman Studies* 27, ed. John Gillingham (2005), 52–67
Benjamin, Richard, 'A Forty Years War: Toulouse and the Plantagenets, 1156–96', *Historical Research* 61 (1988), 270–85
Bennett, Matthew, 'Military Masculinity in England and Northern France c.1050–c.1225', *Masculinity in Medieval Europe*, ed. D.M. Hadley (London, 1999), 71–88
Benson, Robert L., *The Bishop-Elect: A Study in Medieval Ecclesiastical Office* (Princeton, 1968)
_____. 'The Obligations of Bishops with "Regalia": Canonistic Views from Gratian to the Early Thirteenth Century', *Proceedings of the Second International Congress of Medieval Canon Law*, ed. Stephan Kuttner and Joseph Ryan (Vatican, 1965), 127–37
Bettey, J.H., *Wessex from AD 1000* (London, 1986)
Bisson, Thomas N., *Assemblies and Representation in Languedoc in the Thirteenth Century* (Princeton, 1964)
_____. *The Crisis of the Twelfth Century: Power, Lordship, and the Origins of European Government* (Princeton, 2009)
_____. 'The Organized Peace in Southern France and Catalonia, ca.1140– ca.1233', *The American Historical Review* 82 (Apr., 1977), 290–311
Bliese, John R.E., 'Aelred of Rievaulx's Rhetoric and Morale at the Battle of the Standard, 1138', *Albion* 20 (1988), 543–56
_____. 'The Battle Rhetoric of Aelred of Rievaulx', *HSJ* 1 (1989), 99–107
_____. 'St. Cuthbert's and St. Neot's Help in War; Visions and Exhortations', *HSJ* 7 (1997), 39–62
Bloch, R. Howard, *A Needle in the Right Hand of God: The Norman Conquest of 1066 and the Making and Meaning of the Bayeux Tapestry* (New York, 2006)
Bloom, J. Harvey, *English Seals* (London, 1906)
Blumenthal, Uta-Renate, *The Early Councils of Pope Paschal II 1100–1110* (Toronto, 1978)

_____. *Papal Reform and Canon Law in the 11th and 12th Centuries* (Aldershot, 1998)
_____. 'Pope Gregory VII and the Prohibition of Nicholaitism', *Medieval Purity and Piety: Essays on Medieval Clerical Celibacy and Religious Reform*, ed. Michael Frassetto (New York, 1998), 239–68
Bolton, W.F., *A History of Anglo-Latin Literature 597–1066*, Vol. 1: 597–740 (Princeton, 1967)
Bonnaud-Delamare, Roger, *L'idée de paix a l'époque carolingienne* (Paris, 1939)
_____. 'Les institutions de la paix au Aquitaine au XIe siecle', *La Paix. Recueils de la Société Jean Bodin* 14 (Brussels, 1961), 415–87
Bouchard, Constance, 'Laymen and Church Reform Around the Year 1000: The Case of Otto-William, count of Burgundy', *Journal of Medieval History* 5 (1979), 1–10
_____. *Spirituality and Administration: The Role of the Bishop in Twelfth-Century Auxerre* (Cambridge, MA, 1979)
_____. *Strong of Body, Brave and Noble: Chivalry and Society in Medieval France* (Ithaca, 1998)
Bradbury, Jim, *Philip Augustus: King of France 1180–1223* (London, 1998)
_____. *Stephen and Matilda: The Civil War of 1139–1153* (Stroud, 1996)
_____. 'Battles in England and Normandy, 1066–1154', *Anglo-Norman Warfare*, ed. Matthew Strickland (Woodbridge, 1994), 182–93
Brasington, Bruce C., '"Notes from the Edge": Marginalia and Glosses in Pre-Gratian Canonical Collections', *Bishops, Texts and the Use of Canon Law Around 1000: Essays in Honour of Martin Brett*, ed. Bruce C. Brasington and Kathleen G. Cushing (Aldergate, 2008), 165–81
Brett, Martin, *The English Church Under Henry I* (Oxford, 1975)
_____. 'Warfare and its restraints in England 1066–1154', *'Militia Christi' e Crociata nei secoli XI–XIII* (Milan, 1992), 129–44
Bridgeford, Andrew, *1066: The Hidden History of the Bayeux Tapestry* (New York, 2005)
Brooke, Christopher, *Medieval Church and Society* (London, 1971)
Brown, Shirley Ann, 'The Bayeux Tapestry: Why Eustace, Odo and William?', *Anglo-Norman Studies* 12, ed. Marjorie Chibnall (1990), 7–28
Brundage, James, 'Adhemar of Puy: The Bishop and His Critics', *Speculum* 34 (1959), 201–12
_____. 'The Crusade of Richard I: Two Canonical Quaestiones', *Speculum* 38 (1963), 443–52
_____. 'Crusades, Clerics and Violence: Reflections on a Canonical Theme', *The Experience of Crusading*, Vol. I, ed. Marcus Bull and Norman Housley (Cambridge, 2003), 147–56
_____. 'The Hierarchy of Violence in Twelfth- and Thirteenth-Century Canonists', *The International History Review* 17 (1995), 670–92
_____. *Law, Sex and Christian Society in Medieval Europe* (Chicago, 1987)
_____. 'The Limits of the War-Making Power: The Contribution of the Medieval Canonists', *Peace in a Nuclear Ages: The Bishops' Pastoral Letter in Perspective*, ed. Charles J. Reid, Jr. (Washington, D.C., 1986), 69–85

_____. *Medieval Canon Law* (New York, 1995)
_____. Review of *War and Chivalry: The Conduct and Perception of War in England and Normandy, 1066-1217* by Matthew Strickland, *American Historical Review* 103 (1998), 862-3
_____. 'St. Anselm, Ivo of Chartres and the Ideology of the First Crusade', *Les mutations socio-culturelles au tournant des XIe-XIIe siecles* (Colloques internationaux de CNRS, Le Bec-Hellouin, juillet 1982) (Paris, 1984), 175-87
Bull, Marcus, *Knightly Piety and the Lay Response to the First Crusade: The Limousin and Gascony, c.970-c.1130* (Oxford, 1998)
Bur, Michel, *Suger: abbé de Saint-Denis, regent de France* (Paris, 1991)
Burgtorf, Jochen, *The Central Convent of the Hospitallers and Templars: History, Organization, and Personnel (1099/1120-1310)* (Boston, 2008)
Burton, Janet, 'Citadels of God: Monasteries, Violence, and the Struggle for Power in Northern England, 1135-1154', *Anglo-Norman Studies* 31, ed. C.P. Lewis (2008), 17-30
van Caenegem, R.C., 'Chivalrous Ideals and Religious Feeling', *Law, History, the Low Countries and Europe*, ed. Ludo Milis et al (London, 1994), 145-60
Cahen, Claude, *La Syrie du Nord: A L'Epoque des Croisades et la Principaute Franque D'Antioche* (Paris, 1940)
Caie, Graham, D., 'Christ as Warrior in Old English Poetry', *War and Peace in the Middle Ages*, ed. Brian Patrick McGuire (Copenhagen, 1987), 13-24
Callahan Jr., Thomas, 'The Arrest of the Bishops at Stephen's Court: A Reassessment', *The Haskins Society Journal* 4, ed. Robert B. Patterson (1993), 97-108
Carpenter, David, *The Struggle for Mastery: Britain 1066-1284* (Oxford, 2003)
Cazel Jr., Fred A., 'Intertwined Careers: Hubert de Burgh and Peter des Roches', *HSJ* 1, ed. Robert. B. Patterson (1989), 173-81
Cheney, C.R., *The English Church and its Laws 12th-14th Centuries* (London, 1982)
_____. *English Synodalia of the Thirteenth Century* (Oxford, 1968)
_____. *Hubert Walter* (London, 1967)
Cheney, Mary G., *Roger, Bishop of Worcester 1164-1179* (Oxford, 1980)
Chew, Helena M., *The English Ecclesiastical Tenants-in-Chief and Knight Service: Especially in the Thirteenth and Fourteenth Centuries* (London, 1932)
Chibnall, Marjorie, 'La Carriere de Geoffroi de Montbray', *Les eveques normands du XI siecle*, ed. Pierre Boulet et Francois Neveux, *Colloque de Cerisy-la-Salle*, 30 Septembre-3 Octobre 1993 (Caen, 1995), 279-93
_____. *The Empress Matilda: Queen Consort, Queen Mother and Lady of the English* (Oxford, 1991)
_____. 'Military Service in Normandy before 1066', *Anglo-Norman Warfare*, ed. Matthew Strickland (Woodbridge, 1994), 28-40
Chodorow, Stanley, *Christian Political Theory and Church Politics in the Mid-Twelfth Century: The Ecclesiology of Gratian's Decretum* (Berkeley, 1972)
Clanchy, M.T., *From Memory to Written Record, England, 1066-1307* (Cambridge, MA, 1979)

Conedera, Sam Zeno, *Ecclesiastical Knights: The Military Orders in Castile, 1150–1330* (New York, 2015)

Cotts, John D., 'Peter of Blois and the Problem of the "Court" in the Late Twelfth Century', *Anglo-Norman Studies* 27, ed. John Gillingham (2005), 68–84

Cowdrey, H.E.J., 'Bishop Ermenfrid of Sion and the Penitential Ordinance following the Battle of Hastings', *The Journal of Ecclesiastical History* 20 (1969), 225–42

———. 'Christianity and the Morality of Warfare during the First Century of Crusading', *The Experience of Crusading*, ed. Marcus Bull and Norman Housley, Vol. 1: Western Approaches (Cambridge, UK., 2003), 175–92

———. *The Cluniacs and the Gregorian Reform* (Oxford, 1970)

———. 'The Enigma of Archbishop Lanfranc', *HSJ* 6 (1995), 129–52

———. 'The Genesis of the Crusades: The Springs of Western Ideas of Holy War', *The Holy War*, ed. Thomas Patrick Murphy (Columbus, 1976), 9–32

———. *Gregory VII, 1073–1085* (Oxford, 1998)

———. 'Pope Gregory VII and the Chastity of the Clergy', *Medieval Purity and Piety: Essays on Medieval Clerical Celibacy and Religious Reform*, ed. Michael Frassetto (New York, 1998), 269–304

———. *Popes and Church Reform in the 11th Century* (Aldershot, 2000)

———. 'Towards an Interpretation of the Bayeux Tapestry', *Anglo-Norman Studies* 10 (1988), 49–66

Cownie, Emma, *Religious Patronage in Anglo-Norman England 1066–1135* (Woodbridge, 1998)

Crocker, Richard L., 'Early Crusade Songs', *The Holy War*, ed. Thomas Patrick Murphy (Columbus, 1976), 78–98

Cronne, H.A., *The Reign of Stephen 1135–1154: Anarchy in England* (London, 1970)

Crook, John, 'The Physical Setting of the Cult of St. Wulfstan', *St. Wulfstan and His World*, ed. Julia S. Barrow and N.P. Brooks (Aldershot, 2005), 189–217

Crosby, Everett U., *Bishop and Chapter in Twelfth-Century England: A Study of the Mensa Episcopalis* (Cambridge, UK., 1994)

Cross, J.E. 'The Ethic of War in Old English', *England Before the Conquest: Studies in Primary Sources Presented to Dorothy Whitelock*, ed. Peter Clemoes and Kathleen Hughes (Cambridge, 1971), 269–82

Crouch, David, *The Birth of Nobility: Constructing Aristocracy in England and France, 950–1300* (London, 2005)

Cubitt, Catherine, 'Bishops and Succession Crises in Tenth-and Eleventh-Century England', *Patterns of Episcopal Power: Bishops in Tenth and Eleventh Century Western Europe*, ed. Ludger Körntgen and Dominik Waßenhoven (Berlin, 2011), 111–26

Cullum, P.H., 'Clergy, Masculinity and Transgression in Late Medieval England', *Masculinity in Medieval Europe*, ed. D.M. Hadley (London, 1999), 178–96

Curry, Anne, 'The Military Ordinances of Henry V: Texts and Contexts', *War, Government and Aristocracy in the British Isles c.1150–1500: Essays in honour of Michael Prestwich*, ed. Chris Given-Wilson, Ann Kettle, and Len Scales (Woodbridge, 2008), 214–49

Cushing, Kathleen G., *Papacy and Law in the Gregorian Revolution: The Canonistic Work of Anselm of Lucca* (Oxford, 1998)
_____. *Reform and the Papacy in the Eleventh Century: Spirituality and Social Change* (Manchester, 2005)
Damon, John Edward, *Soldier Saints and Holy Warriors: Warfare and Sanctity in the Literature of Early England* (Aldershot, 2003)
Darlington, R.R., 'Æthelwig, abbot of Evesham', *English Historical Review* 48 (1933), 1–22
_____. 'Æthelwig, abbot of Evesham (Continued)', *English Historical Review* 48 (1933), 177–98
Darnton, Robert, *The Kiss of Lamourette* (New York, 1990)
Davis, H.W.C., 'Waldric, the Chancellor of Henry I', *English Historical Review* 26 (1911), 84–9
Davis, Michael R., *Henry of Blois: Prince Bishop of the Twelfth Century Renaissance* (Baltimore, 2009)
Davis, R.H.C., 'The *Carmen de Hastingae Proelio*', *English Historical Review* 93 (1978), 241–61
_____. *King Stephen 1135–1154* (Berkeley, 1967)
DeVailly Guy, *Le Berry du Xe siècle au milieu du XIIIe: Étude politique, religieuse, sociale et économique* (Paris, 1973)
Douglas, David, *William I* (New Haven, 1964; reprint, 1999)
Douie, D.L., *Archbishop Geoffrey Plantagenet and the Chapter of York* (York, 1960)
Draper, Peter, 'King John and Saint Wulfstan', *Journal of Medieval History* 10 (1984), 41–50
Driver, John, *How Christians Made Peace with War: Early Christian Understandings of War* (Scottdale, 1976)
Duby, Georges, *The Legend of Bouvines: War, Religion and Culture in the Middle Ages*, trans. Catherine Tihanyi (Berkeley, 1990)
_____. *The Three Orders: Feudal Society Imagined*, trans. Arthur Goldhammer (Chicago, 1980)
Duggan, Anne J., 'Conciliar Law 1123–1215: The Legislation of the Four Lateran Councils', *The History of Medieval Canon Law in the Classical Period, 1140–1234: From Gratian to the Decretals of Pope Gregory IX*, ed. Wilfried Hartmann and Kenneth Pennington (Washington, D.C., 2008), 318–66
Duggan, Charles, *Twelfth-Century Decretal Collections and Their Importance in English History* (London, 1963)
Duggan, Lawrence G., *Armsbearing and the Clergy in the History and Canon Law of Western Christianity* (Woodbridge, 2013)
Dunbabin, Jean, 'From Clerk to Knight: Changing Orders', *The Ideals and Practice of Medieval Knighthood II: Papers from the Third Strawberry Hill Conference 1986*, ed. Christopher Harper-Bill and Ruth Harvey (Woodbridge, 1988), 26–39
Dvornik, Francis, *The Ecumenical Councils* (New York, 1961)
Earl, James, W., 'Violence and Non-Violence in Anglo-Saxon England: Ælfric's "Passion of St. Edmund"', *Philological Quarterly* 78 (1999), 125–49

Edbury, Peter W., and Rowe, John Gordon, *William of Tyre: Historian of the Latin East* (Cambridge, 1988)

Erdmann, Carl, *The Origin of the Idea of Crusade*, trans. Marshall W. Baldwin and Walter Goffart (Princeton, 1977)

Farmer, Dom Hugh, 'William of Malmesbury's Life and Works', *The Journal of Ecclesiastical History* 13 (1962), 39–54

Field, Rosalind, 'Children of the Anarchy: Anglo-Norman Romance in the Twelfth Century', *Writers of the Reign of Henry II*, ed. Ruth Kennedy and Simon Meecham-Jones (New York, 2006), 249–62

Fleming, Robin, *Kings and Lords in Conquest England* (Cambridge, 1991)

Flori, Jean, 'Ideology and Motivations in the First Crusade', *The Crusades*, ed. Helen Nicholson (Basingstoke, 2005), 15–36

Forey, Alan, *The Military Orders From the Twelfth to the Early Fourteenth Centuries* (Toronto, 1992)

France, John, *The Crusades and the Expansion of Catholic Christendom, 1000–1714* (London, 2005)

———. 'Holy War and Holy Men: Erdmann and the Lives of the Saints', *The Experience of Crusading*, Vol. 1, ed. Marcus Bull and Norman Housley (Cambridge, 2003), 193–208

———. 'Property, Warfare, and the Renaissance of the Twelfth Century', *HSJ* 11 (2003), 73–84

———. *Victory in the East: A Military History of the First Crusade* (Cambridge, 1996)

———. *Western Warfare in the Age of the Crusades, 1000–1300* (Ithaca, 1999)

Franklin, Michael, 'The Bishops of Winchester and the Monastic Revolution', *Anglo-Norman Studies* 12, ed. Marjorie Chibnall (1990), 47–66

Fraser, C.M., *A History of Antony Bek* (Oxford, 1957)

Frassetto, Michael, 'Heresy, Celibacy, and Reform in the Sermons of Adhemar of Chabannes', *Medieval Purity and Piety: Essays on Medieval Clerical Celibacy and Religious Reform*, ed. Michael Frassetto (New York, 1998), 131–48

Gerrard, Daniel, 2010, 'The Military Activities of Bishops, Abbots, and other Clergy in England, c. 900–1200' (Ph.D. thesis, University of Glasgow, 2010)

———. Review of *Armsbearing and the Clergy in the History and Canon Law of Western Christianity*, by Lawrence G. Duggan, *English Historical Review* 130 (April 2015), 410–12

Gibaut, John St. H., *The Cursus Honorum: A Study of the Origins and Evolution of Sequential Ordination* (New York, 2000)

Gibbs, Marion, and Lang, Jane, *Bishops and Reform, 1215–1272: With Special Reference to the Lateran Council of 1215* (Oxford, 1934)

Gibson, Margaret, *Lanfranc of Bec* (Oxford, 1978)

Gilchrist, J.L., 'Canon Law Aspects of the Eleventh Century Gregorian Reform Programme', *The Journal of Ecclesiastical History* 13, No. 1 (April, 1962), 21–38

Gillingham, John, 'The Cultivation of History, Legend, and Courtesy at the Court of Henry II', *Writers of the Reign of Henry II*, ed. Ruth Kennedy and Simon Meecham-Jones (New York, 2006), 25–52

_____. 'Historian as Judge: William of Newburgh and Hubert Walter', *English Historical Review* 119 (Nov., 2004), 1275–87
_____. *Richard I* (New Haven, 2002)
_____. 'Richard I and the Science of War in the Middle Ages', *Anglo-Norman Warfare*, ed. Matthew Strickland (Woodbridge, 1994), 194–207
_____. 'Royal Newsletters, Forgeries and English Historians: Some Links between Court and History in the Reign of Richard I', *La Cour Plantagenêt (1154–1204)*, ed. Martin Aurell (Poitiers, 2000), 171–85
_____. 'War and Chivalry in the *History of William the Marshal*', *Anglo-Norman Warfare*, ed. Matthew Strickland (Woodbridge, 1994), 251–64
Goetz, Hans-Werner, 'Protection of the Church, Defense of the Law, and Reform: On the Purposes and Character of the Peace of God, 989–1038', *The Peace of God: Social Violence and Religious Response in France around the Year 1000*, ed. Thomas Head and Richard Landes (Ithaca, 1992), 259–79
Gossman, Francis J., *Pope Urban II and Canon Law*, The Catholic University of America Canon Law Studies, No. 403 (Washington, D.C., 1960)
Grabher, Jasonne M., and Hoeflich, Michael H., 'The Establishment of Normative Legal Texts: The Beginnings of the *Ius commune*', *The History of Medieval Canon Law in the Classical Period, 1140–1234: From Gratian to the Decretals of Pope Gregory IX*, ed. Wilfried Hartmann and Kenneth Pennington (Washington, D.C., 2008), 1–21
Gransden, Antonia, 'The Chronicles of Medieval England and Scotland, Part II', *Journal of Medieval History* 17 (1991), 217–43
_____. *Historical Writing in England c. 550 to c. 1307* (Ithaca, 1974)
Guide to Bishops' Registers of England and Wales: A Survey from the Middle Ages to the Abolition of Episcopacy in 1646, ed. David M. Smith (London, 1981)
A Guide to British Medieval Seals, ed. P.D.A. Harvey and Andrew McGuinness (Toronto, 1996)
Hahn, Cynthia, 'Proper Behavior for Knights and Kings: The Hagiography of Matthew Paris, Monk of St. Albans', *HSJ* 2 (1990), 237–48
Hallam, Elizabeth, M., *Capetian France 987–1328* (London, 1980)
_____. 'Monasteries as "War Memorials": Battle Abbey and La Victoire', *The Church and War*, ed. W.J. Sheils, *Studies in Church History* 20 (London, 1983), 47–57
Harding, Alan, *Medieval Law and the Foundations of the State* (Oxford, 2002)
Harnack, Adolph, *Militia Christi: The Christian Religion and the Military in the First Three Centuries*, trans. David McInnes Gracie (Philadelphia, 1981; originally published 1905)
Harper-Bill, Christopher, 'Bishop William Turbe and the Diocese of Norwich, 1146–1174', *Proceedings of the Battle Conference on Anglo-Norman Studies* 7, ed. R. Allen Brown (1985), 142–60
Hay, David J., *The Military Leadership of Matilda of Canossa, 1046–1115* (Manchester, 2008)
Head, Thomas, 'The Acts of the Council of Charrouz (989)', *The Peace of God: Social Violence and Religious Response in France around the Year 1000*, ed. Thomas Head and Richard Landes (Ithaca, 1992), 327–8

———. 'The Judgment of God: Andrew of Fleury's Account of the Peace League of Bourges', *The Peace of God: Social Violence and Religious Response in France around the Year 1000*, ed. Thomas Head and Richard Landes (Ithaca, 1992), 219–38

Heath, Peter, 'War and Peace in the Works of Erasmus: A Medieval Perspective', *The Medieval Military Revolution: State, Society and Military Change in Medieval and Early Modern Europe*, ed. Andrew Ayton and J.L. Price (New York, 1998), 121–44

Hehl, Ernst-Dieter, 'War, Peace and the Christian Order', *The New Cambridge Medieval History*, ed. David Luscombe and Jonathan Riley-Smith, Vol. 4 (Cambridge, 2004)

Heintshel, Donald Edward, *The Mediaeval Concept of an Ecclesiastical Office* (Washington, D.C., 1956)

Heiser, Richard, 'The Households of the Justiciars of Richard I: An Inquiry into the Second Level of Medieval English Government', *HSJ* 2, ed. Robert. B. Patterson (1990), 223–31

Hewitt, Herbert J., *The Organisation of War Under Edward III, 1338–62* (Manchester, 1966)

Hill, Joyce, 'Two Anglo-Saxon Bishops at Work: Wulfstan, Leofric and Cambridge, Corpus Christi College MS 190', *Patterns of Episcopal Power: Bishops in Tenth and Eleventh Century Western Europe*, ed. Ludger Körntgen and Dominik Waßenhoven (Berlin, 2011), 145–61

Hill, Rosalind, 'An English Archbishop and the Scottish War of Independence', *The Innes Review* 22 (1971), 59–71

Holdsworth, Christopher J., 'Ideas and Reality: Some Attempts to Control and Defuse War in the Twelfth Century', *The Church and War*, ed. W.J. Sheils, Studies in Church History 20 (London, 1983), 59–78

———. 'Peacemaking in the Twelfth Century', *Anglo-Norman Studies* 19, ed. Christopher Harper-Bill (1997), 1–18

Hollister, C. Warren, *Anglo-Saxon Military Institutions* (Oxford, 1962)

———. 'The Campaign of 1102 against Robert of Bellême', *Studies in Medieval History Presented to R. Allen Brown*, ed. C. Harper-Bill, C. Holdsworth, and J.L. Nelson (Woodbridge, 1989), 193–202

———. *Henry I* (Yale, 2001)

———. *The Military Organization of Norman England* (Oxford, 1965)

Holt, Andrew, 'Between Warrior and Priest: The Creation of a New Masculine Identity during the Crusades', *Negotiating Clerical Identities: Priests, Monks and Masculinity in the Middle Ages*, ed. Jennifer D. Thibodeaux (Basingstoke, 2010), 185–203

Hornus, Jean-Michel, *It is Not Lawful for Me to Fight: Early Christian Attitudes Toward War, Violence, and the State*, trans. Alan Kreider and Oliver Coburn (Scottdale, 1980)

Hosler, John D., 'The Brief Military Career of Thomas Becket', *HSJ* 15 (2004), 88–100

Housley, Norman, *The Avignon Papacy and the Crusades, 1305–1378* (Oxford, 1986)

_____. *Contesting the Crusades* (Oxford, 2006)
_____. *The Italian Crusades: The Papal-Angevin Alliance and the Crusades against Christian Lay Powers, 1254–1343* (Oxford, 1982)
_____. 'Recent Scholarship on Crusading and Medieval Warfare, 1095–1291: Convergence and Divergence', *War, Government and Aristocracy in the British Isles c.1150–1500: Essays in Honour of Michael Prestwich*, ed. Chris Given-Wilson, Ann Kettle, and Len Scales (Woodbridge, 2008), 197–213
Howell, Margaret, *Regalian Right in Medieval England* (London, 1962)
Hunt, Noreen, *Cluny Under Saint Hugh, 1049–1109* (South Bend, 1968)
The Ideals and Practice of Medieval Knighthood: Papers from the First and Second Strawberry Hill Conferences, ed. Christopher Harper-Bill and Ruth Harvey (Woodbridge, 1986)
Innocent III: Vicar of Christ or Lord of the World?, ed. James M. Powell, second edition (Washington, D.C., 1994)
Iogna-Prat, Dominique, *Order and Exclusion: Cluny and Christendom Face Heresy, Judaism, and Islam (1000–1150)*, trans. Graham R. Edwards (Ithaca, 2002)
Jaeger, Stephen, 'The Courtier Bishop in Vitae from the Tenth to the Twelfth Century', *Speculum* 58 (1983), 291–325
_____. 'Courtliness and Social Change', *Cultures of Power: Lordship, Status, and Prowess in Twelfth-Century Europe*, ed. Thomas N. Bisson (Philadelphia, 1995), 287–309
Jedin, Hubert, *Ecumenical Councils of the Catholic Church* (London, 1960)
Jestice, Phyllis G., 'Why Celibacy? Odo of Cluny and the Development of a New Sexual Morality', *Medieval Purity and Piety: Essays on Medieval Clerical Celibacy and Religious Reform*, ed. Michael Frassetto (New York, 1998), 81–116
Johnson-South, Theodore, 'The Norman Conquest of Durham: Norman Historians and the Anglo-Saxon Community of St. Cuthbert', *HSJ* 4 (1993), 85–95
Jones, Michael E., 'The Historicity of the Alleluja Victory', *Albion* 18 (1986), 363–73
_____. 'St. Germanus and the Adventus Saxonum', *HSJ* 2, ed. Robert B. Patterson (1990), 1–11
Jones, Thomas, *War of the Generations: The Revolt of 1173–1174* (Ann Arbor, 1980)
Jotischky, Andrew, *Crusading and the Crusader States* (Harlow, 2004)
Kaeuper, Richard W., *Chivalry and Violence in Medieval Europe* (Oxford, 2001)
_____. *Holy Warriors: The Religious Ideology of Chivalry* (Philadelphia, 2009)
_____. *War, Justice, and Public Order: England and France in the Later Middle Ages* (Oxford, 1988)
Kamen, Henry, 'Clerical Violence in a Catholic Society: The Hispanic World 1450–1720', *The Church and War*, ed. W.J. Sheils, *Studies in Church History* 20 (London, 1983), 201–16
Kapelle, William, *The Norman Conquest of the North: The Region and Its Transformation, 1000–1135* (North Carolina, 1979)

Karras, Ruth Mazo, 'Thomas Aquinas's Chastity Belt: Clerical Masculinity in Medieval Europe', *Gender and Christianity in Medieval Europe*, ed. Lisa M. Bitel and Felice Lifshitz (Philadelphia, 2008), 52–67

Kealey, Edward J., *Roger of Salisbury: Viceroy of England* (Berkeley, 1972)

Kedar, Benjamin Z., 'On the Origins of the Earliest Laws of Frankish Jerusalem: The Canons of the Council of Nablus, 1120', *Speculum* 74 (1999), 310–35

Keynes, Simon, 'An Abbot, an Archbishop, and the Viking Raids of 1006–7 and 1009–12', *Anglo-Saxon England* 36 (2007), 151–220

Kienzle, Beverly Mayne, *Cistercians, Heresy and Crusade in Occitania, 1145–1229* (York, 2001)

King, Andy, 'A Good Chance for the Scots? The Recruitment of English Armies for Scotland and the Marches, 1337–1347', *England and Scotland at War, c.1296–c.1513*, ed. Andy King and David Simpkin (Leiden, 2012), 119–56

King, Edmund, *King Stephen* (New Haven, 2010)

King, James R., 'The Friar Tuck Syndrome: Clerical Violence and the Barons' War', *The Final Argument: The Imprint of Violence on Society in Medieval and Early Modern Europe*, ed. Donald J. Kagay and Andrew L.J. Villalon (Woodbridge, 1998), 27–52

Knowles, David, *The Episcopal Colleagues of Archbishop Thomas Becket* (Cambridge, 1951)

_____. *Saints and Scholars: Twenty-five Medieval Portraits* (Cambridge, 1962)

_____. *Thomas Becket* (Stanford, 1971)

Kreider, Alan. 'Military Service in the Church Orders', *The Journal of Religious Ethics* 31 (2003), 415–42

Krey, August C., *The First Crusade: The Accounts of Eyewitnesses and Participants* (Princeton, 1921)

Kuttner, Stephan, *Gratian and the Schools of Law, 1140–1234* (London, 1983)

_____. *The History of Ideas and Doctrines of Canon Law in the Middle Ages* (London, 1980)

_____. *Medieval Councils, Decretals, and Collections of Canon Law* (London, 1980)

_____. 'The Revival of Jurisprudence', *Renaissance and Renewal in the Twelfth Century*, ed. R.I. Benson and Giles Constable (Cambridge, MA, 1982), 37–67

Landes, Richard, 'Between Aristocracy and Heresy: Popular Participation in the Limousin Peace of God, 994–1033', *The Peace of God: Social Violence and Religious Response in France around the Year 1000*, ed. Thomas Head and Richard Landes (Ithaca, 1992), 184–218

_____. 'Rodulphus Glaber on Events in the Year 1033', *Peace of God: Social Violence and Religious Response in France around the Year 1000*, ed. Thomas Head and Richard Landes (Ithaca, 1992), 338–9

_____. *Relics, Apocalypse, and the Deceits of History: Ademar of Chabannes, 989–1034* (Cambridge, MA, 1995)

Lapina, Elizabeth, *Warfare and the Miraculous in the Chronicles of the First Crusade* (Penn State Press, 2015)

Lapsley, Gaillard Thomas, *The County Palatine of Durham: A Study of Feudal Obligation* (New York, 1900)

Lawrence-Mathers, Anne, 'William of Newburgh and the Northumbrian Constructions of English History', *Journal of Medieval History* 33 (2007), 339-57

Le Goff, Jacques, *The Medieval Imagination*, trans. Arthur Goldhammer (Chicago, 1985)

LeJeune, Rita and Stiennon, Jacques, *The Legend of Roland in the Middle Ages*, Vol. 2, trans. Christine Trollope (Brussels, 1971)

———. *La Legende de Roland dans l'art du Moyen Age*, 2 vols. (Bruxelles, 1966)

Lewis, Michael John, 'Identity and Status in the Bayeux Tapestry: The Iconographic and Artefactual Evidence', *Anglo-Norman Studies* 29, ed. C.P. Lewis (Woodbridge, 2007), 110-20

Leyser, Karl, 'The Angevin Kings and the Holy Man', *Communications and Power in Medieval Europe: The Gregorian Revolution and Beyond*, ed. Timothy Reuter (London, 1994), 49-73

———. 'Warfare in the Western European Middle Ages: The Moral Debate', *Communications and Power in Medieval Europe: The Gregorian Revolution and Beyond*, ed. Timothy Reuter (London, 1994), 189-203

Lifshitz, Felice, 'Beyond Positivism and Genre: "Hagiographical" Texts as Historical Narrative', *Viator* 25 (1994), 95-113

———. 'The Politics of Historiography: The Memory of Bishops in Eleventh-Century Rouen', *History and Memory* 10 (1998), 118-37

Little, Lester K., *Religious Poverty and the Profit Economy in Medieval Europe* (Ithaca, 1978)

Lloyd, Simon *English Society and the Crusade, 1216-1307* (Oxford, 1988)

Loud, Graham A., 'Churches and Churchmen in an Age of Conquest: Southern Italy, 1030-1130', *HSJ* 4 (1993), 37-53

MacMullen, Ramsay, *Voting About God in Early Church Councils* (New Haven, 2006)

Magnou-Nortier, Elisabeth, 'The Enemies of the Peace: Reflections on a Vocabulary, 500-1100', trans. Amy G. Remensnyder, *The Peace of God: Social Violence and Religious Response in France around the Year 1000*, ed. Thomas Head and Richard Landes (Ithaca, 1992), 58-79

Maier, Christoph T., *Preaching the Crusades: Mendicant Friars and the Cross in the Thirteenth Century* (Cambridge, 1994)

Markus, R.A., 'Saint Augustine's Views on the 'Just War'', *The Church and War*, ed. W.J. Sheils, *Studies in Church History* 20 (London, 1983), 1-13

Marritt, Stephen, 'King Stephen and the Bishops', *Anglo-Norman Studies* 24, ed. John Gillingham (2002), 129-44

Marten, Lucy, 'The Rebellion of 1075 and its Impact in East Anglia', *Medieval East Anglia*, ed. Christopher Harper-Bill (Woodbridge, 2005), 168-82

Martindale, Jane P., '"An unfinished business"; Angevin Politics and the Siege of Toulouse (1159)', *Anglo-Norman Studies* 23, ed. John Gillingham (2001), 115-54

Mason, Emma, *Saint Wulfstan of Worcester, c.1008-1095* (Oxford, 1990)

Mastnak, Tomaž, *Crusading Peace: Christendom, the Muslim World and the Western Political Order* (Berkeley, 2002)

Matthew, Donald, *King Stephen* (London, 2001)

Mayer, Hans Eberhard, *The Crusades*, trans. John Gillingham (Oxford, 1988)
McHardy, Alison K., 'The English Clergy and the Hundred Years War', *The Church and War*, ed. W.J. Sheils, Studies in Church History 20 (London, 1983), 171–8
McNab, Bruce, 'Obligations of the Church in English Society: Military Arrays of the Clergy, 1369–1418', *Order and Innovation in the Middle Ages: Essays in Honor of Joseph R. Strayer*, ed. W.C. Jordan, B. Mcnab and T.R. Ruiz (Princeton, 1976), 293–314
Meredith-Jones, C., 'The Chronicle of Turpin in Saintonge', *Speculum* 13 (1938), 160–79
Midmer, Roy, *English Mediaeval Monasteries (1066–1540): A Summary* (Athens, GA, 1979)
The Military Orders: Fighting for the Faith and Caring for the Sick, ed. Malcolm Barber (Aldershot, 1994)
Miller, Andrew George, 'Carpe ecclesiam: Households, Identity and Violent Communication ("Church" and "Crown") under King Edward I)' (Ph.D. Thesis, UC-Santa Barbara, 2003), 204–37
_____. 'Knights, Bishops and Deer Parks: Episcopal Identity, Emasculation and Clerical Space in Medieval England', *Negotiating Clerical Identities: Priests, Monks and Masculinity in the Middle Ages*, ed. Jennifer D. Thibodeaux (Basingstoke, 2010), 204–37
Miller, Maureen, 'Masculinity, Reform, and Clerical Culture: Narratives of Episcopal Holiness in the Gregorian Era', *Church History* 72 (2003), 25–52
Moore, R.I., *The First European Revolution, c.970–1215* (London, 2000)
_____. *The Formation of a Persecuting Society: Authority and Deviance in Western Europe 950–1250*, second edition (Malden, MA, 2007)
Morey, Dom Adrian, and Brooke, C.N.L., *Gilbert Foliot and His Letters* (Cambridge, 1965)
Morillo, Stephen, ed., *The Battle of Hastings: Sources and Interpretations* (Woodbridge, 1996)
_____. *Warfare under the Anglo-Norman Kings 1066–1135* (Woodbridge, 1994)
Morris, Colin, 'William I and the Church Courts', *English Historical Review* 82 (1967), 449–63
Morton, Catherine, 'Pope Alexander II and the Norman Conquest', *Latomus: Revue d'etudes latines* 34 (1975), 362–82
Morton, Nicholas, 'The Defense of the Holy Land and the Memory of the Maccabees', *Journal of Medieval History* 36 (2010), 275–93
Müeller, W.P., 'The Recovery of Justinian's Digest in the Middle Ages', *Bulletin of Medieval Canon Law*, New Series 20 (1990), 1–30
Nakashian, Craig M. '"All my sons are bastards": Geoffrey Plantagenet's Military Service to Henry II', *Ecclesia et Violentia: Violence against the Church and Violence within the Church in the Middle Ages*, ed. Radosław Kotecki and Jacek Maciejewski (Newcastle upon Tyne: Cambridge Scholars Publishing, 2014), 122–40
_____. 'The Political and Military Agency of Ecclesiastical Leaders in Anglo-Norman England, 1066–1154', *Journal of Medieval Military History* 12 (2014), 51–80

_____. 'The Use and Impact of the English Levied Soldiers in Anglo-Norman England', *Comitatus: A Journal of Medieval and Renaissance Studies* 37 (2006), 1–31

Nelis, Suzanne J., 'What Lanfranc Taught, What Anselm Learned', *HSJ* 2, ed. Robert Patterson (1990), 75–82

Nelson, Janet, L., 'The Church's Military Service in The Ninth Century: A Contemporary Comparative View?', *The Church and War*, ed. W.J. Sheils, Studies in Church History 20 (Oxford, 1983), 15–30

_____. 'Monks, Secular Men and Masculinity, c.900', *Masculinity in Medieval Europe*, ed. D.M. Hadley (London, 1999), 121–42

Nicholson, Helen, 'Before William of Tyre: European Reports on the Military Orders' Deeds in the East, 1150–1185', *The Military Orders: Welfare and Warfare*, Vol. 2, ed. Helen Nicholson (Aldershot, 1998), 111–18

_____. *The Knights Hospitaller* (Woodbridge, 2003)

_____. *The Knights Templar: A new history* (Stroud, 2001)

_____. 'The Military Orders and the Kings of England in the Twelfth and Thirteenth Centuries', *From Clermont to Jerusalem: The Crusades and Crusader Societies, 1095–1500*, ed. Alan V. Murray (Turnhout, 1998), 203–17

_____. 'Serving King and Crusade: The Military Orders in Royal Service in Ireland, 1220–1400', *The Experience of Crusading*, Vol. 1, ed. Marcus Bull and Norman Housley (Cambridge, 2003), 233–54

_____. *Templars, Hospitallers and Teutonic Knights: Images of the Military Orders, 1128–1291* (Leicester, 1993)

Nilson, Ben, *Cathedral Shrines of Medieval England* (Woodbridge, 1998)

O'Doherty, J.F., 'Historical Criticism of the Song of Dermot and the Earl', *Irish Historical Studies* 1 (1938), 4–20

O'Donnell, Lindsey, 'Rendering unto Caesar: Ecclesiastical Identity in Thirteenth-Century North Wales' (M.A. Thesis, University of Missouri-Columbia, 2004)

Ortenberg, Veronica, *The English Church and the Continent in the Tenth and Eleventh Centuries: Cultural, Spiritual, and Artistic Exchanges* (Oxford, 1992)

Ott, John Stephens, 'Guardians Upon the Walls of this Terrestrial Jerusalem Bishops, Episcopal Authority, and Community in Northern France, ca. 1070–1150' (Ph.D. dissertation, Stanford University, 1999)

Owen, D.D.R., 'The Secular Inspiration of the Song of Roland', *Speculum* 37 (Jul., 1962), 390–400

Owen-Crocker, Gale R., 'The Interpretation of Gesture in the Bayeux Tapestry', *Anglo-Norman Studies* 29, ed. C.P. Lewis (2007), 145–78

Pacaut, Marcel, *Louis VII et son Royaume* (Paris, 1964)

Partner, Nancy, *Serious Entertainments: The Writing of History in Twelfth-Century England* (Chicago, 1977)

Paxton, Jennifer, 'Monks and Bishops: The Purpose of the Liber Eliensis', *HSJ* 11 (2003), 17–30

Peltzer, Jörg, 'The Angevin Kings and Canon Law: Episcopal Elections and the Loss of Normandy', *Anglo-Norman Studies* 27, ed. John Gillingham (2005), 169–84

Penman Michael A., 'Faith in War: The Religious Experience of Scottish Soldiery, c.1100–c.1500', *Journal of Medieval History* 37 (2011), 295–303

Pennington, Kenneth, 'The Decretalists 1190-1234', *The History of Medieval Canon Law in the Classical Period, 1140–1234: From Gratian to the Decretals of Pope Gregory IX*, ed. Wilfried Hartmann and Kenneth Pennington (Washington, D.C., 2008), 211–45

Pennington, Kenneth, *Pope and Bishops: The Papal Monarchy in the Twelfth and Thirteenth Centuries* (Philadelphia, 1984)

_____. *The Prince and Law, 1200–1600* (Berkeley, 1993)

Pennington, Kenneth and Muller, Wolfgang P., 'The Decretalists: The Italian School', *The History of Medieval Canon Law in the Classical Period, 1140–1234: From Gratian to the Decretals of Pope Gregory IX*, ed. Wilfried Hartmann and Kenneth Pennington (Washington, D.C., 2008), 121–73

Peters, Edward, 'History, Historians, and Clerical Celibacy', *Medieval Purity and Piety: Essays on Medieval Clerical Celibacy and Religious Reform*, ed. Michael Frassetto (New York, 1998), 1–22

Phillips, Jonathan, 'Archbishop Henry of Reims and the Militarization of the Hospitallers', *The Military Orders: Welfare and Warfare*, Vol. 2, ed. Helen Nicholson (Aldershot, 1998)

Pierce, Ian, 'Arms, Armour and Warfare in the Eleventh Century', *Anglo-Norman Studies* 10 (1988), 237–57

Pixton, Paul B., *The German Episcopacy and the Implementation of the Decrees of the Fourth Lateran Council, 1216–1245* (New York, 1995)

Platt, Colin, *The Abbeys and Priories of Medieval England* (London, 1984)

Poggiaspalla, Ferminio, 'La chiesa e la partecipazione dei chierici alla guerra nella legislazione conciliare fino alla Decretali di Gregorio IX', *Ephemerides iuris canoni* 15 (Rome, 1959), 140–53

Pollock, Melissa, *The Lion, the Lily, and the Leopard : The Crown and Nobility of Scotland, France, and England and the Struggle for Power (1100–1204)* (Turnhout, 2015)

_____. *Scotland, England and France After the Loss of Normandy, 1204–1296* (Woodbridge, 2015)

Post, Gaines, *Studies in Medieval Legal Thought: Public Law and the State, 1100–1322* (Princeton, 1964)

Potts, Cassandra, 'When the Saints Go Marching: Religious Connections and the Political Culture of Early Normandy', *Anglo-Norman Political Culture and the Twelfth-Century Renaissance: Proceedings of the Borchard Conference on Anglo-Norman History, 1995*, ed. C. Warren Hollister (Woodbridge, 1997), 17–31

Powell, T.E., 'The "Three Orders" of Society in Anglo-Saxon England', *Anglo-Saxon England* 23 (1994), 103–32

Power, Daniel, 'The Norman Church and the Angevin and Capetian Kings', *The Journal of Ecclesiastical History* 56 (2005), 205–34

Powicke, Michael, *Military Obligation in Medieval England* (Oxford, 1962)

Prestwich, J.O., 'The Military Household of the Norman Kings', *Anglo-Norman Warfare*, ed. Matthew Strickland (Woodbridge, 1994), 93–127

_____. 'War and Finance in the Anglo-Norman State', *Anglo-Norman Warfare*, ed. Matthew Strickland (Woodbridge, 1994), 59–92

Prestwich, Michael, 'Gilbert de Middleton and the Attack on the Cardinals, 1317', *Warriors and Churchmen in the Middle Ages: Essays Presented to Karl Leyser*, ed. Tim Reuter (London, 1992), 179–94

Prinze, Friedrich E., 'King, Clergy and War at the Time of the Carolingians', *Saints, Scholars and Heroes: Studies in Medieval Culture in Honour of Charles W. Jones*, Vol. 2, ed. M.H. King and W.M. Stevens (Collegeville, 1979), 301–29

_____. *Klerus und Krieg im Früheren Mittelalter* (Stuttgart, 1971)

Remensyder, Amy G., 'Pollution, Purity, and Peace: An Aspect of Social Reform between the Late Tenth Century and 1076', *The Peace of God: Social Violence and Religious Response in France around the Year 1000*, ed. Thomas Head and Richard Landes (Ithaca, 1992), 280–307

_____. *Remembering Kings Past: Monastic Foundation Legends in Medieval Southern France* (Ithaca, 1995)

Reuter, Timothy, '*Episcopi cum sua militia*: The Prelate as Warrior in the Early Stauffer Era', *Warriors and Churchmen in the Middle Ages: Essays Presented to Karl Leyser*, ed. Tim Reuter (London, 1992), 79–94

_____. 'A Europe of Bishops: The Age of Wulfstan of York and Burchard of Worms', *Patterns of Episcopal Power: Bishops in Tenth and Eleventh Century Western Europe*, ed. Ludger Körntgen and Dominik Waßenhoven (Berlin, 2011), 17–38

Ridyard, Susan J., *The Royal Saints of Anglo-Saxon England: A study of West Saxon and East Anglian Cults* (Cambridge, 1988)

Rigg, A.G., *A History of Anglo-Latin Literature 1066–1422* (Cambridge, 1992)

Riley-Smith, Jonathan, *The Crusades: Idea and Reality, 1095–1274* (London, 1981)

_____. *The First Crusade and the Idea of Crusading* (Philadelphia, 2009)

Robinson, I.S., 'Gregory VII and the Soldiers of Christ', *History* 58 (1973), 161–92

Rolker, Christof, *Canon Law and the Letters of Ivo of Chartres* (Cambridge, 2010)

Rollason, David, 'The Miracles of St Benedict: A Window on Early Medieval France', *Studies in Medieval History presented to R.H.C. Davis*, ed. Henry Mayr-Harting and R.I. Moore (London, 1985), 73–90

Romig, Andrew, 'The Common Bond of Aristocratic Masculinity: Monks, Secular Men, and St. Gerald of Aurillac', *Negotiating Clerical Identities: Priests, Monks, and Masculinity in the Middle Ages*, ed. Jennifer D. Thibodeaux (Basingstoke, 2010), 39–56

Rosenwein, Barbara H., 'Feudal War and Monastic Peace: Cluniac Liturgy as Ritual Aggression', *Viator* 2 (1971), 128–57

Round, J.H., 'Some English Crusaders of Richard I', *English Historical Review* 18 (1903), 475–81

Rubenstein, Jay, 'Liturgy Against History: The Competing Visions of Lanfranc and Eadmer of Canterbury', *Speculum* 74 (1999), 279–309

Russell, Frederick H., *The Just War in the Middle Ages* (Cambridge, 1975)

Ruud, Maylou, 'Monks in the World: The Case of Gundulf of Rochester', *Anglo-Norman Studies* 11, ed. R. Allen Brown (1989), 245–60

Ryan, Vincent, 'Richard I and the Early Evolution of the Fourth Crusade', *The Fourth Crusade: Event, Aftermath, and Perceptions*, ed. Thomas F. Madden (Aldershot, 2008), 3–13
Saltman, Avrom, *Theobald Archbishop of Canterbury* (London, 1956)
Sassier, Yves, *Louis VII* (Paris, 1991)
Scammell, G.V., *Hugh du Puiset, Bishop of Durham* (Cambridge, 1956)
Schein, Sylvia, *Fideles Crucis: The Papacy, the West, and the Recovery of the Holy Land 1274–1314* (Oxford, 1991)
Schenk, Jochen G., 'Forms of Lay Association with the Order of the Temple', *Journal of Medieval History* 34 (2008), 79–103
Schwyzer, Hugo. 'Arms and the Bishop: The Anglo-Scottish War and the Northern Episcopate, 1296–1357' (Ph.D. dissertation, UCLA, 1999)
_____. 'Northern Bishops and the Anglo-Scottish Wars in the Reign of Edward II', *Thirteenth Century England* 7 (1999), 243–54
Searle, Eleanor, *Lordship and Community: Battle Abbey and its Banlieu 1066–1538* (Toronto, 1974)
Seidel, Linda V., 'Holy Warriors: The Romanesque Rider and the Fight Against Islam', *The Holy War*, ed. Thomas Patrick Murphy (Columbus, 1976), 33–54
Senette, Douglas, 'A Cluniac Prelate: Henry of Blois, Bishop of Winchester (1129–1171)' (Ph.D. dissertation, Tulane University, 1991)
Shean, John F., *Soldiering for God: Christianity and the Roman Army* (Leiden, 2010)
Sizgorich, Thomas, *Violence and Belief in Late Antiquity: Militant Devotion in Christianity and Islam* (Philadelphia, 2009)
Smith, Katherine Allen, 'Saints in Shining Armor: Martial Asceticism and Masculine Models of Sanctity, ca.1050–1250', *Speculum* 83 (2008), 572–602
_____. 'Spiritual Warriors in Citadels of Faith: Martial Rhetoric and Monastic Masculinity in the Long Twelfth Century', *Negotiating Clerical Identities: Priests, Monks and Masculinity in the Middle Ages*, ed. Jennifer D. Thibodeaux (Basingstoke, 2010), 86–110
_____. *War and the Making of Medieval Monastic Culture* (Woodbridge, 2011)
Somerville, Robert, *Councils of Urban II*, Vol. 1, *Decreta Clarmontensia* (Amsterdam, 1972)
_____. *Papacy, Councils and Canon Law in the 11th–12th Centuries* (Aldershot, 1990)
Southern, R.W., *Saint Anselm and His Biographer: A Study of Monastic Life and Thought, 1059–c.1130* (Cambridge, 1963)
_____. *Saint Anselm: A Portrait in a Landscape* (Cambridge, 1990)
_____. *Western Society and the Church* (Harmondsworth, 1970)
Spear, David, 'The School of Caen Revisited', *HSJ* 4 (1993), 55–66
Sprey, Ilicia Jo, 'Papal Legates in English Politics, 1100–1272' (Ph.D. dissertation, University of Virginia, 1998)
Staunton, Michael, 'Eadmer's *Vita Anselmi*: A Reinterpretation', *Journal of Medieval History* 23 (1997), 1–14
_____. *Thomas Becket and His Biographers* (Woodbridge, 2006)
_____. 'Thomas Becket's Conversion', *Anglo-Norman Studies* 21 (1999), 193–212

Stein, Peter, *Roman Law in European History* (New York, 1999)
Strevett, Neil, 'The Anglo-Norman Civil War of 1101 Reconsidered', *Anglo-Norman Studies* 26, ed. John Gillingham (2004), 159–76
Strickland, Matthew, 'Against the Lord's Anointed: Aspects of Warfare and Baronial Rebellion in England and Normandy 1075–1265', in *Law and Government in Medieval England and Normandy: Essays in Honour of Sir James Holt*, ed. G. Garnett and J. Hudson (Cambridge, 1994), 56–79
_____. *War and Chivalry: The Conduct and Perception of War in England and Normandy, 1066–1217* (Cambridge, 1996)
Swanson, R.N., 'Angels Incarnate: Clergy and Masculinity from Gregorian Reform to Reformation', *Masculinity in Medieval Europe*, ed. D.M. Hadley (London, 1999), pp. 160–77
_____. *Church and Society in Late Medieval England* (Oxford, 1989)
Tanner, Norman, 'Pastoral Care: The Fourth Lateran Council of 1215', *A History of Pastoral Care*, ed. G.R. Evans (London, 2000), 112–25
Taylor, Andrew, 'Was there a Song of Roland?', *Speculum* 76 (2001), 28–65
Thomas, Hugh M., *The English and the Normans: Ethnic Hostility, Assimilation, and Identity 1066–c.1220* (Oxford, 2003)
_____. 'Shame, Masculinity, and the Death of Thomas Becket', *Speculum* 87 (2012), 1050–88
Throop, Palmer A., *Criticism of the Crusade: A Study of Public Opinion and Crusade Propaganda* (Amsterdam, 1940)
Tillman, Helene, *Pope Innocent III*, trans. Walter Sax, *Europe in the Middle Ages Selected Studies*, Vol. 12 (Amsterdam, 1980)
Truax, Jean A., 'All Roads Lead to Chartres: The House of Blois, the Papacy, and the Anglo-Norman Succession of 1135', *Anglo-Norman Studies* 31, ed. C.P. Lewis (2008), 118–34
_____. *Archbishops Ralph d'Escures, William of Corbeil, and Theobald of Bec: Heirs of Anselm and Ancestors of Becket* (Farnham, 2012)
Turner, Ralph V., *King John* (London, 1994)
_____. 'King John in His Context: A Comparison with His Contemporaries', *HSJ* 3 (1992), 183–95
_____. *Men Raised from the Dust* (Philadelphia, 1988)
_____. 'Richard the Lionheart and English Episcopal Elections', *Albion* 29 (1997), 1–13
Tyerman, Christopher, *England and the Crusades* (Chicago, 1988)
_____. *God's War: A New History of the Crusades* (Cambridge, MA, 2006)
_____. 'Were there Any Crusades in the Twelfth Century?', *English Historical Review* 110 (1995), 553–77
Ullmann, Walter, *The Church and the Law in the Earlier Middle Ages* (London, 1975)
_____. *Law and Politics in the Middle Ages* (Ithaca, 1975)
Urry, William, *Thomas Becket: His Last Days*, ed. and intro. Peter A. Rowe (Stroud, 1999)
Van Dam, Raymond, *Saints and their Miracles in Late Antique Gaul* (Princeton, 1993)

Van Houts, Elizabeth, 'Latin and French as Languages of the Past in Normandy during the Reign of Henry II: Robert of Torigni, Stephen of Rouen, and Wace', *Writers of the Reign of Henry II*, ed. Ruth Kennedy and Simon Meecham-Jones (New York, 2006), 53–77

Vaughn, Sally N., *Anselm of Bec and Robert of Meulan: The Innocence of the Dove and the Wisdom of the Serpent* (Berkeley, 1987)

———. *Archbishop Anselm 1093–1109: Bec Missionary, Canterbury Primate, Patriarch of Another World* (Farnham, 2012)

Vermeesch, Albert, *Essai sur les origines et la signification de la commune dans le nord de la France (XIe et XIIe siècles)*, Studies Presented to the International Commission for the History of Representative and Parliamentary Institutions 30 (Heule, 1966)

Vincent, Nicholas, *Peter des Roches: An Alien in English Politics, 1205–1238* (Cambridge, 1996)

Vollrath, Hanna, 'Was Thomas Becket Chaste? Understanding Episodes in the Becket Lives', *Anglo-Norman Studies* 27, ed. John Gillingham (2005), 198–209

Voss, Lena, *Heinrich von Blois, Bischof von Winchester, 1129–1171* (Berlin, 1932)

Waley, D.P., 'Papal Armies in the Thirteenth Century', *English Historical Review* 72 (1957), 1–30

Ward-Perkins, Bryan, *The Fall of Rome and the End of Civilization* (Oxford, 2006)

Warren, W.L., *Henry II* (New Haven, 2000)

———. *King John* (Berkeley, 1978)

Watson, Fiona J., *Under the Hammer: Edward I and Scotland, 1286–1306* (East Lothian, 1998)

Webb, Diana, *Patrons and Defenders: The Saints in the Italian City-States* (London, 1996)

Weiler, Björn, 'William of Malmesbury, King Henry I, and the Gesta Regum Anglorum', *Anglo-Norman Studies* 31, ed. C.P. Lewis (2008), 157–76

Weiss, Judith, 'Arthur, Emperors, and Antichrists: The Formation of the Arthurian Biography', *Writers of the Reign of Henry II*, ed. Ruth Kennedy and Simon Meecham-Jones (New York, 2006), 239–48

Wells, Scott, 'The Warrior *Habitus*: Militant Masculinity and Monasticism in the Henrician Reform Movement', *Negotiating Clerical Identities: Priests, Monks and Masculinity in the Middle Ages*, ed. Jennifer D. Thibodeaux (Basingstoke, 2010), 57–85

White, Graeme, *Restoration and Reform 1153–1165: Recovery from Civil War in England* (Cambridge, 2000)

White, Stephen D., *Feuding and Peace-Making in Eleventh-Century France* (Aldershot, 2005)

Williams, Ann, 'The Cunning of the Dove: Wulfstan and the Politics of Accommodation', *St. Wulfstan and His World*, ed. Julia S. Barrow and N.P. Brooks (Aldershot, 2005), 23–38

Winchester in the Early Middle Ages: An Edition and Discussion of Winton Domesday, ed. Martin Biddle (Oxford, 1976)

Winroth, Anders, *The Making of Gratian's Decretum* (Cambridge, 2000)

Wright, Nicholas, *Knights and Peasants: The Hundred Years War in the French Countryside* (Woodbridge, 1998)
Young, Charles R., *Hubert Walter, Lord of Canterbury and Lord of England* (Durham, N.C., 1968)

Index

Acre, siege of (1189–91) 232–3, 236
Adalbero, archbishop of Metz 64–5
Adalbero, bishop of Laon 47, 65
Adalbero, bishop of Verdun 64–5
Adhémar, bishop of Le Puy 73, 77, 79–80, 139, 202
    chanson d'Antioche 116–20
    Bearing the Holy Lance 119–20
Adela, daughter of William I 185
Ælfric of Eynsham 46–50, 260
Ælred, abbot of Rievaulx 193–4
Æthelwald of Wessex 44
Æthelwold, bishop of Winchester 172
Æthelwulf, king of Wessex 44
Æthewig, abbot of Evesham 145, 161–2, 170–2
Aimon de Bourbon, archbishop of Bourges *see* Peace League of Bourges
Alberic, bishop of Ostia 75
Aldred, archbishop of York 131
Alexander, bishop of Lincoln 188, 194, 201–2
Alexander the Minorite 83
Alexander II, Pope 129–30
Alexander III, Pope 85, 159, 222
Alexander VI, Pope 258
Alexiad see Anna Comnena
Alfred, king of England 46–7
Ambroise 232, 235, 237, 239
Andrew of Fleury *see* Peace League of Bourges
Anglo-Saxon Chronicle 45, 147, 152, 170
Angoulême cathedral 102
Annals of Cambrai see Lambert of Wattrelos
Anselm of Bec, Saint, archbishop of Canterbury 136, 140, 158, 163–9, 171, 183, 202, 207, 210, 213, 245
Anselm, bishop of Havelberg, archbishop of Ravenna 84
Anselm, dean and chancellor of Laon 180
Anselm, Saint, bishop of Lucca 72
Antioch, siege of (1098) 79
Arms 42, 51
Armsbearing 118, 134, 134 n. 37, 250

prohibition on clerical 33, 35–6, 38, 42, 48, 69, 72–3, 75, 76 n. 41, 89–90, 221, 254–5, 257
Arundel, castle of 195
Ashingdon, battle of (1016) 46
Asser 44–5
Astronomus 37
Audita Tremendi see Gregory VIII, Pope
Auxerre, bishops of 16–17
Aylmer, Felix 206

Baldwin of Flanders 15
Baldwin of Forde, archbishop of Canterbury 77, 80, 222, 229, 231–3, 235, 236, 252
Baldwin de Redvers, earl of Devon 189
Barbarossa, Frederick, emperor of the Holy Roman Empire 229, 231–2
Bardolph, Hugh 224
Barthelemey de Vendôme, archbishop of Tours 247
Basset, Ralph 255, 257
Bayeux Tapestry 128–30, 133–4, 138
Becket (film-1964) 206
Becket, Thomas, Saint, archbishop of Canterbury 179, 207–15, 228
    Campaign in Aquitaine (1159) 212–13
    Campaign in Gisors (1161–62) 214
Bede, Saint 33
Bek, Antony, bishop of Durham 22 n.74, 116, 255–7
Bella Antiochena 97
Benedict IX, Pope 68
Benevento campaign 67–9
Berengard of Narbonne 60–2
Bernard of Angers 51–5
Bernard of Clairvaux 11–12, 30–1, 71–2, 226
    De Laude Novae Militiae 84
Bigod, Hugh 188
Bigod, Roger (d. 1107) 174
Bohemund, prince of Taranto 79
Boniface, St, archbishop of Mainz 35
Bonizo, bishop of Sutri 66, 68–9
Bouvines, battle of (1214) 240
Brewer, William, bishop of Exeter 251

INDEX 289

Bruno, bishop of Segni 68–70
Bruno, bishop of Toul *see* Leo IX, Saint, Pope
Burchard, bishop of Worms 86, 89–91, 93, 95

Caesar of Heisterbach 19
Canon law 38, 69, 75, 84, 86–99 *see also* Burchard, archbishop of Worms, church councils, decretists, Gratian, Ivo of Chartres
Canterbury, archbishops of *see* Anselm of Bec, Baldwin of Forde, Dunstan, Hubert Walter, Lanfranc, Richard of Dover, Stephen Langton, Stigand, Thomas Becket, William de Corbeil
Capet, Hugh, king of France 64
Carmen de Hastingae Proelio see Guy, bishop of Amiens
Celestine III, Pope 225–6, 229, 240, 244–6
Chanson d'Antioche see Adhémar, bishop of Le Puy
Chansons de geste 100–19 *see also Chanson d'Antioche, Song of Roland, Song of Aspremont, William in the Monastery*
Charlemagne 35, 36
Charles the Bald, king of France 37
Chivalry 8–9, 18, 21, 53, 61, 103, 106, 160, 162, 216, 231, 236, 243
  Mentalité 100
Chretien de Troyes 243
  Yvain 243
Church councils 31, 33–4, 36, 38, 41, 59–60, 66, 69, 72–3, 75, 76 n. 41, 96, 99, 221–2, 249, 251, 257 *see also* Concilium Germanicum (742), Council of Arles (314), Council of Chalcedon (451), Council of Charroux (989), Council of Clermont (1095), Council of Gerona (1068), Council of London (1074–5), Council of Meaux (845), Council of Metz (888), Council of Nablus (1119), Council of Narbonne (1054), Council of Nicaea (325), Council of Paris (846), Council of Rheims (1049), Council of Soissons (744), Council of St. Paul (1268), Council of Ticino (876), Council of Toledo (633), Council of Toulouges (1027), Council of Ver (844), Councils of Vic (1033 and 1068), Council of Vienne (1311–12), Council of Westminster (1138), Council of Westminster (1175),
Council of Winchester (1070), Council of Windsor (1070), Lateran II (1139), Lateran III (1179), Lateran IV (1215)
Churchman/Churchmen
  Definition 5–6
  Fighting 5–7
  Military behavior
    Defense of Christianity 104–7, 230–1, 250
    Defense of the king 104, 107, 165–8, 170–1, 174, 189, 218, 239, 243, 244, 250
    Defense of the patria 7–8, 135–6, 144–6, 161, 163, 170–1, 218, 243, 244–5
    Defense of the region 7, 165–6, 175–6, 244–5
    In battle 1, 3, 32–3, 37, 44–5, 51–4, 75, 79, 100–7, 133, 135, 141, 182, 193, 214, 226–7, 231, 233, 235, 239, 241–3, 246, 249–50, 255, 257–8
    On campaign 2–3, 16–17, 32–3, 44–5, 55–8, 67–9, 70, 75, 77, 79, 132–4, 140–1, 145–6, 155, 170–1, 189–91, 192–4, 212–14, 216–17, 233–4, 240, 248, 251–2, 255–6
    Ordo/ordines 40, 46–47, 48, 58, 62–3, 65, 97, 105, 112, 113, 183, 186–7, 205, 213, 219–20, 228, 239, 240, 241, 258
  Worldliness 10–11, 19–21, 41, 84, 97, 110, 140, 153–4, 156, 158, 163, 181, 184–5, 202–3, 205–6, 208–11, 214–15, 223, 224–5, 228, 237, 243, 250
Cistercians 84, 186
Clement III, antipope 71, 151
Cleric *see* churchman/churchmen
Cluny, Cluniacs 127, 185, 186–7, 206, 226–7
Coleman *see* William of Malmesbury
Comnena, Anna 4–5, 78
Concilium Germanicum (742) 35
Concubinage 41
Conrad II, emperor of the Holy Roman Empire 67, 70
Constantius of Lyon 32–3
Council of Arles (314) 31
Council of Chalcedon (451) 33–4
Council of Charroux (989) 41
Council of Clermont (1095) 60, 72
Council of Gerona (1068) 60
Council of London (1074–5) 74
Council of Meaux (845) 38
Council of Metz (888) 38
Council of Nablus (1119) 96–7
Council of Narbonne (1054) 60
Council of Nicaea (325) 31
Council of Paris (846) 38
Council of Rheims (1049) 66, 69

Council of Soissons (744) 35
Council of St. Paul (1268) 76 n.41
Council of Ticino (876) 38
Council of Toledo (633) 35
Council of Toulouges (1027) 60
Council of Ver 36
Councils of Vic (1033 and 1068) 60
Council of Vienne (1311–12) 257
Council of Westminster (1138) 75
Council of Westminster (1175) 75–6, 221–2
Council of Winchester (1070) 73–4
Council of Windsor (1070) 73–4
Crécy, battle of (1346) 257
Crispin, Milo 159
Crusades 16, 70, 76–9, 80–1, 139, 231–8 see also First Crusade, Second Crusade, Third Crusade

Damian, Peter 65, 66–7, 70
De contemptu Mundi see Henry, archdeacon of Huntingdon
De Nugis Curialium see Map, Walter
Decretists/decretalists 94–6, 243
Dorylaeum, battle of (1097) 79
Draco Normannicus see Stephen of Rouen
Dunstan, archbishop of Canterbury 164

Eadmer of Canterbury 136, 159, 163–8, 171, 177–8
Eadnoth, bishop of Dorchester 46
Eahlstan, bishop of Sherborne 44–5
Ebal, archdeacon of Laon 180
Ecbert, king of Wessex 44
Edgar, king of England 164
Edward I, king of England 255–7
Edward the Confessor, king of England 131, 144, 173
Edwin, earl of Mercia 144, 173
Eleanor of Aquitaine 237
Engelram de Trie 214
Erasmus, Desiderius 259–60
Ermenfrid, bishop of Sion 73–4, 131
Espec, Walter 194
Eustace, bishop of Ely 179
Eustace of Bolougne (son of King Stephen) 197
Eustace, count of Bolougne (d. 1087) 144
Expositio in Apocalypsim see Alexander the Minorite

Fagaduna, battle of (1075) 162
Falkirk, battle of (1298) 255
Fantosme, Jordan 219
First Crusade 72, 78–9, 139
fitzCount, Brian 204
fitzHildebrand, Robert 200
fitzOsbern, William 139–40, 142, 144

fitzStephen, William 208, 210–15
Foliot, Gilbert, bishop of London 209 n. 5, 236
Foy, Saint *see* Bernard of Angers
Francis of Assisi, Saint 254
Frederick, duke of Swabia 233
Frederick II, emperor of the Holy Roman Empire 229, 246, 251–2
Froissart, Jean 258

Gaudry, bishop of Laon 158, 179–83
Gautier, archdeacon of Laon 180
Geoffrey, count of Anjou (d. 1151) 207
Geoffrey de Montbray, bishop of Coutances 20–1, 74, 125–6, 130, 138, 140, 157, 207
  Distribution of fiefs 135–6
  Eulogy 141–2
  Hastings (1066) 132, 139
  Patronage 128, 137, 142
  Rebellion of 1075 145–6, 162, 170–1
  Rebellion of 1088 152, 154–5, 168, 174
Gerald of Cambrai 47
Gerald of Wales 80, 137–8, 230, 238–9
  Speculum ecclesiae 217–19, 221
Gerbert d'Aurillac 64
Gerento, abbot of Dijon 156
Germanus, Saint, bishop of Auxerre 32–3
Gervase of Canterbury 230, 236–7, 239
Gesta Guillelmi see William of Poitiers
Gesta Normannorum Ducum see William of Jumièges
Gesta pontificum Autissiodorensium 16–17 see also Auxerre, bishops of
Gesta Stephani 185, 189–91, 196–7, 199, 200–1, 203, 213–14
Gethsemane, Garden of 29–31, 48–9, 71, 85, 93, 183, 226, 228, 259–60
Gilbert of Assaily, Master of the Knights Hospitaller 85
Gimon of St. Foy *see* Bernard of Angers
Glaber, Rodolphus 42–3
Godfrey, count of Verdun 64
Godwineson, Harold, king of England 130–1, 169, 173, 177
Gratian 30, 75, 87, 96
  Decretum 84, 92–4
Gregorian reform movement 11, 68, 142, 187–8 see also Gregory VII, pope
Gregory VII, pope 11, 65–6, 70–1, 73, 129, 139, 151, 166, 172
Gregory VIII, Pope 231
Gregory IX, Pope 86–7, 98, 252
Grim, Edward 212
Grosseteste, Robert, bishop of Lincoln 255
Guichard de Beaujeu 226–7

Guillaume of Laon 182
Guitmund of La-Croix-Saint-Leufroi 20
Gunbaldus, archbishop of Bordeaux 41
Guy, bishop of Amiens 130
Guy of Le Puy 39–40, 56

Hamericus 228 n.93
Hardrada, Harald, king of Norway 169, 173
Hastings, battle of (1066) 73–4, 102, 127, 129, 131–2, 134–5, 136, 138–9, 141–2, 144, 152
Hattin, battle of (1187) 231
Henry, archbishop of Rheims 85
Henry, archdeacon of Huntingdon 178, 185, 190–1, 201–3, 210
Henry of Blois, abbot of Glastonbury, bishop of Winchester 75, 184–8, 194–6, 203, 206, 210, 213, 223
    At battle of Winchester (1141) 197–8
    At battle of Wilton (1142) 199
    At siege of Exeter 189–91, 214
    At siege of Lidelea 204–5
    Description by Henry of Huntingdon 201–2
    Fighting William Pont de l'Arche 199–200, 201
Henry, count of Champagne (d. 1197) 231
Henry Despenser, bishop of Norwich 258
Henry IV, emperor of the Holy Roman Empire 70–1, 151
Henry V, emperor of the Holy Roman Empire 180
Henry I, king of England 152, 158, 165–8, 171, 179–80, 184, 186, 187–9, 213, 250
Henry II, king of England 80, 102, 184, 205, 207–9, 211, 214, 216–21, 226, 228, 229–30, 231
Henry III, king of England 229, 240, 249, 251, 254
Henry V, king of England 258
Henry the Young King, king of England 217–18
Heraclius, Patriarch of Jerusalem 80
Herbert de Boseham 208, 210, 214–15
Herleva 126
Herluin, vicomte of Conteville 126
Hervé of Saint-Martin 43
Hildebrand *see* Gregory VII, Pope
Hincmar of Rheims, archbishop 14, 45
Historia Anglorum see Henry, archdeacon of Huntingdon
Historia Novorum see Eadmer of Canterbury
Historiarum see Rodolphus Glaber
History of William Marshal 249
Hospitallers *see* Knights Hospitaller
Hubert de Burgh 251

Hugh, archbishop of Rouen 188
Hugh, bishop of Bayeux 126
Hugh, bishop of Coventry 222–3
Hugh, bishop of Langres (d. 1050) 66
Hugh, earl of Chester 148
Hugh of Noyers *see* Auxerre, bishops of
Hugh de Puiset, bishop of Durham 222, 224
Hugh, Saint, abbot of Cluny 185
Huguccio of Pisa 95
Humbert of Silva-Candida 66–7

Innocent II, Pope 185, 199
Innocent III, Pope 15, 169, 179, 234, 240 246–9, 252
Investiture controversy 70, 164 *see also* Gregorian reform movement, Pope Gregory VII
Itinerarium Peregrinorum et Gesta Regis Ricardi see Richard, prior of Holy Trinity London
Ivo of Chartres 93
    Decretum 91–2
    Panormia 89, 91–2

Jobert of Syria, Master of the Knights Hospitaller 85
John of Anagni 222
John I, bishop of Oporto 68
John of Coutances, bishop of Worcester 179
John I, king of England 179, 207, 216, 222–3, 229, 240–1, 247–9, 251
John of Mantua 71–2
John of Salisbury 82, 210–11, 213
John of Worcester 44, 146–7, 154–5, 162, 170–2, 173, 175–8, 185, 197–8
Julian the Apostate, emperor of Rome 55
Julius Excluded from Heaven see Erasmus, Desiderius
Julius II, Pope 259

Knightliness 10–11, 100–1, 105
Knights Hospitaller 83–4, 85–6
Knights of Narbonne 110
Knights Templar 11, 81–3, 226

Lambert of Wattrelos 85
Lanfranc, archbishop of Canterbury 74, 116, 136–7, 138, 140, 163, 164, 169, 172, 183, 202, 207, 210
    Actions during 1075 rebellion 145–6, 153, 158–62, 170
    Arrest of Odo of Bayeux 150–1
Langton, Stephen, archbishop of Canterbury 138, 248
Lateran II (1139) 249

292 INDEX

Lateran III (1179) 1
Lateran IV (1215) 99, 249, 251
Leo IX, Saint, Pope 65–70, 159
L'Estoire de la Guerre Sainte see Ambroise
Liber extra 86–7, 98
Liber Miracula Sancte Fidis see Bernard of Angers
Life of Saint Bruno see Ruotger of Cologne
Life of St. Gerald of Aurillac see Odo of Cluny
Life of Saint Germanus see Constantius of Lyon
Life of Wulfstan see William of Malmesbury
Lincoln, battle of (1217) 250–1
Louis VII, king of France 212, 217
Louis VIII, king of France (as prince) 246, 249
Louis the Pious, emperor of the Holy Roman Empire 37
Lucius II, Pope 185
Lucius III, Pope 219–20
Lupus of Ferrières 37

Maccabees 48–9, 82, 84
   Judas Maccabeus 28 n.4
Malet, Robert 162
Map, Walter 215–16, 226–8
Marshal, William 83, 249–51
Masculinity 9–10
Matilda of Boulogne, queen of England 197
Matilda, countess of Canossa 71
Matilda, empress of Germany 184, 188–9, 195–8, 199, 203, 207
Mauger, bishop of Worcester 179
Melton, William, archbishop of York 257
Mercurius, Saint 55
Military orders 81–6
miles Christi 10, 187
Miles, sheriff of Gloucester 203
Miracula sancti Benedicti see Peace League of Bourges
Moniage Guillaume see William in the Monastery
Montacute, castle of 140
Morcar/Morkar, earl of Northumbria 144, 173
Myton-on-Swale, battle of (1319) 257

Neville's Cross, battle of (1346) 257
Nicaea, siege of (1097) 79
Nicholas I, Pope 38, 75
Nicholas II, Pope 159
Nicholas de Farnham, bishop of Durham 254–5
Nogent, Guibert de 179–82

Odo, bishop of Bayeux 20, 97, 125, 137, 138, 157, 158, 166, 168, 170–1, 174, 187, 189, 210
   Actions during 1075 rebellion 145–7
   Actions during 1088 rebellion 151–5
   Arrest in 1082 147–51
   Bayeux Tapestry 128–9, 133–5
   As earl of Kent 142, 144–5
   Early career 126–7
   Hastings campaign (1066) 74, 129–35
   As Justiciar 139–40, 143–4
   Patronage 127–8
   Serving Duke Robert of Normandy 155–6
Odo of Cluny 11
Odo of Corbie 37–8
O'Toole, Peter 206
Otto, bishop of Freising 84
Otto IV, emperor of the Holy Roman Empire 241
Oxford Charter of Liberties (1136) 188

Pandulf de Masca, bishop of Norwich 251
Paschal II, Pope 180
Peace of God movement 39, 55–7, 90 *see also* Truce of God movement
Peace League of Bourges 40, 55–9
Peter, abbot of Woburn 179
Peter of Blois 5
Peter, Saint 258
Peter the Venerable, abbot of Cluny 185, 186
Philip of Dreux, bishop of Beauvais 97, 216, 223, 229, 248, 252
   At battle of Bouvines (1214) 240–4
   Capture in 1197 244–6
Philip I, king of France 179
Philip II, king of France 229, 231, 240, 244, 246
Philippidos see William the Breton
Plantagenet, Geoffrey, archbishop of York 75–6, 207, 210, 215–26, 228, 230, 238–9
   Actions during the Great Rebellion (1173–74) 216–18
   Campaign on behalf of Richard against John (1193) 223–4
Poer, Roger le 194, 196
Policraticus see John of Salisbury
Pont de l'Arche, William 199–201
Pontius, abbot of Cluny 186–7

Ralph of Coggeshall 231
Ralph of Diceto 231, 234, 235–6
Ralph, earl of East Anglia 145–6, 162, 170
Ralph of Hauterive, archdeacon of Colchester 236

Ranulf Glanvill 229-30, 231
Raymond of Aguilers 79
Raymond of Penafort *see Liber Extra*
Raymond of St.-Gilles, count of
    Toulouse 79
Reginald de Bohun, bishop of Bath 237
Regularis Concordia see Æthelwold, bishop
    of Winchester
Relatio de Standardo see Ælred, abbot of
    Rievaulx
Remigius of Fecamp, bishop of
    Dorchester/Lincoln 20, 125, 158
  Actions at Hastings (1066) 74, 133,
    136-7, 139
  Attempted canonization 137-8
Richard of Dover, archbishop of
    Canterbury 221-2
Richard de Clare 161
Richard, count of Cornwall 14
Richard I, duke of Normandy 126
Richard I, king of England 81, 207, 216,
    218, 221-3, 229, 234, 250
  Fighting Philip of Dreux 240, 243-4,
    246-7
  Third crusade 231-2, 236-8
Richard II, king of England 258
Richard of Devizes 80-1
Richard of Ilchester, bishop of
    Winchester 219
Richard of Poitou 84
Richard, prior of Hexham 192-3
Richard, prior of Holy Trinity
    London 232-5, 237-9
Robert of Bellème 167
Robert de Béthune, bishop of
    Hereford 203
Robert, bishop of Hereford 177
Robert, bishop of Worcester 179
Robert, count of Mortain 125, 134, 140
Robert 'Curthose' II, duke of
    Normandy 137, 152-3, 155, 166-8,
    169, 174, 179-80
Robert I, duke of Normandy 126
Robert, earl of Gloucester 188, 194-7, 199,
    224
Robert of Lewes, bishop of Bath 203-4
Robert de Montbray/Mowbray 154-5, 165,
    174
Robert of St.-Marien 17
Roches, Peter des, bishop of
    Winchester 80, 116, 229, 240,
    246-9, 254-5
  Actions on 1217 campaign 249-51
  On crusade 251-2
Roger, bishop of Salisbury 187-8, 194, 196
Roger de Breteuil, earl of Hereford 145,
    160-1, 170

Roger de Clinton, bishop of Chester 201
Roger of Howden 220-1, 224-6, 231, 244-5
Roger de Lacy 175
Roger de Montbray 217-18
Roger de Montgomery, earl of
    Shrewsbury 174-5
Roger des Moulins, Master of the Knights
    Hospitaller 85
Roger of Wendover 179, 246-7, 250
Royal service 7, 50
  criticisms of 19-20, 228
Rufinus of Bologna 95-6
Ruotger of Cologne 38

Saladin 231, 237
Samson, abbot of Bury St. Edmunds 179
Second Crusade 231
Sicard, bishop of Cremona 96
Simon, dean of York 225
Simon, earl of Northampton 197
Simon of St. Bertin 82
Simony 41
Sinclair, William, bishop of Dunkeld 257
Song of Roland 100, 103-9, 128-9
Song of Aspremont 109-12, 119
St. Calais, William, bishop of Durham 152,
    170
Standard, battle of (1138) 75, 192-4 *see also*
    Thurstan, archbishop of York
Stephen, count of Blois (d. 1102) 185
Stephen, count of Boulogne, king of
    England 184, 187-92, 194-7, 198-9,
    204, 207, 214
Stephen of Rouen 213
Stigand, archbishop of Canterbury 131,
    136, 138, 139, 144
Sylvester II, Pope *see* Gerbert d'Aurillac
Symeon of Durham 146-7, 149, 171, 192

Talbot, Geoffrey 203-4
Templars *see* Knights Templar
Tertullian 28
Teutonicus, Johannes 84
Theobald IV, count of Blois 189
Theobald V, count of Blois 233
Theodred, bishop of London 45
Thierry, duke of Upper Lorraine 64
Third Crusade 76, 80-1, 231-8
Thomas of Bayeux, archbishop of York 136
Three Books Against the Simoniacs 66
Thurstan, abbot of Glastonbury 19-20
Thurstan, archbishop of York 75, 184, 202
  Battle of the Standard (1138) 191-4, 245
Tinchebrai, battle of (1106) 158, 179-81
Tostig, earl of Northumbria 144, 169, 173
Truce of God movement 59
Tuck, Friar 254

Turbe, William, bishop of Norwich 205
Turpin, archbishop of Reims 9 n.28, 80, 100–1, 116–17
  In *Song of Roland* 102–9, 110, 128
    As knight 102–5, 107–9
      Almace 105–6
      Fight with Abisme 102
      Fight with Corsablix 104
      Fight with Roudez 108
      Showing prowess 104–5, 107–9
      Death scene 107–8
  In *Song of Aspremont* 109–112
    Bearing the True Cross 111–112

Urban II, Pope 65, 72–3, 77
Urban III, Pope 231
Urse, sheriff of Worcester 170–1

Vita Anselmi see Eadmer of Canterbury
Vita Lanfranci see Crispin, Milo
Vitalis, Orderic 73, 129, 130, 143, 144, 145, 151, 186
  Arrest of Odo of Bayeux 147–9
  Condemning worldliness 19–20
  Gaudry of Laon 179–80
  Odo of Bayeux and Geoffrey of Coutances 138–41
  Rebellion of 1088 153–6

Wace 101–2
Walcher, bishop of Durham 146, 163
Walter, bishop of Albano 166
Walter the Chancellor 97
Walter de Cantilupe, bishop of Worcester 254
Walter of Guisborough 255–6
Walter, Hubert, bishop of Salisbury, archbishop of Canterbury 1, 76–7, 80–1, 179, 222, 223–4, 252
  Early career 229–30
  Elevation to Canterbury 237–8
  Third Crusade 231–7, 238–40
Walter de Lacy 170
Waltheof, earl of Northumbria 145, 162–3
Wenrich of Trier 71
Wibert, archbishop of Ravenna *see* Clement III, antipope
Wilfrid, archbishop of Narbonne 60–3
William, archbishop of Tours 222

William, archbishop of Tyre 82, 84–5, 97, 232
William the Breton 240–3
William of Canterbury 210–11
William de Corbeil, archbishop of Canterbury 187–8
William I, duke of Normandy, king of England 102, 138, 144, 146, 154, 158, 169, 173, 174, 184–5
  Arrest of Odo of Bayeux 148–9, 150–2
  As duke of Normandy 125–8
  Hastings campaign 132, 134–5, 139
  Rebellion of 1075 161–3, 170
  Regarding Remigius of Fécamp 136–7
William of Jumièges 130
William Longchamp, bishop of Ely 216, 222–3
William Longsword, earl of Salisbury 242
William in the Monastery 113–16
William of Malmesbury 73, 147, 149–50, 185
  Historia Novella 188, 196–7
  Life of Wulfstan/Vita Wulfstani 169–70, 173–4, 177–8
William of Newburgh 1–4, 230, 239
William of Poitiers 127, 129–32, 138, 143
William 'Rufus' II, king of England 137, 151–3, 158, 164–7, 169–70, 174–5, 184, 196
William de Stuteville 224
William of Warenne 161–2
Wimund, bishop of Sodor and Man 1–4
Wulfsige, abbot of Ramsey 46
Wulfstan, bishop of Worcester, archbishop of York (d. 1023) 47, 48–9, 50
Wulfstan, St, bishop of Worcester (d. 1095) 20–1, 140, 145, 158, 161, 169, 183
  Pre-1066 172–4
  Rebellion of 1075 170–2
  Rebellion of 1088 174–6
  Vita Wulfstani 176–9

York, archbishops of *see* Aldred, Geoffrey Plantagenet, Thomas of Bayeux, Thurstan, William Melton, Wulfstan

Zacharias, Pope 35